BIDLICAL AND CLASSICAL MYTHS:
THE MYTHOLOGICAL FRAMEWORK OF
WESTERN CULTURE

In the 1970s and 1980s, Northrop Frye and Jay Macpherson co-taught at the University of Toronto's Victoria College a very influential course on the history of Western mythology in which Frye focused on the Biblical myths and Macpherson on the Classical. *Biblical and Classical Myths* attempts to re-create the remarkable synergy of that course, combining Frye's lectures (published only very recently in the Collected Works of Northrop Frye) and Macpherson's popular 1962 textbook, *Four Ages: The Classical Myths*.

Frye's lectures on the Bible, which make up the first half of the book, expound on a wide variety of topics related to Biblical imagery and narrative. In the second half of the book, Macpherson recounts the major Classical myths, exploring their interconnections and their survival in later European traditions.

By complementing the Biblical tradition with the Classical, this volume provides a comprehensive introduction to Western mythology. Engaging and accessible, *Biblical and Classical Myths* represents a unique achievement in scholarship and is an essential volume for students and others interested in literature and cultural studies.

(Frye Studies)

The late NORTHROP FRYE was a professor in the Department of English at Victoria College, University of Toronto.

JAY MACPHERSON is a professor emeritus in the Department of English at Victoria College, University of Toronto.

Biblical and Classical Myths

The Mythological Framework of Western Culture

Northrop Frye
and
Jay Macpherson

UNIVERSITY OF TORONTO PRESS
Toronto Buffalo London

Symbolism in the Bible
© Victoria University, University of Toronto (lectures), and Robert D. Denham
(foreword, annotation) 2004

Four Ages: The Classical Myths
First published by Macmillan of Canada 1962
© University of Toronto Press 2004
Toronto Buffalo London

ISBN 0-8020-3927-8 (cloth)
ISBN 0-8020-8695-0 (paper)

Printed on acid-free paper

Frye Studies

National Library of Canada Cataloguing in Publication

Frye, Northrop, 1912–1991.
Biblical and classical myths : the mythological framework of
western culture / Northrop Frye and Jay Macpherson.

Includes bibliographical references and index.
ISBN 0-8020-3927-8 (bound).   ISBN 0-8020-8695-0 (pbk.)

1. Myth in the Bible.   2. Mythology, Classical.   I. Macpherson, Jay, 1931–
II. Title.

BL312.F79 2004   201'.3   C2004-902028-5

This volume has been published with the assistance of a grant from
the DeGroote Trust for the Collected Works of
Northrop Frye at McMaster University.

University of Toronto Press acknowledges the financial assistance to
its publishing program of the Canada Council for the Arts and the
Ontario Arts Council.

University of Toronto Press acknowledges the financial support for its
publishing activities of the Government of Canada through the
Book Publishing Industry Development Program (BPIDP).

Contents

Preface to the Combined Edition

The two authors of this book taught at Victoria College in the University of Toronto throughout their careers, Northrop Frye from 1939 to 1991 and Jay Macpherson from 1957 to 1996. Frye was a towering figure in modern criticism, author of more than thirty books, including the influential *Fearful Symmetry: A Study of William Blake, Anatomy of Criticism: Four Essays*, and *The Great Code: The Bible and Literature*. Macpherson has long been known as one of Canada's finest poets, author of *The Boatman* and *Welcoming Disaster*, and as a scholar learned in both Classical mythology (*Four Ages of Man*) and in patterns of romance in European and North American literature (*The Spirit of Solitude: Conventions and Continuities in Late Romance*).

Though very different in style and person, Frye and Macpherson were both unusually committed, effective teachers. Much of their scholarly writing emerged from their work as university lecturers and was designed to help student readers and others. This present book is quintessential Frye and Macpherson. The underlying scholarship is extensive and deep but the presentations of Biblical and Classical myths are readily accessible to any attentive learner. The texts are as fresh as at the time of their first deliveries, in oral and in written forms respectively. The apparatus now made available with each author's work is up-to-date, unobtrusive, and judiciously chosen, to help interested readers go further in the areas of mythological and cultural studies that most interest them. The illustrations and maps, chosen by Jay Macpherson and Margaret Burgess, are simple, informative, and elegant.

Biblical and Classical Myths: The Mythological Framework of Western Culture is the result of particular circumstances and collaborations. I am general editor of the Collected Works of Northrop Frye, a thirty-three-volume scholarly edition being published by the University of Toronto Press. As editor of volume 13 of this project, Robert D. Denham published in 2003 *Northrop Frye's Notebooks and Lectures on the Bible and Other Religious Texts.* In response to enthusiastic external and internal readers' reports on Denham's manuscript, Ron Schoeffel and Bill Harnum, senior officers at the Press, asked us to make available in a paperback edition the famous Frye lectures on the Bible. This request accorded exactly with my thinking about the Frye materials. For more than fifty years the lectures, constantly changing, influenced many hundreds of students and moved them to a state of cultural consciousness they had not previously imagined; I was one of those lucky ones. But I had an additional idea: to complement the lectures with Macpherson's retelling of the Classical myths. This would give a rich account of the two long-interwoven mythologies of the Western world, indicated in the subtitle of this book and chosen because it is the name of the course that Frye and Macpherson co-taught for some years, beginning in 1973–74. The Press liked the idea of the combination and Macpherson readily agreed to help. She has worked assiduously preparing this book for publication, interrupting her own research as she did so. She and I have received expert, detailed assistance from Margaret Burgess, also a co-teacher (later) of Frye's lecture course, and a most knowledgeable, helpful member of our editorial staff.

In a period of human history in which numerous cultures jostle together daily, sometimes creatively and sometimes with fiercely destructive results, it is important to understand the traditions of Western culture, as it combines and recombines with others. This book is dedicated to that end.

Alvin A. Lee

Abbreviations

AC   *Anatomy of Criticism: Four Essays*. Princeton: Princeton University Press, 1957.

AV   Authorized Version

CR   *Creation and Recreation*. Toronto: University of Toronto Press, 1980.

CW   Collected Works of Northrop Frye

DG   *Divisions on a Ground: Essays on Canadian Culture*. Ed. James Polk. Toronto: Anansi, 1982.

DV   *The Double Vision: Language and Meaning in Religion*. Toronto: University of Toronto Press, 1991.

NF   Northrop Frye

NFR   *Northrop Frye on Religion: Excluding "The Great Code" and "Words with Power."* Ed. Alvin A. Lee and Jean O'Grady. CW, 4. Toronto: University of Toronto Press, 2000.

GC   *The Great Code: The Bible and Literature*. New York: Harcourt Brace Jovanovich, 1982.

RSV   Revised Standard Version

Biblia Pauperum 1: ANNUNCIATION
(Luke 1:26–38)

Eve and the serpent
(Genesis 3:1–7)

Gideon's fleece
(Judges 6:36–40)

Symbolism in the Bible

Northrop Frye

EDITED BY ROBERT D. DENHAM

Foreword

The text given here is that of a series of twenty-four lectures Frye gave in his course entitled "The Mythological Framework of Western Culture" in 1981–82. The lectures, transcribed by Anis George and edited by Michael Dolzani, were originally printed in spiral-bound booklets that accompanied the videotapes of Frye's lectures, entitled *The Bible and Literature: A Personal View from Northrop Frye*, a series conceived and produced by Robert Sandler. These booklets included extensive teaching guides for each of the videotapes, prepared by Professor Dolzani, who was Frye's research assistant at the time. The thirty programs in the video series, each twenty-six minutes in length, were issued by the Media Centre at the University of Toronto. Frye had originally asked Sandler if he would be the writer for a TV Ontario series featuring Frye on literature, based on the model of Jacob Bronowski's *The Ascent of Man* and Kenneth Clark's *Civilization*. This project fell through, but Sandler, after having sat in on Frye's Bible lectures, eventually persuaded the Media Centre at the University of Toronto to videotape the lectures. Sandler then edited the lectures, sometimes deleting material to fit the half-hour format and at other times dividing material from two different lectures for a single video. The full texts of Frye's twenty-four lectures are, however, printed in the teaching manuals, and these are reproduced in what follows. The titles of the lectures either follow those of the study guides or are adaptations of them. On six occasions two units in the video series were derived from one lecture, the twenty-four lectures thus resulting in thirty programs. Typographical errors have been silently corrected; emendations to the text have been listed at the end of the lectures as published in volume 13 of the Collected Works, *Northrop Frye's Notebooks and Lectures on the Bible and Other Religious Texts*, but have been omitted from the present paperback edition. It should be emphasized that the copy-text is not from a retranscription of the tapes of the lectures themselves, but is an edited version of the transcription made in the early 1980s. Emendations and editorial changes to the text are therefore not necessarily alterations of what Frye said but of the printed transcription of the lectures.

Courses on "The English Bible" had been offered at Victoria College from the time the Department of Religious Knowledge was established in 1904–5, when two-hour-per-week courses were options in both first and second years. By 1930–31 when Frye was a second-year undergraduate these had been extended to courses in all four years— one hour a week in first year, two hours a week in second year, and three hours a week in third and fourth years for students in the Pass Course, and one hour a week in all four years for students in the Honour course. Frye's first experiments with teaching in this area were conducted under the auspices of the Student Christian Movement over a period of four years. In the early 1940s he conducted small discussion groups on "Mythology and Symbolism of the Bible," "Revelation," "Comparative Religion," and "Symbolism in the Book of Revelation." Sometime in the mid- to late-1940s Frye began teaching a course on "The English Bible" under the auspices of the Religious Knowledge department. Once established, the course continued more or less unchanged until 1966–67, when it was listed as "Symbolism in the Bible." In 1970–71 after the Department of Religious Studies was formed the course was described as "a study of the Bible based on the conception of its imaginative and doctrinal unity, and approached through an examination of its recurrent themes and images. Some attempt will be made to indicate how its traditional view of the Bible has influenced the poetry and thought of the Western world." The final major transformation of the course—although not necessarily of Frye's own lectures—occurred in 1973–74 when he was joined in a co-teaching arrangement by Jay Macpherson. At this time the course was changed to "The Mythological Framework of Western Culture." Macpherson added a sequence of lectures on Classical mythology to run parallel with Frye's on the Bible. She was succeeded by Marguerite Stobo, who filled in for Macpherson in 1978–79 and then took over from her in 1980–81; and Marguerite

Stobo was in turn succeeded by Margaret Burgess, who taught with Frye from 1987–88 until his death in 1991 and to whom I am indebted for this information about the Bible course—and for much of the wording.

Robert D. Denham

Biblia Pauperum 2: NATIVITY
(Luke 2)

Moses and the burning bush   Aaron's rod
(Exodus 3)   (Numbers 17)

1

An Approach to the Bible and Translations of the Bible

My part of this course is a study of the narrative and imagery of the English Bible; and to clarify what I am trying to do in it, it might be worth sketching in a background of the history of the course, to explain why I started giving it in the first place.

It goes back to my days as a junior instructor, when I found myself saying to the head of my department here that I found some difficulty in getting my students to understand what was going on in *Paradise Lost*, which I was trying to teach. And the difficulty was obviously a lack of knowledge of the Bible. My chairman said, "Well, how do you expect to teach *Paradise Lost* to people who don't know a Philistine from a Pharisee?" I was tempted to answer that given the middle-class status of my students, that particular distinction would perhaps not be too important for them. But I didn't often talk that way to my departmental chairman, and I said, "Well, what do I do?" And he said, "You offer a course in the English Bible."

Well, in those days religious knowledge was a college subject at Victoria and Trinity and St. Michael's. University College also had religious knowledge courses, but it had to give them euphemistic titles like "Near Eastern Studies" or "Oriental Languages" so that Queen's Park would not be frightened into thinking that a college with an interest in God was drawing money from the province.[1]

The courses naturally differed a great deal. If you went to St. Michael's you got St. Thomas Aquinas exclusively, with perhaps a course or two in St. Augustine for dessert: so that the religion courses were rather enclosed in the various colleges. When the university Department of Religion was organized, I was able to go on teaching the course within the department. But then, under the new regulations, it became a half-course, and as I think half-courses are nothing but a nuisance for students, I asked colleagues to give a course on Classical mythology as well, and so to round out and expand the original idea of the course, which is to provide for students, whether their main interest is litera-ture or not, some knowledge of the cultural traditions that we've all been brought up in and which we are all conditioned by every time we draw a breath, whether we realize it or not.

It took me some time to hit on the right formula for a course in the Bible. I consulted the curricula of other universities, and found that they gave courses called "The Bible as Literature," which involved chopping pieces out of the Bible like the Book of Job and the parables of Jesus, saying, "Look, aren't they literary?" That approach violated all my instincts as a critic, because those instincts told me that what a critic does when he is confronted with any verbal document whatever is to start on page one at the upper left-hand corner and go on reading until he reaches the bottom right-hand corner of the last page. But many people who have attempted to do that with the Bible have flaked out very quickly, generally somewhere around the middle of Leviticus.

Part of the reason is that the Bible presents the appearance of being, not a book, but a small library of books, a miscellany of various texts: the suggestion is almost that there is no such book as the Bible. In fact, the word "bible" itself comes from the Greek *ta biblia*, which is plural: "the little books." So the possibility arises that "the Bible," as we call it, is only a name we give for convenience to a pile of books that have got bound up in one cover.

So I had to go on to the next stage, which was to establish that there *was* a genuine unity in the Bible, and that that unity was of two kinds. The first was a unity of narrative. As I've said, not everybody gets through the Bible from Genesis to Revelation; but anybody who does will discover that the Bible does at least have a beginning and an end. It starts quite logically at the beginning of time with the Creation, it ends quite logically at the end of time with the Apocalypse, and it surveys the whole of human history—or the part of history that interests it—in between, under the symbolic names of Adam and Israel.

So the narrative unity of the Bible, which is there in spite of the miscellaneous nature of its content, was something that I stressed. And that concern for narrative seems to me to be distinctive of the Bible among other sacred books. In the Koran, for example, the revelations of Mohammed were gathered up after his death and arranged in order of length, which suggests that revelation in the Koran pays no attention to narrative continuity—that's not what it is interested in. But the fact that the Bible *is* interested in it seems to be significant for the study of literature and for many other reasons.

The second way in which the Bible is unified is through a number of recurring images: mountain, sheep, river, hill, pasture, bride, bread, wine, and so on. They echo and re-echo all through the Bible and are repeated in so many ways as to suggest that they have a thematic importance: that they are actually building up some kind of interconnected unity. The present course is really based on this conception of the unity of the narrative of the Bible and the unity formed by its recurrent imagery.

The only form of the Bible that I can deal with is the Christian Bible, with its Old and New Testaments, however polemical those names may sound. In the first place, it's the only version of the Bible I know anything about, and in the second place it is the one that has been decisive for Western culture through the Middle Ages and Renaissance to our own time.

The Old Testament was of course written in Hebrew, except for a few passages in the later language Aramaic, which replaced Hebrew as a spoken language and was probably the language spoken by Jesus and his disciples. In Hebrew, only the consonants are written down, so that all the vowels are editorial. Therefore, the establishing of the text of the Hebrew Bible took quite a long while, and was still going on in New Testament times. Some centuries before that, it had been translated into Greek for the benefit of Jews living in the city of Alexandria in Egypt. The number of translators was traditionally seventy, and so the Greek translation of the Hebrew Old Testament has been called the Septuagint, usually abbreviated LXX. The Hebrew text in the form in which we have it was established later—it's called the Masoretic, the scholarly or traditional text established by rabbis and scholars working mainly around the environs of Lake Tiberius in Galilee. So the Septuagint is in many respects older than the Hebrew text that we have, and sometimes preserves more primitive readings.

The New Testament was written in Greek by writers whose native language probably was not Greek. The kind of Greek they wrote was called *koine*, the popular Greek which was distributed all through the Near Eastern countries as a kind of common language. The writers of the New Testament may have been familiar to differing degrees with the Hebrew text of the Old Testament, but when they quoted from the Old Testament they tended to use the Septuagint. And that is the beginning of a principle which is rather important for the history of Christianity. In any sacred book, there is enough concentration in the writing, and enough attention paid to it by those who accept it as sacred, for the linguistic characteristics of the original language to be of great importance. Any Jewish interpretation or commentary on the Hebrew Old Testament inevitably takes great care to study the linguistic nuances of the Hebrew original, and similarly with the Koran, which is so bound up with the linguistic characteristics of Arabic that in practice the Arabic language has had to go everywhere that the Islamic religion has gone.

In contrast, Christianity as a religion has been dependent from the beginning on translation. After the New Testament period, the centre of power in the Western world shifted to Rome, and with that shift came the need for a Latin translation of the Bible. The Latin translation that appeared was known as the Vulgate, that is, the one in common use. The translation was made by St. Jerome, in what may well be the greatest effort of scholarship ever achieved by a single man. For the next thousand years, the Vulgate Latin Bible *was* the Bible as far as Europe was concerned. There was very little knowledge of Greek or Hebrew through the Middle Ages, and the Vulgate was for the most part as far as anyone could go in reading the Bible.

Already in the Middle Ages, the question had arisen of translating the Bible into the vernacular (or modern) languages. It was resisted by authorities of the Church establishment, partly because the issue very soon got involved with reform movements within the Church. One of these reform movements was led in England by John Wyclif, a contemporary of Chaucer in the fourteenth century. His disciples, working mainly after his death, produced an English translation of the entire Bible, which was of course a translation of the Vulgate Latin text, not of the Greek and Hebrew. Nevertheless, the Wyclifite Bible became the basis for all future English translations. In the sixteenth century, the Protestant Reformation broke out in Germany under Luther, and one of Luther's major efforts to consolidate his position was to make a complete German translation of the Bible, which became among other things a cornerstone of modern German literature.

Similar efforts were made in England. Henry VIII, you remember, declared himself to be the head of the Church, but didn't want to make any alteration in Church doctrine, so he amused himself in his later years by executing Protestants for heresy and Catholics for denying his claim to be head of the Church. Thus, William Tyndale, the first person to work on the translation of the Bible into English from Greek and Hebrew sources, was a refugee and had to work on the Continent. Eventually he was caught by Henry's goon squad and transported back to England, where he was burned at the stake along with copies of his Bible. Henry VIII, with that versatility of intention which is often found in people who have tertiary syphilis, had begun his reign by being called "Defender of the Faith" by the Pope, because he had written a pamphlet attacking Martin Luther—that is to say, his minister Sir Thomas More had written it but Henry had signed it. However, as "Defender of the Faith," he changed his mind about what faith he was going to defend, and in the last years of his reign the English Bible in the hands of various other translators, including Miles Coverdale, had become established as the official Bible for the Church of England of which he was now the head.

Well, in Queen Elizabeth's reign, there were two Bibles. One was very largely the product of the right-wing establishment in the Church of England, and was called the Bishops' Bible. The other was a Puritan Bible, which again had been produced by refugees on the Continent during Queen Mary's reign. It was called the Geneva Bible but is sometimes called the "breeches Bible" because in the story of Adam and Eve it is said that after the fall they knew that they were naked, and so they tried to make for themselves what the King James Bible refers to chastely as "aprons" but the Puritan Bible calls "breeches." The Bishops' Bible was the one that was approved of during Elizabeth's reign: the Geneva Bible was not. The objections against it were less to its scholarship, which was very thorough, than to its marginal notes, which were very copious, and which set out the infallible rightness of the Puritan position and the madness and obstinacy of everyone who opposed it. But both circulated in England, and Shakespeare is believed by scholars to have used—almost certainly by mere accident—the Bishops' Bible for his earlier plays, and the Geneva Bible for his later ones.

Elizabeth died in 1603. Her successor, King James VI of Scotland, moved to London to become King James I of England. King James was the son of Mary, Queen of Scots, who was of course Roman Catholic. He had listened to a lot of Puritan sermons in his youth, and this conditioned him in favour of the more right-wing establishment. In fact "No bishop, no king" was one of his mottoes: he believed that the episcopal system was essential to the monarchy. However, his real motto was "Blessed are the peacemakers," and he thought that he would try to achieve some kind of reconciliation between the Episcopalian right wing and the Puritan left wing: at that time the Puritans did not form a separate Church but were a group within the Church of England. His way of achieving reconciliation was the time-honoured way of calling a conference, which met at Hampton Court in 1604, and after a few weeks broke up with the usual theological hair-pulling. But before it did so, it had passed one very important resolution, which was that there should be an authorized English translation of the Bible, to be done by a committee of scholars who would represent both Episcopalian and Puritan scholarship. These scholars worked on their translation for seven years, and when it finally appeared in 1611 it was known as the Authorized Version, because it was, as the title page says, "appointed to be read in churches."

It is also often called the King James Bible. And please do not refer to it as the "St. James Bible." King James was a remarkable person in many ways: he was a poet, he was a literary critic, he was a diplomat, he was an anti-tobacco pamphleteer, he was strongly homosexual, he was in all probability a bastard, but he was not a saint. ·

The Authorized Version held the field, and nobody else attempted another version of the Bible except the Roman Catholics, who again had to be working outside the country on the Continent. They had done a translation of the New Testament early in Elizabeth's reign, and by also translating the Old Testament produced the complete version known as the Douay Bible, because it was completed at Douay in Flanders. It was finished in 1609, which was a little late for the translators of the 1611 Bible to make much use of it. In contrast to the King James Bible, the Douay Bible is based on the Vulgate, which the Roman Catholic Council of Trent in the sixteenth century had declared to be the authentic version of the Bible, and had stipulated that any Catholic translation of the Bible into English would have to follow the Vulgate original.

The sequence of English Bibles culminating in the King James Bible goes back to the Wyclif Bible, which again was a translation from the Vulgate. After 1611, scholars like Milton or Sir Thomas Browne usually continued to quote the Vulgate in Latin, but the use of the English Bible naturally grew as the language grew.

The King James Bible is the one I want to use for this course. I have various reasons for that. It is the most familiar and the most accessible version, and more importantly, the translators of the King James Bible were not out to make a new translation; they were out to make a traditional one.

There have always been two tendencies in Biblical scholarship, though they have often converged. One is the analytical tendency to try to establish what the original text says, which is the basis of the critical tradition. The other is the attempt to translate the Bible in accordance with what a consensus of ecclesiastical authorities has declared the meaning to be. Most copies of the King James translation in ordinary circulation omit two very important things; and I would like you to procure, if you possibly can, a version of the Bible which contains them both, as this Cambridge edition which I have does. The two things that are usually omitted are, first of all, the sequence of books known as the Apocrypha, which I will explain in a moment; and secondly, the Address to the Reader with which the King James translators prefaced their book. The Dedication to King James, which is almost invariably preserved in copies of the Authorized Version, is only a perfunctory piece of rhetoric, but the Translators to the Reader is a very careful, very lucid, very honest statement of what the translators were trying to do and what their policy in translating was. And they say almost at once that rather than to make a brand new translation, they were trying to produce a version of the Bible that would be in general agreement with the whole tradition of Biblical translation.

What that means in practice is that the King James Bible is a Bible very close to the Vulgate tradition: therefore it comes very close to the Bible with which everyone in England before 1611 was familiar. And that is the main reason I want to use it.

The differences between Roman Catholic and Protestant translations of the Bible have been, I think, greatly exaggerated and are mainly confined to a number of technical terms having to do with the organization of the Church. The disputes turn on whether the word *episcopos* means "bishop" or "apostle"; whether the word *ecclesia* means "church" or "congregation." There are perhaps half a dozen words of that kind, which we will not be concerned with in this course. We are concerned with the imagery of the Bible, with words like "mountain" and "river" and "sheep" and "body" and "blood" and so forth, words which are so concrete that no translator can possibly get them wrong. So there aren't any major difficulties in translation or variety of translation that we need to be worried about.

The great prestige of the King James Bible in literature is largely due to the fact that it was an authorized version appointed to be read in churches. That is, its rhythm is based on the spoken word, and while there are a great many lapses, the ear of the King James translators for the spoken word was extremely acute. And because of that the Authorized Version has held the field even against more scholarly modern translations.

The oral basis of the King James Bible, the fact that this translation was intended primarily to be read aloud, accounts for many of its features, such as the practice of printing every sentence as a separate paragraph, which makes sense for public reading. The result is that the Authorized Version has established itself as part of our oral heritage: the sounds, the cadences of that translation keep echoing through our minds whether we realize it or not.

It was not until the latter part of the nineteenth century that the need for revised versions began to make itself felt, and even then the prestige of the King James Bible rather overshadowed them. There was a British Revised Version in 1885, and an American Standard Version in 1900:[2] both of them, from the literary point of view, were flops. They made very limited headway, partly because the genuine scholars on the translating committee were always being outvoted by the old fuddy duddies opposed to any change whatever; and, more important, they fell foul of the principle of translating that it is not the scholarly knowledge of the original that makes a translation permanent, but sensitivity to one's own language. These translators, in attempting a kind of middle course between the language of the early seventeenth century and the spoken language of 1885 and 1900, fell between two stools. For example, there is a phrase that is repeated very frequently through the Old Testament—"Yahweh Sabaoth"—which in the King James version is "The Lord of Hosts," a magnificent phrase. The American Revised Version renders this "Jehovah of Hosts." Now that is a mistranslation, even if it is more accurate than the King James version. If you doubt that it's a mistranslation, just try it out on your eardrum. "Jehovah of Hosts" reveals a profound insensitivity to English as a spoken language, and no translation that makes a boner like that has any chance of surviving.

Various other translations appeared later in the twentieth century. The Revised Standard Version of 1952 is one that I refer to a good deal myself. If you pick up the annotated version, which is annotated by Bruce Metzger of Princeton for the Old Testament, I forget just who for the New,[3] you get an extremely valuable book that has very unobtrusive comments and footnotes. The New English Bible—which is more British than the RSV, which is largely American scholarship—came out in 1970. And the leading Roman Catholic Bible at present is called the Jerusalem Bible. As I say, I would like to use the King James Bible for my own quotations, and I would like to feel free to refer to the Apocrypha as well, so it would be an advantage to have a Bible that includes it.

The Apocrypha is a group of fourteen books which were almost certainly written originally in Hebrew. But the word "apocrypha" means "hidden" or "concealed": the "cryp" part of it is from the same root as our words "crypt" and "cryptic"—things hidden away. And what was hidden in this case was the Hebrew original. When the rabbinical scholars of the early Christian centuries were making up their canonical books, they excluded the books that had no Hebrew original. Consequently, those survived only in Greek texts or, in one case, a Latin one, though in later years archaeologists have recovered some parts of the Hebrew originals.

St. Jerome, when he made his Vulgate translation of the Bible into Latin, translated the books of the Apocrypha, but he put them in a separate section. The Church of Rome, however, overruled him on this point, and so Roman Catholic Bibles even today have the books of the Apocrypha along with the books of the Hebrew Old Testament. The Apocrypha was also a part of the 1611 enterprise, and was translated along with the Old and New Testaments. But the Protestants tended to go back to St. Jerome's practice of keeping the Apocryphal books separate, and as a result they dropped out of most Protestant Bibles in ordinary circulation. In reading earlier English literature, however, you have to keep in mind the fact that the books of the Apocrypha were quite as familiar to readers in England as the books of the Old and the New Testaments. For example, in Shakespeare's *Merchant of Venice*, which is an extremely Biblical play, Shylock hails Portia as a "Daniel come to judgment" [4.1.23], meaning that she is a very good lawyer. But Daniel does not appear as a lawyer in the Book of Daniel: he appears as a lawyer only in a couple of books in the Apocrypha: the story of Susanna [vv. 44–63], and the story of Bel and the Dragon.[4]

The books of the Old Testament, the books of the New Testament, and the fourteen books of the Apocrypha make up what we ordinarily call the Bible. There are a number of other peripheral books that didn't make it into either the Bible or the Apocrypha, some of which have a good deal of interest in their own right. For example, there is a collection of writings named the Pseudepigrapha, which is Greek for "false writings," because they were ascribed to venerable figures who assuredly did not write them. It's true that a great many of the books in the Bible itself are pseudepigrapha in the same sense, but that is another kind of question. These books are very largely prophecies about the end of the world. They were written in the last three centuries before the Christian era, and are almost certainly Hebrew and Jewish in origin. The best known of them are two books ascribed to the patriarch Enoch. Enoch is referred to in the Book of Genesis as the great-grandfather of Noah [5:18–29]. He is supposed to have written a long apocalyptic prophecy that was accepted in the early Church as authentic. There is a reference to it in the New Testament, in that curious little epistle known as the Epistle of Jude, the second to last book in the New Testament [vv. 14–15]. There is a quotation from the Book of Enoch that speaks of its author as the seventh in descent from Adam [60:8], which Enoch is according to the Genesis genealogies. But it very soon became clear that the Enoch of the Old Testament could not possibly have written this book, so it fell out of favour and disappeared from Western Europe, turning up again in Abyssinia around 1790 in an Ethiopian version. There is a Second Book of Enoch which turned up thirty or forty years later than that in south Russia, and various other books of the same kind in this collection. Some of them are classics in their own right, like the Testament of the Three Patriarchs and the Sayings of the Fathers. A man called R.H. Charles has edited the Apocrypha and the Pseudepigrapha of the Old Testament in two volumes, and that is the version to refer to if you want to know more about them.

There are also a number of writings that didn't get into the New Testament canon. Some of them might very well have done so: there are two letters by Clement—St. Clement, who was a leader in the early Church—and there are a few others of the same quality. But for the most part, a number of apocryphal writings exist that in the Middle Ages were accepted, yet which modern historical scholarship has rejected entirely as having any claim to authenticity. But as long as they were accepted, they had an important cultural influence. For example, if you read Middle English, you'll find there are many references to the "harrowing of hell." Jesus after his death is supposed to have descended to hell and rescued all the people who were destined for salvation, starting with Adam and Eve and ending with John the Baptist. This is accepted as a part of the gospel in, for example, Chaucer, but it is entirely apocryphal. It goes back to a book called the Gospel of Nicodemus, or sometimes the Acts of Pilate. It is an interesting book, but as a gospel it's a fraud, unacceptable as having any historical basis at all.

And then there are a number of infancy gospels, which elaborate legends about the childhood of Jesus. In one of them, Jesus is out

making mud pies and one of his little pals comes along and interferes
with his play, so the infant Jesus strikes him dead. The dead child's
mother comes to complain to the Virgin Mary, and the Virgin Mary says
to Jesus, "Now look, you shouldn't go around killing people, it is bad
for public relations." So the infant Jesus says, "Oh well, all right." And
so he goes back and brings the little boy back to life again and goes on
with his mud pies [Gospel of Pseudo-Matthew 26]. In another part of
the same book, he is represented as being somewhat bewildered that
the other children didn't want to play with him [chap. 29]: and so these
books go prattling on and on, with the inventiveness of second rate
minds. At the same time, it is as gospels that they, for example, assign
an ancestry for the Virgin Mary and make her daughter to St. Anne.[5] St.
Anne was the patron saint, I believe, of the province of Quebec—Ste
Anne de Beaupré.[6] There was a famous shrine there, until it was realized that there is no historical evidence for the existence of St. Anne,
nothing in the Bible about her at all: so the title was transferred to John
the Baptist. In any case, these books have been edited by a man named
Montague James, who calls them the New Testament Apocrypha. M.R.
James was the headmaster of Eton College: he wrote some excellent
ghost stories and was also a Classical scholar.

There are also two secular writers to whom I may be referring quite
frequently. One was a Jewish philosopher living in Alexandria in Egypt
during the time of Jesus, known to posterity as Philo Judaeus. He was a
Platonic philosopher who attempted to derive the doctrine of Forms in
Plato from the account of Creation in Genesis: and while there is a good
deal of straining to make interpretive points in his books, they are also
full of interest for anybody who is interested in the Biblical pattern of
imagery. Also, there is a great Jewish historian, Josephus, who lived at
the time of the Roman destruction of Judaea and who wrote a book
called *Antiquities of the Jews*, which covers much the same ground as the
Old Testament but adds a great deal of detail in the later period. He is,
for example, fascinated by King Herod, who turns up at the beginning
of the New Testament, and a great deal of his book is devoted to Herod
and his doings. He has a later book called *Wars of the Jews*, which deals
with the final struggles against the Roman power. And he is, again,
invaluable as a historical authority for the Old Testament period.

We don't know much about the Gnostic gospels because they survive
only in the works of the orthodox Christians who attacked them. And
of course there were political reasons why the orthodox opponents'
books survived but the Gnostic books themselves didn't. But their

opponents did quote fairly liberally from them, so one can learn a good deal about the Gnostics. The best introduction to Gnosticism is by Hans Jonas: it's called *The Gnostic Religion*. But there were pagan and Jewish Gnostics as well as Christian ones: it was a pretty widespread movement. I'll be coming to the Gnostics later in this course and will deal with some of the issues they raised.

Biblia Pauperum 3: EPIPHANY
(Matthew 2:1–11)

David receives Abner
(2 Samuel 3:6–21)

Solomon receives the Queen of Sheba
(1 Kings 10:1–13)

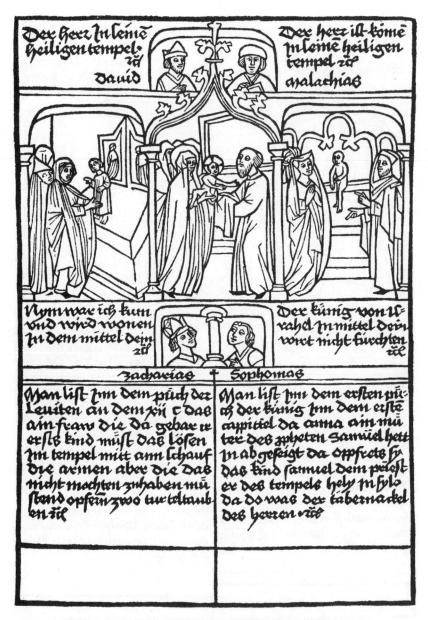

Der Herr In seinē
heiligen tempel·
zū
dauid

Der herr ist kōmē
In seinē heiligen
tempel zū
malachias

Nym war ich kum
vnd wird wonen
In dem mittel dein
zū

Der künig von Is-
rahel In mittel dein
wirt nicht fürchten
zū

zacharias ✝ Sophonias

Man list Jm dem puch der
Leuiten an dem xij c das
ain fraw die da gebar ir
erst kind müst das lösen
Jm tempel mitt ann schauf
die armen aber die das
nicht mochten zuhaben mū
stend opfern zwo turteltaub-
en zū

Man list Jm dem ersten pū-
och der künig Jm dem erste
capptiel da anna ain mū-
ter des propheten samuel hett
in ab geseigt da opfrets sy
das kind samuel dem priest
er des tempels holy In sylo
da do was der tabernackel
des herren zū

Biblia Pauperum 4: PRESENTATION OF CHRIST IN THE TEMPLE
(Luke 2:22–39)

Purification after childbirth
(Leviticus 12)

Samuel dedicated to temple service
(1 Samuel 1:24–8)

2

The Shape of the Bible

The narrative sequences in the Bible that I was speaking of are of a type that make it very difficult to answer the question, Are they histories or fictions? In fact, it might be said that what is distinctive, almost unique, about the Bible is the fact that that question cannot be directly answered at all.

Every sequence in words, just by virtue of the fact that it is a sequence, is a verbal structure in which the words have their own patterns and their own forms. It is impossible to describe anything with definitive accuracy in the outside world by means of words, because words are always forming their own self-contained patterns of subject and predicate and object. They are continually shaping reality into what are essentially grammatical fictions.

It doesn't matter whether a sequence of words is called a history or a story: that is, whether it is intended to follow a sequence of actual events or not. As far as its verbal shape is concerned, it will be equally mythical in either case. But we notice that any emphasis on shape or structure or pattern or form always throws a verbal narrative in the direction we call mythical rather than historical. To give you an example, the Book of Judges is a sequence of stories about leaders who were originally tribal leaders, but the stories have been edited to present the appearance of a united Israel going through a series of disasters and restorations. The actual heroes are different each time—Gideon, Jephthah, Samson, Samuel—and the stories told about them naturally differ in content. But they're all set inside a similar framework: Israel deserts its God, and the result is disaster; an enemy moves in, conquers the country or invades it; the Israelites think better of their infidelity, turn back to their God again; a deliverer or a judge is sent, who brings them back to a position roughly where they were before.

Now that gives us a narrative shape or pattern that we would get either in a history or in a work of literature: roughly a U-shape. And that U-shaped pattern is the typical shape of the structure we know as comedy. If we look at comedy, we find that a situation is presented which gradually becomes more ominous and threatening and foreboding of disaster to the characters with which we are sympathetic. Then there's a kind of gimmick or sudden shift in the plot, and eventually it moves towards a happy ending where everybody gets married, and the hero and heroine's real life is assumed to begin after the play is over. That is why the heroes and heroines of so many comedies are in fact rather dull people. The main character interest is thrown onto the blocking characters, the parents who've forbidden them to marry, for instance.

That curve is also the containing narrative shape of the Bible, because the mythical shape of the Bible, if we read it from beginning to end, is a comic one. It's a story in which man is placed in a state of nature from which he falls—the word "fall" is something which this diagram indicates visually.[7] At the end of the story, he is restored to the things that he had at the beginning. Judaism focuses upon the story of Israel, which in the Old Testament is to be restored at the end of history, according to the way the prophets see that history. The Christian Bible is focused more on the story of Adam, who represents mankind as falling from a state of integration with nature into a state where he is alienated from nature.

In symbolic terms, what Adam loses is the tree and the water of life. Those are images that we'll look at in more detail later. On practically the first page of the Bible we are told that Adam loses the tree and the water of life in the garden of Eden. On practically the last page of the Bible, in the last chapter of the Book of Revelation, the prophet has a vision of the tree and the water of life restored to man. That affinity between the structure of the Bible and the structure of comedy has been recognized for many centuries and is the reason why Dante called his vision of hell and purgatory and heaven a *commedia*.

We owe our great tragedies very largely to the Greek tradition, which has a different outlook. The Bible is not very close to tragedy: when it deals with disaster, its point of view is ironic rather than tragic. While there are many reasons for this, the main one is that in a typical tragedy there is a hero who embodies certain qualities which suggest the superhuman, and the Bible recognizes no such hero except for Jesus himself. The Crucifixion would be the one genuine tragic form in the Bible, but that of course is an episode in a containing comedy.

And this U-shaped pattern of loss and return and deliverance is found all the way through the Bible. It's not only the overall containing form, but appears in many parts of the Bible that have nothing to do with history. It is, for example, the containing form of the story of Job, who is in a state of prosperity, loses everything he has, and at the end of the story is restored to what he had before. It is also the containing shape of Jesus' parable of the prodigal son [Luke 15:11–32]. It's perhaps interesting to notice that of these loss-and-return stories, the prodigal son is the only version we have in the Bible where the decision to return is a voluntary act of the chief character himself. All the others depend on a human confession of helplessness and a divine intervention.

A fact which links onto that is that the central nation of the Bible story is Israel, and the most important historical fact about Israel is that the Israelites were never lucky at the game of empire: the land of Israel was simply a highway between Egypt and the Mesopotamian kingdoms. In the entire historical record, there are only two very brief periods of relative prosperity and independence: the period of David and Solomon and the period just following the Maccabean rebellion, about a century before the time of Christ. The reason was the same in both cases: one world empire had declined, and its successor had not yet arisen. The period of David and Solomon came between the decline of Egypt and the rise of Assyria, and the period of the Maccabees and their successors came between the decline of Syria and the rise of Rome.

So we find that history is always in itself a problem for the Biblical narrators. They are surrounded by kingdoms that are prosperous and powerful and, although awfully wicked, that seem to get away with it. Most of the Biblical writers are writing within an Israel which desperately longs to have this kind of power and influence and prosperity, and would certainly regard it as a mark of signal divine favour if it ever did have it. But throughout the Biblical story, mostly it doesn't.

We can look at the story of Israel, mythically, as a sequence of falls and rises. Sometimes the rise is only to a change of masters, but still, that U-shaped pattern is the way in which the story of Israel is told throughout the Bible. Now, to mention all of these falls and rises at once would be confusing, so I'll select six, in honour of the days of Creation. We start of course with Adam, who is thrown out of Eden and told to go and till the ground, which is cursed in order to make it more difficult. And so, from the garden, we are turned out into a wilderness. To that symbol of the wilderness, two other images are added. One is the image of the sea, which turns up in the story of Noah's flood. The other is the symbol of the heathen city. The first person born outside the garden of Eden is Cain, the eldest son of Adam and the murderer of Abel. He is then sent into a far country, and there he founds a city. That city has always been a puzzle to readers of Genesis, who are reading a narrative which seems to imply that there were only three people alive in the world at that time. But what is interesting is the assumption that cities are the earliest form of human settlement, rather than villages or hamlets or isolated farms.

Cain goes out to what is called the land of Nod. We don't know where that is, but it looks as though it were somewhere in Mesopotamia. We'll pass over the story of the flood for the moment, but the first conspicuous upward movement is the one associated with Abraham, who lives in a heathen city called Ur in Sumeria and is drawn out of there by God and promised a land in the west. And from this the patriarchs succeed: Abraham's son is Isaac; Isaac's son is Jacob, whose later name is Israel. This period seems to be very largely a pastoral one associated with flocks and herds, essentially a ranching economy. But then Jacob (Israel), as a result of a complicated story about his son Joseph, goes down into Egypt.

Now this is the great archetypal event, so to speak: it's the one from which all the others take their form and model. The Israelites did nothing wrong in entering Egypt; in fact, they were welcomed there. But after a century or two, there arose a pharaoh who determined to exterminate them by genocide, and the result was the Exodus. The Exodus, under the leadership first of Moses and then of Joshua, takes them back to the Promised Land. But this time the economy is more of an agricultural one. They are promised a land flowing with milk and honey [3:8], and neither of those is a vegetable product: but the symbol of the Promised Land, when they get there, is a big bunch of grapes [Numbers 13:23–4]. We are told that, with some reluctance, they settled down to an agricultural life, dependent on the crops and on the harvest and vintage.

The crucial event of the Exodus was the crossing of the Red Sea. The Israelites got across it safely, but the Egyptian army pursuing them was drowned in it [Exodus 14]. So the demonic image of the sea recurs in the story of the Exodus, and that is followed of course by forty years' wandering in the wilderness.

There follows the period of the judges, and eventually the Israelites find themselves in bondage to many of the surrounding kingdoms, of which the most powerful and important were the Philistines. The Philistines were probably a Greek-speaking people from Cyprus, and they gave their name, somewhat ironically, to Palestine. By this time, we are getting towards the period of the Trojan War, which is a legendary reconstruction of a period of history in which the Egyptian Empire was declining and was constantly being attacked by sea pirates, most of whom were allied to the Greeks. The armour of the Philistine giant Goliath, which is described in the Book of Samuel [1 Samuel 17:5–7], is rather like the armour of the Homeric warrior. So we're speaking of the period around 1200 to 1100 B.C.

This is followed by a renewed prosperity, where the great leaders are David and David's son Solomon. Here the imagery shifts to urban imagery. David's great feat, from the Biblical point of view, was to capture the city of Jerusalem and to make it the capital of his kingdom. Thus, Jerusalem becomes the central image of this phase of Israelite history, along with the temple on Mount Zion built by his successor Solomon.

Solomon is a curious example of the way in which legend and history are interwoven in the Bible. The historical Solomon was not a wise man, but a weak and foolish and extravagant man who spent seven years building a temple, thirteen years building his own palace, and who then, at the suggestion of some of his seven hundred wives, amiably built two or three more temples to other gods. Well, that's fair enough: historically, Solomon was probably not a monotheist at all. But the memory of his taxation for all these buildings was very bitter, and not long after his death, when his son proposed to continue his policies, he instantly lost ten-twelfths of his kingdom, which split into a Northern Israel and a Southern Kingdom of Judah. After that, it was only a matter of time until another captivity. The great Assyrian war machine rumbled across western Asia and destroyed the Northern Kingdom around 722 B.C. The Southern Kingdom, Judah, had a respite for a little while, but eventually King Nebuchadnezzar of Babylon came and sacked Jerusalem, and the Israelites, now the Jews, were carried away into captivity in Babylon.

The Babylonian captivity lasted about seventy years, until Babylon itself was destroyed by the power of Persia. The first great king of Persia, Cyrus, one of the few authentically great men of the ancient world and a tremendous legendary figure both in Greek literature and in the Bible, permitted—in fact, according to the Bible, encouraged—the Jews to return and rebuild their temple [2 Chronicles 36:22–3; Ezra 1:1–3] . There are two returns prominently featured in the Bible, one of them towards the end of the sixth century, around 516 B.C., and a later one about a century later under Ezra [7–10] and Nehemiah [2:5 ff.]. There were probably others, but symbolically we need only one return, which focuses on the image of the rebuilt temple.

There follows something of a blank. Consecutive Old Testament history stops with the destruction of Jerusalem in 586 B.C., and we have only fragmentary glimpses of the Persian period. You remember that the Persian Empire was destroyed by Alexander the Great, who gets very little attention in the Bible, although the great Biblical historian Josephus has him welcomed into Jerusalem by the high priest with many expressions of mutual esteem.[8] But Alexander's empire of course fell apart instantly after his death. Judah was eventually attached to the largest chunk of it, the Seleucian Empire, with its headquarters in Syria. Finally, around 165 B.C., there arose the persecution of the non-Helle-nized Jews by the king of Syria, whose name was Antiochus and who gave himself the name of Epiphanes, which means "the Glorious." But when he wasn't listening, his courtiers altered it to Epimanes, "the Lunatic." Antiochus seems to have regarded the Jewish religion as a personal insult, and his persecution was so ferocious that it provoked the rebellion of a man of the priestly tribe of Levi, whose five sons, all of whom were also very actively engaged in the rebellion, are known as the Maccabees.

Eventually the Maccabees gained a certain degree of independence for the country, perhaps the most important event symbolically being not so much the rebuilding of the temple as the purification of it. What Antiochus had done that was particularly outrageous to Jewish feelings was to put a statue of the god Apollo in the Holy of Holies,[9] the most sacred part of the temple. Therefore, on the anniversary of this sacri-lege, the temple was purified by Judas Maccabeus [2 Maccabees 10:1–9]. The independence won by the Maccabees lasted until the legions of Rome, headed by Pompey, again came rolling over from Asia Minor and entered Jerusalem in 62 B.C.. That is the historical situation which we meet at the beginning of the New Testament.

In A.D. 70, Jerusalem was sacked and looted by the Emperor Titus. In A.D. 135, the Emperor Hadrian expelled all the Jews from their home-land and changed the name of Jerusalem to a Latin name—Aelia Capitolina—and simply eradicated all geographical traces of the Jewish people. At this point, Jewish and Christian versions of this U-shaped narrative diverge. The Christian interpretation is that Jesus came to achieve all these symbols of peace and prosperity in a spiritual form. In the Jewish belief, that has still to happen, and there has to be also a literal return of the Jewish people to their homeland.

I wouldn't say that this pattern was cyclical. The Bible doesn't like cyclical views of history. The reason it doesn't is that a cycle is a machine, and a cyclical view of history means a machine turning, something impersonal. Such a view would be part of that perverse tendency on the part of mankind to enslave himself to his own inventions and his own conceptions. Man invented the wheel, and so in no time at all he's talking about wheels of fate and wheels of fortune as something that are stronger than he is. That's the Frankenstein element in the human mind, an element which is part of original sin.

The Bible, while its approach to history is a very oblique one, nevertheless has a very strong, even passionate interest in historical sense. And in history, as we know, nothing ever exactly repeats. Every situation is a little different, but what happens is a kind of growing consolidation of these images. So that the image of the final restoration of mankind that we get in the Book of Revelation is not a simple return to a simple garden of Eden, but incorporates the imagery of cities and of harvests and vintages as well. I think that at every phase we get a new aspect, symbolically, of the ideal human life, which is first thought of as a garden where man lives entirely on tree fruits. Then, as history goes on, it incorporates these elements of human work, these elements by which man transforms his environment into something with a human shape and a human meaning. And with the conception of the rebuilt temple, you have the element of time added. It becomes something that takes place in time as well as in conceptual space.

Well now, if we look at this manic-depressive chart,[10] we notice that symbolically there is a certain affinity among all the categories on the top. They are all symbols for the home of the soul, for the ideal situation of human life. Similarly, all the categories at the bottom are recurring symbols of the bondage and tyranny of human history. We've been dealing with the principle of myth at some length, but the next thing we have to do is to invoke another principle, which is the principle of metaphor.

Metaphor is the grammatical figure which says "this is that." If you look at the forty-ninth chapter of Genesis, which is Jacob's prophecy of the twelve tribes of Israel, you'll find a number of metaphors of that kind: Joseph is a fruitful bough; Naphtali is a hind let loose; Issachar is a strong ass; Dan shall be a serpent in the way [vv. 22, 21, 14, 17]. Now that is the grammatical form of the metaphor, in which there are two categories, A and B. They are said to be the same thing, although they remain two different things. Therefore, the metaphor is illogical; or, more accurately, it is insane. That is, nobody can take metaphor seriously except the people mentioned in the speech of Theseus in *A Midsummer Night's Dream*, the lunatic, the lover, and the poet [5.1.7–8]. The Bible is so full of metaphors because it is so intensely poetic.

We'll find later how many of the images of the Bible, and even how many of the central doctrines of the Bible, or the central doctrines of Christianity which evolved from the Bible, can be grammatically expressed only in the form of metaphor. In the doctrine of the Trinity, for example, one equals three. Or, one is three and three are one. The doctrine of the real presence is that the body and blood are the bread and the wine. Jesus, in Christian doctrine, is man and God. All of these are metaphorical in grammatical expression, and they are all statements that completely transcend, or whatever they do, the world of logic. In logic, A can only be A. It can never be B.

We are told in the New Testament by Paul and others that the Bible has to be understood spiritually—*pneumatikos*—and the word "spiritually" means a good many things in the New Testament. But one thing it always means, and always has to mean, is "metaphorically." In Revelation 11:8 we are told of a martyrdom of two witnesses in the last days, as one of the prophecies of what is going to happen at the end of time. And the verse reads: "And their dead bodies shall lie in the street of the great city, which spiritually is called Sodom and Egypt, where also our Lord was crucified." That is, spiritually, metaphorically, Sodom, Egypt, and the earthly Jerusalem are all the same city. And similarly, in the symbolism of the Bible, Egypt, Babylon, and Rome are all symbolically the same tyranny. And the Pharaoh of the Exodus, the Nebuchadnezzar of Babylon, and the persecuting Caesars of Rome, of whom Nero is particularly the type, are metaphorically or spiritually the same person.

But, of course, they are the same person in a way which does not commit you at all to any literal belief in reincarnation or "there's that man again." That is, Antiochus and Nero and Nebuchadnezzar and the Pharaoh of the Exodus are all spiritually the same person. And similarly, the garden of Eden, the Promised Land, Jerusalem, and the temple on Mount Zion are all interchangeable spiritually, the same image of the soul's ideal and the soul's home. The reason this conception is so centrally important in the Christian Bible is that Jesus continually talks about his spiritual kingdom, which he makes quite clear has nothing to do with overturning the Roman Empire. And that is why the word "spiritual" is so much stressed in the New Testament.

I don't mean individual or subjective. The word "spiritual" is something which normally we approach in a rather individual and subjective way, but there's a very strong social interest in the Bible which is part of its historical interest. In the New Testament, Paul, for example, speaks of a moment of private illumination that he had. At the end of the second Letter to the Corinthians, he's extremely apologetic about it, and talks about boasting, which is something he dislikes doing [12:1–12]. He also talks about it very vaguely. He's not sure whether it happened to him or to somebody else. And what he's thinking of, I think, is that a religion which is aimed purely at individual illumination is something of a cop-out. What he is trying to proclaim is a social and a revolutionary thing as well. He wants the world, not individuals here or there, to wake up.

Biblia Pauperum 5: FLIGHT INTO EGYPT
(Matthew 2:13–14)

Rebecca sends Jacob to Laban   Michal helps David escape
(Genesis 28:11–46)   (1 Samuel 19:9–17)

3

Images of Paradise: Trees and Water

I was speaking last day of a number of ups and downs in a chart that looked like the Loch Ness monster: of Israel rising to a certain ideal level, and then dropping to a level of bondage or invasion or exile. And I suggested that the categories on top and the categories on the bottom are all metaphorically identical with one another. One has to understand the extent to which the Bible relies on metaphorical identification. Metaphor in the Bible is not an ornament of language: it is the controlling mode of thought, and metaphor is a statement which grammatically reads, "this is that." As all statements that two things are the same thing while being two things are illogical, or rather antilogical, we have to take into consideration too, as one of the important things about the Bible, that it is not using a language of logic or predication. It is using a language which it has in common with poetry, but using it for a slightly different purpose.

I said that there was, first of all, a story at the beginning of the Bible according to which Adam was placed in the garden of Eden and was then thrown out of it into the wilderness. We can call this, if you like, the paradisal form of existence. On the ideal side we have the apocalyptic: "apocalypse" means "revelation." The last book in the Bible is *Apocalypsis Iohannis*—the Apocalypse, or Revelation of John. What the Bible has to reveal is, among other things, an ideal mode of living, which exists in various categories. The first category that's presented to us is the paradisal one, which is given us in the form of a garden or oasis. The paradisal is represented as the world that God made to put man into, rather than a world which achieved its form through human effort. And of course, for desert dwellers, the oasis, with its trees and water, would be the perfect image of providential creation, of something provided for man, without man's needing to do anything about it.

All these images in the Bible have both a group form and an individual form. The individual form of this garden or oasis imagery is the imagery of trees and water. We are told that there were two trees in the garden of Eden—the tree of life and the tree of knowledge of good and evil. There are certain complications there that we'll come to later: they would be metaphorically the same tree in two different areas or categories of existence. But we can say that there is the tree of life and the water of life. The water of life is not explicitly called that in the Genesis account. But it is quite clear that that is what it is from the use of the image elsewhere in the Bible. There are several interesting things about this. The account in Genesis doesn't speak, as I say, explicitly of the water of life, but it does speak of rivers.

There are two accounts of Creation in the Book of Genesis. The one with which the Bible begins is a much later account: it's known as the Priestly account, and is a kind of semi-philosophical cosmogony. A much earlier account begins in chapter 2, verse 4, beginning with the paragraph, "These are generations of the heavens and of the earth." The way you tell it from its predecessor is that the word for God suddenly changes. In the first chapter of Genesis we read, "In the beginning, the Elohim created the heavens and the earth." That word "Elohim" is plural. The "im" ending is a regular Hebrew plural: and so it would be theoretically possible, though very bad scholarship, to translate the opening verse of Genesis as "In the beginning, the gods created heaven and earth," a fact which greatly amused Voltaire when he learned it. But the fact had been known for many centuries before him, and St. Augustine had explained the plural form as referring to the Christian Trinity—which isn't very much better as scholarship.[11] But actually, the "im" is what is known as an intensive plural, a plural of majesty or impressiveness. When somebody told an off-colour joke in the presence of Queen Victoria, she said, "We are not amused," meaning the British Empire as represented by Queen Victoria: that was the use of an intensive plural.[12] And so you get the plural form of God used in the first chapter of Genesis. Then in the second chapter, beginning in the fourth verse, the name for God shifts to "Yahweh." Nobody knows how it was pronounced: it's four Hebrew letters. As you perhaps realize, in Old Testament Hebrew, only the consonants are written down, and all the vowels—or practically all the vowels—are editorial. The result was that in reading from the Scriptures in public worship, this word "Yahweh" was regarded as too secret to be pronounced so a different set of vowels was substituted from the word "Adonai," which means "Lord," and that gave you a hybrid form that would be something like "Jehovah" and, by way of Luther's German Bible, that got into English as the normal anglicization of this word "Yahweh."

It is only in this second account that you get much emphasis on the story of the garden, the oasis. We are told that there was a river which watered the whole garden. It's spoken of as a single river in chapter 2, verse 10: "And a river went out of Eden to water the garden; and from thence it was parted, and became into four heads." Then the four rivers are listed. Two of them are the Euphrates and Tigris of Mesopotamia. The word "Mesopotamia" means "the land between the two rivers." And the third, the Gihon, apparently is the Nile.[13] The fourth one is more mysterious. According to the Jewish historian Josephus, who lived in New Testament times, the fourth river was the Ganges [*Antiquities of the Jews*, 1.1.3]: he probably meant the Indus. But in any case, you have then a garden stretching from Egypt to India, which would provide a fair amount of space for two people to wander in. And it is watered by four rivers that are explicitly said to have one source.

In fact, the Creation, in the Yahwist (or Jahwist) account, begins with the watering of the garden in verse 6. "But there went up a mist from the earth, and watered the whole face of the ground." The word "mist," though it's a fairly accurate rendering of the Hebrew word, doesn't make much sense in this context. The Septuagint, the Greek translation, has *pege*, "fountain," and the fountain is something that recurs throughout the imagery of the Bible.

What is interesting is the assumption that there are two seas under the earth—a sea of sweet, or fresh water, and a sea of salt water. After all, it's a matter of common observation that fresh water is under the ground, because it comes up in springs and in wells. Therefore you have, scattered through the early books of the Bible, various references to a sea of fresh water under the ground. It is this sea of fresh water that waters the garden of Eden.

In the Ten Commandments, the second commandment forbids the Israelites to make an image of any god, including the god of the waters under the earth. That suggests by implication that there must have been other people living near the Israelites who did have such gods and did have statues and temples erected in their honour. The Sumerians, who are the beginning of Near Eastern civilization, had such a god, by the name of Enki. He was, like many fertility gods, an unwearied seducer of female divinities. But he also seems to have been something of a protector of the human race, and speaks up for it when the equivalent of the flood story turns up and the gods propose to destroy humanity.

The kingdom which replaced Sumeria was the kingdom of Akkad, a Semitic kingdom that spoke a Semitic language and took most of its mythology over from Sumer. They also had a god of the sweet waters, which they called Abzu. Some people have tried to connect it with the Greek word "abyss." His consort Tiamat was the goddess of the bitter waters, the salt waters. According to the Akkadian creation poem, Abzu was killed and his consort Tiamat, now a widow, decided to revenge herself on the gods. The gods were terrified of her, except for the hero god Marduk. Marduk killed Tiamat, split her in two, and made the heavens out of half of her body and the earth out of the other half.

That story of the Creation beginning with the dragon-killing is something that the Hebrew authors of the Old Testament were quite familiar with, though they used it as poetic imagery, not as a matter of belief. Even the late account of Creation in Genesis 1 with which the Bible begins has some faint echoes of an earlier account where the Creation was the result of a victory over a dragon. Genesis begins, "In the beginning God created the heaven and the earth. And the earth was without form, and void": *tohu wa bohu*. "And darkness was upon the face of the deep." The word "deep" is *tehom*. And the scholars tell us that those Hebrew words are connected etymologically with the proper name Tiamat, the goddess of the bitter waters. The Biblical account of Creation makes it out of a chaos, which is a more philosophical version of the salt sea: nevertheless, the sea remains an image of chaos all through the Bible.

In addition to the fresh water sea under the ground, there is also assumed to be a source of fresh water up in the sky, much higher up than the rain clouds. In the first chapter of Genesis we are told that after the creation of light there was a creation of a firmament, that is, a sky which divided the waters below from the waters above [vv. 3–7]. Those waters above the heavens are referred to later in Psalm 148. Only once in history did these two bodies of water, above and below, prove destructive: that was when, at the time of Noah's flood, they poured in to reinforce the rains and the bursting out of the sea, and helped to drown the world. In Genesis 7:11[–12], "In the six hundredth year of Noah's life, in the second month, the seventeenth day of the month, the same day were all the fountains of the great deep broken up, and the windows of heaven were opened. And the rain was upon the earth forty days and forty nights." The windows of heaven suggest a source of water above the rain clouds. If you look at that Psalm that I mentioned earlier, Psalm 148, in the fourth verse: "Praise him, ye heavens of heavens, and ye waters that be above the heavens." Well, it's a matter of common observation that the rain clouds are below the heavens. And the implication of there being water above, or behind the windows of heaven, indicates another dimension of water. So that you are, first of all, presented with a conception of a water of life which is both above and below, and that leads to the suggestion that the water of life that is being talked about here is not quite the same thing as ordinary drinking water. In other words, the suggestion is that man could live in water like a fish: there would be a state of existence in which water does not necessarily drown, in which man can live in water as one of his own elements.

All through the early books of the Bible, particularly in the account of the Exodus, the wanderings in the wilderness, the water supply was naturally a matter of life and death, so there are a great many references to trees and water. One of the most important contrasts in Biblical imagery is the contrast between living water and dead water. The great weakness of the King James Bible as a translation is its fondness for rationalized translations, or what the funeral service calls the "comfort of a reasonable religion":[14] consequently, it is much less metaphorical than the actual Bible is and will say things like "springing water," where the Hebrew original has "living water."

The first event in the Bible, then, is the expulsion from Eden and the loss of the tree of life and the water of life. In Genesis 3:22–3, "And the Lord God said, Behold, the Man is become as one of us, to know good and evil: and now, lest he put forth his hand, and take also of the tree of life, and eat, and live for ever: Therefore the Lord God sent him forth from the garden of Eden, to till the ground from whence he was taken." That's a rather strange verse—that verse 22. It has God addressing an assembly of other gods, and speaking as somebody actually terrified of the power that man has now acquired through his knowledge of good and evil. In fact, he's so terrified he can't even finish his sentence. And the sense of losing the tree of life, at any rate, and by implication the water of life, is certainly very strongly marked in its emphasis.

That is the first event. If you look at the last event in the Bible, that is, in Revelation 22, the very last chapter of the last book in the New Testament that begins, "And he shewed me a pure river of water of life, clear as crystal, proceeding out of the throne of God and of the Lamb. In the midst of the street of it, and on either side of the river, was there the tree of life, which bare twelve manner of fruits, and yielded her fruit every month: and the leaves of the tree were for the healing of the nations." So the opening incident in the Bible is man's loss of the tree and water of life. The closing incident of the Bible is his regaining of the tree and water of life. And you notice that the river of life is described as the "street": that is, it has become an element in which man can live.

Now, at this point, I want to introduce a principle which is going to be very central in this course, which is that of the New Testament's attitude to the Old Testament. The New Testament's view of the Old Testament is that it presents what is essentially a prophecy of what is going to happen later, namely, the coming of Christ. And consequently, everything that happens in the Old Testament is a type of something that happens in the New. What happens in the New Testament explains the Old Testament happening, and therefore it's called an antitype.

If you look, for example, at Romans 5:14, Paul says, "Death reigned from Adam to Moses, even over them that had not sinned after the similitude of Adam's transgression, who is the figure of him that was to come." The Greek word that Paul uses, translated "figure" here, is the word *typos*. The Latin rendering in the Vulgate is *forma*, but the King James Bible has "figure" because, for the most part, it was the word *figura* that had come to be the Latin equivalent of the Greek word *typos*, from which we get "type." And so what Paul is saying is that Adam is a type of Christ. And elsewhere he speaks of Christ as the second Adam [1 Corinthians 15:45–7].

If you look at 1 Peter 3:21, "The like figure whereunto even baptism doth now also save us," here again is the word "figure," but the Greek word is not *typos*, but *antitypos*—antitype. And what Peter is saying, or what the First Epistle of Peter is saying, is that the Christian rite of baptism is the antitype of the saving of Noah's family from drowning.

That means that the New Testament is, among other things, a dense mosaic of allusions to the Old Testament. That's particularly true of some books, of the Book of Revelation and the Epistle to the Hebrews, but there's hardly a passage in the New Testament—I suspect that there is not a *single* passage in the New Testament—that is not related in this type–antitype manner to something in the Old Testament.

Consequently, that passage at the end of Revelation about the tree and water of life being restored to man must come from something in the Old Testament too. You'll find it in the very middle of the Bible, in Ezekiel 47:7. Ezekiel represents himself as being in Babylon during the captivity, and his prophecy is directing the Jews returning from the Babylonian captivity to their homeland to start by rebuilding the temple. The last eight chapters of the Book of Ezekiel are a detailed vision of the proper worship of God being re-established in the forsaken and abandoned temple.

By the time of chapter 47, the temple has been pretty well rebuilt. The angel who was showing him this prophecy also shows him the rebuilt temple, and says that as soon as the temple was complete, a spring of water bubbled up from the threshold and formed a river which flowed eastward. Now a river that arose on the hill of Jerusalem and flowed eastward would flow into the Dead Sea. And the Dead Sea, which is so salty that nothing can live in or around it, is a consistent image of dead water all the way through the Bible. We are told that this fresh water, running into the Dead Sea, will bring it to life. In verse 8, "Then said he unto me, These waters issue out toward the east country, and go down into the desert, and go into the sea: which being brought forth into the sea, the waters shall be healed." I think that he has here a sense, not merely of the Dead Sea being turned into fresh water, but of all salt water being turned into fresh water. That is picked up by the author of Revelation, who says, at the beginning of the twenty-first chapter, just as the final vision begins, that heaven and earth were "passed away; and there was no more sea." And again, one has to think of that metaphorically. What the author of Revelation is saying is that in the final Apocalypse, there is no more Dead Sea, that is, there is no more dead water. That is, there is no more death.

In Ezekiel's vision, you notice that, along with the river, there comes a growth of trees along its bank. In verse 7, "Now when I had returned, behold, at the bank of the river were very many trees on the one side and on the other," which suggests that metaphorically the tree of life in Eden is not so much a single tree as all the trees. He says that these trees are also trees of life in verse 12, "By the river upon the bank thereof, on this side and on that side, shall grow all trees for meat, whose leaf shall not fade, neither shall the fruit thereof be consumed: it shall bring forth new fruit according to his months." "Meat" in 1611 meant any kind of food. And all that is picked up and quoted by the author of Revelation.

Biblia Pauperum 6: EGYPTIAN IDOLS FALL
(apocryphal)

Moses and the golden calf
(Exodus 32)

Dagon falls before the Ark
(1 Samuel 5:1–5)

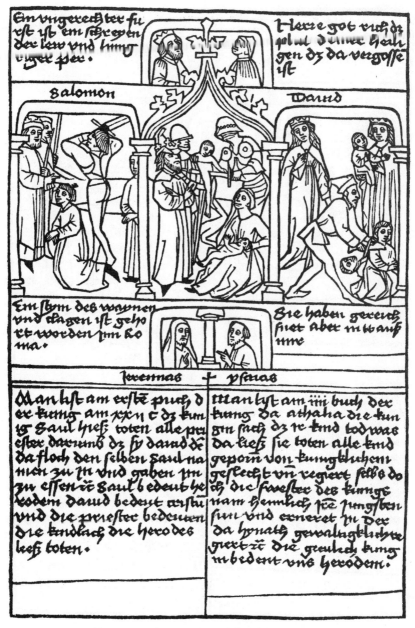

Biblia Pauperum 7: MASSACRE OF THE INNOCENTS
(Matthew 2:16–18)

Saul has the priests killed
(1 Samuel 22)

Athalia kills the princes of Judah
(2 Kings 11:1)

Biblia Pauperum 8: RETURN FROM EGYPT
(Matthew 2:19–23)

David returns after Saul's death
(2 Samuel 2:1 ff.)

Return of Jacob
(Genesis 32–3)

4

Parody and Manifest Demonic: Trees and Water

I was speaking about the structure of imagery of the Bible, and was saying that the imagery tends to split into two opposed categories. One I'm calling the apocalyptic or the ideal, the one that's associated with the garden of Eden, with the Promised Land, with Jerusalem and the temple, with Jesus' spiritual kingdom. The other I am calling the demonic: it's what is associated with the heathen kingdoms of tyranny— Egypt and Babylon, and, in the New Testament, Rome.

Now that means that the whole of Biblical imagery tends to fall into these two sharply opposed categories, and that there is no image in the Bible which does not have both an apocalyptic and a demonic context: or at any rate, which *may* not have both. There is no image in the Bible which is necessarily always demonic or always ideal. In other words, there is no natural image. A serpent, for example, is usually a sinister image in the Bible because of its role in the garden of Eden story, but it's a quite genuine symbol of wisdom in most of the religions and mythologies of the world, and is used that way by Jesus as well—"Be ye ... wise as serpents" [Matthew 10:16]. Therefore, whether an image belongs to one category or the other depends on the context, but that context is never very difficult to determine.

. I was dealing with the various levels of imagery, and we'd started with the paradisal. I said that the great symbol for that was the oasis, which has, in particular, two images—the tree of life and the water of life, which we traced through the Bible. If you look at the Book of Psalms, for example, the very first Psalm applies the same image to the private and individual life. The righteous man, we are told, "shall be like a tree planted by the rivers of water" [v. 3]. The same images recur through the New Testament as well. As we tried to show, they contain the entire action of the Bible, being the first things that man loses at the opening of the narrative and the last things that he regains at the end of it.

It follows, therefore, that these paradisal images would also have to have their demonic counterparts. The complication here is that there are two kinds of demonic imagery in the Bible. In the first place, there is the odd paradox of a fact that the only kingdoms that are consistently successful and prosperous are the evil kingdoms. It is Egypt and Assyria and Babylon and Tyre which have the kind of power and prosperity that Israel itself desperately longed to have, and would have regarded as a mark of divine favour if it had had it. So the prosperity of the heathen kingdoms forms a category of imagery that we can call the parody demonic, which has all the qualities of the real thing except permanence. There is also the manifest or the you-just-wait demonic, which is what all this prosperity and success will eventually and inevitably turn into sooner or later.

We saw that the water of life was associated with four rivers, two of which were the Euphrates and the Tigris of Mesopotamia. The third is usually identified with the Nile in Egypt, and the fourth possibly, as Josephus suggests, with India (the Ganges or the Indus). Clearly, their parody demonic images would be the Nile, the Euphrates, and the Tigris as they came to be in history. They are the rivers that gave prosperity and success and fertility to Egypt, to Babylonia, and to Assyria. Nineveh is on the Tigris, and Babylon is on the Euphrates. To that, you could add the commerce and shipping in the Mediterranean and the Persian Gulf, which increased the success and prosperity of the Mesopotamian kingdoms and also of Phoenicia. Phoenicia occupied the northwest part of Israelite territory, and in contrast to the Israelites, who never consistently held a port on the Mediterranean, they were great seafarers and traders. And so these rivers of history are the water of life for these heathen kingdoms. They sustained their prosperity and their commercial prestige and their fertility, which is an important recurring image of a slightly different category.

There's been a great deal of work done on the Bible and its relationship to comparative folklore and mythology. The general underlying assumption is that there's nothing in the Bible that can't be found in some form—or to which some analogy cannot be found—in some mythology or folklore elsewhere. But we could reverse the axiom and say that there is nothing really essential in the folklore or mythology of any civilization whatever that cannot be found in some form in the Bible. If we do reverse the axiom in that way, we'll find a great many images in the Bible which are parody images of very widespread myths. One of these is the "world tree."

The "world tree" is sometimes the same thing as the tree of life, and as such, it belongs to mythologies far older than the Bible. As it develops in mythology, it comes to be a form of what is called the *axis mundi*, the vertical aspect of existence. Its roots form the lower world below this one, and its fruits and branches are in an upper world above this one. The surface of this world has usually been, in mythology, a middle earth, with an upper world in the sky and a lower world underground. The *axis mundi* or world tree extends all through these three worlds, and in more sophisticated developments, the planets are the fruits hanging from its branches. You'll find it practically everywhere you look, from Norse mythology, where it is called Yggdrasil, to nursery tales like Jack and the Beanstalk.

So we're not surprised to find that when the prophets start denouncing the apparent prosperity of Egypt or Assyria or Babylon, they will use an image of this kind in a parody context. Look, for example, at Ezekiel 31. This is an oracle against Egypt which applies to Egypt the same image that is applied to Assyria. The story of Assyria was a particularly dramatic one for the Old Testament writers. Nineveh, the capital of Assyria, was the greatest city of the ancient world, and according to the book of Jonah, it was a three-day's journey to cross it from its western suburb to its eastern one [3:3]. And yet, quite suddenly, Nineveh just vanished. It disappeared under the sands, where it remained until the middle of the nineteenth century. Almost immediately after it was destroyed, it was impossible for anybody else even to find the site of the world's greatest city. So the suddenness with which heathen power could vanish almost overnight was naturally a favourite theme of prophecy.

Ezekiel says, in 31:3[, 5]: "Behold, the Assyrian was a cedar in Lebanon with fair branches, and with a shadowing shroud, and of an high stature; and his top was among the thick boughs. ... Therefore his height was exalted above all the trees of the field, and his boughs were multiplied, and his branches became long because of the multitude of waters, when he shot forth." Now, here is a parody description of a world tree, identified with the Assyrian power, which is nourished by the water of life fertilizing its roots. And in verse[s] 8[–9]: "The cedars in the garden of God could not hide him: the fir trees were not like his boughs, and the chestnut trees were not like his branches; nor any tree in the garden of God was like unto him in his beauty. I have made him fair by the multitude of his branches: so that all the trees of Eden, that were in the garden of God, envied him." But, of course, the Assyrian kingdom falls with a great crash. In verse 16, there's a significant comment: "I made the nations to shake at the sound of his fall, when I cast him down to hell with them that descend into the pit: and all the trees of Eden ... shall be comforted in the nether parts of the earth." The great Assyrian tree has fallen to the level of the vanished garden of Eden before the beginning of history.

There is probably a fairly specific allusion there to Assyrian mythology, because you find the world tree on Assyrian monuments. In the much later Book of Daniel there's a very similar tree associated with Nebuchadnezzar and the power of Babylon. The language used about that tree is even more explicitly a description of a world tree, an *axis mundi*. In Daniel 4:20[-2]: "The tree that thou sawest, which grew, and was strong, whose height reached unto the heaven, and the sight thereof to all the earth: Whose leaves were fair, and the fruit thereof much, and in it was meat for all; under which the beasts of the field dwelt. ... It is thou, O King, that art grown and become strong: for thy greatness is grown, and reacheth unto heaven, and thy dominion to the end of the earth." The world tree is here explicitly said to reach to heaven and to be visible from all over the world.

That is the image, then, of temporary prosperity, and it is contrasted with the manifest demonic, which is the more direct parody of the ideal image. What we get, then, as the main units of the manifest demonic, are the tree of death and the water of death.

Now as I said earlier, the most obvious and dramatic image of the water of death is the Dead Sea, because it is quite literally dead water in which nothing lives—too much salt in it. And traditionally, though not explicitly, the evil cities of Sodom and Gomorrah were destroyed by fire from heaven and sunk under the Dead Sea. Similarly, the Red Sea is also an image of the water of death, largely for political reasons. At the time of the Exodus the Israelites crossed the Red Sea, but the Egyptian army was drowned in it, so that symbolically and metaphorically Egypt is sunk under the Red Sea, as Sodom and Gomorrah are under the Dead Sea.

Ezekiel directs an oracle against Tyre, the great commercial city of Phoenicia, and says that eventually Tyre will turn into a rock [26:4, 14]. The words "Tyre" and "rock" are very close together in Hebrew—they make a pun—and the rock will be, again, sunk under the sea. So the image of the kingdom sunk under water, which is what happened of course to the whole of the earth in the time of Noah's flood, is an image of the demonic water of death.

Now, remember that metaphorical thinking is not logical thinking. What you are dealing with when you are thinking in metaphors is not a world of solid blocks or obstacles, not a world of nouns that can be kicked around by verbs: it's a world of metaphors, and metaphorical imagery is a world of forces and energies which often modulate into one another. And so the tree of life in the garden of Eden before the fall may be thought of as a tree in a garden, or it may be thought of as all the trees in the garden, or it may be thought of as the body of the unfallen Adam himself. And that imagery of the divine man, or the man with the divine destiny who is metaphorically identical with the tree of life, runs all through the Bible, and accounts for a very central metaphorical expression. That is the Hebrew word "Messiah," of which the Greek equivalent is "Christ." And what that word means is "the anointed one," the person who has been confirmed as a royal figure by an anointing ceremony which symbolically and metaphorically identifies him with the tree of life. That is, assuming that something like olive oil or a vegetable oil or a tree oil of some kind would be used in the anointing ceremony, because I doubt that they would use petroleum in such an instance.

The identification of the Messiah with the tree of life remains fairly constant throughout the New Testament. I say New Testament, because in the Old Testament the word "Messiah" simply means a legitimate ruler, whose right to rule has been confirmed by some anointing ceremony, whether real or assumed. King Saul, who was rejected, is still called the Lord's anointed, the Messiah, and, once, a person outside the Israelite community altogether, King Cyrus of Persia, was called the Lord's anointed by Isaiah [45:1]. But by the time of Jesus, with the Maccabean victory still fresh in the Jewish mind, there was a good deal of speculation about a figure called *the* Messiah, and that figure is of the type that theologians call eschatological: that is, a figure concerned with the ending of history and the evolution of man out of time into some other kind of existence entirely.

Thus came the question, Who is *the* Messiah? And that, of course, is still the question that divides Judaism and Christianity. But what I'm concerned with at the moment is not that, but the metaphorical identification with a tree of life.

In the story of the Exodus, the water of death has two aspects. It is in the first place the water that drowns the Egyptians, and in the second place the water from which the Israelites escape, becoming a nation by doing so. Similarly, the flood of Noah is an event in which everybody gets drowned except the family of Noah, which escapes by floating on top of the flood with the ark. That is carried over into the Christian symbolism of baptism, where again the same ambiguous imagery occurs: symbolically and metaphorically, the person who is baptized dies in one world and is reborn in another.

If we apply such a principle to the imagery of trees, the tree of death would be represented by such a thing as the barren fig tree that would later crucify Jesus at the time of the Passion [Matthew 21:19–21]. The tree of the knowledge of good and evil is clearly a sinister tree as far as the results of eating it are concerned. And this tree of knowledge quite clearly has something to do with the discovery of sex as we know it. That is, as soon as they ate of the tree of knowledge, Adam and Eve knew that they were naked. This inspired a feeling of shame, which meant that the present, rather frustrating experience we know as sexuality came into the world when man fell into a lower state of being. And so, if Adam before his fall was metaphorically a tree of life, then after his fall, he would metaphorically be a tree of death, or of moral or sexual knowledge.

We find as one of the laws written in the Book of Deuteronomy, for example, in Deuteronomy 21:22[–3]: "And if a man have committed a sin worthy of death, and he be to be put to death, and thou hang him on a tree: His body shall not remain all night upon the tree, but thou shalt in any wise bury him that day; (for he that is hanged is accursed of God)." And again, the symbol of the tree of death, which is under the curse of God, like the barren fig tree cursed by Jesus, is here associated with a hanged criminal.

Now, what is true of the word "sea," which is both a symbol of death and a symbol of renewed life, depending upon whether one is looking at it from the Egyptian or the Israelite point of view, is true also of the cross, which is a tree of death insofar as it expresses the human reaction to God, and a tree of life for members of Christianity. So we're not surprised to find, perhaps, that Paul quotes this law of Deuteronomy and applies it to the Crucifixion. In Galatians 3:13: "Christ hath redeemed us from the curse of the law, being made a curse for us: for it is written, Cursed is every one that hangeth on a tree." This is all part of symbolism that is consistent in the New Testament of the Messiah or Christ figure as simultaneously a figure of triumph and transcendence and also a victim, a scapegoat figure.

As we'll coo later, there are many Old Testament prototypes (as Christianity interpreted them) of the Jesus of the Gospels. One of them is King Solomon, the king who built the temple and was traditionally the teacher of wisdom. Solomon, however, was only one of David's many sons. David had another son called Absalom, who rebelled against his father. His manner of death is described in 2 Samuel 18:9[–10]: "And Absalom met the servants of David. And Absalom rode upon a mule, and the mule went under the thick boughs of a great oak, and his head caught hold of the oak, and he was taken up between the heaven and the earth; and the mule that was under him went away. And a certain man saw it and told Joab, and said, Behold, I saw Absalom hanged in an oak." And so David's general, Joab, came up to him and thrust darts into his side and killed him while he was hanging on the tree. Well, Absalom's curious helplessness in what seems a relatively easy situation to get out of perhaps indicates a certain ritual element in his death. Traditionally, he was hung from the tree by his beautiful golden hair, reminding one of certain cults connected with the oak tree and the mistletoe, where a human sacrifice would be initiated by cutting the mistletoe, the golden emblem from the branches of an oak. But however that may be, the symbolism of Absalom hanging on a tree and having darts thrust into his side is something as essential to the story of Jesus as the aspect of the "King of kings and Lord of lords" [Revelation 19:16].

Well, then we find that Israel goes through the three stages that I mentioned earlier [Lecture 2], the pastoral stage, the agricultural stage, and the urban stage. These are all images of a nature which is transformed by human effort and energy into something with a human shape and a human meaning. What man really wants is what his work shows that he wants, whenever he gets a chance to work, and doesn't have to waste his life making war or feeding a parasitic class. When he gets a chance to work, he is transforming the animal world into a world of flocks and herds; the vegetable world into a world of crops, of harvest and of vintage; and the world of stones and minerals into a world of cities and buildings and highways.

Let us take for example the pastoral world. The Bible invariably uses the sheep as the typical apocalyptic or ideal animal. I suggested in one of my books that the reason for that is that sheep societies are perhaps more like human societies than those of any other animal: because the sheep is gregarious, stupid, and easily stampeded.[15] It is consequently the appropriate animal to describe in pastoral metaphors—words like "pastor" and "flock" still survive in language about the Church. But as far as pure metaphor is concerned, there's no earthly reason bulls and cows should not be as appropriate images as sheep.

Here we have to consider the importance and influence in the Bible of what one might call negative ritual: the fact that the Israelites are so frequently forbidden to do things quite obviously because their neighbours did them. For example, we are told many times in the Mosaic code: Thou shalt not seethe (i.e., boil) a kid (i.e., a baby goat) in his mother's milk [Exodus 23:19, 34:26; Deuteronomy 14:21]. That is the basis for the Jewish kosher rule about not mixing milk and meat dishes. But boiling a kid in his mother's milk is not something that would occur to anybody off the top of his head: so it looks as though it must have been a fertility rite on the part of the neighbouring Canaanites, from whom the Israelites were required to separate themselves.

Similarly, the bull was a favourite fertility image in neighbouring countries, and for that reason is regarded with some suspicion as an appropriate emblem for the faithful and obedient Christian. In the Old Testament, for example, there is a story in the Exodus that while Moses was absent conversing with God on Mt. Sinai, his brother Aaron, the high priest, led the tribes of Israel into idolatry by making a golden calf as an idol [Exodus 32:1–6]. "Calf" there means bull. That is a type of the later split in the kingdom between the ten tribes of Northern Israel and the tribe of Judah, when the king of Northern Israel, Jeroboam, set up local shrines with the emblem of a golden calf, again meaning a bull, as indicating departure from the line of religious orthodoxy [1 Kings 12:28–9]. And in New Testament times, the great rival of Christianity through the Roman Empire was the religion of Mithraism, where the chief event of the year was a celebration of the birthday of the sun on December 25. Mithraism went everywhere with the Roman Empire: a Nazi bomb falling in London exposed a Mithraic temple during the war, and if you go to Rome, one place that you should definitely not miss is the church of San Clemente, where there is a series of four or five churches of different periods, and a Mithraic temple lying at the very bottom of the whole structure. The great emblem of Mithraism was the bull, and its great rite was the sacrifice of the bull, which was a repetition of an original creation myth, and forms again an exact parallel of the Christian sacrifice of a lamb who is, according to the Book of Revelation, "slain from the foundation of the world" [13:8]. It is this affinity of the bull with heathen kingdoms that knocks it out as a normal image of a pastoral world; and in effect, one can almost class it as a parody demonic image.

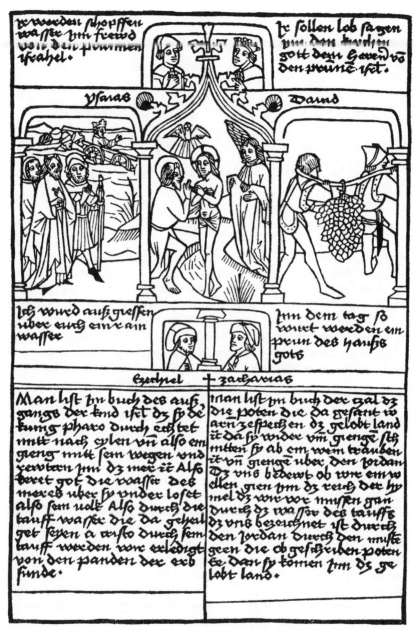

Biblia Pauperum 9: BAPTISM OF CHRIST
(Matthew 3:13–17)

Israel crosses Red Sea
(Exodus 14:15–31)

Scouts bring grapes from the brook
Eshcol (Numbers 13:17–27)

5

Sexual Imagery: The Bride and the Bridegroom; The Great Whore and the Forgiven Harlot

We've been looking at various categories of Biblical imagery: the paradisal and then, below that, the organization of the animal world. The first gives us the garden of Eden, and the second the pastoral world, more particularly the sheepfold. Of course, pastoral and garden imagery have overlapped, both in Biblical and secular literature, all through the history of human imagination. It's easy to see in such things as the 23rd Psalm, "The Lord is my shepherd," how the pastoral ideal and the paradisal ideal really blend together and form the same thing.

I'll be filling out various stages of this table as we come to them. There is, however, the intervening category of the human world, which is a much more complicated one. Now if we ask what is the ideal human form for existence, we find that there is no simple or single answer, because our answers keep shuttling between a social ideal and an individual one. That is, the human ideal is a paradoxical mixture of a belonging and an escape.

According to Jean-Paul Sartre, "hell is other people,"[16] but I'm not sure that Sartre wanted to spend the whole of eternity by himself. Similarly, Andrew Marvell can write a poem, *The Garden*, in which he suggests that the fall of man really began when a stupid and blundering God created Eve in order to be a companion for Adam. And as he says, "Two Paradises 'twere in one / To live in Paradise alone" [ll. 63–4]. But you cannot think of a human ideal consistently either in social terms or in individual ones. So we seem to be in a deadlock, and the only solution is that human life, like Greek nouns, seems to have a dual as well as a singular and a plural.

Thus we have the individual life, the sexual, erotic relation between two people, and the social. The sexual relation is given an emphasis in the Bible which, like so many things in the Bible, is unintelligible in anything but metaphorical terms. We are told that in the sexual relation, two people are actually the same person while remaining two people, which is not possible, but is therefore the cornerstone of Biblical imagery. Thus, the ideal of human life becomes an ideal in which the sexual relationship has become the pattern for the identification of the individual and the social.

The imagery of a wedding, of the union of the bridegroom and the bride, is one of Jesus' favourite images for the apocalyptic or ideal world. It is essential to realize that in this case, the bride is actually the entire body of Christian followers. In the Book of Revelation, this bride is identified with Jerusalem [21:2], or Israel, meaning the people of God.

That suggests, first of all, that sexual imagery has relatively little to do with the actual relations of men and women. Thus, in this relationship where Christ is the bridegroom and the bride is the people of Christ, it follows that Christ is symbolically the only male. He is also symbolically the only individual, the only person with a right to say "I am." That means that the souls of the people of God, whether they are souls of men or of women, are all symbolically female and make up a single bride figure.

Now again, metaphorical thinking is not logical thinking, and we have to proceed to make a series of identifications that we would find it hard to follow in other contexts. The Song of Songs is a series of wedding songs in which both the bridegroom and the bride are presented: they both have their songs. The opening verse says: "The song of songs, which is Solomon's." Now there is no more reason for ascribing the authorship of the Song of Songs to Solomon than there is for ascribing it to the Witch of Endor. But the poem is symbolically associated with Solomon because the symbolism expands from songs about a rural wedding where the bride is called "sister," which is the conventional Oriental term for the loved one, into a symbolic wedding of the king with the land over which he rules.

That is why the bride describes herself as "black but comely" [1:5]: that is, she represents the black fertile soil of the land. We are told that her body is to be compared to various aspects of the country: her nose, for example, is "as the tower of Lebanon which looketh toward Damascus" [7:4], which might seem to be a rather doubtful compliment to a bride whose charms were less symbolic. But the wedding of the king and the fertile land is an image for what the word "testament" itself indicates. The word that we translate as "testament," which is *berith* in Hebrew and *diatheke* in Greek, means a covenant or a contract, specifically the contract between God and his people Israel. So that Solomon and his bride, the Shulamite woman of the Song of Songs, expand by a further range of symbolism into the relationship of God and his people, which is why in Christian typology the Song of Songs was interpreted as a song of the love of Christ for his bride, his people. Of course, Christianity was a big-city religion which expanded from one city to another, and consequently the image of the black fertile land is not as immediate in Christianity as it is in Judaism. But the same symbolic shape is nevertheless there.

If you look at Isaiah 62:4, you see the same prophecy being applied to the restored Israel: "Thou shalt no more be termed Forsaken; neither shall thy land any more be termed Desolate: but thou shalt be called Hephzibah, and thy land Beulah: for the Lord delighteth in thee, and thy land shall be married." "Married" is the meaning of the word "Beulah." And the image of the land married to its king expands into the image of the people of God married to its God.

In the demonic world, the demonic counterpart of the bride would be the figure described in the Book of Revelation as the Great Whore, and the male figure of whom she is the mistress would be the figure who in the New Testament is described as Antichrist, the figure opposed to Christ. Just as the bride is identified with Jerusalem, so the Whore would be identified with the heathen city of Babylon.

In Revelation 17:2, she is the figure, "With whom the kings of the earth have committed fornication, and the inhabitants of the earth have been made drunk with the wine of her fornication." And then in verse 5: "And upon her forehead was a name written, Mystery, Babylon the Great, the Mother of Harlots." And later on, in verse 9, she is associated with seven mountains which are clearly the seven hills of Caesarean Rome, so that Babylon and the Rome of the persecuting Caesars are symbolically the same demonic city, where the power opposed to that of Christianity is established.

It's important perhaps to realize that the word "whore" in the Bible almost always refers to a theological and not a sexual irregularity. One person who is associated with whores in the Old Testament is Jezebel, the wife of Ahab, and that is not because she is supposed to have cuckolded King Ahab—the narrator of Kings could hardly have cared whether she did or not—but because she introduced the worship of Baal into Israel [1 Kings 21].

The reason for the epithet, apart from the symbolic contrast to bride, is not just that it's abusive, but that it has a more specific reference to the custom in Canaanite religion of maintaining prostitutes in the temple, which is a practice that the Israelites in Deuteronomy are forbidden to have anything to do with, but which was obviously extremely familiar to them. Tamar, for example, in Genesis, disguises herself as a cult prostitute in order to get back her inheritance as a forsaken wife [38:1–30]. The story would be unintelligible if the practice were not familiar to Israel as well as to the surrounding nations.

Antichrist in his turn is the secular ruler. And as a society grows from a tribal community into a nation and from a nation into an empire, the ruler of the empire tends to think of himself as the ruler of the world. The Bible does not regard the world ruler as necessarily an evil person, but he rules over the kind of world in which, sooner or later, one of his descendants is going to become so. Jesus' axiom about spiritual and temporal authority, "Render to Caesar the things that are Caesar's, and to God the things that are God's" [Mark 12:17] runs into a difficulty as soon as Caesar begins to claim what is due only to God, that is, divine worship. It's only when he does that that he becomes the Antichrist figure referred to both in one of Paul's letters [2 Thessalonians 2:3–4] and in the Book of Revelation itself.

In the Book of Revelation, the Antichrist is characterized by a cipher, the number 666 [13:18]. Ciphers of that kind usually turn on the fact that the letters of the alphabet were also used as numbers: and there has never been a cipher in history solved as often as that one has been. It has been solved in Hebrew; it has been solved in Greek; and it's been solved by Robert Graves in Latin. And it always spells out the name of Nero, who is the type of the persecuting emperor. He was the first emperor to institute a persecution of Jews and Christians, according to Tacitus, in order to have somebody to blame for the burning of Rome. And although the author of Revelation probably lived under a later emperor, Nero is still the type. As the type, he is spiritually, that is, metaphorically, identical with other persecuting figures in the Bible, such as Antiochus, who is the villain in the Book of Daniel, the Pharaoh of the Exodus, and Nebuchadnezzar.

There is a more comprehensive picture of female figures in the Bible that we might look at at this point. I have been dividing images into the apocalyptic, or ideal, and the demonic. Those are a contrast. There are also intermediate figures, who represent human nature in the sense that they are neither wholly evil nor wholly ideal, but are imperfect

figures undergoing the process of redemption. You can divide the female figures of the Bible into two groups, the maternal and the marital,
that is, the mother figures and the bride figures.

The ideal maternal figures include the Virgin Mary and a mysterious
woman who appears at the beginning of Revelation 12, and who is said
to be a woman "clothed with the sun, and the moon under her feet, and
upon her head a crown of twelve stars." She is a Queen of Heaven, like
so many maternal goddesses, but she is also described as the mother of
the Messiah, like the Virgin Mary. So there are really three accounts of
the birth of the Messiah in the New Testament: the one in Matthew,
which has the wise men and Jesus born in a house; the one in Luke, the
pastoral one, which has the shepherds and Jesus born in a manger; and
this account in chapter 12, which is so obviously mythical and metaphorical that it has never succeeded in getting on our Christmas cards.

In the intermediate, or analogical, category you have the specifically
human mother, who of course is Eve, "our general mother," as Milton
calls her [Paradise Lost, bk. 4, l. 492], the representative of humanity
going through sin and redemption; and also Rachel, who, though only
one of the wives of Jacob or Israel, is symbolically the mother of Israel
and is so referred to in Matthew in connection with the Slaughter of the
Innocents [2:18]. Ideal bride figures would then include the bride of the
Song of Songs and the Jerusalem bride, who appears at the end of the
Book of Revelation, chapter 21, where it is said that she is "the holy city,
New Jerusalem," descending to earth "as a bride adorned for her hus-
band" [v. 2].

Now there doesn't appear to be a demonic maternal figure, but this
blackboard demands one.[17] We often find that if the Bible does not
supply what is needed diagrammatically, it will invariably be supplied
by later legend. So later legend obliged by constructing the figure of
Lilith. Lilith is mentioned in Isaiah 34:14—the King James version calls
her a "screech owl," which is one of the bad things that the Authorized
Version is continually doing, that is, making rationalized translations.
But in later legend, Lilith became the first wife of Adam. There are two
accounts of Creation in the Book of Genesis, and the effort to reconcile
those two accounts wound up by giving Adam two wives, the first one
being Lilith and the second Eve. Lilith, we are told, was the mother of
all the demons and the fallen angels. Being that, she had a very flourish-
ing career in Romantic literature: she appears in Goethe's Faust and as
the heroine of a romance of George Macdonald,[18] and in many other
places.

The demonic marital figure is of course the Great Whore of Revelation, identified with Babylon as the other bride is with Jerusalem, and with such Old Testament prototypes as Jezebel introducing the cult of Baal. It follows therefore that there needs to be an intermediate marital figure, and that that intermediate figure would represent the human race going through the process of sin and redemption.

We have said that the word we translate "testament" has the primary meaning of a covenant or contract between God and his people. The contract is represented as something drawn up with Israel by God's initiative. It is also represented as a contract which God could break but won't, because of his nature, but as a contract which man, strictly speaking, cannot break but is forever trying to break. So symbolically, the female figure of this category would be the Forgiven Harlot, the bride figure who is unfaithful to her Lord but who in spite of that is to be forgiven and brought back again. That harlot figure appears in various parts of the Old Testament, in Ezekiel for example, chapter 16, verse 3: "Thus saith the Lord God unto Jerusalem; Thy birth and thy nativity is of the land of Canaan; thy father was an Amorite, and thy mother an Hittite ..." and so on: the whole chapter goes on to describe the unfaithfulness and forgiveness of Jerusalem. The Canadian poet James Reaney has a poem called *Rachel* which is in effect a very beautiful and very eloquent paraphrase of this chapter in Ezekiel.[19] The same image turns up later in Hosea, where Hosea is ordered by God to marry two harlots, one after the other [1:2, 3:1]. These represent the apostasy of both north and south Israel.

The same figure turns up in the New Testament as the woman usually identified as Mary Magdalene. There is an anonymous woman in the seventh chapter of Luke described as a sinner whose sins are forgiven because "she loved much" [v. 47]. Mary Magdalene appears in the next chapter of Luke, and is generally identified with her. A similar female, who has the same symbolic role whether she is the same person or not, has firmly established squatter's rights on the opening of the eighth chapter of John. She is actually a bit of floating folklore associated with Jesus, and in the early manuscripts she appears in various places. The modern translators of the Bible, who are much more distinguished for scholarship than for common sense, try to get her out of John 8 and put her in an appendix, but nevertheless she's still there. She represents perhaps one of the most eloquent and moving episodes of the gospel, the woman who, because she was a harlot, is condemned to be stoned to death. Jesus interferes and suggests that those who have never committed any sins at all might take the lead in throwing the stones. Hence, in paintings of the Crucifixion, you usually see the cross of Christ flanked by two female figures, the Virgin Mary and Mary Magdalene, one in blue and the other in red.[20]

In a polytheistic mythology, you can have the maternal figure and the bridal figure identified. That is, you can have a female goddess figure who is both the mother of a god and, later on, his mistress. You find that in the cults associated with dying gods in Mediterranean countries. And you have such counterparts as the relations, say, of the Virgin Mary and the infant Jesus with the relations of Venus and Cupid in Classical mythology, where Venus is the mother of the God of Love and can also be a bride figure. In Christianity, however, the two figures of the mother and the bride obviously have to be separated, although they are still very close together symbolically. The bride of the Song of Songs for example is described as "a garden inclosed" and "a fountain sealed" [4:12]. Or, as the Vulgate says, *hortus conclusus, fons signatus*. And the "garden inclosed" and the "fountain sealed" have always been traditionally identified with the Virgin Mary, who from one symbolic point of view is the bride of the Holy Spirit as well as the mother of the Logos. We are also told that Christ is the Son of a Father who is a spiritual Father, and that his death reconciles man with the Father.

Now if you constructed a demonic parody of all that, you would get something very close to the story of Oedipus, who kills his father and makes a wife out of his mother. The status of the Oedipus story as a kind of demonic parody of the Christian story was striking enough for the poet Yeats to construct an elaborate theory of history according to which civilizations of Oedipus and civilizations of a Christ figure alternate all through time, one being tragic and heroic, the other comic and altruistic.[21] But it's perhaps easier to see the Oedipus story as either a demonic parody of the Christian story, as it is in some aspects, or as an intermediate analogy of it, as it is in certain other aspects. In the story of the creation of Adam for example, the older story which begins in the second chapter of Genesis, the Yahwist account as it's called, Adam is made from a female, *adamah*, or mother earth. And when, after the fall, he goes back to the ground from which he was taken, he returns to that earth-mother after making the break with his Father. So the Oedipus legend is not quite removed from the story of Adam itself.

This account of the human symbolism in the Bible is of course closely linked to the account of city symbolism, because the city is the emblem of the people or the group. So if you go to the urban image, you have

Jerusalem on the one side and Babylon on the other. That brings us up again against the question of the ambiguity between the social image and the individual image.

Now there's another dimension of this relation of the social to the individual which we've already run into. We saw that the paradisal imagery of the Bible is in the first place a garden and in the second place a single tree, a tree of life. That leads to a general principle of imagery in the Bible, to a special kind of metaphor where the individual is identified with the class or group of things to which it belongs. That is the type of metaphor that I sometimes call a royal metaphor, because it underlies one of the most pervasive of human institutions, the institution of kingship. We've already seen how the king, Solomon, inevitably interposes himself in the symbolic expansion of the Song of Songs. Similarly, Elizabeth II can draw crowds wherever she appears, not because there is anything remarkable about her appearance, but because she dramatizes the metaphor of society as a single body. That has been the function of the king in all ages, to represent in an individual form the unity of his society.

The corporate or class image, like the city, would also be, on the principles of this royal metaphor, identified with a single building. That building would most naturally be the house consecrated to the city's god, in other words, the temple. Thus the city is the bride and the temple is the bridegroom.

We are told several times in the Gospels that the temple is to be identified with the body of Christ. In the Gospels, Jesus is represented as saying, "Destroy this temple, and in three days I will raise it up" [John 2:19]. The narrator adds that he was speaking of the temple of his body. The author of Revelation, in describing the New Jerusalem, is very emphatic that there was no temple therein, because, as he explains, the place of the temple has been taken by the body of God [21:22]. There is, consequently, in this metaphorical symbolism, the unity of the bridegroom and the bride in which all the buildings of the city are one building, the house of many mansions. And the corresponding demonic image is of course the Tower of Babel.

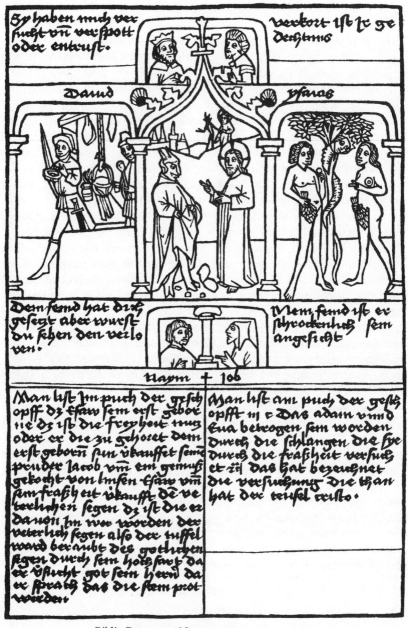

Biblia Pauperum 10: TEMPTATION OF CHRIST
(Matthew 4:1–11)

Esau sells birthright
(Genesis 25:21–34)

Fall of Adam and Eve
(Genesis 3:1–7)

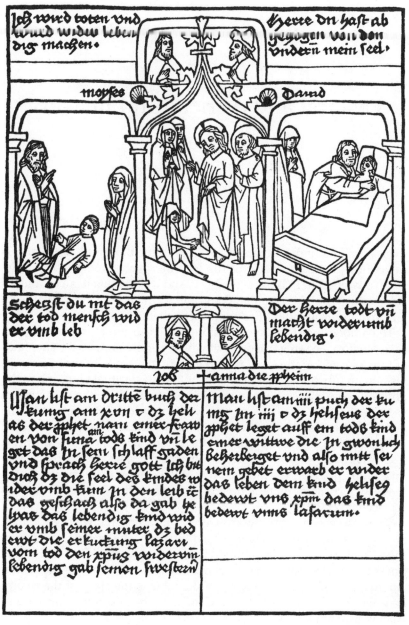

Biblia Pauperum 11: RAISING OF LAZARUS
(John 11)

Elijah raises widow's son
(1 Kings 17:17–24)

Elisha revives child
(2 Kings 4:8–37)

6

Pastoral and Agricultural Imagery

I was speaking of the pattern of imagery in the Bible and of its various categories, and particularly of the way in which three phases of history[22] are reflected in Biblical imagery. And we saw that it is a characteristic of this type of image that the group form and the individual form are metaphorically identified with each other.

The ambiguity of the symbolism attached to the Messiah is that in each category he is regarded as both master and victim, as the shepherd of the flock and at the same time the sacrificial lamb. In the same way, his human function is that of a king, but he's a spiritual king, and in the physical world he is only a mock king put to death. In the urban phase we saw that the city is identified with the bride, Jerusalem, and the temple that is the house of the god in the middle of the city is identified in the Gospels and in the Book of Revelation with the body of Christ. Jesus says in the Gospels: "Destroy this temple, and in three days I will raise it up" [John 2:19]. And the Book of Revelation was insistent that in the New Jerusalem there is no temple because the Body of Christ has replaced it [21:22].

There are various ramifications of this imagery that we need to look at. For one thing, the archetypes, so to speak, the original models of these three phases of Israelite civilization, are established before the time that Israel appears on the historical scene: that is, before the time of Abraham. Almost the first story of the Bible is the story of the rivalry between the two sons of Adam, Cain and Abel. Cain is a farmer and Abel is a shepherd.

Disputes between a farmer and a shepherd are thousands of years older than the Bible. They go back to Sumerian times, but usually in Sumerian times it's the farmer who has the best of the argument, as

would be very natural for a country that's dependent entirely on irriga-
tion and is primarily an agricultural country. But in the Old Testament,
the original pastoral relationship of wandering herds is idealized as the
time when Israel was united with its God, and we find that idealizing of
the pastoral life in the 23rd Psalm, in the imagery of the Good Shepherd
attached to Christ, and elsewhere.

Abel was murdered by Cain. He was a shepherd and his offering, we
are told, was accepted by God; whereas Cain was a farmer, and his
offering of the firstfruits of the crops was not accepted. We are not really
told why this is so, but it establishes the types of a later liturgical
pattern. The primary sacrifice is the sacrifice of the lamb, and that is the
one that is first laid down for us in the story of Abraham's command to
sacrifice his son Isaac, where at the last minute he is stopped from
doing so and a ram is substituted [Genesis 22:1–14]. That story indicates
that for Israel the sacrifice of a lamb is to replace the sacrifice of a son or
of a human being.

And that is confirmed later on by the story of the Passover, which is
the primary rite in the Jewish liturgy. The Passover offering is the
offering with blood, which is the fundamental reason, at least insofar as
there is a reason, why Abel's sacrifice is acceptable and Cain's is not.
Eventually of course, the farmer's offerings of firstfruits were added,
and the calendar developed three major festivals: the Passover, which is
pastoral in imagery; the festival of the harvest, which developed into
the Jewish and Christian Pentecost; and the vintage festival, which
became the Feast of Booths and, eventually, of the New Year in Judaism.
But this imagery of harvest and vintage becomes established rather
later, and apparently the story of Noah has something to do with the
establishing of an agricultural pattern of life.

That is, after the flood Noah institutes a tremendous massacre of
animals in honour of God, and God, we are told, highly approves of the
smell: he says, that smells pretty good: I'd better take the curse off the
ground that I put on it at the time of Adam's fall. Then he promises
Noah that there will be an unfailing cycle of seed time and harvest
[Genesis 8:21–2], the basis of an agricultural program of life. So Noah
turns into a farmer.

His first accomplishment—human nature being what it is—is to
discover wine and get drunk [Genesis 9:20–1]. But nevertheless, the
harvest and the vintage remain apocalyptic symbols, along with the
symbolism of the Good Shepherd and of the city. And if we look
through the Gospels we see very frequently how fond Jesus is of these

metaphors of harvest and vintage for the coming of the Last Day, and the extent to which the animal elements of body and blood are identified with the corresponding vegetable ones of bread and wine. That comes into the pattern of the Eucharist that Jesus is recorded as establishing at the Last Supper, where he specifically identifies the wine with his blood [Matthew 26:27–8; Mark 14:23–4; Luke 22:20].

After the pastoral period of the patriarchs, Israel descends into Egypt. There, God promises Moses from the burning bush that he will lead his people into a land flowing with milk and honey [Exodus 3:8], which are not vegetable products. But what they eventually come into is a Promised Land in which they enter upon an agricultural economy. That of course meant that they were exposed to what the Old Testament writers regarded as contamination from the agricultural rites of the surrounding peoples.

It is with a certain amount of reluctance that Israel enters the Promised Land and embarks on an agricultural economy. If you look, for example, at Joshua 5:12: "And the manna ceased on the morrow after they had eaten of the old corn of the land; neither had the children of Israel manna any more; but they did eat of the fruit of the land of Canaan that year." Corn is seventeenth-century English for any kind of grain. And the first symbol of Canaan was an enormous bunch of grapes which the spies brought back from the Promised Land [Numbers 13:23–7]. In fact the word "Canaan" itself means more or less "the red land," and its Greek equivalent is *phoenicia*. It is supposed to have derived its name from another source, the purple dye from the murex shell fish. But the association of redness with the earth and the agricultural economy is fairly consistent throughout the Bible.

As for the urban life, the Israelites are represented first of all as apparently desert dwellers like the Bedouins. Yet their leaders, Abraham and Moses, are described as having come from the cities, one from Mesopotamia and the other from Egypt. There even seems to be some evidence that the word "Hebrew," which used to be a somewhat pejorative term when used by outsiders, originally meant something more like "proletariat" than the conventional name for a people. And certainly that is the role in which they appear in Egypt.

In any case, they are compelled to live beside neighbours with agricultural rites. I mentioned the law about not boiling a kid in its mother's milk [Lecture 4], suggesting that it was a negative ritual, something that the Israelites were forbidden to do because their neighbours did it. That is true also of the various agricultural cults which had to do with encouraging the fertility of the soil by various rituals founded on the principle of sympathetic magic. That is, if you want it to rain, you pour water on the ground: that kind of imitation by magic and a ritual is the basis of what might have been called the dying-god cult.

I take the phrase "dying god" from Frazer, who investigated this question back in the 1890s.[23] His thesis has been refuted so often that it is now time for it to come back into style again. He speaks of many Mediterranean religions as having been founded on the cult of a god who was fundamentally a god of the fertility of the earth, and more particularly of the vegetable fertility, though it is connected with animals as well. He was as a rule a male god, though there are exceptions, such as Persephone in Greek religion; and he is represented as related to a female principle of whom he is sometimes the son, sometimes the lover, and sometimes the victim. He has various names in various countries. His name in Babylonia was Tammuz; in Syria, Adonis; in Asia Minor, Attis; in Egypt, Osiris; in Greece, Dionysus or sometimes Hyacinthus.

Now the myth associated with this god usually tells of his death. He is a victim either of the female principle he's attached to or of something representing the dead or sterile part of the year. Thus Adonis is killed by a boar who apparently represents the winter. In Ezekiel 8:14 we are shown one of the central rites of these dying god cults. Ezekiel represents himself as being in Babylon along with the captive Jews, and as being shown in a vision what is happening in the temple of Jerusalem. The death of the god was each year ceremonially and ritually mourned by a group of women who represented the female principle of the dying god; and the female goddess represented in her turn the continuing fertility of the earth, which remained dormant throughout the winter or the late part of the summer. It was the chorus of women representing this female principle—the mother or the mistress, whichever she was thought of as being—that formed a central part of the ritual for the dying god. In verse 14, the angel who is showing Ezekiel all this in a vision "brought me to the door of the gate of the Lord's house which was toward the north; and, behold, there sat women weeping for Tammuz." That is, they were carrying on the cult of the dying god. That ritual maintained itself in surrounding countries down to the time of Christ; and even in the very late Book of Daniel, the persecution of the Jews just before the Maccabean rebellion is associated with the cult of the god beloved of women, that is, Tammuz or Adonis [11:37, RSV].

The cult was extremely common all over the Mediterranean. You can't look in Classical literature without seeing that. Theocritus of Sicily has an idyll on the festival of Adonis [Idyll 15]; and the cult of Attis, whose female principle was Cybele, was transferred to Rome during the Punic Wars of Hannibal, largely for political reasons. There it took the form, as most of these cults did, of a three-day spring festival. On the first day, an effigy representing the god was hung on a tree, and the effigy was supposed to die. The second was the day when the god was absent from the world, and the priests lashed themselves into orgiastic frenzies and castrated themselves as part of their sacrifice to their god: there's an ode of Catullus about that, which is a very powerful and very terrible poem [*Carmen 63*]. And then on the third day there was a ritual procession to the marshes or somewhere where the reborn god was supposed to be discovered.

There were other rituals of the same general type, connected with promoting the fertility of the soil. Again the women took the initiative in these cults, and would grow plants in pots and bring them along by forced growth. They would then throw the pots with the plants in them into the water as a rain charm. These were known as gardens of Adonis, and the throwing of the plants into the water was a regular part of the fertility ritual. You would expect the Hebrew prophets to take a very dim view of this practice. If you look at Isaiah 17:10–11: "Because thou hast forgotten the God of thy salvation, and hast not been mindful of the rock of thy strength, therefore shalt thou plant pleasant plants, and shalt set it with strange slips: In the day shalt thou make thy plant to grow, and in the morning shalt thou make thy seed to flourish: but the harvest shall be a heap in the day of grief and of desperate sorrow." So the gardens of Adonis were obviously familiar to the Israelites, and the prophet here is attacking the practice as something that has nothing to do with the Israelite religion.

One of the great confrontations between the two cults is that between Jehovah and the fertility god Baal of the Syrians on the top of Mount Carmel. There is a great contest between Elijah and the priests of Baal as to which god is capable of bringing rain. 1 Kings 18 contains a wonderful scene in which the priests of Baal first of all knock themselves out trying to get their god to deliver rain out of an absolutely cloudless sky. And Elijah makes fun of them in the most approved charitable manner in verse 27: "And it came to pass at noon, that Elijah mocked them, and said, Cry aloud: for he is a god; either he is talking, or he is pursuing, or he is in a journey, or peradventure he sleepeth, and must be awaked."

"Pursuing" is a euphemism which means, perhaps he is making water after all. But the priests are thereby moved to greater and greater efforts. In verse 28: "And they cried aloud, and cut themselves after their manner with knives and lancets, till the blood gushed out upon them." This is sympathetic magic again: if you prick yourself and the blood flows, it suggests that what you need very badly at that point is rain.

Similarly, in Hosea 7:14—only here the King James translation lets you down, because the King James translators didn't know very much about dying god cults—"And they have not cried unto me with their heart, when they howled upon their beds." Then the King James Bible has: "they assemble themselves for corn and wine," but that's wrong. What Hosea is saying is that they *gashed* themselves for corn and wine: that is, they cut themselves until the blood flowed.

Now the root of all this, which you can trace in the Bible also, is that the firstfruits of the crop should be offered to the god. It is assumed that the god, like the God of Noah, lives off the smell of the offerings: and he has to be fed first, otherwise disaster will result. Some of these cults seem to involve an original cult where the sacrificial victim was a human being. The human being might have been the leader of a society, the divine king, according to Frazer, or his eldest son, or later on, a criminal or a prisoner taken captive in battle.

And so we find a certain sequence of sacrificial victims. The original victim would be the divine king himself. That is, the king would be regarded as containing within himself the fertility of the land over which he rules, so that it would be only common sense to put him to death as soon as his strength begins to fail, because his virility and the fertility of his country are bound up together by sympathetic magic. But if you're going to put him to death as soon as his strength fails, there's no sense letting all that divinity go to waste; and so there could be a ritual banquet at which his body was eaten and his blood drunk, so that the divine essence passed into the body of his worshippers.

Well, whether that rite ever existed or not as an historical fact could not matter less. The point is that it is symbolically the right one to have there at the beginning of the sequence. Then follows the sacrifice of the king's eldest son, because it leads to a certain amount of social insecurity—for reasons I don't need to go into—if you keep putting a king to death as soon as his strength is alleged to fail. That is the stage recorded in the story of Abraham's order to sacrifice his son Isaac, an order which at the last moment is rescinded and the sacrifice transferred to the ram.

This is incorporated into the Israelite code, in the list of commandments given in Exodus 34. This is a set of commandments much older
than the more familiar Ten Commandments in Exodus 20. Verse 19
says, "All that openeth the womb is mine; and every firstling among
thy cattle, whether ox or sheep, that is male."[24] Then it goes on to say
that "the firstling of an ass thou shalt redeem with a lamb: and if thou
redeem him not, then shalt thou break his neck. All the firstborn of thy
sons thou shalt redeem" [v. 20]. That is, every firstborn son is technically an offering to God. But the actual sacrifice is not to be carried
through: he is to be redeemed, usually by a lamb, that being the pattern
established in the story of Abraham and Isaac and in the story of the
Passover.

We can see at work here the principle that offering to God as a
sacrifice what you most want yourself gets to be inconvenient after a
while, so various substitutions are made. In fact, it is one of the motifs
in Greek mythology associated with Prometheus. Prometheus' real sin
was in persuading men that the gods didn't want any of the real meat
when they offered a sacrifice: they'd be quite content with the entrails
and the offal. And they were not. And so, every so often there comes the
feeling that the deity wants the full payment and without cheating.

We get an example, which is ascribed again to one of the surrounding
nations, in 2 Kings 3:2[6–]7. Here Israel is attacking the central city of
Moab, one of the neighbouring enemies—"neighbour" and "enemy"
were practically the same word in the ancient world. And we are told
that "when the king of Moab saw that the battle was too sore for him, he
took with him seven hundred men that drew swords, to break through
even unto the king of Edom"—who was his ally at the time—"but they
could not. Then he took his eldest son that should have reigned in his
stead, and offered him for a burnt offering upon the wall. And there
was great indignation against Israel: and they departed from him, and
returned to their own land." So when he is in a desperate situation, he
makes the original offering of his own eldest son that should have
reigned in his stead. And the last sentence is very clearly a clumsy
editorial effort to conceal the fact that in the original story the stratagem
worked, and the Israelites were in fact driven off.

The sacrifice of human beings in that context is what is prohibited in
the Bible. Archaeologists have discovered an inscription by this King
Mesha of Moab who sacrificed his eldest son, and it's obvious from that
inscription that his piety towards his god Chemosh was just as authentic as the Israelite piety towards Jehovah. But that was how his mind

worked and how, in some context, the Israelite mind would have worked too: we are also told that after Jericho was taken by Joshua, a curse was put on the city that whoever rebuilt it would have to sacrifice his eldest son at the beginning and his youngest son at the end of the rebuilding of the city. Which is a terrible curse: the only thing is that trade routes are much more important than children; and Jericho is apparently one of the world's oldest inhabited sites. So the city was rebuilt, and the person who rebuilt it sacrificed his eldest son to begin the operation and his youngest son to finish it [1 Kings 16:34].

I suspect that the original cannibal feast, which is original in the sense of being symbolically original, may not have actually been practised by any society. I think human beings only tend to cannibalism when they run out of other supplies of protein. And even a ritual banquet as solemn as that one would be might not have been carried through in quite so literal a way: we don't know. In any case, the Israelites were extremely familiar with the cult of human sacrifice, particularly the sacrifice of firstborn sons. And although that is condemned, they are much more neutral on the question of a sacrifice which is to fulfil a vow or a sacrifice of a prisoner taken in a war. That may be a sacrifice not merely acceptable to God but actually demanded by him. We find such a story in the Book of Judges, in the eleventh chapter.

We notice that in the commandment in Exodus 34, female animals, whether animal or human, are lawfully ignored. But in the story of Jephthah, it says that he made a vow to sacrifice to God the first thing he saw when he came back from his battle if he won the battle. Notice that the psychological basis of sacrifice is very frequently a bargaining basis. The formula is *do ut des*, I give that you may give. That is what prayer in Homer, for example, very largely consists of. It consists of reminding the gods very pointedly that they have been very well fed by the hero's sacrifices in the past, and if they wish the supply to be continued, they'd better come through with some more victories. This is a typical folk tale of a rash-vow type, where Jephthah says he will sacrifice the first thing that comes to meet him returning from the battle if he's victorious. And of course, the first thing to meet him is his only daughter.

In 11:37[-8], his daughter says that he has to go through with the sacrifice, seeing that he has made the vow. "And she said unto her father, Let this thing be done for me: let me alone two months, that I may go up and down upon the mountains, and bewail my virginity, I and my fellows. And he said, Go." Then, at the end of the chapter, we are told that it was a custom in Israel that the daughters of Israel went yearly to lament the daughter of Jephthah four days in the year. So there are two things to notice there: one is her virginity, which makes her the unblemished and consequently acceptable sacrificial victim; and the other is the fact that she becomes the centre of a cult of mourning women. So the original religion associated with this story is clearly something much older than the Mosaic Code.

If you look at the Book of Zechariah, the second to last book in the Old Testament, right at the end in 12:10[–11]: "And I will pour upon the house of David, and upon the inhabitants of Jerusalem, the spirit of grace and of supplications: and they shall look upon me whom they have pierced, and they shall mourn for him, as one mourneth for his only son, and shall be in bitterness for him, as one that is in bitterness for his firstborn. In that day shall there be a great mourning in Jerusalem, as the mourning of Hadadrimmon in the valley of Megiddon."

Now Hadadrimmon is simply another fertility god of this type, whose cult took the form of his death's being mourned by a group of women. One thing that is interesting about this prophecy in Zechariah is that the phrase "they shall look upon me whom they have pierced" [12:10] is quoted in the Gospel of John [19:37], which means that the authors of the Gospels were thoroughly familiar with the symbolism of dying god cults, and incorporated that symbolism into their accounts of the Passion. You remember that Jesus is followed to his execution by a mourning chorus of women, whom he addresses as "daughters of Jerusalem" [Luke 23:28].

In the Book of Micah, which is in the middle of the minor prophets, there is another reference which contains a verse often regarded—I think with considerable justification—as one of the great moral breakthroughs in history. In 6:6[–8], Micah says: "Wherewith shall I come before the Lord, and bow myself before the high God? shall I come before him with burnt offerings, with calves of a year old? Will the Lord be pleased with thousands of rams, or with ten thousands of rivers of oil? Shall I give my firstborn for my transgression, the fruit of my body for the sin of my soul? He hath shewed thee, O man, what is good; and what doth the Lord require of thee, but to do justly, and to love mercy, and to walk humbly with thy God?"

Now what is fascinating about that seventh verse is that the question of whether one should not fall back on the original demand of the firstborn son as the sacrificial victim was still familiar enough for the prophet to refer to it as a moral problem. Of course what he was saying was that this whole bargaining basis of sacrifice, of making a reparation for something he'd done wrong and so forth, is utter nonsense and that one has to get to a new level of apprehension altogether. But before he says that, he says that it is possible that people around him are still wondering whether, in the event of a sufficiently difficult situation, they ought not to fall back on the original rite.

Biblia Pauperum 12: TRANSFIGURATION
(Matthew 17:1–13)

Abraham and the three angels
(Genesis 18:1–22)

Three young men in the furnace
(Daniel 3)

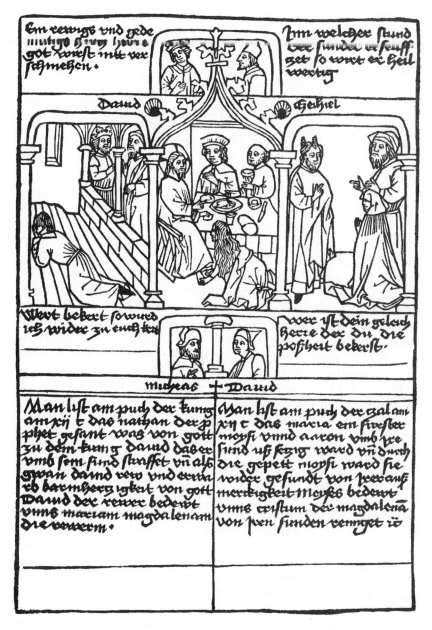

Biblia Pauperum 13: REPENTANCE OF MARY MAGDALENE
(Matthew 26:7–13; partly legendary)

David repents
(2 Samuel 12:1–25)

Miriam repents
(Numbers 12)

7

The World of Angels;
Leviathan, Dragons, and the Antichrist

I was speaking about some of the sacrificial images in the Bible associated with its agricultural symbolism, which form part of the general table of imagery we've been dealing with. We've said that these symbols on the idealized side have both a group form and an individual form. Now in that table, all of these categories are metaphorically identical with one another, and the group form and the individual form are united by what I've been calling the royal metaphor, the metaphor which combines identity *as* with identity *with*. So that the individual and the group forms are likewise identified: the garden and the tree of life are essentially the same thing.

In the New Testament, Jesus is represented explicitly, when instituting the Eucharist, as identifying the bread and wine of the Eucharist supper with his own body and blood, as both a human and an animal victim: the shepherd giving his life for the sheep, and the sacrificial lamb, which is the antitype of the Passover. Now the statements in the New Testament are too explicit for historical Christianity to avoid, considering what these metaphors mean in that context. And of course any consideration of a principle like that in historical Christianity leads eventually to persecution and heretic burning and everything else. But such things merely muddle the actual picture of what's going on. There have been various doctrines: the Roman Catholic doctrine, which is the pure metaphor, that the bread and wine of the host are the body and blood of Christ; and the Lutheran consubstantial theory that the bread and wine are the body and blood of God because God is universal, and so on. These are all conceptualized or rationalized translations of a metaphor into another kind of language. Unfortunately there's a very strong smell of intellectual mortality about these rationalized translations: sooner or later they disappear and we're right back to the meta-phor. Nobody can deal with a metaphor except by something like Saint Patrick's shamrock expounding the doctrine of the Trinity. The actual statement is a metaphor, and the function of the metaphor is to release the imagination by paralysing the discursive reason. It's like the koan in Zen Buddhism. The general tendency in historical Christianity is, so far as is possible, to consider these other metaphorical identifications as "just" metaphors. That is in keeping with the rationalistic distortions of Biblical imagery, which is essentially a metaphorical structure.

The identification of the categories with one another is clear enough: the city is described as Jerusalem, the bride adorned for her husband [Revelation 21:2], and consequently identified with the human cat-egory. And if all the buildings in a city are one building—a house of many mansions [John 14:2]—it follows that all the buildings are one stone. Consequently, you find in Biblical imagery the body of Christ identified with the one stone. There's a verse in the Psalms saying, "The stone which the builders refused is become the head stone of the corner" [118:22]. That's quoted three or four times in the New Testa-ment [Matthew 21:42; Mark 12:10; Luke 20:17; Acts 4:11; 1 Peter 2:7]: it obviously was a very important verse to them. But the cornerstone of the temple is again part of this metaphorical structure. And as this is a world in which nothing can ever be dead, it follows that the stones are as much alive as anything else.

In the Book of Revelation, the churches are told "To him that over-cometh will I give ... a white stone" [2:17]. But the white stone there has a metaphorical connection with the man's body. We are told later on that an angel came out who was clad in what the King James Bible calls "white linen" [15:6], but "linen," again, is a rationalized translation, because there's far better textual evidence for *lithon*, stone. Conse-quently, you have to include a dimension of symbolism in which human beings are also, as the Epistle of Peter says, lively stones [1 Peter 2:5].

We've already seen various identifications of the body of Christ with the tree of life, as in the word "anointed," and various other explicit references. That gives a special importance in the Gospels to those metaphors where Jesus says, "I am the vine, ye are the branches" [John 15:5], "I am the door" [John 10:9], "I am the Way" [John 14:6], and so on. These metaphors "I" are insisting on the metaphorical identification of all these categories of reality in the world that he's talking about—his spiritual kingdom.

This isn't all the universe, of course. There is also the world between

God and man, the spiritual world. The group form of the spiritual world consists of angels or messengers. Now the function of angels in the Bible is of some interest and importance. In the hierarchy of existence they are above human life, but in the Apocalypse, all these categories are not a hierarchy anymore: they are all interchangeable, and consequently all equal. Therefore, there are some sharp warnings in the New Testament against the dangers of worshipping angels [e.g., Revelation 19:10, 22:9]. Angels are fellow creatures of man: their function is that of messenger, and they are not to be regarded with the feelings of adoration that one would reserve for God.

The question is, where does the imagery of angels come from? And the obvious answer is that it comes from "up there." That is, the imagery of this world is derived from the categories of ordinary existence, and the categories of ordinary existence are permeated by the conceptions of up and down. You can raise all kinds of both theological and scientific objections to such a story as that of the Ascension of Christ in the first chapter of Acts, where he sails up into the air and "a cloud received him out of their sight" [v. 9]. We are by no means the first generation to ask, Well, where did he go from there? Did he just sail into outer space, or what? The answer is that this is the mythological universe, and there is no outer space in the mythological universe. In the universe of nature, there is no such thing as up or down: in the mythological universe, there is nothing else.

And so, the tendency to think of hell as "down there" and of heaven as "up there" is built into our mythological ways of thinking. I think as long as the human body has a top and a bottom it's likely to be read into the symbolism of the mythological universe that man lives in. The temple, for example, in all the nations surrounding Israel, the holy building, the ziggurat in the Mesopotamian or Persian cities, was thought of as a tower stretching from earth to heaven, and as, consequently, a connecting point between man and God. I imagine that the basis for the imagery is the human body. The spatial difficulties in the matter, of course, do give trouble in rationalizing the imagery, but as long as it remains metaphorical it doesn't have to be rationalized.

Consequently, the only place for the imagery of the angels to come from is the sky. Now there are two levels of the sky: the upper level, which is the fire level, and the lower level, or the air level. The fire level is derived from the sun and the stars, the fiery bodies in the sky. The other level is the level of clouds and the air and birds.

There are two kinds of angels mentioned in the Bible, the seraphim and the cherubim, and in later iconography they were associated respectively with tongues of flame and with birds in the sky. Later iconography got very elaborate and developed a system of nine orders of angels, but they retained those two as the spirits of love and contemplation. In medieval pictures where angels appear, you will see the seraphim coloured red and the cherubim coloured blue.

The seraphim come into the vision of Isaiah in Isaiah 6[:6–7], where again the seraphim were associated with fire: they take a hot coal off the altar and put it on the prophet's lips to make him articulate. The cherubim are seen in Ezekiel's vision at the beginning of the Book of Ezekiel of a curious vehicle that has wheels within wheels and is drawn around by four living beings: that is, angel figures which have the forms of a man, a lion, an ox, and an eagle. Those four living beings of Ezekiel's vision reappear in the Book of Revelation, where they are seen surrounding the throne of God [4:6–9].

From a Christian point of view, what Ezekiel saw was the Son or Word of God. Consequently, these living creatures that drew his chariot could be typologically identified with the writers of the four Gospels, who carried the message of Christianity all around the world. And so, if you look again at medieval pictures of Christ, you will usually see these four living beings in the corners, representing the four Gospels— Matthew the man, and Mark the lion (as you will remember if you've ever been to Venice, which is under the patronage of Saint Mark), Luke the ox, and John the eagle. The opening words of the Gospel of John, "In the beginning was the Word," are regarded as the most sacred utterance in Christianity, and it is very largely because of that that churches still have lecterns in the shape of an eagle.

The group of angels is, of course, all one Spirit, later considered to be the Holy Spirit, the third person of the Trinity. And so there are two aspects to the imagery of the Holy Spirit also: fire imagery and cloud, air, and bird imagery. He is associated with tongues of flame descending from the sky like lightning, and also with the wind and birds, typically the dove, which has been the chosen bird just as the sheep has been the chosen animal.

The dove has a reputation for chastity that I think would soon be exploded with any careful observation of them. As a matter of fact, I suspect that the reason for choosing them is precisely the opposite: doves were the birds that were sacred to Venus, and whether it's Christian love or pagan love, the dove's qualifications for being the typical bird of love are always in the foreground. We are told in the Synoptic

Gospels that at the baptism of Christ, the spirit of God in the form of a dove was seen descending on him. Jesus says to Nicodemus, "The wind bloweth where it listeth" and goes on to associate wind and spirit [John 3:8].

You notice that quite a lot of things happen to the four elements in apocalyptic imagery. We've already dealt with the water of life: we've said that the description of the garden of Eden seems to assume a fresh-water sea below the actual salt sea and waters above the heavens which are much higher up than the rain clouds. So the suggestion is that man is in the middle of the water of life, and that in a higher state of being, he could live in the water of life, which has a good deal to do with the fishing imagery connected with Christianity and the identification of Jesus with the fish in some contexts.

Similarly, it's a world where the inanimate no longer exists, where the stones are alive, so that earth becomes a part of a living world. It follows, therefore, that there must be a fire of life as well as a water of life, and that all of these elements can be seen as living in the fire of life in the apocalyptic vision. The fire of life is a fire that burns without burning up. At the beginning of the Book of Exodus, Moses sees a bush burning, which nevertheless doesn't burn up. This puzzles him, so he turns aside to see why: it turns out to be the place of the theophany, of the revelation of the future of Israel. The burning tree is also symbolized by the candlestick so important in Jewish ritual—and in Christian too, in another context.

When John the Divine, in the Book of Revelation, has a vision of the city of Jerusalem, he sees it as glowing with gold and precious stones [Revelation 21:10–21]. He takes that from the account of the building of Solomon's temple. The account of Solomon's temple, by the narrator of the Book of Kings, says that nobody thought of silver in those days; they only put gold on [1 Kings 10:21], and several centuries later we have the same thing in the Book of Chronicles where the author is using the Book of Kings as a source [2 Chronicles 9:20], but is so far away in time from what he's describing that it's become a kind of romantic fairy tale. The Chronicler tells you that the temple of Solomon, though in its dimensions a rather modest building, actually was constructed with something like twenty tons of gold [2 Chronicles 9:13]. Similarly, in the Book of Revelation, the New Jerusalem is described in terms of gold, and as having twelve gates which are each one a precious stone or jewel [Revelation 21:18, 21]. That in its turn is the antitype of the breastplate of the high priest Aaron, which contained the twelve precious stones for the twelve tribes of Israel [Exodus 28:15–21]. So this city, glowing with gold and precious stones, is not there because the narrators are vulgar, and it's not there solely to be the antitype of certain things mentioned in the Old Testament. The gold and the precious stones are there to suggest a city burning in the fire of life: a city which is constantly burning, but is not burning up. The fire is an image of life and exuberance and energy, but not of torment or destruction.

If you set a bird on fire, you'll get of course a phoenix, which is not in the canonical Bible except for a reference in the Book of Job, which the cautious King James translators have rendered something like "sands" [29:18]. But the phoenix comes into folklore very early, both in the books surrounding the Bible, the Pseudepigrapha, and in Classical mythology from Herodotus on, and the bird that burns and rises from it to be a bigger and better phoenix consequently becomes an image of the Resurrection. The phoenix appears on the coat of arms of Victoria College. It ought to represent the Faculty of Theology, but again the original designers were more cautious and put it there as a symbol of medicine: they knew that *that* at least might do you some good. There's also a wonderful poem by an Elizabethan poet, a Jesuit, Robert Southwell, who was martyred—tortured about a dozen times by the secret police, and finally killed. His poem called *The Burning Babe* is a poem about Christmas Day, in which the rising sun is identified with a burning babe who is the newborn Christ.

I don't know how familiar you may be with Mozart's *Magic Flute*, which is built on a symbolism that's said to be derived from Freemasonry, but at the very end of the story the hero goes through the final ordeal, which is the ordeal of water and fire. And evidently the assumption is that he acquires, symbolically at least, the power to live in all four elements and not simply on earth and in air.

I've been constructing a table of imagery in which in each category one has an idealized or apocalyptic and a demonic side. There is the paradisal imagery of trees and water, and on the demonic side the wasteland imagery of dead trees and dead water. There are angels, with their imagery derived from the fire world of heavenly bodies, and the air world of birds, and on the demonic side there are fire demons, the jack-o-lanterns, will-o'-the-wisps over marshes, and spirits of storm and tempest.

On one side we have Christ, who is the unifying figure of the apocalyptic world, and opposite him Antichrist, the world ruler who demands divine worship. The latter is, of course, a figure that is pre-

Christian: it's in the Old Testament as well. Its types are the Pharaoh of the Exodus, Nebuchadnezzar, who destroyed Jerusalem, and Antiochus Epiphanes, the persecutor of the Jews just before the Maccabean rebellion. And the imagery carries on into the New Testament period, where the type of the persecutor is Nero, although a predecessor of Nero, Caligula, also expressed a strong desire to place his statue in the Holy of Holies. In the animal category, there is the sheepfold, with the sheep and the lamb as the typical animals of the apocalyptic world, as in the 23rd Psalm and elsewhere; and opposed to that there is the beast of prey, the sinister animal, of which perhaps the best example is the dragon. The dragon is a particularly useful demonic animal not just because of its antisocial habits of breathing fire and eating virgins, but also because it doesn't exist, and is consequently an admirable animal for illustrating the paradox of evil, which is a very powerful moral force in human life as we know it, but in the apocalyptic world becomes simply nothingness, simply cannot exist at all. And that, perhaps, is why the author of Revelation speaks of the dragon as the beast that "was, and is not, and yet is" [17:8]. That last "is" in Greek is *parestai*, which means continuing for the time being.

There is a myth in which Creation takes the form of a dragon-killing. The Hebrews were quite familiar with the story: they constantly employed it, and by no means always in a demonic context. They used it simply as poetic imagery, that is, not as a myth that they believed to be factual, but simply as decorative. The dragon of chaos has various names in the Bible, but the most common is the name Leviathan and sometimes Rahab.

And the leviathan is portrayed as, again, an image of chaos, of the still uncreated which survives in the human world incarnate in the heathen kingdoms of Egypt and Babylon and Rome.[25] In Ezekiel 29[:3–5]: "Thus saith the Lord God; Behold, I am against thee, Pharaoh king of Egypt, the great dragon that lieth in the midst of his rivers, which hath said, My river is mine own, and I have made it for myself. But I will put hooks in thy jaws, and I will cause the fish of thy rivers to stick unto thy scales, and I will bring thee up out of the midst of thy rivers, and all the fish of thy rivers shall stick unto thy scales. And I will leave thee thrown into the wilderness, thee and all the fish of thy rivers: thou shalt fall upon the open fields; thou shalt not be brought together, nor gathered: I have given thee for meat to the beasts of the field and to the fowls of the heaven." Now here, the prophet is prophesying to the Pharaoh of Egypt, whom he identifies with the dragon which is also the River Nile—"my river is mine own." And remember that on the principles of metaphor, a monster in the sea *is* the sea. And whatever the origin of this dragon might be—a crocodile or whatever you like—still, a crocodile in the Nile metaphorically *is* the Nile. So that the prophet is saying that the dragon will be hooked and landed and thrown into the open fields, which is metaphorically the same thing that John is saying in the Book of Revelation when he says that in the last day "there was no more sea" [21:1]. Because to hook and land a sea monster is metaphorically to bring up the sea as well.

In Isaiah 27[:1]: "In that day the Lord with his sore and great and strong sword shall punish leviathan the piercing serpent, even leviathan that crooked serpent; and he shall slay the dragon that is in the sea." The next verse seems to have no logical connection with it: "In that day sing ye unto her, A vineyard of red wine." But it's more logical than it looks, because the hooking and landing of Leviathan is also the destruction of the sterile and the chaotic in the world, and consequently, a great outburst of fertility would follow it. We come much closer to the centre of this kind of imagery if we turn to Isaiah 51[:9–10]: "Awake, awake, put on strength, O arm of the Lord; awake, as in the ancient days, in the generations of old. Art thou not it that hath cut Rahab, and wounded the dragon? Art thou not it which hath dried the sea, the waters of the great deep; that hath made the depths of the sea a way for the ransomed to pass over?" Now here the prophet adopts as a poetic image the account of Creation as the dragon-killing; and we'll come to verses in the Psalms that praise God for having brought Creation into existence by destroying the dragon of chaos.

Then he says that God twice won this victory over the dragon. He did it the second time at the crossing of the Red Sea, where the dragon was Egypt. And now he's calling upon God to make a third exhibition of his power, and this third is the Day of the Lord, to quote the King James version of it, which the prophets are constantly referring to as that time in the future when Israel will be restored and those who have been, well, listening to the prophets will be happy, but the vast majority of people will be anything but happy. The prophecy of the Day of the Lord is in practically all the prophets, and it is here connected in imagery with the two great victories over chaos and evil, the victory at the original Creation and the victory at the creation of the nation of Israel.

The most eloquent of all these prophecies of the Day of the Lord is in the prophecy of Zephaniah, which is the ultimate basis for the medieval hymn *Dies Irae*. It's a mad, magnificent poem, and has been incorporated into the Requiem Mass, but its origin is in these Day of the Lord prophecies.

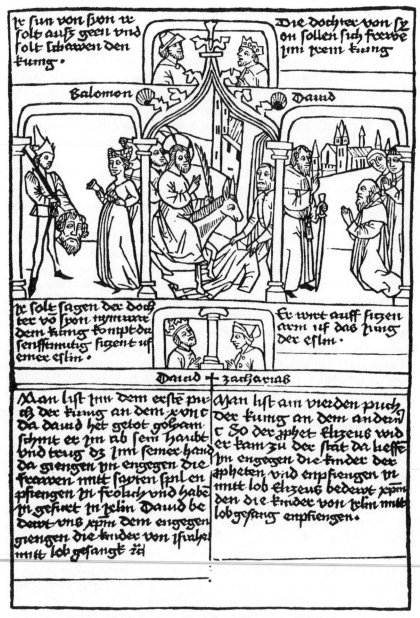

Biblia Pauperum 14: ENTRY INTO JERUSALEM
(Matthew 21:1–11)

Women of Israel greet David	Sons of prophets honour Elisha
(1 Samuel 18:6–9)	(2 Kings 2:1–15)

8

Demonic Parodies and
the Hero from across the Sea

I've been constructing a table of imagery in which each category has both an idealized or apocalyptic side and a demonic side. Above the paradisal category in this table is the spiritual world, whose two angelic orders are derived from the two levels of the upper regions of the heavens. The imagery of fire spirits is derived from the sun and the stars, that of the air spirits from the clouds and wind and birds of the lower sky; and this distinction is reflected in the later iconography of the seraphim and the cherubim, which are painted red and blue, and to whom attach the imagery of tongues of flame and of wind and birds.

In the demonic parody of this situation, the spirits would again derive from the different regions of the sky. Traditionally, the demonic spirits live in a kind of prison of heat without light, and this imagery of hell as a place of fire, which is derived from the New Testament, largely again has the same kind of origin. And the air spirits in their turn are the demons of storm and tempest.

Ariel and Puck in Shakespeare are derived, not from the conception of spirits inhabiting an upper region, but from a conception of elemental spirits. There were four kinds of elemental spirits: the fire spirits are salamanders, the air spirits are sylphs, the water spirits are undines, and the earth spirits, the gnomes, are the kobolds. Shakespeare takes the old word "puck" and applies it to a character in *A Midsummer Night's Dream*, Robin Goodfellow, *the* Puck. A puck, in Shakespeare's day, was the kind of fire spirit that is called an *ignis fatuus*, that is, the phosphorescent light over marshes that people going astray in the dark would take for habitations. Ariel, as his name indicates, is an air spirit or sylph, although in earlier magic and legend the word "ariel," which means "lion of God," is usually an earth spirit. Puck is a mixture of fire spirit and air spirit, and Ariel is an air spirit, but they are not demons. They belong to an intermediate fairy world that is neither demonic nor apocalyptic. It is significant perhaps that these two characters in Shakespeare both act under orders from an older and more responsible person. They are mischievous but not evil.

As I said, evil spirits inhabit the upper air as well, and in astrological speculation there are malignant planets and malignant settings, or positionings, of planets and signs, and St. Paul in Ephesians 2:2 speaks of the devil as the prince of the power of the air. All this demonic imagery, of fire spirits and air spirits, the phosphorescent lights and the *ignis fatuus* and the demons of storm and tempest, now survives only in the playful symbolism of Halloween—of course, there was a time when it was not playful at all. The popular imagery of witches is also derived from some such source.

In pastoral imagery there is the sheepfold, and in the parody demonic category the beast of prey. In the manifest demonic there is more particularly the dragon, and the dragon in the form of the leviathan who is a sea serpent or a sea monster, and who is sometimes called Rahab. In the human world, you have the Antichrist and whore figures, who are opposed to the Christ and bride figures; and just as the bride is called Jerusalem, so the whore is called Babylon. By the principle of metaphor, the demonic categories are all identical, so that the city of Babylon, the Whore of Babylon, and Nebuchadnezzar are to be identified with sinister animals like the dragon and leviathan, or with these fire or storm demons.

The reason they are so readily identifiable is that, while all images on the ideal side can be identified in Christian imagery with the body of Christ, there cannot be a demonic divinity. No demonic principle can exist on the divine level: one may call himself a god, he may be worshipped as a god, but he can't be a god. Consequently, these sinister cosmological figures, these sea monsters and dragons, are identifiable with the rulers of heathen kingdoms, and can be identified also with the gods that the heathens worship. But their root is a political root, because the actual godhead cannot be present on the demonic side.

Thus, Biblical symbolism asserts of heathen kingdoms what many people today would claim is true of both sides, that the reality is political and that the religious is the projection. The gods of Egypt are metaphorically identical to the Pharaoh of Egypt, but the Pharaoh is the reality, though of course in Egyptian religion he in fact was the reality because he *was* an incarnate god.

I suggested that in this world of sinister animals, as we go further out into the manifest demonic, the desert places in the ruins which are the wasteland, we begin to approach a world where we can't say where the sinister animals stop and the evil spirits begin. If we look, for example, at Isaiah 13, we are told that Babylon eventually, like Sodom and Gomorrah, will become a ruin or a wasteland. In verse 21: "But wild beasts of the desert shall lie there; and their houses shall be full of doleful creatures; and owls shall dwell there; and satyrs shall dance there." Verse 22: "And the wild beasts of the islands shall cry in their desolate houses, and dragons in their pleasant palaces: and her time is near to come, and her days shall not be prolonged."

Well, the King James translators have made a valiant effort with these words, many of which don't occur elsewhere in the Old Testament. And consequently their renderings of them are sometimes little better than guesswork. For we can't tell where the animal stops and the evil spirit begins. The doleful creatures are the *tziim* who are the dwellers in the *tziyya*, the dry places. In a parable of Jesus, an unclean spirit passes through dry places seeking for rest and finding none [Matthew 12:43; Luke 11:24]. The two dead times of the year, depending on the climate involved, are the winter or the late summer after the crops are harvested, when there is no more rain: it's that time of year particularly that is thought of as presided over by the god of death—the time of the waterless places.

I said previously [Lecture 3] that in many mythologies which are older than the Biblical one, the Creation takes the form of the killing of a dragon or a monster, as in the creation hymn of the Babylonians, the hymn that begins with the words, *enuma elish*, "when on high," and which tells how the god Marduk killed the monster of chaos Tiamat and split her in two, and made heaven out of half of her and earth out of the other half. I said that this conception of the act of creation as a dragon killing was known to the writers of the Old Testament, who used it as a poetic image, though not as a canonical story. And I pointed out various references to Leviathan or to Rahab in Isaiah and Ezekiel in which these monsters are identified with the power of Egypt and Babylonia.

In the Gospels, the ability of Jesus to command the raging of the waves and the storms of the sea is a point very early made about him in the Gospel of Mark [4:37–41]. This repeats the original act of Creation as the bringing of life and order and stability out of chaos. In Psalm 89:9, this process is presented in the form of the killing of a dragon named

Rahab: "Thou rulest the raging of the sea: when the waves thereof arise, thou stillest them." Verse 10: "Thou hast broken Rahab in pieces, as one that is slain; thou hast scattered thine enemies with thy strong arm." And if you look back at Psalm 74:13: "Thou didst divide the sea by thy strength: thou brakest the heads of the dragons in the waters." Verse 14: "Thou brakest the heads of leviathan in pieces, and gavest him to be meat to the people inhabiting the wilderness."

Now here again is the conception that we glanced at in Ezekiel 29, where the dragon is identified with the river Nile, the source of the fertility of Egypt. It is prophesied that in the last day, Jehovah will hook and land Leviathan and throw him into the wilderness. As the leviathan in the form of the Nile River is the source of Egypt's fertility and therefore the source of food in Egypt, it follows that the body of Leviathan thrown into the wilderness becomes food for the nation of Israel, which is inhabiting the wilderness. And so the legend arises, which is still known in Judaism, that in the day of the Messiah Israel will have the flesh of the leviathan to eat.

One of the oldest stories in the world is the story of an aged and impotent king who rules over a wasteland. That king had been around for hundreds of thousands of years before there was any writing. He is still there in Wagner's *Parsifal*, and he will keep going until the end of time. He already represents a number of metaphorical identifications: that is, he goes back to the identity of the virility of the king with the fertility of the land over which he rules; and it's because he is old and impotent that his land is a wasteland. The wasteland is ravaged by a sea monster, who is another symbol of sterility and waste and impotence. The sea monster demands human victims for his dinner, and the victims are chosen by lot. For a while, all goes relatively well: people don't particularly mind that one of their inhabitants is disappearing every day; but when the lot falls on the king's daughter, things begin to get serious. She nevertheless has to be tied to a rock and left there to await the monster's coming. At that point, the youthful hero arrives from the sea, kills the dragon and frees the young lady, marries her—is given her in marriage by her grateful father—and becomes the next king by marrying the king's daughter. This story is so old that it goes back to the custom of mother-right, where inheritance is through the female line. This was the practice in Egypt, and was a great encouragement to incest, because obviously what the Pharaoh had to do to legitimize his power was to marry his sister.

Anyway, this is the story behind the St. George legend and the Perseus legend in Greek mythology. It is easy to see in it the overtones of a myth of renewal of the seasons, the old king, the wasteland, and the sea monster all being images of sterility, the winter, and cessation of all life; and the young hero coming from over the sea, killing the dragon, and marrying the daughter being identified with the renewing powers of the spring. This was in fact acted as a folk play in England. The actual choice of St. George as the patron saint of England comes from the Crusades; but the symbolism of St. George and the dragon was already very well established: Spenser in the first book of *The Faerie Queene* has already identified the St. George and the dragon story with the similar patterns in the Bible.

If you turn from the New Testament to the story of Christ as recorded in later Christian art and legend, you notice that they make certain alterations, or rather additions, to the New Testament story. The general progression of events through which Christ goes in the Bible is, first of all, that he is in heaven; then that he creates the world, because in the Book of Genesis, God said, "Let there be light," and there was light: in other words, the creative agent is the Word that speaks. Then there comes the Incarnation, or the entry into the world of flesh, and then there is the death of Christ on the cross. He descends to the lower world, and then follows the "harrowing of hell." He returns to the surface of the earth in the Resurrection, and after forty days ascends back into heaven.

Now, there's a considerable foreshortening of time in this sequence: an infinity between life in heaven and the Creation, something like 4,000 years between the Creation and the Incarnation, about thirty years between his birth and his death in this world, and three days and three nights (that is, by our counting, two nights and one day) between his death and his Resurrection, forty days to the Ascension, and then back to eternity.

You notice also that of these eight stages, two are really not there in the New Testament. There are a few vague hints of a descent to hell, but the New Testament evidence for this motif is very weak [Ephesians 4:9–10]. And the "harrowing of hell" does not belong in the Bible at all: it was added to Christian legend by an apocryphal work called The Acts of Pilate, or the Gospel of Nicodemus, which was accepted during the Middle Ages as at least semi-canonical. According to the Gospel of Nicodemus, Jesus, after his death on the cross, descended into hell on the Saturday between Good Friday and Easter; and from hell, he extracted all the souls that were destined to be saved, from Adam and Eve down to John the Baptist.

What is interesting from our present perspective about the quest of Christ is the imagery with which it is presented by painters. In pictures of the descent of Christ to hell, hell is often presented as the open mouth of a monster: Jesus walks through the open mouth of this monster, whose body is the body of hell, and then returns with the redeemed behind him. In the interests of general decorum, he is assumed to be returning by the same route by which he entered. But of course other routes are possible, and one is strongly hinted at—in fact much more than hinted at—at the end of Dante's *Inferno*.

In any case, this iconography incorporates into the Christian legend the St. George and the dragon symbolism, where Jesus has the role of St. George, hell is the dragon, and the recreation of the world takes the form of redeeming mankind from death in hell, which is metaphorically identical with the dragon. Similarly, the heroine of the story, the king's daughter who gets rescued, is the bride of Christ, the Christian Church, corresponding to Andromeda in the Classical story. It follows therefore that the aged and impotent king who is her father is the first Adam, that is, human nature in its fallen and impotent form. Such a structure underlies T.S. Eliot's *The Waste Land*, where a figure from the Grail romances called the Fisher King, an aged and impotent king who sits by the sea "fishing, with the arid plain behind me" [l. 425], is identified as the first Adam.

Now, if we start thinking mythically and metaphorically about this story, rather than logically, the principle of metaphor will take us quite a long way. When the sea monster coming out of the sea is sterility and death and chaos, it follows that he must be the whole world, the whole scene of that story, its setting in the state of death. In other words, if we go on thinking metaphorically, we can see that Andromeda or the heroine must already have been swallowed by the monster; and in order to save her, the hero would have to walk down the open throat of the monster just as Christ is represented as doing in the "harrowing of hell" paintings.

If you look at the book of Jonah, you'll find that Jonah is a prophet who is told to go and prophesy to Nineveh, one of the heathen kingdoms, and tell its people that if they don't mend their ways, they are in for it. Now it's all very well for Isaiah and Ezekiel to do this sort of thing when they are safe in Israel, but Jonah, if he has to go to Nineveh, might get in a lot of trouble. Jonah has no taste for martyrdom, and consequently gets a ship and proceeds in the opposite direction upon the Mediterranean Sea. Well, it's an inviolable rule of romance that if you go to sea in the Mediterranean, your ship is going to be wrecked: so Jonah's ship, before long, is subjected to a tremendous storm. The sailors draw lots to see who is responsible, and it appears that Jonah is, so they toss him overboard. And the Lord "prepared a great fish to swallow up Jonah" [1:17]. He is inside the fish three days and three nights—again, it's two nights and one day by our counting—and is coughed up again onto dry land. Now, with the amount of coaching in metaphor which you have had in this course, you should be able to see that the sea and the storm and the monster and the foreign country which Jonah goes to are all metaphorically the same thing—and the same place. And what this same thing and same place are is quite explicitly stated in the Book of Jonah itself. In 2:1[–2]: "Then Jonah prayed unto the Lord his God out of the fish's belly, And said, I cried by reason of mine affliction unto the Lord, and he heard me; out of the belly of hell cried I, and thou heardest my voice." Well, the word translated as "hell" here is *sheol*, the grave: so Jonah is where he says he is, in the world of death.

Christ descending into the belly of a monster for three days and three nights following his death on the cross is the antitype of which the story of Jonah is the type; and Jesus in the Gospels accepts the story of Jonah as a type of his own Passion where he says, "as Jonas was three days and three nights in the whale's belly; so shall the Son of man be three days and three nights in the heart of the earth" [Matthew 12:40].

There is no heroine in the Jonah story. But Psalm 87:4 says, "I will make mention of Rahab and Babylon to them that know me: behold Philistia, and Tyre, with Ethiopia; this man was born there." We can see the implications of this verse if we remember that for most of the Old Testament period, the people of Israel were living in the middle of a heathen power. It was sometimes Babylonian, sometimes Assyrian, sometimes Persian, sometimes Greek, sometimes Roman, but they were always in the middle of a heathen power metaphorically identical with the body of Rahab or Leviathan. So if we ask what corresponds to the already swallowed Andromeda, it's the bride, the people whom the hero goes down into the monster to rescue. If we ask where we are in relation to Leviathan, the answer clearly is that we're inside him: we've all been swallowed by him. In Old Testament imagery, the primary identification of Leviathan is with the heathen kingdoms: but all kingdoms are more or less heathen. And so again, these monsters expand until they become essentially the world that we are all living in and want to be delivered from.

We begin to understand now why there is so much about fishing in the Gospels, and why Jesus is so persistently associated either with a fish or with a dolphin, which has a reputation for saving people out of water. The salvation out of water comes into the story of Peter on the Lake of Galilee, again with the same general overtones. The world in which we live is mythologically a subterranean world or a submarine world, depending on which element we choose. So from one point of view the flood of Noah has never receded. There's an old puzzle about what happened to the fish at the time of the flood. One of the simplest and most direct answers is that *we* are the fish. We didn't drown, but we have had our oxygen supply severely curtailed.

I'll wait to deal with the Book of Job later, but right now there is one thing we should look at, a long speech by God to Job, which ends with two lyric poems in praise of Leviathan and, according to tradition, another great hulking brute, Behemoth. I say "according to tradition" because *behemoth* is the intensive Hebrew plural of a word for "beast." Thus, because of that, the translators of the New English Bible think that there is only one animal involved. But traditionally there have always been two animals, a land animal and a sea animal. Likewise, there are two dragons, one from the land and the other from the sea, which appear in the Book of Revelation. Behemoth and Leviathan are also mentioned in the Apocrypha, in the Book of Esdras [2 Esdras 6:49]. These two animals correspond to the demonic world thought of either as subterranean or as submarine, though the one does not exclude the other.

In chapter 40 of the Book of Job, there is the poem on Behemoth as traditionally rendered; in chapter 41, the poet turns to Leviathan. The fact that these monsters can be pointed out to Job means that at the end of the poem, he is outside them and able to contemplate them. The implications of that statement will take us quite a while to reach, but I wish to end merely with the suggestion that these two monsters have cosmological dimensions as well as political ones, in which they represent the world as the prison of time and space that encloses us.

Biblia Pauperum 15: CLEANSING OF THE TEMPLE
(Matthew 21:12–13)

Darius approves rebuilding of
Temple (Ezra 5–6)

Judas Maccabaeus cleanses Temple
(1 Maccabees 4:36–59)

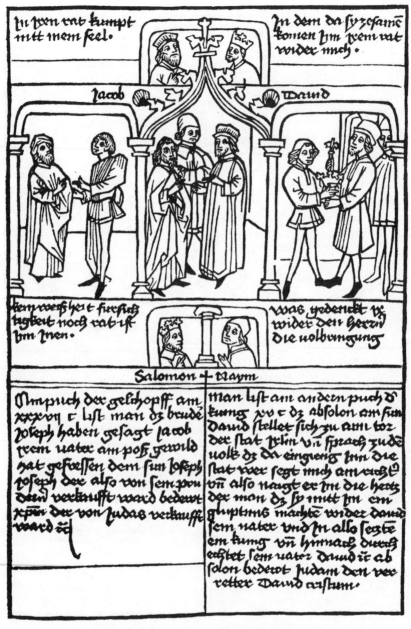

Biblia Pauperum 16: PLOTTING AGAINST JESUS
(Matthew 26:1–5)

Joseph's brothers deceive Jacob   Absalom conspires against David
(Genesis 37:12–35)   (2 Samuel 15:1–12)

9

The Double Mirror:
Exodus and the Gospel

I've been building up a pattern of imagery in the Bible, and the pattern of imagery is necessarily somewhat static as I outline it. But of course the Bible is a narrative as well as a structure of imagery: things happen; and I think we are at the point now where we need to examine some of the narrative structures in the Bible as well.

Now you remember that in almost the first lecture [Lecture 2] we suggested that the history of Israel in the Old Testament presents a series of falls and rises where Israel turns to apostasy and gets into trouble, is invaded or conquered by another country, is then sent a deliverer after the Israelites have changed their minds, and is brought back to something approximating its former state. And this you might represent as a U-shape of falling and rising. That U-shape is found everywhere in the Bible, not only in the historical parts, but in such things as the Book of Job and Jesus' parable of the prodigal son.

We saw that there was a series of these narrative movements, and that the first historical one, that is, the one following the "fall" out of the garden of Eden, is the descent into Egypt and subsequent deliverance of Israel. That sequence is the model for all the others. The captivity and the return from Babylon are thought of simply as a repetition of the deliverance from Egypt. Over and over again, in the Psalms and else-where, Jehovah says, "I am the Lord thy God which brought thee out of the land of Egypt."

Jehovah has actually been described by a German scholar as the "out-of-Egypt-bringing-God," which is the kind of thing Germans do. The deliverance from Egypt therefore is the model for everything else that happens. Part of the reason is that although usually the descent is an error or a sin—that is, an apostasy—on the part of Israel, this is not true with the Exodus account. The Israelites seem to have done nothing wrong, as far as we can see, in entering Egypt. But once they got there, the Pharaoh changed from the one to whom Joseph was an advisor to a later Pharaoh who was determined on genocide.

Once again, the Biblical account is a story, not a history, and it is not the historical Egypt that is the "furnace of iron" [Deuteronomy 4:20] from which Israel is delivered, but the spiritual Egypt. The deliverance from Egypt, which is where the history of Israel properly speaking begins, is the theme of the Book of Exodus. Now in a sense, the descent—whether it's caused by apostasy or not—is really not an event at all. If it's caused by infidelity to God, it's a pseudo-event; it's a failure to act. The deliverance, consequently, is the one thing that happens. As the Exodus is the model for every deliverance in the Old Testament, we can say that, metaphorically, the Exodus is the only thing that really happens in the Old Testament. Hence, in the Christian Bible, the Exodus would be, more than any other event in the Old Testament, the type of the most important antitype of Christianity, that is, the Resurrection of Christ.

I've tried to show that the progression of events in the Old Testament, although it deals with historical material, is not anything that we would call a history. Similarly, the life of Christ as portrayed in the Gospels, though it is the life of a real person, is not presented in any recognizable form of biography. The life of Christ is presented as the antitype, as the real form, the real meaning, of the story of the Exodus.

We begin with the story of the birth of the hero where life is threatened. That is a story very much older than the Bible: it was told about a Mesopotamian king, Sargon, centuries before the time of the Exodus. The story of Moses is that his birth was a threatened one: the Pharaoh of Egypt says that all male Hebrew children that are born are to be killed, which corresponds to the Slaughter of the Innocents in the New Testament, the two characters involved being the Pharaoh of the Exodus and Herod.

Now as a matter of fact, there were various massacres of children ordered by Herod, and one of his own sons was killed in one of them. The Emperor Augustus when he heard the news, remarking on the fact that Herod, although he was not a Jew, nevertheless observed the Jewish dietary laws, said that it was obviously much safer to be Herod's pig than Herod's son. But in any case, one of these slaughters of innocents is identified with a particular slaughter from which Jesus escapes, just as Moses escapes in the earlier account.

You notice the similarity of Moses' being concealed in what is called an ark, a *kibotos*, and Jesus' being born in the manger. And then you remember that in the Gospel account, Jesus is taken to Egypt by Joseph and Mary. In the earlier account, Moses grows up in Egypt, and the names "Joseph" and "Mary" recall the "Joseph" who led the Israelites into Egypt in the first place and the "Miriam" who was Moses' older sister. In fact, there is a sura of the Koran that identifies the "Miriam" of the Exodus story with "Mary" of the Gospels [19:28]. Naturally, Christian commentators on the Koran say that this is ridiculous: but we must remember that the Koran is speaking from a totally typological, ahistorical point of view; and from that point of view, the identification makes sense.

According to Matthew, Jesus was taken to Egypt to get him out of the way of Herod, but also to fulfil the prophecy in Hosea: "Out of Egypt I called my son" [11:1, RSV]. It is quite clear that Hosea is talking about Israel, so that again the fact is established that the life of Jesus is being presented as an individualized form of the Exodus.

Moses organizes the twelve tribes of Israel and Jesus gathers twelve disciples. The crucial event of the Exodus is the crossing of the Red Sea, where the Egyptian army is drowned, the event in which the nation of Israel is born, so that the story of Israel symbolically starts with the passing over the Red Sea. The corresponding event in the life of Jesus is the baptism in the Jordan, where he is recognized audibly as the Son of God. It is at the baptism that the two oldest Gospels, Mark and John, begin: the infancy stories of Matthew and Luke are later material. I don't mean that John is the oldest Gospel as we now have it, but that the kernel of it is in fact older.

There follows the forty years' wandering in the desert, as, immediately following the baptism, Jesus wanders forty days in the desert, the period which is commemorated in Lent and which was the period, according to the Synoptic Gospels, of the Temptation. By withstanding the Temptation, Jesus fulfils the law, which was also the reason for the forty years in the desert for the Israelites.

The law is received from the top of a mountain. So, in Matthew, is the Sermon on the Mount, which contains the kernel of so much of the gospel. And if you look carefully at the Sermon on the Mount, you will see that a great deal of it consists of a commentary on the Ten Commandments. There is also the miraculous provision of food, similar to the miraculous feedings during the ministry of Christ.

The Old Testament types of Judas are Korah, Dathan, and Abiram, the people who are swallowed up in the earth because they led rebellions [Numbers 26:9–10]. The type of the Judas story is not so much in the Exodus as in the prophecy of Zechariah. In 11:12[–13], God is represented as breaking his contract with his people: "And I said unto them, If ye think good, give me my price; and if not, forbear. So they weighed for my price thirty pieces of silver. And the Lord said unto me, Cast it unto the potter: a goodly price that I was prized at of them. And I took the thirty pieces of silver, and cast them to the potter in the house of the Lord." Those two themes, the potter's field and the thirty pieces of silver, are connected in this prophecy of Zechariah, in which God is represented as being betrayed by his people and sold for thirty pieces of silver, which according to the Book of Exodus is the symbolic price of a slave [21:32].

In Numbers 21[:6], there is an account of a rebellion of the Israelites against their leadership. And the Lord, who is always on the side of the establishment, "sent fiery serpents among the people, and they bit the people; and much people of Israel died." Verse[s] 8[–9]: "And the Lord said unto Moses, Make thee a fiery serpent, and set it upon a pole: and it shall come to pass, that every one that is bitten, when he looketh upon it, shall live. And Moses made a serpent of brass, and put it upon a pole, and it came to pass, that if a serpent had bitten any man, when he beheld the serpent of brass, he lived." In the Gospel of John [3:14], Jesus refers to this lifting up of a serpent in the wilderness as a type of his own Passion. In other words, the brazen serpent on the pole is an Old Testament type of the Crucifixion, and is accepted by Jesus as such. The dead body of Christ on the cross is symbolically the body of the serpent of death and hell which Christ leaves behind him. Or as Michael explains to Adam in *Paradise Lost*: "But to the cross he nails thy enemies, / The law that is against thee, and the sins / Of all mankind" [bk. 12, ll. 415–17]. Thus, the natural body dies on the cross and rises a spiritual body: the analogy is the serpent that sheds its skin.

We are then told that Moses dies in the wilderness. He climbs a mountain from which he can see the Promised Land, but he has already been told he cannot enter it because of the fact that he performed one of his miracles in a fit of bad temper [Deuteronomy 32:48–52, 34:1–6], so his successor Joshua is the one who invades and conquers Canaan. Now the hidden link in the typology here is that Joshua and Jesus are the same word: "Jesus" is simply the Greek form of "Joshua." Consequently, the conquest of the Promised Land is the same thing as Jesus' opening up of the spiritual Promised Land in his conquest over death and hell. From the point of view of Christian typology, the fact that Moses dies in the wilderness means, among other things, that the law alone, which Moses personifies, cannot redeem mankind. Thus, when, at the beginning of the Gospel of Matthew, the angel Gabriel tells the Virgin Mary to call her child Jesus, or Joshua, the typological meaning is that the reign of the law is now over, and the assault on the Promised Land has begun.

Now this is the long version. There is also a short version, and the short version is even more important typologically. You remember that I gave you an account of the quest of Christ in the Bible that had him descending metaphorically from the sky down to the surface of this earth in the Incarnation: then came his death on the cross, descent to hell, harrowing of hell, return to the surface of this earth, and the Resurrection and the Ascension back to heaven again. Now that can split in two, if you like, and what we've been dealing with is very largely the parallel between the Exodus story and Christ's life in the upper air, that is, his descent to the Egypt of this world, his ministry, his death, and his Resurrection. But then there is this whole underworld sequence which takes the three days and two nights of the Easter weekend. That sequence corresponds to the crux of the Exodus account, which consists of three main events. One is the Passover; the second is the passing through the Red Sea; and the third is the reaching of the other side. These correspond in the Gospel account to the Crucifixion and death; the descent to hell, which is usually given in subterranean rather than submarine imagery, but is still the same imagery; and the Resurrection from the tomb on the third day.

I brought in a translation of an Easter hymn by St. Ambrose, which dates from the fourth century A.D. And it says: "For these are our paschal solemnities, in which the very lamb is slain, by whose blood the doorposts of the faithful are made holy. This is the night in which thou, Lord, didst first lead our fathers, the children of Israel, out of Egypt and make them cross the Red Sea on dry foot. This is the night in which Christ broke the bonds of death and rose again as a victor from hell." There's another hymn of the sixth century: "Protected from the destroying angel on the eve of the Passover, we have been snatched from the harsh rule of Pharaoh. Now Christ is our Passover, the lamb that was sacrificed. Christ is risen from the grave, returning as a victor from hell."[26] The typology on which those hymns are based is this parallelism between the killing of the lamb as the sacrificial victim, which saves the life of the Hebrew children; the descent to hell, where the Egyptian firstborn were all killed, and later their army was drowned in the Red Sea; and then the passing through the sea, the deliverance from the water to the other side.

The Gospels could hardly insist more strongly than they do on the parallelism between the feast of the Passover and the time of the Crucifixion of Christ. That's written all over the Passion accounts in all the Gospels, and it contrasts rather strikingly with the determination of the time of Jesus' birth. There is no New Testament evidence whatever about what time of year Jesus was born, and as far as we can see, the Church seems to have been content to take the winter solstice festival from other religions. The great rival of Christianity in the early days was Mithraism, which was a sun-god religion; and in Mithraism, the most important event of the calendar was the winter solstice, the birthday of the sun, which was celebrated on the twenty-fifth of December. There are many reasons why the winter solstice date is a very good one for Christmas as well, but it's just possible that the fact that there's no Gospel authority for it accounts for the fact that Christianity has never established anything more than squatter's rights on Christmas. It's been a pagan festival from the very beginning.

I'm trying to get out from under that either/or dilemma, which I don't believe in. I think that it seems utterly clear that the Gospel writers are trying to tell us something: they are not trying to prevent us from knowing something else. But what they are trying to tell us is what, from their point of view, really happened. Now, a historian tries to put you where the event was. If he's talking about the assassination of Caesar, he tries to make you see what you would have seen if you'd been present at the assassination of Caesar. But if you'd been present at the Crucifixion of Christ, you might not have seen what the Gospels portray at all, because what you would have seen might have missed the whole point of what was really going on. You and I would have seen only a mentally unstable political agitator getting what was coming to him.

I don't think the Gospels are very interested in reliable witnesses. The only witnesses they care about are the early group of primitive Christians that formed around the Resurrection. They disregard the normal kind of historical evidence, accounts of travellers coming by and that sort of thing. That's what a biographer would pick, but the Gospel writers are not biographers. Mostly, the people like Thomas who wanted evidence were told to read the Scriptures, that is, the Old Testament. With Thomas, of course, the desire for visible and tangible evidence of the Resurrection was granted [John 20:24–9]. But Thomas was also told that if he hadn't bothered with that kind of evidence, he might have understood the Resurrection more clearly. What I think that means is not that an uncritical attitude is closer to the truth than a critical one: I think what it means is that the more trustworthy the evidence, the more misleading it is.

The point that I want to return to when we come to the Book of Job is that no serious religion ever tries to answer anybody's questions, because in any serious or existential matter the progress in understanding is a progress through a sequence of formulating better questions. An authoritative answer blocks off progress; it blocks off all advance. The answer consolidates the assumptions in the question, and brings the process to a dead stop. That is what I mean when I say that the more trustworthy the evidence, the more misleading it is. Trustworthy evidence means a kind of authority that stops you from asking any more questions.

10

The Metaphor of Kingship

I was speaking of the parallel between the Exodus events and the events in the gospel. And I was saying that the life of Jesus is evidently being presented to us in the Gospels as a progress of the spiritual Israel in the form of an individual. Now that means of course that in terms of type and antitype, the story of Israel in the Old Testament, which is the story of a society, is a type which has as its antitype in the New Testament the story of an individual.

That leads to the form of metaphor in which the individual is identified with the group. I have previously suggested that there are two forms of identification [Lecture 7]. There is in the first place identity *with*, the kind of identification that you get in the ordinary metaphor. If you look at Jacob's prophecy of the twelve tribes of Israel in Genesis 49, you will find a series of metaphors of that type: "this is that." That is, "Joseph is a fruitful bough," "Naphtali is a hind let loose," "Issachar is a strong ass," and so on [vv. 22, 21, 14]. In that form, the this-is-that form where two things are said to be the same thing and yet remain different things, we have the ordinary poetic metaphor, which is, as I said earlier, not simply illogical but antilogical, because two things could never be the same thing and yet remain two things.

There is also the identity *as*, which is the basis of all ordinary categorical thinking, where you identify an individual by placing it within a class. If somebody who has just come in from Mars comes into my office and says, "What's that brown and green object outside your window?" and I say "That's a tree," I am identifying the individual object he's pointing to with the class to which it belongs. That is, I'm identifying it as a tree.

There is a third kind of metaphor which unites the antilogical identity *with* and the categorical identity *as*; and that is the kind of metaphor that you have when you identify all the trees of Eden with the tree of life, and all the cities of the world either with Jerusalem or with Babylon. And it is that peculiarly powerful and subtle metaphor which you get by identifying a thing *as* itself and also *with* its class that the metaphor of kingship belongs to. That is why kingship is one of the most pervasive of human institutions.

The society that went furthest in identifying the entire society with and as the king was ancient Egypt. If you look at, say, the Tutankhamen collection, you would say to yourself that it would be absolutely incredible that all that labour and expense went into the constructing of the tomb for a pharaoh. We'd never believe it without direct evidence. And yet, when we understand how very pervasive royal metaphors are in Egypt—that Pharaoh is not only a king, he is an incarnate god, identical with the god Horus before his death and with the god Osiris after it, and that he was called "the shepherd of his people"—it becomes more conceivable. And unlike the Hebrew practice, he was high priest as well as king. So it is possible that the ordinary Egyptian found an identity for himself within the mystical body of Pharaoh which was of a kind that our mental processes simply cannot recapture.

There is something of that feeling in the typical king figure of the Old Testament, who is usually identified either with David or Solomon and who is not spoken of as an incarnate god but as somebody under the special protection of God and in a special relationship to him. In Psalm 2, for example, you have an imagery attached to the king which is more common among the Semitic peoples of Western Asia. In verse 7: "I will declare the decree: the Lord hath said unto me, Thou art my Son; this day have I begotten thee." This of course is taken in a much more precise sense in Christianity [cf. Acts 13:33; Hebrews 1:5], but in this context, the king is being regarded as chosen of God, and therefore the son of God. He is, strictly speaking, the adopted son of God, but the ceremony of adoption is symbolized by the physical term "begetting": "This day have I begotten thee." That gives the king a special connection with divinity on the one hand and with his people on the other; because by the principles of metaphor, the king does not represent his people, he *is* the people in the form of a single body, which is why the conception of the line of David is so central in the Messianic imagery of the Bible.

This 2nd Psalm is one of the two psalms—the other one is Psalm 110—which were of greatest importance to the New Testament writers in defining their conception of the royalty of Jesus. They used the term "begotten" to mean that Christ is the Son of God, proceeds from the Father, and is the only element or aspect of experience that is not a creature. Everything else has been created, but Christ was not created; he was begotten. That's the Christian reading of it, and it is an even more intensive identification than is, I think, intended in the 2nd Psalm.

Now we remember that the typical narrative structure in the Bible was of a U-shape where, in the Old Testament, the society of Israel usually starts in a position of relative peace or prosperity, does something wrong or meets with a hostile ruler as it did in Egypt, and plunges into a state of bondage or servitude from which it is delivered. Now, if the king is his people in an individual form, it follows that the legendary kings of glory, David and Solomon, don't exhaust the metaphorical imagery of the king. The king also is his people in their shame and humiliation.

The Book of Lamentations has to do with the sacking of Jerusalem by Nebuchadnezzar of Babylon and the carrying away of the people of Israel into captivity. And we are told that the unlucky last king of Judah, whose name was Zedekiah, had his eyes put out by Nebuchadnezzar. In 4:20: "The breath of our nostrils, the anointed of the Lord, was taken in their pits, of whom we said, Under his shadow we shall live among the heathen." Now that phrase "breath of our nostrils" could hardly say more explicitly than it does that the king is not a representative of his people, but *is* his people in an individual form.

Of course, Israel spent most of its time during the Old Testament period in a state of humiliation and foreign conquest. Consequently, the king figure has a good deal of this kind of imagery attached to him. I was speaking of the Semitic peoples of Western Asia, who had somewhat similar attitudes to kingship. Even when those kings were strong and successful, they would have to go through certain ritual ceremonies in which they assumed the opposite role. We are told that in Babylon at the time of the New Year festival a king, such as Nebuchadnezzar, would go through a ceremony of ritual humiliation, have his face slapped by the priest and that sort of thing, and then his title would be renewed for another year. Nebuchadnezzar was a strong and successful monarch: but if this ceremony were omitted, it might provoke the jealousy of his tutelary deity.

So we're not surprised to find that rather similar imagery is sometimes attached even to the glorified kings of Israel. 2 Samuel 6 describes not only an episode from the very successful and glorious reign of King

David, but also the particular episode which, from the Biblical writer's point of view, was the greatest moment in David's life, the moment at which the ark of the covenant, which had gone through the desert with the Israelites, was brought into Jerusalem—because the greatest military feat of David's reign was the capture of Jerusalem and the making of that city the capital of Israel. In verse 17: "And they brought in the ark of the Lord, and set it in his place." You have to watch out for seventeenth-century locutions in the King James Bible: "his" there is the genitive case of "it." In other words, the word "its" did not exist in the English language when the King James translators were at work; or if it did exist, it was only coming into being as a neologism, which no respectable person like a Biblical scholar would use. That's why the translations have to twist all around corners sometimes to avoid the word "its," as in Psalm 19[:6]: "There is nothing hid from the heat thereof" instead of saying "There is nothing hid from its heat." So here, "his place" means "its place."

"And they brought in the ark of the Lord, and set it in his place, in the midst of the tabernacle that David had pitched for it." David showed his sense of the importance of the occasion by, in the first place, holding a communal meal—in verse 19, he gave to everybody in Israel a cake of bread and a piece of flesh and a flagon of wine—and also by dancing in front of the ark with all his might. His wife, Michal, who is Saul's daughter, sneered at him as having made an exhibitionistic fool of himself in front of the servants [v. 20]. David's answer is very interesting from our present point of view: he says, in verse 22: "And I will yet be more vile than thus, and will be base in mine own sight: and of the maidservants which thou hast spoken of, of them shall I be had in honour." He is speaking of the necessity of his own humiliation, even in his own eyes, as a part of his royal responsibility. So you can understand from that how it was that David got to be the traditional author of the Psalms. In the Psalms you get phrases like "I will praise the Lord," where the "I" is the author of the hymn, but also all the singers of the hymn. That is, the individual and the group are not linked in any logical relationship at all: they are identified. And it makes the identification that much more vivid and intense if the "I" who speaks as the author of the hymn is, in fact, the king. That certainly would account for the number of psalms that are associated with David and yet are confessional psalms which express the need for forgiveness, or the need for deliverance, or a need of rescue against the slanders of enemies, and that kind of thing. All these are things which the king goes through as the individuality of his people.

I think you'll find this kind of metaphor used wherever you find royalty and the institution of kingship, or at least the equivalent of royalty. I remember seeing a movie about forty years ago which had to do with a group of émigrés from revolutionary Russia. They were arguing with a Communist in the revolutionary Russian government, and one of them said, "What the Tsar was is something that you could never begin to understand. He *was* Russia." That is an example of the royal metaphor being used in its full weight. There are even hymns to Stalin in later Russia which apply the same imagery to him, because of course anything that can be applied in a religious context can also be applied in an Antichrist context. The only mark of any genuine distinction in Hitler was the seriousness with which he took his Antichrist role, in identifying himself as the individual who *was* Germany. You can find the royal metaphor, like every other image, in either an apocalyptic context or a demonic one. And you can get it also in any society which has accepted that view of royalty, kingship, leadership, dictatorship, or whatever it is, whether it's explicitly religious or not.

Of course, the theory of democracy, insofar as it has a theory, is of a somewhat different kind. The metaphor of kingship is one which can be very appealing in certain contexts, and extremely regressive and sinister in certain other contexts. If Queen Elizabeth II were to go by on Charles Street,[27] you would all be rushing to the window, not because there is anything unusual in her appearance, but because she enables you to see yourselves as a group in the form of an individual. There is a particular intensity or even a pathos about a figure who has acquired that status purely by accident, as a result of birth, and hasn't any executive power. That is the kingship metaphor as an attractive icon. But of course there are many other contexts where the kingship metaphor is a very dangerous idol, and it is because of the dangers in it that democracy has replaced the ritual humiliation of the king with the annual election in which, according to the theory, if you get enough individual imbecilities added together, you get a collective wisdom.

There can be other metaphors of individuality. The person is the most direct and the most intensive form of metaphor, because a person is of the same category as the people. Whereas if you identify yourself with the flag or with something which is really a metaphor for a person, you are using a secondary metaphor. Legally, there is such an entity as a Crown, but if Joe Blow were to walk along Charles Street carrying a crown, it would not arouse more than a casual interest on your part. That's a secondary metaphor. The primary metaphor is the one which is of the same category as ourselves.

The most eloquent passage anywhere in the Bible containing this identification of the king with his people in moments of humiliation comes from what is called the Second Isaiah. Isaiah 40–55, because he is writing many centuries later than the Isaiah who appears in the beginning of the book, represents himself in fact as writing during the Babylonian captivity. The prophecies of the Second Isaiah revolve around a conception that scholars call the "suffering servant," and the pronoun suggests that he's talking about an individual person.

In 53:3: "He is despised and rejected of men: a man of sorrows, and acquainted with grief: and we hid as it were our faces from him; he was despised, and we esteemed him not." The distinction is quite clearly drawn between the "he" and the "we." That is, the suffering servant is spoken of as an individual, and the "we" represents the society that has rejected him. But the point is, that even in the act of rejection, the individual *is* the identity of the society that has rejected him.

This identification probably goes back to the ritual described in Frazer's *Golden Bough*. Whether it was actually a ritual at the very beginning of human society or whether Frazer was writing a piece of science fiction doesn't really matter. But in the original rite as he describes it, the central figure of the community is regarded as both divine and human. And because he is that, the tribe's success is bound up with him. Consequently, you can't have an unsuccessful or humiliated godman, or the tribe would go to pieces. So when he shows signs of losing his dominance, you put him to death, eat his body, and drink his blood; and thereby he passes into the bodies of his worshippers and creates a single body out of them. His successor is immediately appointed, and is cheered up in this office by having his predecessor's blood smeared over him. However, as I say, I don't know to what extent that is more than a reconstruction. What is behind it is this metaphorical identification of group and individual, society and king, and the fact that the death or humiliation of the king figure is something into which our own identity is drawn.

In the Exodus–Gospel parallel, the Joshua who conquers the Promised Land is the type of Jesus, who has the same name, and who achieves the conquest over death and hell. Joshua, in his conquest of Canaan, fights against certain enemy kings, and after winning the battle and capturing these kings, he hangs them on trees and then buries them and rolls great stones against the tomb. Similarly, we are told that the successor of the glorious David who captured Jerusalem was the equally glorious Solomon who built the temple: but David also had a son called Absalom who rebelled against his father, and who was, in fleeing from David's armies, caught by his hair in a tree; and who hung there until David's general came up and thrust darts into his side [2 Samuel 18:9–15]. In telling the story of the Passion of Christ in the Gospels, the Gospel narrators needed the imagery of the defeated kings of Canaan and the defeated Absalom as much as they needed the opposing figures of Joshua the conqueror and Solomon the king of wisdom hailed by the wise men.

Now this process of the humiliation of the king, at the bottom of the U-curve, is something that can be expressed symbolically in ritual. As I remarked earlier, it would make for political instability if you went through with that Frazer rite in its unadulterated form. When man is required by religious contract to give everything he most wants himself to God, it's a natural tendency—and in most contexts an extremely healthy tendency—for man to say, "The hell with this," and put in a substitute instead. Similarly, in the Mosaic law there is a very clear conception of the people of Israel celebrating at their New Year the same kind of ritual humiliation that Nebuchadnezzar would have gone through in Babylon. But it is not here associated with a royal figure; it is purely a matter of ritual, and of sacrificial victims chosen for ritual.

Now you remember that the "suffering servant" in Isaiah is described as "despised and rejected." That is, he is not simply a person who bears our griefs, but also a person driven out of the community: "we esteemed him not" [53:3]. And I've already suggested, I think, the significance for Christianity of the fact that Christ was the kind of prophet that no society could put up with. So there are these two aspects of the Passion: one is that of being the pure victim put to death; the other is that of being an exile sent out into the desert.

In Leviticus 14, there is a ritual to be observed by the priest if there is a suspected outbreak of leprosy. The priest is to take two birds and, in verse 50, "He shall kill the one of the birds in an earthen vessel over running water." And the other bird, in verse 53, is to be let go "out of the city into the open fields." So you avert a plague of leprosy by choosing two sacrificial victims, of which one is to be killed, the other sprinkled with its blood and driven out or exiled.

The underlying symbolism of this ritual becomes clearer in chapter 16 in the ceremony for the Day of Atonement. We saw that in the New Year festival in Babylon the king went through a rite of humiliation. This is the corresponding rite for the people of Israel, and here again there are sacrificial victims, in the form of two goats. And again, one of the goats is killed, and the other is to be driven away from the people, symbolically carrying all the sins of the community on its head into the wilderness. The King James translators here came up with one of the most ingenious and inspired mistranslations in history and said, this goat is to be sent as "a scapegoat into the wilderness" [Leviticus 16:10], thereby giving the English language an essential word. It is not what the text says. The text says that this goat is to be driven out "to Azazel," who is the demon of the wilderness. The goat is sent to the devil; or, more precisely, to Azazel, the devil of the wilderness. And obviously, this is a development of a rite in which the original goat would actually have been offered *to* Azazel. There's a passage in Leviticus, another chapter further on, that indicates that [17:7]. This corresponds again to elements in the Passion, where Jesus is both killed on the cross and, immediately after, descends to the kingdom of the devils.

But there is another aspect of the same imagery. We are told that at the time of the Passion there were in fact two prisoners, Jesus and a robber named Barabbas, whose name is quite interesting because it means "son of the father." And Pilate said to the crowd, "It's your custom to release a victim at the Passover feast. So choose one of these";[28] and they chose Barabbas to be released. But as I say, it's symbolically clear that Jesus has both roles.

The rejection theme comes also into the context of mockery. A great deal is made of the fact that although Jesus was a genuine king, even if a king of the spiritual kingdom, he was given royal attributes by his persecutors in a context of mockery: hence the crown of thorns, and the reed put in his hands, and the inscription over the cross: "THIS IS THE KING OF THE JEWS" [Luke 23:38].

Biblia Pauperum 18: LAST SUPPER
(Matthew 26:17–30)

Melchisedek meets Abraham   Fall of manna
(Genesis 14:17–20; Hebrews 7:1–5)   (Exodus 16)

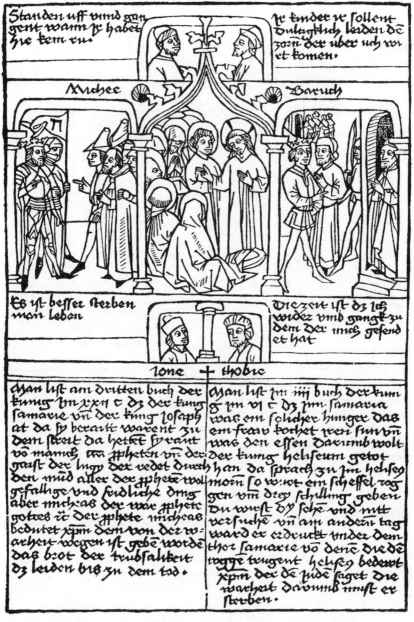

Biblia Pauperum 19: CHRIST IN GETHSEMANE LEAVES THE DISCIPLES
(Matthew 26:36)

Ahab sentences Micaiah to prison   Elisha mocked for his prophecy
(2 Kings 22:1–38)   (2 Kings 6:24–7:20)

11

King, Priest, and Prophet

I was speaking of the relation of the Exodus story in the Old Testament
to the shape in which the life of Christ is presented in the Gospels, and
was saying that the account of Jesus in the Gospels is not a biography
and not conceived as one, but is a setting forth of the life of a person
who is the spiritual Israel in an individual form. One rather striking
thing about Hebrew society in Old Testament times is the very clear
recognition of the difference between spiritual and temporal authority.
That recognition is fairly late, and originally the king must have had a
great many priestly functions, as well as his royal functions: the association of the Psalms with David goes back to that. You can see also
from such things as Solomon's prayer at the dedication of the temple
that the king was originally assumed to be somebody with important
priestly functions. But for the most part the priestly authority and the
royal authority were distinguished. The Israelites embarked on monarchy with a great many misgivings. But the role of the priesthood is
set out in the instructions given to Aaron, the archetypal priest in the
Mosaic code.

In other countries, such as Egypt, the king was always the high priest
as well, but that was not true of the Old Testament period. And this
division of authority between priest and king is accompanied by a
certain autonomous authority given to the figure of the prophet. The
three elements of authority, of prophet, priest, and king, are, however,
all associated with the figure of Jesus in various symbolic ways.

I've spoken of Jesus' role as king, which means he's both the king of
glory like Solomon in the temple and also the king of exile and humiliation like Zedekiah and in the symbolism of the "suffering servant" in
Isaiah. The Queen of Sheba coming to hear the wisdom of Solomon is

the Old Testament type, in the Christian reading, of the Magi coming to the infant Christ: the connecting link is the prophecy in Isaiah 60:6: "The multitude of camels shall cover thee, the dromedaries of Midian and Ephah; all they from Sheba shall come: they shall bring gold and incense; and they shall shew forth the praises of the Lord." But, of course, Jesus as the Messianic figure is associated with all three of these aspects of authority; and there are certain figures in the Bible that have a symbolic importance for that reason.

If we look, for example, at Genesis 14:18, we learn that after Abraham came back from a successful foray, he was greeted by a figure called Melchizedek, who is said to be the priest of El Elyon in Salem. Now, "Salem" is probably Jerusalem. "El Elyon" means, more or less, "the most high God." And "Melchizedek" means "the king of righteousness," or "the righteous king"; and he is here said to be the priest of El Elyon. He greets Abraham, pronounces a blessing on him, and brings forth bread and wine. If Salem is Jerusalem, then this figure, who is the priest of a god very readily identifiable with the Biblical Jehovah, El Elyon, the most high God, seems to be introduced to establish Israel's claim to the city of Jerusalem, which it didn't actually possess until the time of David.

In the 110th Psalm, a psalm which was always regarded by Christian typology as an extremely important psalm in setting forth the royal functions of the king: "The Lord said unto my Lord, Sit thou at my right hand, until I make thine enemies thy footstool" [v. 1]. And in the fourth verse: "The Lord hath sworn, and will not repent, Thou art a priest for ever after the order of Melchizedek." So here we have the priest, Melchizedek, identified with the royal figure, David. In the very late Old Testament period, the Maccabean rebellion was led by a priest named Mattathias, who was of a priestly family of the tribe of Levi and who had several sons that came to power one after the other, first Judas Maccabeus, then Jonathan, and then Simon. Because they came from a priestly family, all of these brothers as they came to leadership were made high priest. Simon, the third one, was also made high priest, but he took on a good many of the attributes of royalty as well, because he achieved independence for Judah, and his successors formed a dynasty where the kings were priests. Thus, for a very brief time, a little over half a century, before the time of Christ, the royal and priestly functions were united. And for that reason a great many scholars think that Psalm 110 originally referred to Simon Maccabeus. One scholar has proposed to work out an acrostic with Simon's name spelled out in it,[29] but I don't have enough expertise in Hebrew to know whether he is right or not. I can merely say that most scholars think he isn't.

The Melchizedek figure becomes prominently associated with Jesus, and in the Epistle to the Hebrews in the seventh chapter [v. 2] the author of Hebrews etymologizes his name in the way I did a few minutes ago, as "king of righteousness in the city of peace," connecting "Salem" with the word "shalom." He makes him, again, a prototype of Christ, as uniting the functions of king and priest in a figure of both spiritual and temporal authority.

The function of a prophet seems to be peculiar to the West Semitic nations in Asia, and represents an authority that is extremely difficult for any society to absorb. Nobody wants a prophet around. Kings and priests are all right, because they represent an established authority, and most of the prophets in the Old Testament were very well broken-in functionaries of either the court or the temple. Those who were not had a long record of persecution and martyrdom.

In the time of Jesus Scripture, that is, what we call the Old Testament, was not in its complete form: the status of some books was still undetermined. But in general, the Torah, the first five books of Mosaic law, was regarded as sacrosanct, and so were most of the historical and prophetic books or what are called the Former Prophets and the Latter Prophets in the Hebrew arrangement: so that the Scriptures in Jesus' day were the law and the prophets. The symbolic names attached to these two elements of the Bible were Moses, representing the law, and Elijah, representing the prophets. At the same time, although Moses is the secretary of the law, he is explicitly described in Deuteronomy [34:10] as a prophet, and his functions are quite clearly discriminated from those of the priest Aaron, his brother.

Still, Moses and Elijah become the symbolic figures of the Old Testament, and in the Septuagint arrangement of Old Testament books, apart from the Apocrypha, the Old Testament ends with the book of Malachi, as it does in the King James Bible. If you look at the last two or three verses of Malachi, you'll see that Malachi winds up the Old Testament from this point of view by an exhortation to remember Moses and to wait for the rebirth of Elijah before the coming of the Messiah. Verse 4: "Remember ye the law of Moses my servant, which I commanded unto him in Horeb for all Israel." Verse 5: "Behold, I will send you Elijah the prophet before the coming of the great and dreadful day of the Lord." Moses and Elijah are thus regarded as the continuing pillars of Scripture. At the beginning of the New Testament, you meet the figure of John the Baptist; and according to Jesus' own statement, the prophecy of Malachi that Elijah will come again was fulfilled by the coming of John the Baptist [Matthew 11:14].

At the same time, when John the Baptist is asked if he is Elijah, he says that he is not. Now, there is no difficulty there, unless you want to foul yourselves up over a totally impossible conception of literal meaning: reincarnation in its literal there's-that-man-again form is not a functional doctrine in the Bible. At the same time, metaphorically, which is one of the meanings of "spiritually" in the New Testament, John the Baptist is a reborn Elijah just as Nero is a reborn Nebuchadnezzar or Rameses II. So it is not surprising that the great scene of the Transfiguration in the Gospels should show Jesus as flanked by Moses on one side and Elijah on the other—that is, the Word of God with the law and the prophets supporting him. Again, that has its demonic parody in the figure of the crucified Christ with the two thieves flanking him on each side.

If you turn to the Book of Revelation, chapter 11, it begins with the commandment to the author to measure the temple of God. Then he speaks of two witnesses in verse[s] 3[–4]: "And I will give power unto my two witnesses, and they shall prophesy a thousand two hundred and threescore days, clothed in sackcloth. These are the two olive trees, and the two candlesticks standing before the God of the earth". The reference there is to the Book of Zechariah, which has a vision of a Messianic figure flanked by two olive trees and two candlesticks [4:1–3]. So here again the author of Revelation has introduced the Messianic figure flanked by two witnesses, as he calls them, which is one of the meanings of course of the word "martyr."

Then he goes on to tell us that these two witnesses are martyred in the last days, and it is quite clear from his description of them that they again represent Moses and Elijah. In verse 6: "These have power to shut heaven, that it rain not in the days of their prophecy"—that is what Elijah said, you remember, breaking the drought on Mt. Carmel [1 Kings 17:1]—"and have power over waters to turn them to blood, and to smite the earth with all plagues." That of course is Moses, striking Egypt with plagues. Then they will be killed—verse 8: "And their dead bodies shall lie in the street of the great city, which spiritually is called Sodom and Egypt, where also our Lord was crucified." Metaphorically, the demonic city is Sodom and Egypt, which both are sunk under the sea, and also the earthly Jerusalem, which had probably been sacked by the Emperor Titus shortly before this book was written.

There is a certain confusion in the New Testament and elsewhere between Moses and the figure in Genesis, the great-grandfather of Noah, who was called Enoch, and who is said not to have died; and you remember that Elijah went up in a chariot into heaven, so that traditionally Enoch and Elijah were the two people who didn't die. Enoch has some role to play here, although he has quite obviously been replaced by Moses. The thing is, that in Deuteronomy, there is clearly a certain ambiguity about the death of Moses. There is a suggestion at the end that Moses also did not die, at least didn't die as other men do. In Deuteronomy 34:5: "So Moses the servant of the Lord died there in the land of Moab, according to the word of the Lord." Verse 6: "And he buried him in a valley in the land of Moab, over against Beth-peor: but no man knoweth of his sepulchre unto this day." We're not quite sure what the antecedents of these pronouns are, but it looks as though God himself buried Moses. It became later a test of faith for people to believe that Moses was the author of the account of his own death, writing with one hand and shovelling with the other, but I don't know if we need that.

Howsoever, a legend grew up, already established by New Testament times, that Moses was, in the technical term, *assumed*, that he didn't really die; and that curious little Epistle of Jude, which is tucked in just before the Book of Revelation, speaks of a dispute between Michael and Satan over the body of Moses [v. 9]. So evidently the point of the author of Revelation is that anybody who is said not to have died has to come back and do it before the end of all death.

For Paul, the sacrament of baptism was a symbol of two things, a symbol of the fact that everybody without exception dies and a symbol of the fact that nobody has to die. That is, every part of you that can die is better off dead. And the part of you that doesn't die is the part that goes through the Red Sea to the dry land on the other side. Paul is certainly emphatic that it is possible to participate in things like the Resurrection before physical death. But again, it's a matter of what is mortal and what is not. There is, incidentally, no doctrine that I know of in the New Testament like that of Plato, which says that the soul is immortal by nature. I think the Biblical attitude is rather that immortality is something that is created by the power of God, but is not something inborn in man by his nature as a human being.

The Platonic idea, of course, also goes with the notion of the soul, which is thought of in terms of the metaphor of "in." Human consciousness feels that it is inside a body that it knows next to nothing about, and so it adopts figures like those of a bird in a cage or a prisoner in a cell to express it. Then, at death, the soul separates from the body: but although the doctrine of the soul certainly influenced Christian theology to a very considerable extent, I don't think it's a Biblical doctrine; I think it's a Greek one. As far as I can read it, the centre of Christianity is not the salvation of the soul, but the Resurrection of the body.

All the languages relevant to the Bible distinguish between the soul and the spirit. In Hebrew, they are usually *nephesh* and *ruach*; in Greek, they are *psyche* and *pneuma*; in Latin, they are *anima* and *spiritus*; and you have similar distinctions in modern languages, as in English between soul and spirit, and German *Seele* and *Geist*, and so on.

Paul, in speaking of how to read the Bible, in 1 Corinthians, 2:14–15, says: "But the natural man receiveth not the things of the Spirit of God: for they are foolishness unto him: neither can he know them, because they are spiritually discerned." Verse 15: "But he that is spiritual judgeth all things, yet he himself is judged of no man." He's discriminating there between the spiritual man, the spiritual body, the *pneumatikos*, and what the King James version translates as the "natural man." But the King James version is struggling with the fact that there is no adjective in English for "soul" corresponding to "spiritual." Because what Paul says is the *soma psychikos* for "natural man," the man with the soul; in other words, Paul is drawing the essential line not between the physical body and the soul, but between the soul and the spirit. And the *soma psychikos*, the soul-body complex, seems to be a part of what he means elsewhere by "flesh and blood" as distinct from "spirit," which is of course a metaphor from "breath" and expresses the sense of a life which includes the bodily life.

As he calls it natural, I suppose he means that he's thinking of the soul as part of the whole mortal complex in the human makeup. Elsewhere, I think in Thessalonians, he tells his correspondent that he prays for his body and soul and spirit [1 Thessalonians 5:23], so evidently he does have a three-tiered conception. By the soul he seems to mean something like consciousness, which human beings have by virtue of the fact that they are human beings. That is something that a man does have by nature.

It is a matter of our habitual categories of expression. We think of, for example, life after death. Now the word "after" is a metaphor indicating that we are still clinging to our ordinary conceptions of time; or we say, "is there something beyond": that's a metaphor from space, meaning that we are still clinging to our metaphors of space. The notion of something like the ego surviving indefinitely in something like time, in something like a place, is, I think, a slightly hazier notion than the New Testament is thinking of.

Jesus' teaching centres on his conception of the spiritual kingdom. We experience time in such a way that everything is either past or future. But when Jesus says something like "before Abraham was, I AM" [John 8:58], in a remark like that, time simply vanishes and you have to think in terms of a pure present, which is not in accord with our normal mental categories. And if that is true of the past, it must also be true of the future. While undoubtedly many of the early Christians thought of the Second Coming as simply a future event which would take place for the benefit of the faithful, perhaps next Tuesday, I think a rather subtler conception of time than that is involved both in Jesus' teaching and in the mind of the author of Revelation.

For Paul, the real individuality is the spirit, and the spirit is Christ in man. In other words, Christ is the genuine individuality of each individual. Without that, man is still primarily generic, primarily a member of a species. The spiritual life would, if it is a spiritual body, naturally include the soul as well as the body. He distinguishes later in Corinthians between the spiritual body of the Resurrection and the natural body [1 Corinthians 15:44]. So the natural body apparently includes the soul, or consciousness or whatever was incorporated in the conception of soul.

Biblia Pauperum 20: CHRIST RETURNS TO THE DISCIPLES
(Matthew 26:37–45)

Foolish virgins
(Matthew 25:1–13)

Fall of rebel angels (Isaiah 14:10–15;
Luke 10:18; Revelation 12:9)

12

The Question of Primogeniture

There are patterns in the Bible whereby the Messianic figure, who is Jesus in the Christian Bible, has absorbed the Old Testament types of authority, including the prophet, the priest, and the king. And yet, as we saw all along, these attributes of authority are accompanied by other attributes, those of a suffering victim, and both seem to be essential to the rounding of the figure.

There is one pattern in the Bible that recurs so often that it must obviously be very deeply connected with the narrative and imagery of the Bible. In the life of Israel, as also in the surrounding nations, the ordinary rule was that of primogeniture. That is, the eldest son usually inherited the title, if there was a title, the property, or the general rights of succession. That is something which of course has run all through human history, and the nations that have observed it are often more successful than the nations that haven't. In France, there was the tendency for aristocratic families to divide up their property among their various sons, whereas in England it was the eldest son who got everything, with the result that the younger son had to go into business, and eventually built up a bourgeois family which made so much money that he was able to buy out his elder brother's descendants. That is perhaps an aspect of the pattern that's not wholly missing from the Bible either. But we notice how often the firstborn son is explicitly passed over in favour of a younger brother.

The very first man born, according to the Biblical story, was Cain, who represents the agricultural economy, which the Hebrews idealized much less than the pastoral one. So the firstborn son of Adam, Cain, becomes the first murderer through the death of Abel. He also becomes an exile, is sent out and founds cities. I think I've touched on the fact that the Cain stories come from a variety of sources, so no one needs to ask the question of where Cain found the people to put in his city. But it's the dispossession of the eldest son, and the fact that the line of succession goes through the third son, Seth, that is the important thing.

Then we have the story of Noah, who curses one of his sons: he is not said to be the eldest son, but the same pattern is clearly recurring. The story ends in the transfer of the curse of Noah's son Ham to Canaan, a story which rationalizes the treatment of the Canaanites by the Israelites. Abraham has a son Ishmael, and Ishmael is sent in exile into the desert. Sarah, Abraham's wife, is told that she will have another son. As she is long past menopause, she thinks that this is impossible and bursts into a laugh. Well, God was somewhat miffed at this, but he was relatively good-natured about it, and Isaac is born at an impossibly late age and is called by a name which means "laughter." So Isaac is the one who succeeds to the inheritance. Isaac has two sons, the hunter Esau and the rancher Jacob. Jacob, whose name is later changed to Israel, is again the younger son with the line of succession going through him. Esau is gypped out of it through some extremely dubious manoeuvres on Jacob's part, many of them connived at by his mother. Jacob has twelve sons, the eldest of them being Reuben. But Reuben is done out of the patrimony because he committed the worst crime that it is possible to commit in a patriarchal society, which was that of approaching one of his father's women. It was not his own mother, although there is an Oedipal theme in the background; but nevertheless he is pushed out of the inheritance, which passes to the fourth son, Judah, and the eleventh son, Joseph. Of Joseph's two sons, Ephraim and Manasseh, again the elder son Manasseh is passed over and the preference given to Ephraim.

In all of these cases, the law of primogeniture is set aside, and the. inheritance goes through a younger son. If one asks why this theme should be so emphatically repeated in the early books of the Bible, the answer seems to have something to do with the fact that so much human anxiety is bound up with the straight line of succession, preferably through the eldest son. If you look at Shakespeare's history plays, for example, you will see how intensely the anxiety of continuity is built into society, how intensely the preserving of the legitimate line of succession seemed to the people of Shakespeare's day part of the necessary order of things. Consequently, the passing over of the natural heir for a younger one symbolizes the opposite, the direct intervention by the deity into human events.

In all these cases, we have the straight primogeniture situation of the elder son passed over for a younger son. But you can expand the pattern into other forms where it becomes more suggestive. For example, the Israelites entered on monarchy, as I remarked earlier, with many misgivings. The first king chosen was King Saul, and although he is said to have been chosen by God, the judge Samuel was very grumpy about surrendering the authority that he would lose by the choosing of a king. He never liked Saul and was out to do him in from the beginning. Still, there is also a suggestion that Saul was the popular choice and that consequently too much of the popular will was involved in selecting him as king. In any case, Saul is rejected and set aside. He and his son Jonathan are killed in a great victory of the Philistines, and the line of succession is passed over from Saul to David, a person of quite obscure parentage who is nevertheless explicitly pointed out by God to Samuel as representing the line that he is going to establish. Now from that time on, the law of primogeniture goes from David without change.

David's son and successor of course was Solomon; Solomon's was Rehoboam. As I have previously remarked [Lecture 2], the great legendary figure of wisdom, Solomon, was actually so weak and so foolish and so extravagant a king that when his son Rehoboam proposed to carry on his policies, he instantly lost five-sixths of the kingdom as the ten tribes in the north revolted and set up their own king. Well, it appears to the Deuteronomic narrators of the Book of Kings that it was somehow wrong to upset the line of David. That was partly of course because Jeroboam, the king of the Northern Israelites, refused to have anything to do with the Jewish claim that all worship should be centred at Jerusalem. He realized that that would simply make his kingdom a vassal kingdom of Judah, and so according to the historians, he set up a local cult of golden calves or bulls, which was regarded as idolatrous.

But the line goes straight through David until the destruction of Jerusalem by Nebuchadnezzar, and from that time it can still be traced. It is an unquestioned assumption in Messianic times, that is, in post–Old Testament and early New Testament times, that the Messiah would be sprung from the line of David, and that he would in fact be born in David's birthplace of Bethlehem.

We find this same pattern of an older person or generation set aside in favour of a younger generation elsewhere too. For example, the actual redemption of Israel by the Exodus is split between Moses and Joshua: Moses, remember, dies in the desert, and it is his successor Joshua who achieves the conquest of the Promised Land. That transfer of the work of redemption from one figure to another fits this same pattern, where Moses, though the greatest prophet of Israel, as he is called, is nevertheless set aside for the crucial act. Similarly, even David, the most glorious figure in the Old Testament, is set aside as far as the building of the temple goes, and is told that that is to be reserved for his successor.

You can find different traces of that pattern in the wandering in the desert, which took forty years. The reason it took forty years to cover so relatively small a space was that the first generation, we are told, was hardhearted and disobedient, so that God resolved that the entire generation that had entered the desert from Egypt would have to die in the desert, and that a new generation would be allowed to enter the Promised Land. So Moses, to some extent, represents the entire generation of Israel which he led into the desert, all of whom had to die before a new generation would enter the Promised Land. In the 95th Psalm there is the verse, "Unto whom I sware in my wrath that they should not enter into my rest" [v. 11], which is a verse quoted by the author of Hebrews [3:11] for reasons of his own that we'll come to in a moment.

After the Babylonian captivity the same pattern is picked up by Jeremiah, who says the old generation and its contract with God has been destroyed and abrogated. A new contract will be made with the new generation, an inner or spiritual contract which will be the new covenant or, as you might translate, the new testament [31:31–3]. Of course, Christianity promptly seized on this prophecy of Jeremiah as referring to its own teachings. And again, the author of Hebrews quotes Jeremiah on that conception of a new covenant or a new testament [8:8–10].

There are many examples, therefore, of this pattern of setting aside the oldest son or older generation and making them either exiles or victim figures. In Exodus 4:22, God is represented as saying, "Israel is my son, even my firstborn." Anybody belonging to Israel who had read through the Bible might feel a chill in his heart at those words, because it's the most ambiguous blessing, according to the general fate of first-born sons in the Bible.

Here again, one has to take into account the law which we've already referred to in connection with the doctrines of sacrifice of the Old Testament [Lecture 6], that every firstborn male is theoretically to be sacrificed to God and is to be redeemed with a lamb instead, the law of Exodus 34:19[–20]: "All that openeth the womb is mine; and every firstling among thy cattle, whether ox or sheep, that is male ... all the firstborn of thy sons thou shalt redeem."

We've already gone into the practice of sacrificing the eldest son as a particularly desperate attempt to attract the attention of one's god, as in the case of Mesha of Moab, who offered his son as a burnt offering on the wall when he was besieged by Israel [2 Kings 3:27]. But in the general context of the symbolism attached to firstborn sons, one would expect Israel to be passed over and to become either an exiled figure or a victim figure. And as a matter of fact, that is precisely the inference that Paul draws in what is probably the earliest of his letters, the letter to the Galatians. If you can find Galatians 4:21: "Tell me, ye that desire to be under the law, do ye not hear the law? For it is written, that Abraham had two sons, the one by a bondmaid, the other by a freewoman. But he who was of the bondwoman was born after the flesh; but he of the freewoman was by promise. Which things are an allegory." The Greek word is *allegoria*, and it's very important, I think, that Paul is telling you explicitly that he reads the Old Testament allegorically. "For these are the two covenants; the one from the mount Sinai, which gendereth to bondage, which is Agar" [4:24]. That's the mother of Ishmael and the first wife of Abraham.[30] "For this Agar is mount Sinai in Arabia, and answereth to Jerusalem which now is, and is in bondage with her children. But Jerusalem which is above is free, which is the mother of us all" [4:25–6].

Well, from the point of view of Judaism, of course, Paul's interpretation of the story of Abraham could hardly be more preposterous. He is saying that Judaism belongs to Ishmael, who represents the wandering Bedouin tribes outside Israel. Isaac represents the New Testament, the new covenant of Christianity. But the author of Hebrews makes the same claim, that Christianity is in fact the inheritance promised to Israel.[31] In both Paul and the author of Hebrews, there is a polemic streak which identifies the legalism which Christianity is supposed to transcend with Judaism. So far as I can see, that is not part of the teaching of Jesus, but it is certainly written into some parts of the New Testament.

Now this being born of the flesh and being born of the promise means that the eldest son, Ishmael, represents the normal, natural succession by primogeniture, where the right passes from the father to the eldest son; and that Isaac, being born of the promise, is the result of a deliberate divine intervention into human affairs. If you turn in the New Testament to the accounts of the Nativity in Luke, you will find that the New Testament counterpart or antitype of the birth of Isaac is attached to John the Baptist, who again is born at an impossibly late period of his mother's life. His father does not believe that this can happen, and is therefore struck dumb until the child is born [Luke 1:5–25, 57–79].

Now it is clear that Jesus is the firstborn son of his family. He is quite explicitly said in the New Testament to have brothers [Matthew 13:55], but there is no doubt from the Gospel account that he is the firstborn of his family. And he is a devoted sacrificial victim partly in consequence of being so.

If we look at the opening of the Gospel of Matthew, we see again this curious paradoxical relationship of the line of descent with the divine intervention which passes over the line of descent. You can't have it both ways except in the Gospel of Matthew. Well, you get the same thing in Luke in a different form, but Matthew begins with a genealogy of Jesus from Abraham to Joseph the husband of Mary, of whom was born Jesus who is called Christ. Now the purpose of that genealogy is to show that Jesus conforms to the pattern of a Messianic figure in being born of the line of David. Matthew sums up his genealogy in verse 17 and counts fourteen generations. Then he begins verse 18, "Now the birth of Jesus Christ was on this wise," and proceeds to tell the story of the Virgin Birth, according to which Joseph is not Jesus' father at all, and the entire genealogy from Abraham is pointless.

The way to overcome these apparent difficulties and contradictions in sacred stories was provided by the discovery of continuous prose. In continuous prose, if you only write enough sentences, any statement can be reconciled with any other statement whatever. You just have to put in enough intervening sentences, which will eventually connect A with Z. So we're not surprised to find that many hundreds of volumes have been written reconciling the difficulty in these two accounts of the descent of Christ in Matthew; and as it would take a lifetime to read through all these books, it is much simpler to assume that the difficulty has been somehow or other taken care of. But if you go back to the Gospel of Matthew, you can see that he just leaves a gaping, yawning paradox; and the paradox is in fact part of his whole conception of Christ, who is born after the flesh like Ishmael but also after the promise like Isaac. So that his birth in the line of David—he is occasionally addressed as the son of David in the Gospels—fulfils the law of primogeniture, but his actual birth represents a divine entry into history. So that you have in addition to the horizontal line of hereditary succession the vertical line of divine entry into the pattern of human life.

There is another story of a very late birth, which begins 1 Samuel and describes the birth of Samuel. We're told that his mother Hannah had prayed for a son for a long time, until it became reasonably clear that, in the normal course of events, she would not have one. She had made a vow that is in accord with the whole symbolic pattern of the Bible, that if she had a son, she would devote him as a sacrificial victim to the service of the Lord; but that of course meant putting him in the temple as a priest, rather than carrying out the original sacrificial ritual [1 Samuel 1].

Samuel is born, and Hannah sings a song of triumph that is very interesting, because one of the things it stresses is that this birth at a late, late age is a symbol of the continuously revolutionary activity of God in human affairs, of God's intervening with special acts which upset all the normal standards of procedure and hierarchy.

The Song of Hannah is in chapter 2[:1–10], and the theme of the reversal of social fortunes in 1 Samuel 2:6[–8]: "The Lord killeth, and maketh alive: he bringeth down to the grave, and bringeth up. The Lord maketh poor, and maketh rich: he bringeth low, and lifteth up. He raiseth up the poor out of the dust, and lifteth up the beggar from the dunghill, to set them among princes, and to make them inherit the throne of glory." So that this revolutionary activity of God, which means a complete overturning of social standards, where the poor are raised up to become rich and powerful, is something symbolized by the birth of Samuel at that late stage of his mother's life.

In the New Testament, if you look at the beginning of the Gospel of Luke, you find again the story that I referred to about the birth of John the Baptist, which picks up and repeats the theme of late birth. The birth of Jesus is not said to be a late birth of the same kind, but again a triumphant hymn of thanksgiving is ascribed to the Virgin Mary at the time of the birth of Christ, the hymn which we know as the Magnificat [1:46–55]. The Magnificat has obviously been influenced by, if not modelled on, the Song of Hannah, and repeats this theme of social overturn.

In Luke 1:46: "And Mary said, My soul doth magnify the Lord." Verse[s] 51[–53]: "He hath shewed strength with his arm; he hath scattered the proud in the imagination of their hearts. He hath put down the mighty from their seats, and exalted them of low degree. He hath filled the hungry with good things; and the rich he hath sent empty away." That overturn of society, which is repeated in some of Jesus' parables, like the parable of Dives and Lazarus [Luke 16:19–31], indicates again this vertical movement down into human society and up again, overturning its values.

The Bible is thrown into the form of a narrative which, as I have so frequently remarked, resembles the general structure of comedy, in that it passes through tragic events but passes out of them again into a final deliverance. It follows therefore that we don't look to Biblical culture for patterns of great tragedy. The Biblical view of man does not accommodate that conception of the semi-divine hero which gives such tremendous power to Greek tragedy. So one doesn't really find tragedies in the Bible. The Book of Job is very often classed as a tragedy, but it's not one, at least not according to the Greek pattern.

What you do find is that certain nodes, so to speak, of the tragic form around these rejected and passed-over figures, who have often been made exiles or victims for no fault of their own that they can possibly discern. There is, for example, Cain's bewilderment at the fact that his offering was not accepted, whereas his brother Abel's was; and he's not very convinced by the rather bumbling answer he gets from God [Genesis 4:5–7], which has probably gone through several editorial expurgations in any case. So the state of mind which leads him to murder Abel is at any rate intelligible. But the Biblical focus on such scenes is ironic rather than tragic. It is only if you are willing to stop and look between the lines for a moment that you can see certain tragic patterns potentially taking form.

Similarly with Ishmael driven out into the desert to starve with his mother [Genesis 16:5–8], and Abraham's feeling of—regret is too mild a word—but he says to God, "O, that Ishmael might live before thee!" [Genesis 17:18]. It is a terrible blow to him to lose a son at a time of culture when the preserving of the line of succession meant infinitely more than it does now.

Even one of the purposes of the story of Isaac, apart from his connection with the Passover and the redeeming of the eldest human child by a lamb, is to indicate that Isaac is being adopted into the line of succession by being at least potentially a sacrificial victim of his father. The story of Abraham and Isaac is the theme of some of the most powerful and eloquent of the medieval mystery plays, and it owes its pathos and its eloquence partly to the audience's realization that this story of Abraham and Isaac is being set in a larger framework in which the God who commands the sacrifice actually has later to sacrifice his own son and to carry it through without any reprieve. Similarly with the cry of Esau when he finds how callously he's been treated and thrust out of the inheritance, and that the blessing has gone to the younger brother: "Bless me, even me also, O my father" [Genesis 27:34]: he becomes at that moment, as I say, a potentially tragic figure.

In the story of Saul, who is another person first chosen and then rejected, you have what comes nearest, I suppose, to being the one great tragedy of the Bible. Because Saul, in the first place, is a man of heroic stature and proportions—he is said to be head and shoulders over every other man in Israel, he is an able king, and he seems to be a decent and humane one. But he is under some kind of curse according to which he could do nothing right. We can see that his inability to do anything right has a good deal to do with the jealousy of Samuel, but, then, Samuel seems to have a remarkably unpleasant God on his side. When King Agag is taken as a prisoner in warfare, Saul spares Agag out of ordinary human decency: he is bound and helpless and a prisoner. Samuel says that this is a mortal offence to the God who demanded Agag as a sacrificial victim; and therefore Samuel hews Agag in pieces before the altar of God. He says that God can never forgive Saul for this, because God is not a man, that he should change his mind. It's the only time in the Bible where God is spoken of as unforgiving [1 Samuel 15]. And so the narrator at this point, by sheer consistency and blundering, has added the one element to the story of Saul that makes it a genuine tragedy: that is, the suggestion of malice inherent in the divine nature. Normally, there is no room for that in the Bible. In Greek culture, where you have a polytheistic religion, you can have any number of vicious and bad-tempered gods. They are drawn from nature, and they reflect the irrational and amoral qualities of nature. But you very seldom get it in the Bible: it is perhaps only in this one passage that one does.

Absalom has again the rudimentary makings of a tragic hero [2 Samuel 18]. His beauty is stressed in the narrative, and certainly David's mourning over Absalom is in the general tonality of tragedy; but there again, the moral slant, the moral emphasis in the narrative, is so strong that the sense of the fall of a semi-divine hero, like the crash of a great oak tree, which you get in the great tragedies of Ajax or Prometheus, is rather muffled and muted. It's one of the inevitable ironies of royal succession that Absalom finally represents. But he is certainly an example of the passing over of one for another.

You may find this a bit of a digression, but it's rather curious how at the time of the Romantic movement in the nineteenth century all these exiled figures come back again as tragic heroes. Byron writes a tragedy on Cain, and *Moby Dick* begins with the sentence, "Call me Ishmael," and Saul and Esau and others are Romantic favourites. It has something to do, I think, with the nostalgia for a passing aristocracy, the sense of the rightful heir who has been driven into the desert.

You can carry back the pattern of the two brothers rather further than the Bible itself warrants if, for example, you think of Satan as the original firstborn son of God who is set aside for the younger son, Christ; and in fact, if you look at the fifth book of *Paradise Lost*, you can see exactly that scene: the jealousy of the older brother at being supplanted by this upstart of a younger brother, who, for reasons totally mysterious to him, has been preferred. Byron, who wrote a poem on the tragedy of Cain, also wrote a poem called *The Vision of Judgment*, in which Lucifer comes back to look at the Heaven constructed by the younger Son; and we're not surprised to find that Lucifer in Byron's poem is an icily polite aristocrat, and that, while his Messianic younger brother does not appear directly, he is clearly running a much more bourgeois establishment, where people like King George III can feel at home.

The emphasis in the Judas story is an ironic rather than a strictly tragic one. He hangs himself, and comes to the same kind of end as a tragic hero, but the emphasis is so strongly on the feeling that he got what was coming to him that there isn't so much of the sense of the fall of the hero. The tragic combines the heroic and the ironic, and in the Judas story I think you have only the ironic.

The expulsion of Adam from paradise is again another example of God's passing over the elder son—that is a point that Paul again seizes on. The first Adam is the rejected Adam, and the second Adam in Christ is the deliverer; but of course in this case the first Adam and the second Adam are the same person because of the Incarnation [1 Corinthians 15:45–9]. Consequently, the tragedy of Adam's expulsion from paradise is an example of the Bible's passing through a tragic episode on its way to a comic conclusion. Similarly with the Crucifixion of Christ, which is certainly a tragedy, but is followed immediately by Resurrection. The annulling of a line of succession by a new choice and a new action is again one of the elements that give to the Biblical narrative that curious revolutionary quality which is part of our own cultural inheritance.

Der mensch meyner
fride Jn den ich ho-
fnet

Der sein zungen v-
kert felt ein fm
die posheit

Dauid

Salomon

we dem poshafftige
zm vbel wirt zm
wider geltung sein
hend.

Er wirt reden feid
mitt seinem nachste
vnd sein herz wirt
sein poshafftig.

ysaias + ieremias

Man list am dritte puch
der kung iij c dz Joab am
furst der ritterschafft ist ko
men zu abner vnd so er mit
zm also redet poslich durch
stach er zn mitt am schwert
Joab bedewt Judam der xpm
durch den kuss verriet vnd
gab zn tod den Juden

Man list am ersten puch Ma
chabeorum am xij c dz triphõ
ist komen zu Judas macha
beo das er mitt zm redet
zm posheit vmb zn also
fieng zu Triphon bedewt zu
dam den verretter.

Biblia Pauperum 21: BETRAYAL OF CHRIST
(Matthew 26:45–52)

Joab slays Abner
(2 Samuel 3:22–30)

Tryphon's treachery
(1 Maccabees 12:39–52)

Biblia Pauperum 22: CONDEMNATION OF CHRIST
(Matthew 27:24)

Jezebel threatens Elijah   Daniel accused
(1 Kings 19:1–3)   (Daniel 6)

Biblia Pauperum 23: MOCKING OF CHRIST
(Matthew 27–31)

Ham mocks Noah's nakedness   Children mock Elisha
(Genesis 9:20–7)   (2 Kings 2:23–4)

Biblia Pauperum 24: CHRIST BEARING CROSS
(John 19:17)

Isaac carries wood
(Genesis 22:3–9)

Widow of Zarephath (Sarepta)
(1 Kings 17:1–16)

Biblia Pauperum 25: CRUCIFIXION
(Matthew 27:33–54)

Sacrifice of Isaac
(Genesis 22:1–14)

Brazen serpent (Numbers 21:4–9;
John 3:14–15)

13

Genesis: In the Beginning

Last term, I was concerned with trying to build up a unified picture of the narrative and imagery of the Bible, and the emphasis consequently was on its imaginative unity, the unity as revealed by the myth and metaphor that form its structure. But the Bible's disregard for unity is quite as impressive as its observance of it: it's just as possible to look at it as a large miscellaneous heap of badly established texts. Everything that could possibly go wrong with a book has gone wrong with the Bible at some stage or other in its history. So the Bible, therefore, is a unity which has passed beyond unity. It's not a matter of its having failed to achieve it, but of its having got past it to something which includes it.

There are two senses, in other words, in which we can use the word "imperfect." We can think of it as a limited or inadequate quality which falls below perfection, or we can think of it, as the tenses of the Hebrew language suggest, as the difference between the perfected, that which is finished and complete, and that which is still continuous and alive. The Bible has tried to present its unified message in that deliberately imperfect way: I'll try to show you something of that in the ending of the Book of Revelation, which as I said is a remarkably open ending for a book of that length.

Now what I want to do this term is to examine a series of what seem to me to be phases in what the Bible has to say, phases of what is traditionally called revelation. It's a rather tricky business to try to understand what the Bible means by revelation, because in the course of centuries, we have eventually realized that its revelation is not the communicating either of historical knowledge or of scientific and natural knowledge. At the same time, revelation does seem to imply the communicating of some kind of knowledge, and the real nature of that knowledge is what I want to examine.

It seems to me that there is a progressive sequence in the Bible of stages, not so much of revelation itself, as of the understanding of it. First, Creation; then revolution, which is the Exodus from Egypt; then law, which follows the Exodus; then wisdom, or the individualizing of the law; then prophecy: those five stages all have their centre of gravity in the Old Testament. There are two others with their centre of gravity in the New Testament: the gospel, and the Second Coming or Apocalypse. That will be our general outline for this term, which means of course that we have to begin with the conception of Creation in the Bible as it's set out at the beginning of Genesis and referred to elsewhere.

There are certain questions that obviously come to mind when you're reading the Biblical account of Genesis. One is, why is there such an insistence on days of the week, and why does the Bible talk about the first, the second, and the third day before the sun was created to measure time? Another one is, why is the account of Creation in the Bible so intolerably patriarchal? The creating God in the Bible is assumed to be male, which obviously must be a metaphor, because he is the creator of both male and female. We are also told that at the beginning of things, the first woman's body was created out of the body of the first man, in a violent reversal of everything that has happened since. For questions like that, there are always immediate answers: the emphasis on the seven days was put in to rationalize the law of the Sabbath, and the emphasis on the maleness of the creating agent was put in to rationalize the doctrines of male supremacy in ancient society. Now I have no doubt that those answers are true as far as they go. They don't go far enough to be very interesting, so I'm going to ignore their truth and try to get a little further.

First of all, in the beginning—the Hebrew simply says, in beginning, *beresheth*—God created the heaven and the earth. Now one of the first questions that's likely to come to a child's mind is, What happened before that? Or, more accurately, what was God doing sitting around all that time before making the world? Saint Augustine said that what God was doing before Creation was preparing a hell for those who asked questions of that kind:[32] which perhaps tells you more about Saint Augustine than it does about God. But to be told that we should not ask a question of course merely increases its urgency in any healthy mind.

So what took place before the Creation? Well, in the first place, that question has got fouled up with the category of time, because the category of time is the fundamental way in which we perceive reality. Considering that the category of time is divided into three dimensions, the past, the present, and the future, that none of these dimensions actually exists, because the past doesn't exist any longer, and the future doesn't exist yet, and the present never quite exists at all, it seems a funny way to grasp reality. But that's the way we do grasp reality: we grasp it with a category which is totally nonexistent.

Further, you will see if you try it that it is entirely impossible to think of the beginning of time. You can talk about a beginning of time, talk about it forever, but you cannot actually think of the notion. A beginning of time is unthinkable. Consequently, all notions of the eternal in religion which mean endless time are notions which have not got clear of the category of time. Popular Christianity tells us that after death we live forever either in heaven or in hell, meaning endlessly in time. But in saying eternal when you mean endless time, you are not getting clear of the category of time at all. Jesus uses the term *aionios*, which the King James Bible translates as "everlasting"; and if you think carefully about that word "everlasting" as a translation for *aionios*, you'll see that it's a little masterpiece of question-begging. "Everlasting" means persisting indefinitely in time.

However, early Christianity discovered that Christianity would be much more saleable if you perverted its good news into bad news, and in particular if you put at the centre of your teaching the doctrine that after death, unless you did what you were told at this moment, you would suffer tortures for eternity, meaning endlessly in time. Every system of organized priestcraft has had a doctrine of that kind, and the only thing to be said in favour of it is that it makes sin creative: that is, we owe a great deal more to the people who went on sinning in spite of it than we do to the people who tried to restrain sin by threatening it. But that is merely an example of what John Bunyan says, that the mouth of hell is open at the gate of heaven,[33] and that turning God into the devil is one of the commonest of all theological errors. So whatever the word "eternal" means, try to think of it as something that transcends the category of time altogether, and then you'll get a little closer to what the Bible is talking about.

So, negatively, that brings you to a partial and tentative answer to the question, Why does the Bible insist on an absolute beginning? Clearly, it is trying to assert that the category of time is not the ultimate category, and that the activity of God as the Bible understands it in Genesis cannot be put on the same level as this moving belt of past, present, and future that we experience as time. The doctrine of an absolute beginning, which is something you cannot think of as long as you are talking about the category of time itself, is there to indicate that the Creation comes out of a world which is above time.

In the seventeenth century, the age of Galileo and Newton, Biblical scholars, including Newton himself, were gravely explaining to each other that the Creation probably took place in 4004 B.C., probably at the spring equinox, probably around ten in the morning. So the discoveries in the nineteenth century in geology, which eventually pushed the age of the earth back to about two billion years, if not three—but as the government will be saying in the future, what's a billion?—made an impact that was out of all proportion to their importance. But scientists, of course, like anybody else, find that they can't get along without creation myths; and eventually we have a Big Bang creation myth, which says that the world exploded, oh, say fifteen billion years ago or thereabouts, and has been scattering in all directions ever since.

Well, that's fine: what happened before that? And you immediately are up against the fact that as long as you are thinking of the order of nature, the conceptions of beginning and end do not apply. But we begin and we end, and because of what Thomas Pynchon calls creative paranoia in the human consciousness[34] we insist that because we begin and we end, beginnings and endings must be much more deeply built into the scheme of things. And so we start out the Biblical creation myth with an absolute beginning, associated at the end of Revelation with an absolute end.

The first phenomena of Creation were light and sound; and in one of Chaucer's poems, an eagle picks up the poet and takes him on a flight to the House of Fame, and keeps talking the whole time, which makes Chaucer very nervous because he is held in the eagle's mouth, and he doesn't want the eagle to drop him. The eagle gives him a long speech on the nature of sound and of words, and he says, among other things, "Sound is naught but air abroken" [*The House of Fame*, l. 765], that is, words are air. It's a traditional enough association.

My point here is that the Creed speaks of God as having made all things visible and invisible, and there are systems of thought, including some Christian ones, which assume that there are two orders of existence, one invisible and the other visible, and that the invisible world is a higher order of reality. That doesn't seem to be the way the Bible thinks of things at all. As soon as you start trying to think of things that you can't see but know exist, the first thing you would think of would be the air. You can't see the air. If you could, you could see nothing else. You'd be living in a dense fog, and fog is in fact an extremely important metaphor in the Bible, as we'll see when we get to the Book of Ecclesiastes. It's the basis of the word which is translated in that book as "vanity." And in a sense, paradoxical as it sounds, we don't really see light either, as distinct from seeing a source or a reflection of light. What we see is symbolically and metaphorically fire, the source of light, rather than light itself. So the Bible doesn't think of the invisible world as a superior order. It thinks of it as that by means of which the world becomes visible: that is, the invisible world is the medium of the visible world. It is the emptiness that permits things to exist. The twentieth-century philosopher Heidegger says that the first question of philosophy is, Why are there things rather than nothing?[35] And he eventually winds up with the answer that, if there were not nothing, there would be no things.

God is invisible for the same reason that air is invisible. If he were directly visible, well, then he would have been an entirely different metaphysical setup: but when Isaiah says that he saw the Lord high and lifted up [6:1], or when Ezekiel has the vision of the chariot [1:15–21], they mean that they see a source of visibility, just as when we look at the sun we see the source of visibility. That's what I mean by the doctrine of the invisible in the Bible, that the invisible is the medium by which the world becomes visible. If God were not invisible, the world would not be visible; that is, God would not then be a Creator.

Now I've said that myth and metaphor, rather than the historical and doctrinal, are the basis of literal meaning in the Bible. So the question arises, what is the metaphorical kernel, let us say, of this conception of beginning? It might be, as I suggested a few moments ago, the metaphorical kernel of getting born: we begin when we join a continuum of living creatures, and we end when we drop off it. But actually, a much clearer metaphorical basis is that of the experience of waking up in the morning, where you dismiss a dark, chaotic, confused world. You simply abolish that world, and, with the help of your alarm clock, you enter a world which you consider for practical purposes more real, though any philosopher could tie you in any number of knots about its reality. Still, as far as you're concerned, it's the real world, and you get up and get dressed. This metaphorical kernel of abolishing a world of chaos and finding a world which for practical purposes is your real world in front of you is as close as we get to the experience of an actual beginning.

Now, I previously said that many creation myths begin with a hero-god killing a dragon, who represents the chaos of the world before the Creation, and I've cited the Babylonian poem *Enuma Elish*, where Marduk, the hero-god of Babylon, kills the sea monster Tiamat, chops her in two, makes heaven from half of her and earth from the other half. We have tried to suggest that this dragon fight, which is referred to many times in the Old Testament, lies closely behind the account of Creation in Genesis. One reason why it is not mentioned there is that the dragon by this time is being conceived in negative terms as pure inertness. That is, you don't have to kill the dragon: the dragon is death, and to kill death is to bring to life.

And I suspect that it is this immediate connection with the experience of waking up that accounts partly for the metaphor of days in the Creation. Of course, there are historical and cultural reasons. There's the law of the Sabbath. The law of the Sabbath itself derives probably from an original lunar cult, and in a sense, the symbolic or metaphorical moon is older than the sun. A tribe of desert wanderers would find that the sun was a killer, and that the moon was a friendly guide on their night journeys, and hence they would be very apt to make a friendly deity out of the moon. There are many traces of a very early lunar cult among the Hebrews in pre-Biblical times, and one of these traces is the emphasis on the numerical unit of seven days of the week, which marks the phase of the moon. In the Gospel of John, the Word of God is spoken of as a light shining in darkness [1:5], and of course a light shining in darkness suggests the moon, or a bright star like the star of Bethlehem, rather than the sun. So the moon is to that degree a more eloquent symbol of beginning even than the sun. We're told that words like "hallelujah," which have to do with the praising of God, were in pre-Biblical times connected with new moon festivals and with the greeting of the new moon in the sky. The three-day rhythm of the old moon, the dark night, and the new moon has woven itself very intricately into the Christian Passion symbolism.

And so, as I say, I think it is the metaphorical connection between the idea of a beginning and the experience of waking up that accounts for the emphasis on the day, which begins, you'll notice, with the evening, "And the evening and the morning were the third day" [Genesis 1:13], and so on, even though the machinery to regulate days did not appear until the fourth day.

So far I've been talking about the account of Creation in the first chapter of Genesis. That comes from what scholars call the Priestly narrative, which is much the latest of the major documents that make up the first five books of the Bible. A second and much older account of the Creation begins in Genesis 2:4: "These are the generations of the heavens and of the earth when they were created, in the day that the Lord God made the earth and the heavens." The one that comes first is the later, the more philosophical account, where Creation is thought of metaphorically as the creation of dry land out of the waters: that is, chaos is metaphorically identified with the waters or the face of the deep, and practically the first act of the Creation is a separating of the dry land from the sea. In the older account, you begin with a universal drought, and the creative act starts with what the King James Bible calls a "mist" in verse 6 but which in the Septuagint is *pege*, "fountain," which makes a great deal more sense.

Now if you examine creation myths across the world, you will find that certain recurring types seem to sort themselves out, and one very common kind of creation myth is the sexual creation myth, which says essentially that the world came to be in the first place in the same way that it still comes into being in the springtime, when lambs are born from sheep, and new seeds sprout out of the ground. You have in that kind of myth a sexual creation myth, and it is essentially a myth which accounts for the origin of life, for the beginning of things that live, animals and plants. They first came into being in the same way that they still do. Now in the world that we know, everything that lives has been born from a female body, and so in mythology the sexual creation myth is very frequently and very naturally associated with some kind of earth-mother. This earth-mother has both a cherishing and a sinister aspect: cherishing because everything comes to birth from her body, and sinister because everything that dies returns to her body. She is both the womb and the tomb of all forms of life, the mother of life and the mother of death. There is no rule without many exceptions in mythology, but that is a very common type of creation myth.

Now you'll notice that that creation myth has underlying it the notion of an endlessly turning cycle. The new life comes in the spring. What was before that? There was the winter. What was before the winter? The last spring, and so on back. It's a myth which conforms to the facts of nature to the extent that it does not try to answer the question about an absolute beginning. Sexual creation myths turn on the question, Which came first, the chicken or the egg? and there is no answer to that question. You simply go back in an endless cycle of time.

I've tried to show in my analysis of its imagery and narrative that the Bible strongly resists this conception of cyclical fatality. It talks more about absolute beginnings and absolute ends, and this tendency goes back to the particular kind of creation myth that it has. In the Bible, the creation myth is an artificial one. That is, the world originally was made. In a play of Bernard Shaw's, somebody quotes the Horatian tag that poets are born and not made. Somebody says that that's a silly thing to say because everybody's born and not made. But not according to the Book of Genesis: everything at first, including the first man and woman, was made, and the cycle of birth was instituted later. Just as it is natural to associate a sexual creation myth with an earth-mother, so it is natural to associate this artificial creation myth with a sky-father. It is easy to think of God as a father because he's a mysterious being who goes to his work in some office to which you can't follow him, and doesn't nurture his children. I've spoken of the Biblical resistance to the idea of cyclical fatality, and the mother is the parent that we have to break from in order to get born. The creation myth of the Bible associates this conception of the break from the mother, in this case the earth-mother, with that cycle that goes around and around forever without ever stopping.

Then again, I said that the sexual creation myth was a myth about living things, whereas, if you put some kind of mythmaking Robinson Crusoe into a landscape by himself and took all his social conditioning away from him—it isn't possible, but we could think of it experimentally—and said, now you produce a creation myth, the kind of creation myth he would produce would depend on whether he was looking up or looking down at the point at which you've released him. If he were looking down, he would see the cycle of animals and plants coming out of the ground in the springtime, the sap moving in the trees, the new lambs being born, and so forth; and that would condition him in the direction of an earth-mother, a sexual creation myth. But if he looked up, he would see the sun going across the sky, and what was unmistakably the same sun coming back again the next morning. So if he looks down to the cycle of animals and plants, he sees what Plato would call the cycle of the different, because the new life is never the same as the old life. The flowers that bloom in the spring are never the same flowers that bloomed the previous spring. But up in the sky, there is the sun with its daily recurrence, the moon with its slower recurrence, and eventually the planets with theirs; and that suggests something more like planning and intelligence. Hence, the artificial myth tends to become associated with the upper cycle, the cycle of the same rather than of the different.

The cycle of the same suggests a sense of planning and intelligence and ordering. That is, this sexual creation myth suggests what Spinoza would call the *natura naturans*, nature as a living organism; whereas, what you collect from the movements of the sun and moon in the sky is rather the sense of *natura naturata*, of nature as a structure or system, where all things return to their sources.[36] It depends, of course, on the social organization that man belongs to. The notion of a sky-creator is said to be an extremely ancient one, but in early or primitive societies, this sky-creator doesn't do anything. He leaves the government of the world to inferior beings, a pattern that reflects a kind of tribal organization of society. But when you get into more highly developed societies like the late Roman Empire, you find that all the effective gods have retreated into the sky, and that a connection is then formed between the sense of a natural order and a moral order.

If you are in a cycle that goes around without stopping, then you are in a sense an embryo: there's a bigger womb that you never escape from; and what's more, this endlessly turning cycle is, when you analyse it closely, a mechanical symbol. The Hebrew word for embryo is *golem*, and in Jewish legend the *golem* became a mechanical monster like Frankenstein's. This means that Jesus' emphasis on the Father has a great deal to do with this sense of an order higher than that of time and with the sense of the urgency about waking up into this order above time and above the area of mother nature. That's what Christianity calls Resurrection.

Biblia Pauperum 26: CHRIST'S SIDE PIERCED
(John 19:34–7)

Creation of Eve   Moses brings water from the rock
(Genesis 2:20–5)   (Exodus 17:1–7)

14

Genesis: Creating the Sexes;
Exodus: A Revolutionary Heritage

I've suggested that while there is a great variety of creation myths, if you look at the creation myths of Mediterranean countries in the general cultural orbit of the Bible, you find certain typical forms emerging. One of these we described as the sexual creation myth, which simply assumes that the Creation was the beginning of the natural cycle. While there are many exceptions in mythology, one very natural figure for this kind of creation myth to focus on would be an earth-mother. And that seems to be, as far as we can see, the common type of creation myth in the east Mediterranean countries, in pre-Biblical times at any rate.

The one that we find in the first chapter of Genesis is an artificial creation myth, where the world is originally made, rather than simply coming into being, and where the focus is a sky-father, rather than an earth-mother. I've suggested that one significant element in that contrast is that an earth-mother or sexual creation myth is simply the cycle of nature and the seasons extended, but that in the Bible there is a belief in a historical process, a sense of time going somewhere and meaning something, which involves a revolt against all cyclical conceptions of reality.

A cyclical conception of reality is essentially the deification of a kind of machine: that is, it illustrates the ineradicable tendency of the human mind to invent something and then abase itself in front of it. No sooner has the human mind invented the wheel than it starts inventing projections of a wheel of fate or a wheel of fortune, of something ineluctable and mysterious and stronger than man himself. It seems ironic that these projected images should almost invariably be taken from man's own inventions.

Anyway, the first chapter of Genesis, the later or Priestly account of Creation, seems to think in terms of a cosmos as emerging from chaos, and as being associated with an awakening of consciousness that seems to be symbolized in the emphasis on the metaphor of days of a week. The second, or Jahwist account, which begins in the second chapter, is much older, and not all the old sexual mythology has been eliminated from it. The second account begins with the watering of a garden, and we've already seen a suggestion in the Song of Songs and elsewhere of the garden as the bride's body. It's in this older account that Adam is made from the dust of the ground, *adamah*, which is a pun in Hebrew, and *adamah* is feminine. So there's a sense in which Adam had a mother as well as a divine father.

What is more important in this contrast for us at the moment is this: a sexual creation myth focused on an earth-mother has no problem with the conception of death, because it is a myth which concerns, very largely, living things, animals and plants, all of which die. In a sexual creation myth death is built in. It is not only an inevitable part of the myth; it is in some respects the only element that really makes sense of it. But we suggested that the artificial myth thinks more in terms of sky metaphors, of the sun that sets in the evening and comes up again as the same sun the next morning. The bodies in the sky—the sun, the moon, the planets—are not living things in the same way, though they may be deified, as animals and plants are, and they suggest also a sense of planning and of intelligence, a control of affairs in which the same recurring phenomena are brought back.

So it's clear from this and from many other considerations as well, that in the Biblical account of the Creation, God could have created only a perfect and model world in which there could be no death or sin or misery or pain. That is the reason we are told in that account in the first chapter of Genesis that God made something and then saw that it was good. As Bernard Shaw says in one of his essays, "What would he say now?"[37] The answer is of course that he would say, according to the traditional Christian interpretation, "This is not the world I made. This is the world you fell into, and it's all your fault, and not the least little bit my fault. See *Paradise Lost*, books 1 to 12."

Now obviously we can only get to that interpretation by doing a certain violence to the Biblical account. For one thing, it is traditional— you'll find it in *Paradise Lost* as well as elsewhere—that everything we find inconvenient in nature, from mosquitoes to earthquakes, is the result of a fall in nature which accompanied or was part of the original fall of man. But that is of course pure reconstruction: there is nothing about a fall of nature in Genesis. It is said that God cursed the ground, but he removed the curse after the flood, so that doesn't count either.

The essential point is that it is a matter of belief in Judaism and Christianity that the original world created by God must have been a model world: consequently, an artificial creation myth must have an alienation myth like that of the fall of man to account for the difference between the world as such a God must have made it and the actual world that we're living in now.

Of course, this implies that the perfect or model world was made primarily for man's benefit: that is a belief which has obvious psychological links with paranoia. But as Thomas Pynchon remarks in his very remarkable novel *Gravity's Rainbow*, man cannot live except in a paranoid state. He has only the choice between creative and destructive paranoia. So it is not the fact that the world was created for man's sake which is the difficulty, but simply that for an artificial creation myth which assumes an intelligent and planning God, one needs, to complete it, the myth of the fall of man.

The fall of man is described very obliquely in the Book of Genesis. There are two trees, we are told, a tree of life and a tree of knowledge; according to the principle of metaphor, they are clearly the same tree. The forbidden tree has a cursed serpent crawling limply away from it on his belly; and as the serpent is very frequently a sexual or a phallic symbol, one would expect that the tree of life, in an original version of the story, would have had an erect serpent climbing up through its branches, as it still does in certain symbolic systems, like those of kundalini yoga in India. Elsewhere, too, the serpent is the symbol of wisdom, so that the knowledge that man gained by the fall through the subtle serpent, the deceiving serpent, must have been in some respects an illusory knowledge.

It is also of course a knowledge which has something to do with the discovery of sex as we know it, because as soon as the knowledge was acquired, Adam and Eve knew that they were naked and looked around for clothing. Thus, the original unfallen state is apparently conceived as being a sexual ideal of a kind that we have since lost the key to. The Freudian psychologist Jacques Lacan speaks of the "myth of the lost phallus" as being one of the most widespread of human conceptions,[38] and it certainly seems involved in the Genesis account as well.

I'm passing over, for the moment at any rate, the flood story, which in a sense completes the account of the fall of man, and would like to go on to the next phase of Biblical revelation, the phase known as Exodus, or the revolutionary phase.

In the first chapter of Exodus we are told that the Hebrews had entered Egypt under the patronage not merely of Joseph as the advisor to the Pharaoh but of the Pharaoh himself. That is consistent with what we find all through the Bible, that the world ruler is not necessarily thought of as an evil or wicked man, but simply as one who rules over the kind of world in which sooner or later a successor of his will be evil. The Pharaoh who welcomed the family of Jacob into Egypt was a benevolent pharaoh, but in the course of time there was a pharaoh who "knew not Joseph" [1:8] and attempted to get rid of the Hebrews by genocide. The first Persian monarchs, Cyrus and Darius, are spoken of with the greatest respect, but before long we have Ahasuerus in Esther, who attempts another pogrom of genocidal proportions. At the time of the Roman Empire, Paul insists that "the powers that be are ordained of God" [Romans 13:1], but in no time at all we have Nero and the other persecuting Caesars; and although Alexander the Great is represented by Josephus as being welcomed into Jerusalem by the high priest [*Antiquities of the Jews*, 11.8.4], in the course of time, the Syrian Seleucian Empire produced Antiochus Epiphanes.

In many respects, the account in the Bible might have been simpler if it had begun where the story of Israel in effect begins, with God appearing in a burning bush to Moses. Moses in Egypt, having escaped from the original massacre of Hebrews and having been brought up as an Egyptian, looks over the landscape and sees a bush burning, yet without burning up. The emphasis is on the ear rather than the eye: the fact that the bush burns without burning up is merely there to attract Moses' attention; but it is the voice that speaks from within that is important.

Now if you begin the story there, you have immediately wiped out that whole dreary chess game that is known traditionally as theodicy. That is, how are you going to reconcile the existence of a perfectly good God with a horribly bad world, and yet without involving the good God in the bad world in any causal way? It's a problem of white not to move and win: a silly problem, I think, and a made-up one. The scene that begins the Exodus story is much more intelligible. Here, there is a situation of tyranny and exploitation going on to start with: the first datum is injustice, tyranny, and exploitation. God then announces that he is giving himself a name and a highly partisan role, and is going to enter history on the side of the oppressed classes. Never mind how you got into this situation: how you get out of it is the important thing.

So Moses grows up and gathers Israel around him, and there occurs the story about the plagues, the hardening of Pharaoh's heart, and then the crossing of the Red Sea, the event which separated Israel from Egypt. All through the rest of the Bible this separation of Israel from Egypt is one of the major tonalities, a theme which comes back again and again and again. And it is a matter of the highest importance for our understanding of our own cultural traditions that the tradition we have derived through Judaism and Christianity from the Bible has this revolutionary factor which the Exodus story gives to it. All the characteristics of the revolutionary mind are adumbrated right there, and you find most of them repeated in Marxism today.

One of those characteristics is the belief in a specific historical event as the starting point. That is, the story of Israel begins with Moses and the Exodus, and the story of Christianity begins with the birth of Christ. It doesn't begin with the Essenes or anything else that might have looked vaguely similar. The story of Communism begins with Marx and Engels and not with Fourier, Owen, St. Simon, or any of the other utopian socialists. Islam begins with Mohammed and the flight from Mecca to Medina.

That historical consciousness is something that I have stressed already, because it gives to us the typological way of reading the Bible that I have been concentrating on in this course. As I tried to explain, typology is not a form of allegorical interpretation: it is a theory of history, or more accurately of the historical process, one which says that in spite of all the chaos and confusion in human events, nevertheless those events are going somewhere and meaning something, and that eventually something will happen which will indicate what their meaning is. That is what is distinctive about the Biblical tradition and is what that tradition has contributed to modern theories of history, both progressive and revolutionary. It is something which, so far as I know, is confined to that tradition. I don't find it in the Orient or in the classics.

Another characteristic of the revolutionary tradition is the dialectical habit of mind, in which everything that is not for us is against us, so that all the middle ground is progressively eliminated. The Hebrews made their great contribution to our own cultural traditions, as is the wont of human nature, through their least amiable characteristic. It was not their belief that their God was true that became influential: it was their belief that all other gods were false. That conception of false god again is something that would have been almost unintelligible to, say, an educated Greek or Roman. A Greek merchant travelling in Babylon would naturally commend himself to the gods of Babylon before going to sleep. And we can see various traces in the Old Testament of an original belief, ascribed to other people such as the Syrians, that there was nothing nonexistent about other peoples' gods.

I think I may have called your attention to a passage in the Book of Kings in which the Syrians say among themselves when they're going to war with Israel, "Well, Israel is a hilly country; consequently, Jehovah must be a God very good at hill fighting. If we can only get the Israelite army out of the hills and onto the plain, then we'll clean up on them."[39] And of course this resulted in disaster, because Jehovah, thin-skinned as ever, took offence at the notion that he wasn't equally good in valleys. Similarly, if you look at the Trojan War, you'll see that when the Trojans are defeated, the Trojan gods are defeated with them, and have to be taken by Aeneas to Italy to get refurbished for another period of power. All that is extremely remote from something like the contest between Elijah and the priests of Baal on Mount Carmel [1 Kings 18:17–40], where the object is to prove, not that Jehovah is stronger than Baal, but that Baal does not exist at all. He is not really a god, but a figment of the human imagination. That dialectical separation between *the* God and no god is something which seems to have come in with the teachings of the prophets, and which again is almost unintelligible to a polytheistic mind.

I think I mentioned earlier that in a tribal organization of society, the gods are local epiphanic gods. Like the nymphs and the satyrs and the fauns of later mythology, they are immediate deities of trees and stones and mountains. When tribes are organized into nations, the gods become an aristocracy, and usually sit on tops of mountains. When the nations grow into world empires, where the ruler thinks of himself as the ruler of the world, then you do get a kind of monotheism in which all the effective gods retreat into the stars except usually one supreme god. All through history you find this type of monotheism associated with world rulers: with an early pharaoh of Egypt, Akhenaton, who practically wrecked his empire in quest of his one god, and the early rulers of Persia, Cyrus and Darius, who were very fervent and devout monotheists. But that kind of imperial monotheism is totally different from the revolutionary monotheism of the Bible.

Imperial monotheism is a very eclectic religion that tends to identify local cults with the service of the supreme god, as they are all the same god anyway. A liberal-minded person in the late Roman Empire, for example, might even go to the point of collecting gods, and would have no objection whatever to having statues of Jehovah and Jesus in his collection. That is, he would think of any number of gods equally as ways of reaching the truth of one God. That is again an attitude of mind that is totally opposed to the kind of monotheism one finds in the Bible, where God has a specific name and a specific role in history, and is not simply a god in whom every other conception of deity may be absorbed.

Another feature of the same revolutionary mentality, I think, is the tendency to do precisely what the Israelites did, to build up a sacred book, and to mark it off clearly from other books that are apocryphal or secular or in some other respect peripheral. The conception of a sacred canon is something that seems to have grown up uniquely with the Israelite tradition. It's possible that there is a scene in the Bible that catches the moment of its birth. In 2 Kings 22, we have one of the last kings of Judah, and one of the few kings that the narrator approves of. One of the first things he does is to repair the temple, and in the course of repairing the temple, a document is found, the book of the law. In verse 8: "And Hilkiah the high priest said unto Shaphan the scribe, I have found the book of the law in the house of the Lord. And Hilkiah gave the book to Shaphan, and he read it." Then they report this fact to the king, verse 11: "And it came to pass, when the king had heard the words of the book of the law, that he rent his clothes." And then he said, verse 13: "enquire of the Lord for me, and for the people, and for all Judah, concerning the words of this book that is found: for great is the wrath of the Lord that is kindled against us, because our fathers have not hearkened unto the words of this book, to do according unto all that which is written concerning us." Now what is of special significance in this passage is the king's conviction that it was a matter of the highest importance for the people as a whole to know the contents of a written document. We're a long way from democracy here, but democracy is founded on the basis of public access to documents, so you can see history turning a rather decisive corner at this point. Such a book would have to be in the first place a law book, because it is the laws which are almost invariably regarded as sacred, as of divine origin and as something that it concerns everyone to know.

Now it's been practically the only thesis in Biblical scholarship that the majority of Biblical scholars are agreed on that this book of the law which was then discovered either was or was very closely related to the existing Book of Deuteronomy. And that means, therefore, that the Book of Deuteronomy was the germ, the core, out of which the entire canon developed. It was probably later than that that the priests began to conflate the older accounts which they already had in temple records, and which survive in such things as the earlier account of Creation and the Genesis stories. The authors of Samuel and Kings are known as the Deuteronomic historians because they follow the general dialectic of Deuteronomy in their historical attitudes.

The Book of Deuteronomy itself seems to have been influenced by the writings and teachings of prophets who came before it, or at least before the time of its discovery. That seems to leave us with the conclusion that such people as David and Solomon had never heard of Moses, that the notion of the contract at Mount Sinai which gave the Israelites the law is a post-Deuteronomic idea and grew up some time after this discovery of the book by Josiah in the seventh century B.C.

The notion of a canon, of books that seem to belong together as especially sacrosanct, seems to be taking shape. We don't know very much about the way it operated, but that it was there seems inescapable. And there's a curious symbolic contrast between the fact that the successful and prosperous empires of Egypt and Babylon and Assyria produced the great temples, whereas the Israelites, who were never lucky at the game of empire, produced a book. To the people who wanted the kind of success that Assyria, Persia, and Babylon had, production of a book must have seemed a good deal like a booby prize. But if you think of the relative durability of a book and a monument, you'll see that the facts are very different.

There's a wonderful scene in the Book of Jeremiah where Jeremiah's secretary is reading to what is practically the last king of Judah a prophecy of Jeremiah consisting very largely of denunciations of the king's very foolish and obstinate policy of resistance to Babylon. We're told that it was a cold day, and there was a fire burning in the room in the palace. Every so often, the infuriated king would cut a piece off the scroll with his knife and throw it in the fire [36:20–32]. Well, that means that it was a papyrus scroll, because if it had been parchment, it would not only have bankrupted the prophet, but it would also have been tough enough to spoil the king's gesture. But we have the contrast between the prophecy of Jeremiah, entrusted to the most fragile and combustible material that the ancient world produced, and the king's palace, built presumably out of the stones of Solomon's palace, which had taken him thirteen years to build. After 2500 years, not the slightest trace remains of the king's palace, whereas the book of Jeremiah remains in reasonably good shape.

The contrast between producing a book which can be wiped out by the merest breath of accident and the great stone monuments that are there to endure forever and actually crumble in a few years, is rather like the difference between life and death perhaps, because any form of life can also be snuffed out very quickly.

The final item in this list of revolutionary characteristics I'm discussing is the tendency to regard your near neighbour, who is separated from you only by a very slight heresy, as a much deadlier and more detestable enemy than the agreed-on common enemy. Early Christianity, for example, didn't so much attack the pagans as the Gnostics or the Arians, whom they *called* pagans. In a Marxist struggle for power today, the people attacked are not capitalist reactionaries: it is the Trotskyites or supporters of the Gang of Four who are called agents of the bourgeois counter-revolution. And with Judaism similarly, there is a much greater bitterness against the Northern Kingdom for its secession, and later on with the Samaritans who occupied the same place, than there is against, say, the Persians.

The word "canon" is an interesting one. In the prophecy of Ezekiel, Ezekiel is told to take a reed and measure the temple of God [chaps. 40–2]. The word for reed is *qaneh*, and it's from that word ultimately, through Greek intermediaries, that we get our word "canon." And so symbolically, at least, there seems to be some connection between this symbol of measuring the temple and constructing a verbal canon. If you look at the eleventh chapter of Revelation, you will see that it begins with the angel giving the narrator a reed like a rod and telling him to measure the temple of God. Immediately following is the account of the martyrdom of the two witnesses who, as we saw, are connected with Moses and Elijah, the two pillars of Scripture, the symbolic law and prophets.

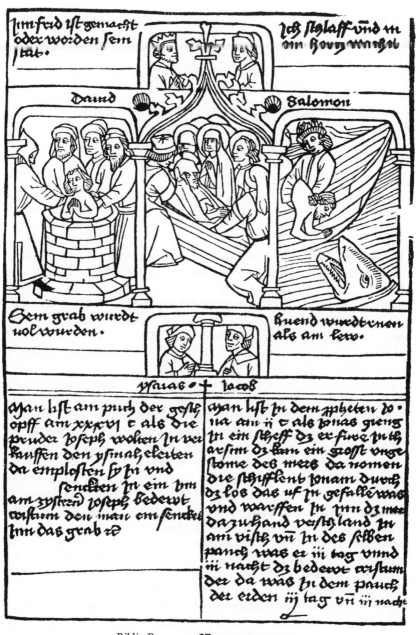

Biblia Pauperum 27: ENTOMBMENT
(Matthew 27:57–61)

Joseph put in the well
(Genesis 37:18–24)

Jonah cast overboard
(Jonah 1)

15

Law: Ordering a Society

I've been dealing with two phases of the Biblical revelation: first of all, with the Creation, and the conceptions of fall and deluge that are part of that complex; then with the revolutionary spirit that crystallizes around Israel in Egypt, and during the Exodus from Egypt. What follows, the third stage, is the stage of law, which for Judaism became the crucial one. The first five books of the Bible in Judaism are called the Torah, a word which is often translated "law," although it means something much broader than that.

The shape of the New Testament turns on its conception of itself as a reformulation of the notion of law in the Old Testament. What one finds in Paul and the Epistle to the Hebrews particularly is a conception of the gospel as having set man free from the law. The legal material in the Old Testament is usually divided into three groups, the judicial, the ceremonial, and the moral; and one of the first controversies in the Christian Church was over the question of whether the first generation of Christians, who were all Jews, would be subject to the ceremonial law or not. You can read about that in the Book of Acts, where Paul is the main spokesman for the view that the gospel breaks with all three aspects of the law. Of course, Christianity immediately set up a ceremonial law of its own; and although Paul says twice that circumcision is nothing [1 Corinthians 7:19; Galatians 5:6, 6:15], the Church in his day was saying something much more like, baptism is practically everything—and Paul himself supports that view. Similarly, the day of rest simply shifts from Saturday to Sunday. It isn't a question of getting rid of a ceremonial code, but of adopting a new one.

There was a good deal of controversy in Christian theology as to how much of this law one got set free from; and there were views that while the judicial part   the years of jubilee [Leviticus 25.0-12], that sort of thing—and the ceremonial code were not binding on Christianity, the moral law as set out in the Ten Commandments still was. Luther makes it a cardinal principle of his teaching that the Christian gospel makes a break with all three; but one has to understand what is meant by that. What he means by it is that the law becomes internalized, and consequently becomes something beyond the reach of a legal code. To say that the gospel set one free of the law doesn't mean breaking the law. It doesn't mean criminal action, because you don't get set free from the law by breaking the law: you get more fouled up with it than ever. You get free of the law by transforming it into an internal principle. As a result, the principles in the teaching of Jesus are concerned with the inner state of mind rather than with the social consequences of action. And so in his commentary on the Ten Commandments that forms a part of the Sermon on the Mount, the negative formulation "don't kill" becomes a positive enthusiasm for human life; and "don't commit adultery" becomes a habitual respect for the dignity of the woman; and "don't steal" becomes an enthusiasm for sharing goods. In all this, of course, there was nothing that a legal code could be formulated to touch. If you think for example of the seven deadly sins as they were set out in the Middle Ages—pride, wrath, sloth, envy, avarice, gluttony, and lechery—those were regarded as the mortal sins, the deadly sins that destroyed the soul; but not one of them necessarily ends in, or results in, criminal or antisocial acts.

That is, in the teaching of Jesus, the conception of sin is totally unintelligible except in a religious context. It is not antisocial behaviour, nor is it anything that a law can regulate. So the transmutation of the law into an inner state of the soul leads to a much stricter and more intensive morality: if you tried to legalize the teachings of Jesus, for example, you would get the most frightful tyranny, because the things that offend your own self-respect are usually things that are of too fine a mesh for any kind of legal code to catch.

There are aspects of this question of law which are of some interest. For one thing, the conception of law is, in general, moral. The moral is the category which to some degree includes the judicial and ceremonial. It relates to the observances that God is represented as prescribing for Israel, laid down on top of a network of social obligations, customs and penalties, and so on. There is also the conception of natural law. Both principles are called "law," but they really have nothing to do with each other. Yet the whole Biblical tradition, and Western culture in general, has revolved around a strained and illegitimate pun on the word "law" as meaning, first of all, the morality of human action, and secondly as meaning the observed phenomena of nature.

Now in the moral sphere you have a commanding personality—God—and you have those who have the choice of obeying or disobeying. If that is law, then what we call natural law has nothing to do with law, because laws of the phenomena of nature cannot be broken. You don't break a law of nature, you only manifest it. If you're standing on the edge of a precipice and jump over, you don't break the law of gravitation. You merely manifest the law of gravitation, and the law of gravitation breaks you. There could be no question whatever of feeling that you have a choice of obeying or disobeying a natural law; and in the course of time, we've come more and more to feel that nature is an impersonal order.

Now, we derived this illegitimate association of law both with human moral behaviour and with the phenomena of nature through a kind of conspiracy between the Biblical and the Greek aspects of our cultural tradition. In Greek polytheistic religion, the gods had separate personalities, and consequently could fall out and disagree. The most obvious example is the Trojan War, where, to give them their Roman names, Juno, Minerva, and Venus turned up all together in front of Paris with a golden apple and said, "We want you to give this to the most beautiful of the three of us." So he had to choose one out of the three; and the other two said, "Well, to hell with you," and went off and took the Greek side in the Trojan War; whereas poor old Venus or Aphrodite, who, being what she was, had no talent for fighting at all, was the only one left on the Trojan side.

She did, according to the *Iliad*, try to get into the melee on one occasion, and one of the Greek warriors, Diomedes, gave her a whack over the wrist, which bruised it; and she went squalling back to Olympus and said to her father Zeus, "Now look at what that awful man did to me: you've got to do something to him." And Zeus said, "Well you got just what you deserved: you have no business on a battlefield. You have to leave that to Athene, who knows how to wear armour" [bk. 5, ll. 334–430].

So in a polytheistic religion you obviously have to have something overruling these clashes of divine wills; and there are suggestions that the will of Zeus is being manifested no matter how the gods and goddesses disagree. But that's hardly consistent, because at one time, when it looks as though the Trojans are about to win over the Greeks,

Hera, or Juno, who is on the Greek side, seduces Zeus by getting him into bed, and so put out of action. Zeus manages to scramble out of bed in time to help the Trojans, whom on the whole he prefers. But it is clear that while Homer does say from time to time that the will of Zeus is being accomplished, he is also saying that there is another force which has already determined what is going to happen, a force that is superior to the will of Zeus in power and that Zeus must obey. This force is the conception that we often translate very badly as "fate." It is really a conception derived from the sense of the regularity and invariability of natural law. Thus, we get most of our scientific tradition from the Greeks because they had a polytheistic religion. The power to overrule the clashes of divine wills in fact became the germ of the conception of natural law. And, as men are put there to serve the gods, and to behave more or less as the gods want them to, moral and natural law become associated even in the Greek tradition.

One place where they are so associated with particular eloquence and power is in the last of Aeschylus' three plays about the murder of Agamemnon, and about the revenge taken on his mother by Agamemnon's son, Orestes. In the third of those plays of Aeschylus, *The Eumenides*, there are two levels of balance or order. There is first the purely mechanical level, represented by the Furies, who are pursuing Orestes to avenge his murder of his mother. Actually, it was a good thing that Orestes did murder his mother: she had it coming to her. But that couldn't matter less to the Furies, who had been given orders that when this kind of thing happens, they automatically take vengeance.

The whole thing comes into a court of the gods; and eventually the goddess of wisdom, Athene, explains that one has to consider certain aspects of equity in the situation. That introduces a superior moral principle. But it is also part of a conception of an order in which men and the gods and nature are all involved. The gods ultimately have to ratify the order of nature: otherwise they'll lose their divinity and become something else. Therefore, in the Greek tradition, moral and natural law here become united.

In the Biblical tradition, the same thing happens, but for quite different reasons. There is also a contract involved; but in the Biblical version, nature is not a party to it. Therefore, there is no order of nature that is thought of as representing or manifesting an aspect of law. In the Biblical tradition, the same God controls both the moral and the natural orders. That means in effect that there is no natural law as we understand it, except as the functioning of nature under God's permission.

The law of gravitation works because God wants it to, but strictly speaking, in the Biblical tradition there is no way of distinguishing a natural event from a miraculous one except by the rarity of the miracle.

If the same God controls both, and if his will is manifest in both moral and natural orders, then in both moral and natural orders you have a commanding personality and an agent who can either obey or disobey. In the nineteenth century, Nietzsche made his famous statement that God is dead. That statement, in spite of all the attention it has aroused even in theology, is still subordinate to Nietzsche's main purpose, which was to demonstrate that there is no personality in charge of nature, that nature consequently has no option of obeying or disobeying, and that all such notions are pure superstition.

The Eumenides ends almost as though it were a comedy. That is, the Furies acquire the name of Eumenides, which means "the kindly spirits," because they are absorbed into a higher and more just conception of law that considers the factor of equity; Orestes is acquitted, and the whole play ends in an atmosphere of serenity. But in the whole context of Greek thought and of Aeschylus' dramatic form, I don't think that that calm and serene conclusion really turns the trilogy of Agamemnon into a comedy. What it does is to render a vision of an interlocking order in which man, the gods, and nature are all involved; and it is that sense of interlocking order which lies behind Greek tragedy. It doesn't lie behind the Bible, and that is one reason Christian tragedy is a difficult form—something of a tour de force when it does appear—and often its success, in Shakespeare for example, is the result of such devices as making the setting pre-Christian in *King Lear*.

The conception of tragedy in Greek literature rests on the notion of *hubris*, or *hybris*. You usually see it spelled with a "u," but that's just illiteracy.[40] This act of *hybris* is an act of aggression that upsets the balance in the order of nature that the gods are there to ratify. Consequently, because it upsets the balance, a counterbalance must be set up, which is what is called *nemesis*. The action of aggression and counterbalance is symbolized by the scales, the emblem of justice, and is what makes the tragic conclusion not merely morally intelligible but almost physically intelligible. In fact, one of the earliest and profoundest of all Greek philosophers, Anaximander, said that getting born was an act of *hybris*, and death was its *nemesis*, the re-establishing of the balance in the scheme of things.[41]

One of the words in Greek drama that we translate as "fate" is *moira*. As I say, it's a very crude and approximate translation: it means more than that. At the opening of the *Odyssey*, Zeus is represented as saying, "It's too bad that men are so ready to blame the gods for their own disasters, because for the most part they bring their disasters on themselves." The example that he gives is that of the man who murdered Agamemnon, Aegisthus: he, Zeus says, went *hyper moron*, beyond fate [bk. 1, ll. 5–49, Loeb]. And because he went beyond fate, fate had to catch up: it had to make the counterbalancing movement that destroyed Aegisthus.

I think that tragedy arose in Greek literature at a certain period, largely in connection with the notion of justice or *dike*, as it's called, where the poets were concerned with this Greek interaction of gods and men and the order of nature. And so tragedy, which dramatized that interaction, really fitted the fifth-century period in Athenian culture. But as it manifests a very fundamental fact about the human situation, it is consequently a structure that can work in any culture, although it is more difficult if the assumptions are Christian ones. As I say, Shakespeare sometimes adopts special devices: because *King Lear* is pre-Christian, the characters keep swearing by Apollo and Jupiter and other gods that the audience knew didn't exist. Even as attentive a student of Shakespeare as Samuel Johnson says that Shakespeare's tragedies are almost miraculously clever stunts, almost a tour de force, and that his instinctive and temperamental bent was for comedy.[42] Whether that is true or not, it is true that most religions tend towards some kind of goal for which the literary model is comedy. Greek religion was one of the very few exceptions that I know of.

There's another by-product of this that is perhaps worth looking at. If you look at the shape of the Biblical story, you can see what we have been pointing out all along, that man is thought of as living on two levels, as a man and as a creature of God. There is the level reached by Adam in the garden of Eden before the fall of man; and there is the lower level, represented by the fall and by all human history since. The higher level manifests itself in things like resurrection and apocalypse.

It follows, then, that in the Christian era there were two levels of the order of nature. The lower level was the level which man fell into, the level of physical nature, a level to which the animals and plants seem to be fairly well adjusted. But man before the fall, in the garden of Eden, was in the state in which God intended him to live. That is an upper level of nature, the true level of human nature. In teaching Milton's *Paradise Lost*, I've often had occasion to notice how the description of the life of Adam and Eve in the garden of Eden makes them seem like a couple of suburbanites in the nude, preoccupied with their own sexual relations and with domestic details of housekeeping and gardening. Adam looks in the sky and says, "There's an angel up in the sky"; and Eve says, "How nice, maybe he'll stay to lunch," which he in fact does. He can't eat anything in paradise except a fruit salad, but then he likes fruit salads. He explains how, being an angel, he can eat without the bother of excretion, which his skin pores take care of [bk. 5, ll. 308–505]. All of that has, naturally, aroused ridicule among some of Milton's readers. But the point is that Milton thought of Adam's life in the garden of Eden as the state in which God intended man to live; so that, therefore, man's original state was civilized. There are no noble savages for Milton until Adam has fallen. Adam turns into a noble savage *after* he's fallen; but before that, he was on the level of human nature.

Thus, there are two levels of nature, one appropriate to man, the other to beings without consciousness. It follows that many things are natural to man that are not natural to animals, and many things are natural to animals that are not natural to man. It is natural for man to wear clothes, to be in a state of social organization, to have degrees of rank, and so on. And so, as Edmund Burke was still insisting in the early nineteenth century, on the human level, nature and art are really the same thing.[43] It is natural to man to be in a state of art.

In Milton's *Comus*, Comus is an evil spirit who captures a virtuous lady and holds her immobile in a chair, then tries to seduce her. His argument for seduction rests on the analogy with physical nature. The animals, he says, don't show the least self-consciousness or sense of sin about sexual intercourse: what's holding you up? And the lady tells him, in effect, that on her level of nature, chastity is what is natural to her.

On this basis, the question, What is natural to man? has a completely circular answer. What is natural to man is natural on the level of human nature, and the level of human nature is what custom and authority have decided to be the level of human nature. Homosexuality, for example, was often said to be condemned because it is unnatural: the animals don't do it. That is, it was asserted that the animals didn't do it, and they didn't examine animals very closely to see whether it was true or not. But the argument doesn't work on this upper level. There, what is unnatural is what the voice of custom and authority has decreed to be unnatural. There is nothing that you can define as inherently unnatural. In the Reformation, many Protestants took the position that nothing was wrong unless the Bible forbade it. And the Bible obligingly comes through with condemnations of most vices, but it forgets polygamy. It never once condemns polygamy, or suggests that there's anything wrong with that state of social organization. As the voice of custom and authority was determined to have a monogamous society to keep the sexual instinct properly regulated, it had to fall back on a conception of natural law for that one thing. But as I say, the argument is totally circular. We don't know what is natural to man as long as we are working on these two levels of nature. What we have inherited since the eighteenth century, coming very largely from issues raised by Rousseau, is the question, Does this upper level of custom and authority represent the reality of human nature, or is it merely the façade which a structure of power has thrown up? We're still trying to figure out the answer to that one; but what I'm trying to get at is its origin: it is the shape of the Biblical myth that seems to imply that there are two levels of the natural.

Since the fall of Adam, man has been born into this middle world, the world of physical nature, the world to which animals and plants are adjusted but to which he is not. So he's confronted from birth with a moral dialectic. Either he moves up as close as he can to what was intended to be his state, or he goes down to the level of sin, which is a level that the animals cannot reach. Everything that is good for man—law and morality and education and virtue—all those things are agents that tend to raise man from the physical level he was born in to the human level he belongs in. Milton explicitly defines education as the attempt to repair the fall of our first parents; and he is referring to secular as well as to religious education.

Another inference from the Biblical story that Western culture has adopted is the conception of what is called "original sin." Original sin arises from the fact that man is born into a world which is alien to him: it really arises out of the fact that man is going to die. His consciousness is, before it is anything else, a consciousness of death. And so, in man, as he is born in this alien world, there is a force of inertia pulling him down. It was out of that general view, not out of the specific doctrine, which came much later, that Jeremiah said that the heart is desperately wicked [17:9].

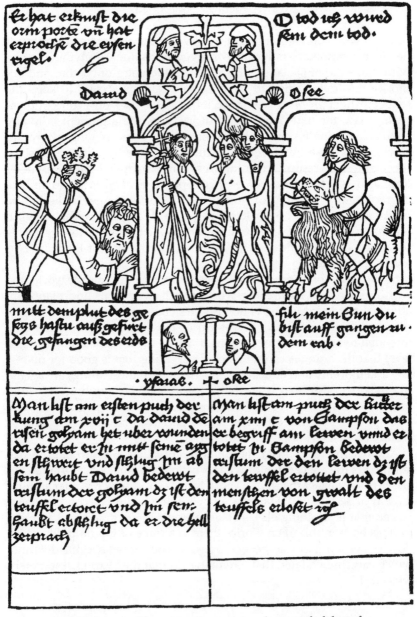

Biblia Pauperum 28: HARROWING OF HELL (apocryphal, but cf.
Psalm 107:8–16; Hosea 13:14; Ephesians 4:9–10; 1 Peter 3:18–19)

David kills Goliath
(1 Samuel 17)

Samson kills the lion
(Judges 14:5–6)

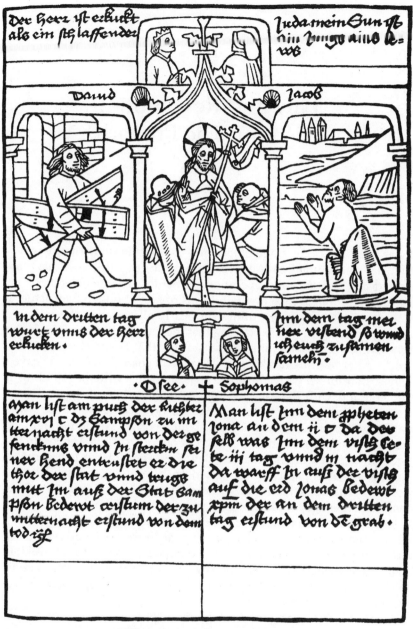

Biblia Pauperum 29: RESURRECTION
(Matthew 28:1–10)

Samson with the gates of Gaza
(Judges 16:1–3)

Jonah released from the whale
(Jonah 2)

16

Law and Revolution;
Wisdom: The Proverb

I was speaking of the stage of law, and of a peculiar inheritance which that has bequeathed to Western civilization, by which we have assumed that the observed operations of nature and the obligations incurred in human society are both forms of law, although they actually represent totally different things. In nearly all societies, the laws are accompanied by myths explaining that they are of divine origin. In the *Enuma Elish* epic, for example, the story is that of the creation of the world. After Marduk has killed the dragon of chaos and formed heaven and earth from her body, the poem goes on to deal with the founding of Babylon and with the establishing of the laws there. It goes directly from the creation myth to the myth of the origin of law because law is naturally conservative, and a myth about its origin would naturally be concerned with the establishing of order out of an original chaos. In the *Oresteia*, which I mentioned last day, the origin of the law court of Athens, the Areopagus, is connected with resolving the feud in the house of Atreus, which had climaxed with Orestes' murder of his mother in revenge for his mother's murder of his father.

In the Bible, however, law follows immediately upon a revolutionary phase. The Israelites rebel against Egyptian authority. They eventually escape from Egypt and become a separate nation in the desert, and it is in the desert that they receive the law. The fact that in the Biblical myth the stage of law follows the stage of revolution has a significance that we have to look at.

A nation which has gone through the experience of a revolution is often one in which the sense of participation on the part of the people is very strong. And so, there is a curious ambiguity in what happens. If you take for example the American Revolution, when Tocqueville came to America in the nineteenth century and looked at it, one of the things that struck him most forcibly was the sense of popular participation and involvement with the social order, and with what has since been called "the American way of life." That does not mean of course that there is a close connection between the revolutionary experience and the reign of law as such, because the moral of a successful revolution is: "violence pays." Hence, a great deal of lawbreaking and violence might be a quite normal outgrowth of the revolutionary experience.

What Tocqueville felt, however, was that this sense of participation and involvement with the American national experiment might eventually produce another kind of tyranny, a kind of tyranny that would not be imposed from above, but would extend within. It would be of a kind which, with the hindsight of another century, we would call totalitarian.

Now, whether that is true or not, you can see, I think, if you follow the narrative of the story of the Exodus, that the progression from the revolution against Egypt, the Exodus, to the imposing of the law, is accompanied by a strong sense of this total participation and involvement in the new national experiment with the new community of Israel.

Now, in the first place, a successful revolution, once it establishes its authority, frequently becomes very strongly repressive about any further revolutions. The thirteen colonies revolted in the eighteenth century, but they fought a civil war a century later over the issue of whether there should be any further revolutions or separations. In the story of the Exodus, we are told that there were many rebellions within the Israelite community in the desert. They were tired of living in the desert; they were tired of this inane pastry that God kept raining down from heaven to feed them; and many of them wanted simply to go back to Egypt. The community of Israel in the desert is presented as a theocratic dictatorship under the direct eye of God. God of course is the perfect counter-revolutionary because he always knows when there's a conspiracy against him. And so we read in the Book of Numbers about the rebellion of Korah and his fellow conspirators, Dathan and Abiram, who were swallowed up by the earth [Numbers 16:1–35]. We read of murmurings among the children of Israel, and of God's sending fiery serpents among them to bite everybody who complained [Numbers 21:4–6].

Moses in this situation has the role of a field commander who is on the inside track to the supreme command headquarters: he goes and reports to his superior officer and issues communiqués about his people's morale, and at times will take responsibility for what Israel does wrong. I have a friend who came back from the Italian campaign in the Second World War saying that the most perfect description of that kind of campaign that had ever been recorded was the story of Moses in the desert. Very concerned about his people's morale, in constant touch with his supreme commander, issuing orders about the next move and the next encampment, and all the time he hasn't the faintest notion where the hell he is or how he got there or where he's going or why he's there in the first place. That sense of a total organization, along with the kind of confusion that only a military atmosphere can induce, is something that runs all through the early books of the Bible.

When we reach the Book of Joshua, we find another modulation of the same kind of thing. If you look at the seventh chapter of Joshua, here we are told that the Israelites take a Canaanite stronghold known as Ai; and God's rule is that everything that they take from a plundered and sacked city shall be devoted to him as a sacrifice. But there is one person among the Israelites who decides to keep something back for himself: his name is Achan. The result is that the next time the Israelites attack a Canaanite stronghold they get taken to the cleaners. Joshua says to God, "Now what's this? After all, we're supposed to win this war." And God says, "Yes, I know, but you stole something from me at Ai, and you've got to look after that before anything else can be done." So they draw lots, and the lot falls on Achan. In verse[s] 24[–5], "And Joshua, and all Israel with him, took Achan the son of Zerah, and the silver, and the garment, and the wedge of gold, and his sons, and his daughters, and his oxen, and his asses, and his sheep, and his tent, and all that he had: and they brought them unto the valley of Achor. And Joshua said, Why hast thou troubled us? the Lord shall trouble thee this day. And all Israel stoned him with stones, and burned them with fire, after they had stoned them with stones." In other words, Achan's whole family was wiped out with him. The line of thinking is that such a person as Achan represents a cancer in the community, and the cancer has to be cut out.

There you get a glimpse of the terrorism of an incorruptible society, and the fact that a society set up in such a way is something that humankind can endure for only a very short time. Corruption is an essential aspect to social living, because the people who take advantage of corruption are not invariably the criminals, but also those who find this kind of omniscient purity a trifle exacting to live under.

Naturally, you would expect the same kind of thing to recur in the primitive Christian community; and the New Testament counterpart to the story of Achan is in the Book of Acts, the fifth chapter. "But a certain man named Ananias, with Sapphira his wife, sold a possession, And kept back part of the price, his wife also being privy to it, and brought a certain part, and laid it at the apostles' feet. But Peter said, Ananias, why hath Satan filled thine heart to lie to the Holy Ghost, and to keep back part of the price of the land?" [vv. 1–3]. And Ananias and Sapphira are struck dead for their atavistic bourgeois habits, and for running counter to the perfect communism of primitive Christian society.

Well, the stage of law, when it follows a revolution, is often accompanied by purges. The story of Achan is an excellent example of a purge, because the entire family of Achan is wiped out with him. But eventually, God decides that the purge, if it's going to be effective, has to be total. And so he lays it down that all the old-line revolutionaries, that is, all the people involved in the Exodus from Egypt, would have to die off in the wilderness, and that a new generation would have to grow up before they could enter the Promised Land. That is in the Pentateuch itself, but it's also referred to later in Psalm 95:11. I refer to that because it's quoted in the Epistle to the Hebrews [3:11] and becomes an important Christian argument as well. "Unto whom I sware in my wrath that they should not enter into my rest." The Christians of course elaborated this argument symbolically, and said that the first generation that came out from Egypt, all of which had to die off, represented Judaism, and that the next generation, which was allowed to enter the Promised Land, symbolized Christianity.

After the return from Babylon, the same symbolic theme is repeated by Jeremiah, in Jeremiah 31:31–3: "Behold, the days come, saith the Lord, that I will make a new covenant with the house of Israel, and with the house of Judah: Not according to the covenant that I made with their fathers in the day that I took them by the hand to bring them out of the land of Egypt; which my covenant they brake. ... But this shall be the covenant. ... After those days ... I will put my law in their inward parts, and write it in their hearts; and will be their God, and they shall be my people." So that Jeremiah is applying to the return from Babylon, which he's prophesying, the same principle, that the old covenant, or the old testament, is to be done away with, and a new covenant, or a new testament, which will be an inward matter, a spiritual matter rather than a matter of ordinances, will replace it. And Christianity, of course, promptly applied this prophecy to its own teachings, and called its own gospel the New Testament.

The next stage on from law, if you're ready for me to make that transition, is the stage of wisdom. The root of wisdom, as it is presented in the Bible, is the individual absorption of the law, the law as permeating the individual life, and as transferring from the community to the individual the law's sense of logical consistency, the obedience to certain principles, and a continuity in observing them. This appears in some of the Psalms, for example that long one, the 119th, which is so long because it's an acrostic poem with every section of it beginning with a successive letter of the Hebrew alphabet. The general theme of that psalm is the individual's confession that he loves the law, and that the law has become a motivating part of his own nature. From there, we develop towards the more primitive conception of wisdom, which is that of practical sense. You can see glimpses of this conception of wisdom as practical sense if you look, for example, at the *Odyssey*. Ulysses is the crafty man of many devices, and when he comes back to Ithaca, he spends almost an entire book telling a completely fictitious yarn to a very faithful old servant of his, the swineherd, in which he represents himself as a Cretan and tells a story about himself totally at variance with everything else in the *Odyssey* [bk. 14]. There's one place where he's really stuck in a corner, and according to Homer, on this occasion he told the truth, not because he loved the truth—in fact, it hurt him like hell to have to tell the truth—but there was really no help for it. There was nothing else he could do.[44]

For it was such devices that got him out of tight spots, as when he told the Cyclops Polyphemus, who asked for his name, that his name was "nobody," *outis* [bk. 9, ll. 380–4]. He is guided in all his affairs by the one goddess who is consistently friendly to him, and that is the goddess of wisdom, Athene. Athene on one occasion appears to Ulysses and says, "You know, I've got a lot of respect and affection for you: you are so superbly crooked. You're such a wonderful liar. And you're very like me, because among all the gods and goddesses, I hold the preeminence for subtle devices" [bk. 13, ll. 350–66, 387–9]. And so we see that even the goddess of wisdom goes back to one of the most ancient categories of gods, the trickster god. And it's Athene who gets him back to Ithaca by a series of disguisings and by putting false appearances on him.

Well, that kind of practical sense is really a search for the means which from day to day does preserve your balance and your sanity and your well-being. Closely connected with this is the literary genre of the

proverb. The proverb is very ancient, and nearly all the ancient kingdoms of the Near East, Egypt and Sumeria and Babylonia, cultivated
the proverb very extensively.

There are two general kinds of proverbs, depending on their social
context. There's the proverb addressed to people who do not have
great advantages in birth or wealth. These proverbs are counsels of
prudence. They tell you how to get along without antagonizing your
superiors: you have to be polite to them, you have to study their moods
and make sure you operate on them when they're in the right mood.
But when it comes to your inferiors, don't be insolent or arrogant to
them because you never know, they may become your superiors some
day. And that is a form of proverb which has always been popular: it's
still going strong in Benjamin Franklin in eighteenth-century America;
it's still going strong in Sam Slick in nineteenth-century Nova Scotia.[45]
Whenever Haliburton at the end of his sketches writes down a proverb
that he thinks is particularly wise and shrewd, he prints it in italics.
That is again a sign of popular literature, and the proverb and very
closely allied fable are the two literary genres that come nearest to being
what we might call democratic. The most celebrated collectors of fables,
Aesop and Phaedrus, were both slaves.

There is another type of proverb. It is very similar as far as content
goes, but is rather a series of maxims handed down by a king to his son
to emphasize the continuity of the principles of order in society. This
kind is found in ancient Egypt, and some of this ancient Egyptian
proverbial material reappears many centuries later in the Book of Proverbs in the Old Testament. The context it is placed in is different, but it
is recognizably the same set of proverbs. This pattern of the father's
handing on the accumulated wisdom of his years to his son is something that goes on all through literature. You'll find it in *Hamlet* when
Laertes is about to leave for Paris and Polonius reaches into his mental
filing cabinet and pulls out the accumulated wise saws which Laertes
must remember when he's in Paris.

It was still surviving in the eighteenth century when Lord Chesterfield wrote a series of letters to his son. Lord Chesterfield was a para-
gon of elegance and politeness and courtesy: his son was a lout. Lord
Chesterfield felt that if he wrote enough letters to him he might make
something better of him, and as a result we have the letters of Chesterfield to his son, which, according to Samuel Johnson, combined the
morals of a whore with the manners of a dancing master.[46] But that's
perhaps not too uncommon in that genre.

That leads us to another aspect of wisdom, which is that wisdom traditionally is something that depends on the accumulated experience of a community, and therefore is especially the property of the elders and seniors. Therefore, the virtue of wisdom goes along with the respect for the authority of the elders, and for the transmission of their principles in as unchanged a form as possible.

You notice that in the Book of Proverbs, which was assigned to King Solomon, there's a verse about "Chastise thy son," which is a verse that has probably been responsible for more physical pain than any other sentence ever written.[47] But it's consistent with this whole conception of wisdom. Wisdom is what the elders know: the young people must be broken in to it. The elders are wiser because they have had more experience in that wisdom of prudence that maintains their stability from one day to the next.

Thus, wisdom is dominated throughout by the anxiety of continuity, the feeling that the same things ought to persist in as unchanged a pattern as possible. It's the kind of thing that makes our continuous institutions, like the law courts and the churches, so sacrosanct: the feeling that the continuity of the institution represents something superior to the individual, who drifts in and drifts out of life. And that is perhaps the normal functioning level of most societies, where the supreme law is the law of tradition and custom, of doing things the way they have been done. In some teachings, like those of Confucius in China, these precepts of wisdom are carried to very great lengths. There's a very popular story in the Near East which is called *The Story of Ahikar*. The "h" is some kind of Near Eastern gargle that I don't know anything about. It isn't quite "Ahikar," but that will do. Ahikar, according to the story, is a counsellor of a king of Nineveh in Assyria, and so, naturally, an elderly man. He's a very wise and trusted counsellor; but he has no son, so he adopts a nephew. The nephew turns out to be a scoundrel who plots against his father and denounces him to the king of Nineveh as a traitor. The king of Nineveh orders his execution, and Ahikar is taken off by the executioner to be murdered.

But the executioner, as happens in so many romances, finds he can't go through with it, and lets him go. Ahikar escapes to Egypt and there becomes a trusted advisor of the Pharaoh of Egypt. Meanwhile, the king of Nineveh finds himself getting into difficulties without his counsellor and says audibly at a council that he wishes he had his Ahikar back again. At that point, the executioner speaks up and says, "Well, it just so happens that I did let him go: he is in Egypt and is now a counsellor there." So the king of Nineveh says, "Offer him anything, but bring him back here."

So Ahikar comes back to Nineveh and is reinstated. He then proceeds to take the most terrible revenge on his nephew and adopted son. He sits him down and keeps reciting one proverb after another to him, an appreciable number of them naturally concerned with the inadvisability of ingratitude. After several hundred of these proverbs, the nephew says, "Well, I think I've got the point now: couldn't you let me off the rest of them?" But Ahikar keeps on placidly reciting proverbs, until, so the text demurely informs us, the nephew blows up and bursts.[48]

Well, with a story like that, of course, you can't miss. You have the authority of the elders; you have the dangers of trusting anybody under thirty; you have the hundreds and hundreds of proverbs to improve the mind of the reader who consults the story. And so we're not surprised to find that the story of Ahikar has embedded itself in all the literatures of the Near East. It is quoted in the Old Testament, and the Book of Tobit in the Apocrypha concerns a man who is said to be the nephew of Ahikar [1:21], thereby establishing a link with another popular tale. It is said to be echoed in the New Testament, though some scholars disagree with that. Ahikar found his way into Greek literature under the name of Aesop; and there's even a sura in the Koran which bears his name, or at least another version of his name, although the Koran for the most part is even less interested in secular literature than the New Testament, which is saying a good deal.

So there you have, perhaps, the typical social attitude which goes with the more primitive forms of wisdom: the prudent trusting to experience, the taking of short views, and getting around the next corner. Even some of the aphorisms in the Sermon on the Mount seem to spring out of the same cultural root. When Jesus says, "Take no thought for the morrow" [Matthew 6:34], he means a great many other things, but one of the things he means is: take short views, and do the immediate practical thing which you know will keep your balance for the time being. It's a pragmatic counsel, and later becomes the basis of the more contemplative and disinterested attitude that we think of as typical of the wise man.

The proverbs, you notice, are an extremely popular and widely read form. There seems to be something about the proverb that stirs the collector's instinct; and there are many books, including two or three books of the Bible, which are essentially collections of proverbs. The Book of Ecclesiasticus in the Apocrypha is said to be a collection of proverbs made by the editor's grandfather, which he has inherited and has added to.

This collecting of proverbs also occurs in non-Biblical literature. In the *Anatomy of Melancholy*, for example, Burton says that among the cures for melancholy, which he is treating as a disease, there are certain consolatory proverbs, or what he calls remedies against discontent. It's true, he says, that nobody was ever helped in the least by any of these proverbs, but nevertheless, I've made my collection, so you're going to get it. And for the next sixty pages we have Burton's remedies against discontent in the form of his collection of proverbs [pt. 2, sec. 3].

The proverb is popular partly because it is believed to be a valid maxim of conduct. At this point you can see the distinction establishing itself between wisdom and knowledge. Knowledge is of the actual: wisdom is rather a sense of the potential, a sense, rather, of the *kind* of thing that one should know. The wise man is not necessarily the man who knows the answer, but the kind of person who knows potential situations, who knows the way to deal with the kind of thing that may happen.

Biblia Pauperum 30: WOMEN AT THE SEPULCHRE
(Mark 16:1–8)

Reuben looks for Joseph
(Genesis 37:29)

The Bride seeks her beloved
(Song of Solomon 5:2–8)

17

Wisdom: Playing before God;
Ecclesiastes: Vanity of Vanities

I was speaking of the development of the conception of wisdom in the Bible, and of its being in its more elementary forms the individualizing of the law that appears in Psalm 119 and various other Psalms, speaking of the love of the law and of its permeation of the individual life. That leads to a sense of wisdom as founded on a sense of social continuity, and in particular of its being embodied in institutions. The continuity and the dignity of the institution is greater than that of the individual; and a great deal of our sense of wisdom is still bound up with a sense of continuity as embodied in institutions of the nation, university, church, and law courts.

Wisdom as continuity of institutions goes back to the fact of a social contract, to the fact that we belong to something at least nine months before we are anything. Consequently ninety-five per cent of what our lives are going to be is already predestined in the instant of conception: we were all predestined to be middle class twentieth-century Canadians before we were born. That sense of continuity is also embodied in many conceptions of education. I was speaking of the curiously penal quality of education down to our own century, which is not founded really on sadism so much as on the sense that the existing tradition or custom is that to which the individual has to be assimilated, and if the individual does not succeed in accommodating himself to it, then so much the worse for him.

On that basis, wisdom is distinguished from knowledge, knowledge being knowledge of particulars, and most of those particulars being derived from nature, from the objective world, from human society, or from whatever else is objective to the person being educated. Wisdom is rather a sense of the potential, a sense of the ability to deal with the kind of situation that may emerge, and from this emerges a more subtle

conception of wisdom. The primitive basis of wisdom is the acceptance
of the permanent continuities of society. But society isn't permanent,
and it isn't continuous: things happen. So the question arises, What is
the quality of mind that deals with changes in society or with unfore-
seen circumstances?

If you look at the conception of wisdom as dominated by an anxiety
to preserve the continuity of doing things as they have been done, you
can see that in many societies, such as Confucian China, that can be a
very powerful basis of ethics. And yet, if you look at the history of
Israel, with that manic-depressive chart of ups and downs that I drew
for you at the very beginning of this course, you will see that that is a
different kind of sequence altogether. A person who is going to live in
that society needs something a bit more than a sense of the preservation
of tradition and custom: because one moment you may be in a relatively independent and prosperous country; the next moment, you may
be in a country which is occupied by an enemy, where your social
circumstances and status may be totally different.

And so you will find yourself living in a very insecure world, and
will find that you have to rise above this fixation on continuity with the
past and realize that what is continuous from the past is a more flexible
thing. That is the difference, precisely the difference, between religion
and superstition. Superstition is persisting in a thing out of habit without investigating whether it is worth persisting in or not. There is
continuity in wisdom, and there is consistency in behaviour as one of
the sources of genuine human dignity; but of course there is always
inorganic consistency, a persisting in things out of what is really an
automatic habit.

If you look at the Book of Proverbs, in the seventh and eighth chapters particularly, you find the conceptions of wisdom and folly symbolized by two women, wisdom represented by a wise woman and folly
by a harlot. Wisdom speaks in the beginning of chapter 8 of Proverbs:
"Doth not wisdom cry? and understanding put forth her voice? She
standeth in the top of high places, by the way in the places of the paths.
She crieth at the gates, at the entry of the city, at the coming in at the
doors. Unto you, O men, I call; and my voice is to the sons of man" [vv.
1–4]. Verse 12: "I wisdom dwell with prudence, and find out knowledge of witty inventions." Here, wisdom is being spoken of as the
power out of which knowledge emerges, as an attitude of mind that
drives one to seek knowledge, even though one realizes that the knowledge itself is not at all what one is after.

Verse[s] 14[–15]: "Counsel is mine, and sound wisdom: I am understanding; I have strength. By me kings reign, and princes decree justice." Thus, wisdom is associated also with the permanence of authority, when the authority is embodied in justice. And as she goes on, it becomes clear that wisdom is essentially a preservation of the community; and that the distinguishing characteristic of folly is its tendency to turn its back on the community, to be self-seeking, to regard the ego as the basis of all one's interest.

If you look at chapter 9[:1–5]: "Wisdom hath builded her house, she hath hewn out her seven pillars: She hath killed her beasts; she hath mingled her wine; she hath also furnished her table: She hath sent forth her maidens: She crieth upon the highest places of the city, Whoso is simple, let him turn in hither: as for him that wanteth understanding, she saith to him, Come, eat of my bread, and drink of the wine which I have mingled." Thus, wisdom calls to people to partake of a communal meal of bread and wine, symbolizing again the actualizing of a community; because in the long run the basis of the wise individual is the wise community. It is that aspect of wisdom, of which the social and the individual cannot be separated, that genuine wisdom is addressing. Then in verse 13, there is the contrasting figure, the foolish woman who represents folly. Her sales pitch begins with the same formula as that of the wise woman. Verse[s] 16[–17]: "Whoso is simple, let him turn in hither: and as for him that wanteth understanding, she saith to him, Stolen waters are sweet, and bread eaten in secret is pleasant." That is the sense of egocentric knowledge, of the possession that nobody else is to have, the secret knowledge which is being associated in the Bible with folly.

In the latter part of chapter 8 in Proverbs, wisdom, still being personified as a woman, goes back to the beginning of Creation, when she was presumably a child, and says in verse[s] 22[–4]: "The Lord possessed me in the beginning of his way, before his works of old. I was set up from everlasting, from the beginning, or ever the earth was. When there were no depths, I was brought forth; when there were no fountains abounding with water." Then she goes on to describe the process of Creation, and herself as a part of the process of Creation; because in the Biblical theory, wisdom is an essential part of the creative act. In it, wisdom is again spoken of as female, as a daughter of God, present with him at the time of the Creation.

In verse 31, she says, "Rejoicing in the habitable part of the earth; and my delights were with the sons of men." That's the King James, but the King James Version is an extremely weak form of the tremendous

Vulgate phrase that has haunted the imagination of Western Europe for centuries, which doesn't say "rejoicing," but comes much closer to what the Hebrew means, and says "playing"; and speaks of wisdom as *ludens in orbe terrarum*, playing throughout the earth. That notion of wisdom as playing before God at the time of the Creation I think throws an entirely new light on the more subtle forms of wisdom that are taught in the Bible.[49]

If you distinguish work and play, I think you may see that work is energy expended for a further aim in view; whereas play is the expression of energy for its own sake, or the manifestation of what the end in view is. A tennis player or a chess player may work very hard to win a match or to improve his game, but what he is doing when he actually comes in contact with chess or tennis is playing. As I have tried to show in dealing with Biblical imagery, the images of the revealed world in the Bible are the images of human work: the city, the garden, the sheepfold, the farm, and so on. But the word "play" as associated with wisdom is the living in a way which is a manifestation of these forms when they are completed. Whenever a thing exists as an end in itself, rather than as a means to a further end, that thing is associable with play rather than with work. That is why even such terrible and horrifying works as *King Lear* and *Macbeth* can still be called "plays": because they manifest the way human life is as it is, and are not presented to you with any further end in view.

The wisdom playing before God at the Creation again suggests a girl child; so that while the Greek goddess of wisdom is a woman in plate armour with a petrifying gorgon's head on her shield, the Biblical conception of wisdom is something much more like a little girl with a skipping rope. And it's arguable, I think, that that is a far more convincing picture of genuine wisdom, of the expression of energy for its own sake. Certainly it is closer to Matthew's vision of the infant Christ as the goal of the journey of the wise men.

While wisdom is unattained, it doesn't follow that the thing which is unattained is essentially unattainable. It is certainly true that the history of Israel recorded in the Old Testament is not a history of continuous wisdom. But it is possible to attain it, if only for brief moments at a time. The Bible insists all the way through that wisdom is not something you get or something you have: it is something that you are; and consequently its basis has to be an existential basis. In the hymn to wisdom in the twenty-eighth chapter of Job, for example, it says in verse 14: "The depth saith, It is not in me: and the sea saith, It is not with me." That is, it is not something you can find, it is not something that is "there." It begins in a "here" consciousness, and genuine wisdom is defined at the end by the fear of the Lord and the departure from evil. As I say, the basis is an existential basis, and that kind of life is nowhere presented as unattainable, difficult as it is to attain it.

The primitive conception of wisdom is the permeation of the individual life by the communal tradition and prudence. But there are different degrees of absorption of that: and complete absorption comes at the point of complete spontaneity. That is why I said that the figure of wisdom in the Bible suggests the little girl with the skipping rope, and why Jesus places a child in the middle of his disciples, not as a symbol of uncritical intelligence, but as a symbol of genuine wisdom, where the absorption has gone to the point of complete spontaneity. There are many Eastern religions, like Taoism in China and some aspects of Zen Buddhism, that also stress the recovery of the child's spontaneity, that complete integrity of the rhythm of thinking and of doing, as the goal of what they are teaching. In practically all of our ordinary life, action comes first, and thinking about the action comes a second or two later, as in T.S. Eliot's *The Hollow Men*, where the shadow falls between the idea and the response [pt. 5, ll. 5–23]. That split second of time between acting and thinking about acting is part of what is meant, in Christianity at least, by the fall. It's the shadow thrown over life that is bound up with the passing of time, and that makes it so difficult for us to live the purely spontaneous life exhorted by the Sermon on the Mount, where the comparison is drawn with lilies of the field [Matthew 6:28].

I think that in Paul's argument, one works for a further end in view, but that is not the central thing that he's talking about, because that becomes a kind of donkey's carrot. You chase a retreating goal, and eventually find that the means don't lead to the end because the means replace the end, and eventually you lose sight of the end. Certainly some of the things that the New Testament means by faith correspond to what the Book of Proverbs means by wisdom: it's the same integrity of action and reflection on the action, the process no longer schizophrenic but the activity of a conscious being. That is why the Book of Proverbs says, "I wisdom dwell with prudence, and find out knowledge of witty inventions" [8:12]. I think the sound of that in English is right: I don't know how close it is to the Hebrew. But the sense of creativity is, I think, included in the whole conception of wisdom.

If we turn to the Book of Ecclesiastes, we get a little closer to a fuller treatment of the conception of wisdom. The word *Ekklesiastes* is an attempt to render in Greek the Hebrew word which means preacher, *koheleth*, and the Preacher, who identifies himself with the legendary Solomon, actually lived many centuries later than the actual King Solomon. He is also, like so many wise men, a collector of proverbs; but he has a kind of touchstone, a phrase which is translated in the King James Bible as "Vanity of vanities; all is vanity," which he applies to all the proverbs that he collects and quotes, and which means: practically all of this is baloney anyway, and you don't need to take it too seriously.

The phrase "vanity of vanities" is from the Hebrew way of forming the superlative, as in the holy of holies, or Song of Songs. The word "vanity" has a metaphorical kernel which means "fog" or "mist"; from there it developed a derived sense of "emptiness," and it's from the sense of "emptiness" that the Vulgate gets the word *vanitas*, which is the source of the King James "vanity." So that to put the essential position of Ecclesiastes into the form of its central paradox, one would say that all things are full of emptiness.

I think that there is no book in the Bible worse served by its translators than the Book of Ecclesiastes, and the King James Bible is I think particularly misleading. A translation of anything is likely to be, and certain to be if it's a translation of the Bible, much more homogeneous than the original. The King James Bible is extremely good when it comes to the solemn and rather sombre eloquence that you get in so many of the prophets and the legal parts of the Pentateuch. But the closer the Bible comes to expressing a distinctively human tone, the further the King James goes astray, not so much in its rendering of the sense as in its rhythm and its sound. When you get to Paul, for example, with his very lively conversational style and his abundance of commercial and business metaphors, you often find that modern translations are really closer to the mood of Paul than the King James, simply because they are modern—simply because the kind of English we speak now is closer to the kind of Greek that Paul spoke.

Ecclesiastes is a very late writer, and so his style is on the whole much less oracular than the earlier parts of the Old Testament. For example, if you look at chapter 2, verse 3, the King James Bible says, "I sought in mine heart to give myself unto wine, yet acquainting mine heart with wisdom." Now what that means is that the Preacher went through a stage in which he tried to be a sensible Epicurean. That is, he tried to get pleasure without hangover, so he experimented in drinking without getting drunk. But when that is presented in language that sounds like something out of an *oraison funèbre* by Bossuet,[50] the reader is badly misled, not so much about the sense of what he's saying as about the tone.

And so, when you read in the commentaries that the author of Ecclesiastes is really an old, pessimistic man who is tired of life, (a) throw the book in the basket, and (b) read the Book of Ecclesiastes again, because you are being totally misled about the actual emotional attitude of a shrewd and humorous and tough-minded writer. Being tired of life is the very last thing he is, and in fact being tired of life is the one disease for which he has no remedy to suggest. You should get rather the impression of somebody determined to tear off all the veils of illusion and superstition that keep repressing our mental processes. We often speak of being disillusioned as something that leaves us feeling dismal. But of course we shouldn't feel dismal if we get disillusioned: we ought to feel as though we've been let out of jail. Illusions are a prison.

There was a time when we went to school to learn the three R's. But we now go to learn the three A's: anxiety, absurdity, and alienation. That is the primer of twentieth-century man: if a person knows the meaning of those three words, he knows all the wisdom that the twentieth century can teach him, which, God knows, is little enough. Anyway, the author of Ecclesiastes is aware of all these three A's, and he tells you how to get through them. Most of it, of course, consists simply of ignoring them; but there are other things to do as well.

I think I've said before, in commenting on the imagery of the Bible, that in the Bible as in other works, you find the world divided between visible and invisible reality. There are many thinkers for whom the invisible world forms an order of reality superior to that of the visible world. In commenting on Creation, I've suggested that while the Bible recognizes an invisible world, it doesn't think of it as a superior order of reality. It thinks of the invisible world rather as the means by which the world becomes visible. That is, if you start to think of things that you can't see but know to exist, the first thing you might think of is the air. You can't see the air because if you did, you could see nothing else. If you could see the air, you would be living in a dense fog or mist, which is one of the metaphorical meanings of this word "vanity." You can't see the air because its being invisible enables you to see what is not air. In the account of Creation at the beginning of Genesis, the first things created are light and the firmament, that is, the basis of vision and sound. Because there is a sense in which you don't see light either: you see a source or reflection of light.

Thus, when the author of Ecclesiastes speaks of vanity, he has in mind a conception rather like what some Oriental religions are talking about when they speak of the void—*shunyata* I think is the Buddhist term. That is, everything is there, but everything is in nothingness. The objective world is neither there nor not there. It is rather a forest that man has got lost in, and his schedule of behaviour is connected with finding a way out of it. If he is oppressed by the objectivity, by the thereness of the forest, he will find himself tramping around in a circle, which is the inevitable symbol of lost direction. If on the other hand he assumes that the forest is not there, he will very soon find himself bumping into trees. So to find the way out, you have to steer a middle course. There is something in the forest which is there, and something which is not there. When you find a wedge between those two things, you've started to find your way out.

That, I think, is what the author of Ecclesiastes means primarily by vanity. It means that he is abandoning all the things that I've called donkeys' carrots: for one thing, the value judgment that wisdom is better than folly. He says that he decided that wisdom was better than folly; then he found that *that* was vanity, because the wise man and the fool both die, so there's no advantage in wisdom. "Then said I to myself, this also is vanity" [cf. 2:15]. That is, once you stop with the notion that there is no difference between wisdom and folly, you're in as bad a muddle as you are when you assume that there *is* a difference. If I can give an example of what is meant here, we may say of the village saint and the village sinner in a small community that the saint is the better man than the sinner, and that all our moral standards would collapse into chaos unless we assumed that the saint was the better man than the sinner; and that if they were both threatened with peril or disaster, the saint would be the more important man to save. That's all right, except that the saint himself would be very unlikely to take such a view, and would certainly in a crisis be more likely to try to save the sinner than to save himself. Consequently, the axiom of his behaviour is not at all that sanctity is better than sinning: he has got to a position where "this" and "this not" are equally meaningless. That is the basis of the ethic of the Book of Ecclesiastes, which is very close to that of the Sermon on the Mount.

Then went Satan forth from the presence of the Lord
(William Blake, *Illustrations of the Book of Job*, pl. 5)

18

Job: A Test

I would like to approach the Book of Job at this point in the course as a work that pertains to the categories of both wisdom and prophecy. If you look at the sequence of books of the Old Testament in the King James order, that is from Genesis to Malachi, with the Apocrypha in a separate section, you see an order which is derived from the Septuagint translation—the Hebrew order is a much more schematic one—and it seems to be pure accident that it actually makes its own kind of sense.

The books from Genesis to Esther are concerned with three themes: law, history, and ritual; the closing one, Esther, is a story which explains the latest of the Hebrew rituals to be established, the feast of Purim. The second half of the Old Testament, from Job to Malachi, is concerned also with three different themes: with poetry, prophecy, and wisdom. In that order, which as I say may be pure accident but still is an order, Job would occupy the place of a poetic and prophetic Genesis. It deals with the theme of how man was plunged into his present alienating situation, but deals with it in terms of poetry and prophecy and wisdom rather than of law and history and ritual.

When Milton, after pursuing the English Revolution of the seventeenth century through four of its stages, was finally checkmated completely by the restoration of the monarchy, he settled down to ask himself why the bid for liberty among the English people had met with so inglorious a failure, and why the great Exodus which had been undertaken in 1640 should have ended, in his phrase, with "a captain back for Egypt."[51] That was why he told the story of the fall of man, which is based on the Christian conception of original sin, the notion that man, being born in a state of mortality, is conditioned from birth with a kind of inertia that makes it impossible for him to achieve any of the things that he really wants to do without divine assistance. Man says he wants freedom and—still paraphrasing Milton—thinks he wants freedom, but as a matter of fact, he does not want freedom: and if he gets it, it is only because freedom is something that God is determined he shall have.[52]

Well, the story of the fall of Adam is a story of a breach of contract, which has always made it dear to the heart of theological lawyers, because it provides them with what passes for an explanation of the human situation. Why do we live in a world where we all die, and where we suffer various inconveniences ranging from earthquakes to mosquito bites? The answer in the Book of Genesis is: well, it was like this: many years ago, a hungry girl long past her lunch time reached for an apple on the wrong tree, and as a result, all this has taken place. The answer is insane, it's psychotic, but then, so is most theology; and at any rate, it is a kind of answer. The advantage of studying the Book of Job is that it deals with the same question: how has man come to be in this alienating situation? But there is no contract; there is no alleged explanation. There is no quasi- or pseudo-historical element in it. It is given simply in purely imaginative terms.

When I was dealing with wisdom, I said that wisdom is conceived in the Bible existentially as more of an attitude of mind than as anything connected with knowledge, because knowledge is specific: it is knowledge of this or that; whereas wisdom deals more with the potential. We think, for example, of Jesus as a wise man, but not necessarily as a knowledgeable man: that is not the point about him. Wisdom, we said, was the conception of law in individualized form, the way in which law permeates society.

Prophecy, we found, was an individualizing of the revolutionary spirit which seems to be peculiar to the Biblical tradition. The prophet is typically a figure who is isolated because of the unpopularity of the message he brings, and who is very frequently persecuted. He is a figure whose authority no society knows how to deal with, because society by itself has no standards for distinguishing an authority above the law from an authority below it. That is, the prophet who denounces society cannot be distinguished from the troublemaker or the subversive, and not only in the Hebrew tradition, but in Greek culture as well. As the figure of Socrates reminds us, most societies have difficulty distinguishing the authority of prophecy.

Consequently, the assumption arose very early in both Judaism and Christianity that the age of the prophets was over; and this assumption

was accepted with a great deal of relief. In medieval Europe, for ex
ample, there was a High King and a High Priest, a Pope and an Emperor. But there was no place for prophetic authority as such; and the
fates of such people as Joan of Arc and Savonarola indicate the same
difficulty that society has always had. The liberty of prophesying was
one of the things that the Protestant Reformation was supposed to be
all about, but Protestantism can hardly be said to have succeeded in
establishing a prophetic authority. That is, its prophets never strayed
very far away from pulpits: they were not really a distinct class from the
priesthood. Nevertheless, that position of the prophet as an isolated or
alien figure who has an authority very difficult for his own society to
accommodate enters into the structure of the whole Bible.

The moral significance of the life of Jesus has been traditionally
assumed to be his perfect conformity to a moral code, as the one man
who did not sin. But perhaps equally important is his significance as a
figure that no organized or established society could possibly have
tolerated. That is, the Christian teaching about who crucified Christ is
not that the Romans or the Jews or whatever people happened to be
there did, but that you and I did, and that all human societies without
exception are involved in the Crucifixion of Christ. That sense of the
figure who was negatively as well as positively outside history is something that has to be taken into account in trying to see what the importance of prophecy is. Society, in order to preserve itself, has to assume
the priority of its interests to those of any individual; and what the high
priest Caiaphas says in the Gospel of John, "it was expedient that one
man die for the people" [cf. 18:14], is a statement that has been echoed
by every human being without exception at some point or other. I want
to approach Job primarily as an example of a book of wisdom which
cannot be satisfactorily understood without some reference to this conception of prophecy as well.

The Book of Job is relatively late among Old Testament books, I
suppose around 300 B.C. It seems to be dramatic in construction: there
are even things in it that remind us of certain things in the great
tragedies, such as having the catastrophe announced by a messenger,
though it is extremely unlikely that the author of Job was thinking of
any kind of theatrical presentation. In fact, it is unlikely that he had
seen a theatre or knew what a theatre was. It is more likely that the
particular idiom in which Job is cast is, insofar as it is dramatic, something of an accident, because the dramatic form to which it is closest is
not so much that of acted plays, whether tragedies or comedies, but to

the Platonic dramatic form of the symposium, the discussion in which certain themes are pursued from different points of view.

The story is an ancient folk tale; and this ancient folk tale, which is in prose, appears at the beginning and at the end of the Book of Job that we have. But the author of Job simply cut the tale in two with a pair of scissors—that is, if scissors had been invented by that time: I'm a very sloppy scholar in some respects—and between the first and the second half put this enormous expansion of the theme which is the book that we know.

According to the story, then, we begin with Satan in the court of God, and that, at once, is unique. It's not just that it's a tremendous act of poetic originality that has haunted the imagination of every great poet ever since, down to Goethe's *Faust* and beyond. It is also because it illustrates something I've mentioned before, that in the account of Creation at the beginning of Genesis God is said to have separated the light from the darkness and the firmament from the chaos, the deep. So you can think of darkness and chaos as outside the Creation, and therefore as enemies of God. But the Creation actually incorporated darkness as an alternate to light, and it incorporated chaos in the form of the sea, as distinct from the land. Consequently, we can also think of chaos and darkness as incorporated dialectically within Creation, and as creatures of God rather than enemies. In most of the prophets, the forces of chaos and darkness are thought of as God's enemies, as certainly Satan is. But in the Book of Job, and there alone, both Satan and the powers of darkness are treated primarily as creatures of God, as things which he tolerates within his Creation.

We've already seen that a legal metaphor runs all through the Bible, and that it is appropriate therefore that we should speak of the end of all things as a Last Judgment, as a trial in which God is thought of as the judge, in which there is a defendant and a prosecutor. The role of the prosecutor is the traditional role of Satan. The word means "adversary," and his primary function is that of the accuser of mankind. The Greek word *diabolos*, which is the origin of our word "devil," originally meant or included the meaning of the person opposed in a lawsuit.

So all through the Book of Job, this metaphor of a trial and a judge is hovering in the background. If you were killed in a feud, the person whose duty it was to avenge your death would be called your *go'el* or avenger, and the same word could be applied to someone who would go bail for you if you were accused, or who in general would take the part of the accused person. In the Book of Job, Job expresses his own confidence that he has such a defender. In Job 19:25, he says, "I know that my *go'el* liveth." The King James translation is "redeemer," which is perhaps an overly Christianized translation: but the general sense is that he is sure that there is somebody on his side in this lawsuit. Then the question is, who is his accuser, and much more important than that, what is he being accused of? Because if there is anything particularly nightmarish about a tyranny or a rule of terror, it is the possibility of being arrested and held without being told what the charge is. That is a situation that one finds in Kafka's novel *The Trial*, and almost all of Kafka's writings form an extended commentary on the Book of Job.

And so Job says, Why hasn't my adversary written a book? Why hasn't he stated the case against me? [cf. 31:35]. That is of course the question to which the poem mainly addresses itself. First of all comes a disaster which wipes out his family, his goods, and his possessions—all but his wife, and his wife turns against him as well. Then comes another disaster, which takes the form of boils. We are told in the opening scene that Satan is taking his usual part of prosecutor, and is telling God that according to the code of the Book of Deuteronomy and elsewhere, he has really set things up in such a way that he can't lose. If it is in man's interest to obey the law and to follow the precepts of God, then man is an incredible fool if he does not do so. And if it is true that the good man is always rewarded, and that it is only the bad man who is punished, then God has really created a race of automata who are not free beings at all. God says, Well, maybe that's true: but there is one man called Job, and I think that he would stick to me no matter what happened [cf. 1:18]. And Satan says, All right, let's try. And so the disasters fall.

At that point, Job's three friends come to see him. The three friends have become proverbial as stupid and unimaginative people. We get this impression partly from Job himself, who says, "Miserable comforters are ye all" [16:2]; and so we tend to think of them simply as replicas of Satan in the lower world, and as carrying on the whole process of accusation. On the other hand, whatever one thinks of them, they are certainly not fair-weather friends. They have nothing to gain from coming to see Job in his utter destitution. In chapter 2, the last verse ends, "So they sat down with him upon the ground seven days and seven nights"—that's the ritual period of mourning—"and none spake a word unto him: for they saw that his grief was very great" [v. 13]. And so, if we are tempted to think of the three friends as stupid and unimaginative, we should not forget either those seven days of silent sympathy.

At the same time, the three men, while they are devout, pious, and

eloquent men—they are all fine poets—still are very heavily conditioned by their own understanding of the law and the way it operates:
that if you obey the Deuteronomic code, you will be happy and prosperous, and if you don't, you'll be miserable. Job is quite clearly unhappy and miserable: so he must have done something to break the
law. They begin to suggest this more and more deviously as time goes
on: there is even a suggestion that Job might have done something
unconsciously, as Oedipus did in Greek drama. But it is also said that
Job has taken care of unintentional offences by the sacrifices that he has
made before he fell into this state of things. And in any case, Job
eventually begins to understand what they are saying; and he feels
outraged, not because of the imputations of divine justice, but because
what he is really saying is that what has happened to him does not bear
any kind of sane relationship to anything he could conceivably have
done. If it is a question of punishment for wrongdoing, the situation is
utterly insane, and raises more questions than it could possibly solve.

The three friends and Job remain devout and pious men. Consequently, the one explanation that never once occurs to them, and never
possibly could occur to them, is the one that has already been given to
the reader: namely, that Job is not being punished at all, but that he is
being tested for something. And the reason it couldn't have occurred to
them is that the bet with Satan suggests that God has a stake of his own
in the matter. That just doesn't come into their conception of the universe anywhere. But we have in fact been told that God is actually
risking something, and risking it on Job's fidelity. In the kind of view of
God that both Job and the friends have, he could never be as vulnerable
as that in his relationships with human beings.

The discussion reaches a deadlock, and we're told that these three
men cease to answer Job because he was righteous in his own eyes
[32:1]. That is an extremely unfair comment to make about Job, and is
perhaps expressed only from their point of view. Then Elihu comes in.
Elihu is a later writer's addition: he came two or three centuries later
probably. He says he is a young man, and consequently is following the
custom which says that the old fools have to speak until their senility is
fully exposed, and then he will get into the discussion himself. However, though he is a fine and eloquent poet, he doesn't really add much
to the argument: he really just sums it up again. Job lets this go by
without any comment at all, partly because it is a later addition. Then
God himself enters the discussion, and speaks to Job out of the whirlwind.

Now at first we are deeply disappointed in what God says. He is a pretty fair poet too: he's not as good as Elihu, but he begins by saying, "Who is this that darkeneth counsel by words without knowledge?" [38:2]. If he means Elihu, he's a bit ungrateful, because he's cribbed a great deal of his speech from Elihu. But in any case, his speech seems to consist of a number of rhetorical questions, all of which, as they say in Latin grammars, expect the answer "no." The questions are all to the same effect: Were you around when I made the world? Do you know how it was made? No? Then why are you questioning the justice of my ways? And Job says, "Yes, Lord, I know nothing, and you know everything." Whereupon God says, "Well, that's better," and proceeds to restore to him everything that he had before.

Now, if that is what the Book of Job actually means, then we can only conclude that some bungling and terrified poet took over the conclusion and spoiled what was originally one of the great visionary dramas in the world's history. That is the view of it that Bernard Shaw takes when he speaks of the ignoble and irrelevant retort of God at the end of the book.[53] Bernard Shaw also has a story called *The Black Girl in Her Search for God*, where a young African woman armed with a big stick goes out to find God. The first god she meets is the God of Noah's flood, who makes thunderous noises at her, so she whacks him over the head with her knobkerrie and he disappears. Then she meets a god who says, Now I do love to have my creatures argue with me, so I can tell them how much wiser I am than they are. Do you have any questions? She doesn't ask any questions, she just whacks him over the head and *he* disappears. Well, this is a conceivable view of the Book of Job. I don't think it is the right one: but if the King James Bible is right when it puts in its marginal headings at the top of the page that "God convinceth Job of ignorance," then it seems to be almost the only moral that we can take from the story. So maybe we should retrace our steps a bit.

In this speech of God, there is the series of rhetorical questions that I mentioned, followed by two lyrical poems at the end: at least I am going to assume that there are two. They are about two fabulous monsters that we have met already in the imagery of the Bible, a land monster named Behemoth and a sea monster named Leviathan. The New English Bible notes that *behemoth* is simply the intensive plural of the word for "beast" in Hebrew, and consequently, it reduces them to one, to Leviathan only, but I am going to ignore that. Traditionally, there have always been two, a land monster and a sea monster: you'll find them referred to even as early as 2 Esdras in the Apocrypha [6:49].

God says in 40:15, where the two great hymns start, "Behold now behemoth, which I made with thee," and then goes on to talk about Leviathan in chapter 41. The two animals seem to have developed out of the kernels of the hippopotamus and the crocodile. That is, they are both Egyptian animals, and it is perhaps significant that Job, although he observes the Israelite law, comes from Uz in the kingdom of Edom, and so is strictly speaking outside the jurisdiction of the Biblical countries.

But we remember that the account of the Creation at the beginning of Genesis, where God creates light from darkness and the firmament from chaos, is a later development of what was originally a dragon-killing myth, and that the dragon-killing myth has been referred to many times in the Old Testament, though always as a poetic myth rather than as a matter of belief. And we see that of these two creatures, Satan and Leviathan, one appears at the beginning of the poem, the other at the end of it; and that everywhere else in the Bible, Satan is the enemy of God, and Leviathan the dragon who is to be hooked and landed in the last day. But here, Satan is a tolerated guest in the court of God. And I imagine that Goethe sums up the feeling of Job rather accurately in his Prologue in *Faust*, where Mephistopheles walks out of heaven saying to himself, I like to talk to the old boy now and again; it is really very decent of him to talk to me [ll. 350–3]. Similarly, Behemoth and Leviathan are not spoken of here as enemies of God, or as outside his order. God is pointing to them with something of the nervous admiration of an artist, saying, Look, Job, aren't they splendid, aren't they wonderful? I made them, you know: don't you like them? And if you think of them in that context, you'll see that it is not really a problem in the poem that we hear no more about Satan, and that at the end of the poem, God makes no reference to the original deal that he made with Satan. According to our table of demonic symbols which we drew up last fall, Satan and the leviathan are metaphorically the same thing, but are simply seen from different points of view. And by pointing out these two monsters to Job, God is implying, or at least the author of the poem is implying, that Job is outside them. He *must* be outside them, or he couldn't see them. You remember that we are mythologically all born inside the belly of the leviathan, and that the whole fishing imagery of the Gospels is connected with that fact.

So it's possible that Job is getting a genuine enlightenment and is not being told just to shut up. Further, if the conventional understanding of Job were right, that Job is merely being bullied by God into silence, then his three friends must have been right about God all along; because their point of view throughout has consistently been that God rewards the righteous and punishes the disobedient. And if that doesn't happen, then all we can say is that the ways of God are mysterious and too high for us to understand. As I say, if that is the meaning of the poem as a whole, then the friends' conception of God is vindicated. But God says explicitly that the friends are wrong in what they said about him. What they said is forgivable—they are welcomed into the community at the end—but what they have said is wrong. Another thing which seems clear is that if Job had suffered in silence all the way through the poem, there would have been no revelation either to him or to anybody else at the end. It is only because Job yells bloody murder that there is a Book of Job at all. Job's protests, his loud demands to know why this has happened, are the kind of things which indicate the integrity that God insisted he had from the first.

Let the Day perish wherein I was born
(William Blake, *Illustrations of the Book of Job*, pl. 8)

19

Job and the Question of Tragedy

I was looking at the Book of Job, and suggesting that because the dramatic form is closer to the Platonic symposium than it is to the typical tragedy or comedy, we often tend to assume that the Book of Job is a problem; and of course a problem is something that ought to have a solution. I think there are many wrong things about looking at Job as a problem, even though that is the point of view of Job himself and of the four people who are talking with him.

I suggested that, in the first place, Job is not being punished for anything, but is being tested for something, that God himself appears to have some kind of stake in the matter, as seems indicated by his colloquy with Satan at the beginning; and while it is no doubt true *a priori* that God knew the outcome in advance, we shouldn't let ourselves get too tangled up with ordinary conceptions of time. If God foreknows the end of an action, then it is just like a fixed horserace. There is something about it which is not quite genuine, and even Milton in *Paradise Lost* fell into that difficulty. But certainly the Book of Job does not impress us as a fixed race, as something which has been all worked out in advance.

One of the principles involved has to do with the relation of question and answer. When you answer a question, you accept the assumptions in the question, so that the answer, if it is a satisfactory answer, consolidates the mental level on which the question is asked. If it is the answer, it also annihilates the question. If you ask me where the nearest telephone is, I can accept the assumptions in the question, answer it, if I know where the nearest telephone is, and consequently annihilate or abolish that particular problem which the question symbolizes. But if you ask me, Where is God? I can say only that conceptions of "where" do not apply to God, and that the only way of answering such a question is to refuse to answer it. I cannot answer the question because I cannot accept the assumptions in the question. It's one of those Have you quit beating your wife? questions, in which the matter of accepting the assumption in the question is primary.

Now it is for that reason that no serious religion ever attempts to answer questions. Because seriousness, whether it is in religion or in art or in science, is a matter of proceeding steadily to better and more adequate questions. In religion, the questions that you raise are not answered except in the most perfunctory ways because, if you think about it for a moment, you will see that to answer such a question as, Why do innocent people suffer? or, Why is there evil in a world created by a good God? really cheats you out of the right to ask the question, and certainly blocks your further advance. It prevents you from reformulating a question with rather better assumptions in it, and so proceeding in the way the human mind does proceed in dealing with very large and serious issues, by trying to make the assumptions in the questions it asks more and more adequate.

There is a very touching story about Gertrude Stein that on her death bed, feeling that she was going, she called over her lifelong friend Alice B. Toklas and said, "Alice, what is the answer?" And Alice said, "Well, Gertrude, I'm afraid we don't know that." Gertrude Stein thought this over, and said, "Well, then, what is the question?"[54] That, I think, is something of what is involved in the argument of Job. If you are looking for an answer to a question or for a solution to a problem, then you start this dreary chess game of whether God is or is not doing the right thing, which of course leads to a superego starting to scream that of course he must be and you're a wicked blasphemer for questioning it; and another part of your mind remains quiet and doesn't comment, but is not convinced.

Another aspect of this problem is that if there is an answer, you will never get out of the world of the question. The answer of God at the end of the Book of Job has, as I said last day, been very much criticized as a kind of bullying and hectoring response. But suppose there had been an explanation which took you back to the beginning to the original scene with Satan in heaven. Then you would have had a God who said, Well, you see, Job, it was like this. And a God full of glib explanations for what happened would be more contemptible than even a bullying or hectoring God would be. If there is one thing the Book of Job cannot end with, it's God producing out of a hat a number of satisfactory explanations for the problems which have been worrying you. Job hasn't got problems, he's got tragedy and misery and boils. Intellectual problems or questions with answers do not get very close to where he is.

If a scientist is conducting a dialogue with nature, and nature doesn't say anything, somebody has to fill in the silence. That somebody is obviously the scientist, who is driven by the silence of nature to keep reformulating what he is investigating and observing. Now this is not quite what happens in the Book of Job, because here there is a dialogue. Job is in the world of time, which you can represent by a horizontal line. When we live in the world of time, we're being dragged along this line backwards, with our faces to the past and our backs to the future. And so, naturally, any question like, How did this happen to me? or, Why did it happen to me? is instinctively, according to all our normal mental processes, thrown backwards into the past. We're really asking questions about the origin or the cause of what happened. Well, the origin or cause of what happened to Job can only have been the origin or cause of everything that has ever happened—in other words, of the Creation itself. And everything follows from that original act of Creation.

What God appears to be saying to Job is, You weren't around when I made the world; therefore you don't know what's in my mind. Therefore you shouldn't be questioning the judgment of my ways. What I think he may actually be saying is something like this: You were not around at the time of the Creation. You were trying to find your way back there, to understand what has happened to you. Don't try it. There's no answer there. I'm not there, or at least no part of me is there that you can get hold of. And bound up with that, first of all, is the fact that how Job got into this mess is far less important than the question of how he is to get out of it. And secondly, that all you can see of a divine purpose when you're looking along the horizontal line, back to the beginning of time, is that of fatality or causation; and those are pretty chilly attributes of a God who is represented as taking an active interest and concern in Job's situation.

That is why the speech of God ends with the two poems on Behemoth and Leviathan, which look irrelevant to the problems of Job's boils and miseries and dead daughters but are actually less irrelevant than they may seem. We saw in our analysis of the imagery and narrative of the Bible that Leviathan, used as a poetic image in the Bible, expands into the entire world of time and space in which we are living, a world in which Satan has a good deal of control. We are all born inside the belly of the leviathan, which is why there is so much about Jesus as a fisherman in the Gospels. And for God to point out these two monsters to Job at the end can only mean that Job is outside them. And because he is outside them, he has been delivered from their power.

Let's look at the final chapter, the forty-second chapter, just at the end of the speech of God. "Then Job answered the Lord, and said, I know that thou canst do everything, and that no thought can be withholden from thee. Who is he that hideth counsel without knowledge? therefore have I uttered that I understood not; things too wonderful for me, which I knew not. Hear, I beseech thee, and I will speak: I will demand of thee, and declare thou unto me. I have heard of thee by the hearing of the ear: but now mine eye seeth thee. ... Wherefore I abhor myself, and repent in dust and ashes" [vv. 1–4, 6].

The tone seems to be one of unquestioning submission—Yes, Lord, you know everything; I know nothing; you've got all the trump cards in your hand, and have had from the beginning, and so on. And yet I think we shouldn't be taken in too much by this Oriental manner of speaking, because Job also manages to say a few other things. He says, "I will demand of thee, and declare thou unto me" [42:4] He still retains the right to speak and even to argue with his Creator.

And then he says, "I have heard of thee by the hearing of the ear: but now mine eye seeth thee" [v. 5], which is a tremendous statement to make, because all through the Bible, the doctrine that God cannot be seen is invariable. The closest we get is Isaiah's saying that he saw God high and lifted up in the temple. There is a very ancient legend that Isaiah was put into a hollow log and sawn in two on the charge of having claimed a direct vision of God. Yet this is what Job is claiming. There is only one reference to the Book of Job that I know of in the New Testament, and that is in the Epistle of James, where James says, "Ye have heard of the patience of Job, and have seen the end of the Lord" [5:11]. And that picks up the same metaphor—"I have heard but I now see." Of course, in James, there is still a Christian sting in the tail: what James's readers have seen is the coming of Christ; and that can hardly be within the historical context of the Book of Job itself.

Let's go on to the end of the folk tale, in chapter 42. "And it was so, that after the Lord had spoken these words unto Job, the Lord said to Eliphaz the Temanite, My wrath is kindled against thee, and against thy two friends: for ye have not spoken of me the thing that is right" [v. 7]. Therefore he commands a sacrifice. And in verse 10, "And the Lord turned the captivity of Job, when he prayed for his friends."

God is traditionally regarded as a trinity of power and love and wisdom. There's a great deal about the power and the wisdom of God in the Book of Job, and it seems curious that there should be so little about love. Various people have adapted the Book of Job, including William Blake in the series of illustrations that he did at the end of his life, and Archibald MacLeish in his play *J.B.*, and it is interesting to notice that Blake and MacLeish make the same alteration in the story of Job: they both make Job's wife faithful to Job throughout, and they both caricature the friends. In Blake, the three friends are simply incarnations of moral virtue, which for Blake means something like a lynching mob. And in *J.B.*, Job's three friends come to see him only because they are spiritual vampires attracted by the smell of misery. In other words, the notion of a Job cut off even from his wife is too tough for reasonably kind and humane people like MacLeish and Blake to take in. Similarly, they can come to terms with the friends only by thinking of them as malignant.

While it is true that for Job not to have even the support of his wife during this trial is tough enough, it is more important that this is the only place where an image of love would naturally emerge. Likewise, he has dismissed his friends as "miserable comforters" [16:2], and yet we are told that the Lord "turned the captivity of Job, when he prayed for his friends" [42:10]. So that perhaps the love which is based on the love of these three blundering and blinkered and yet utterly well-meaning old buffers is perhaps closer to genuine love than any other image that would be available to the poet.

In any case, the redemption of Job is the same thing as the re-establishing of his community. We are apt to forget, perhaps, that this drama is not being carried out in solitude. Job is a patriarch of the whole society in the background. That society disappears from the foreground of the action during most of the book, but it comes back again into existence at the end. "And the Lord turned the captivity of Job, when he prayed for his friends: also the Lord gave Job twice as much as he had before. Then came there unto him all his brethren, and all his sisters, and all they that had been of his acquaintance before, and did eat bread with him in his house: and they bemoaned him, and comforted him over all the evil that the Lord had brought upon him: every man also gave him a piece of money. ... So the Lord blessed the latter end of Job more than his beginning: for he had fourteen thousand sheep, and six thousand camels, and a thousand yoke of oxen, and a thousand she asses. He had also seven sons and three daughters. And he called the name of the first, Jemima; and the second, Kezia; and the name of the third, Keren-happuch. And in all the land were no women found so fair as the daughters of Job: and their father gave them inheritance among their brethren" [42:10–15].

Now, in your experience of drama, you notice that it is characteristic of tragedy that it points to the inevitable. Because it points to the inevitable, it points to the credible as well. Even if you don't believe that Hamlet actually saw the ghost of his father, or that Macbeth saw the ghost of Banquo, you can still understand what state of mind Hamlet and Macbeth were in. Tragedy normally does not conceal anything from the audience. That is, we know who murdered Hamlet's father and Banquo, and we know what Iago's honesty amounts to, though the characters on the stage do not. That is why tragedy is always associated with irony, a perspective in which the audience sees more of what is happening than the actors in the play do. And so, when the tragic ending comes, it impresses us as inevitable, and we say to ourselves, yes, that is the kind of thing that can and does happen. That is how we reconcile ourselves to a tragic ending, through the fact that this portrays things as they can and sometimes do happen.

In a comedy, what we often get is some card up the writer's sleeve, some gimmick that he's thought up whereby the action is suddenly twisted from approaching complications and trouble into a happy ending. What happens in the ordinary New Comedy that was the tradition behind Shakespeare is that boy wants girl; girl is a slave or, that is, she's a prostitute; boy's father says, Nothing doing. It then turns out that the girl was kidnapped or stolen by pirates in infancy and is really the daughter of somebody respectable, so that the hero can marry her without loss of face; and boy gets girl.

Well, in this comic action, there is a gimmick produced to which a normal reaction is to say that this kind of thing doesn't happen in ordinary life. But it happens in plays, and is rather nice when it does happen. Accepting it, therefore, is based on your own preference for a happy ending, but not on your sense of probability in the scheme of things. Fate specializes in practical jokes in bad taste: fate very seldom pulls out a card from the pack to help you.

So, reading the Book of Job, we are reading a drama which has always been classified with the world's tragedies, and yet it is technically a comedy by virtue of the fact that everything is restored to Job at the end. We can understand Job's miseries and trials: there is nothing about that which violates our sense of the probability of what happens in life. But can we actually accept his quite sudden restoration to prosperity? That is what is incredible.

Now, in the first place, there is a rule in comedy expressed in the title of one of Shakespeare's plays, *All's Well That Ends Well*. That's the only title in Shakespeare with a predicate, and it is a statement that is true of the structure of comedy. But it is utter nonsense as a statement about human life. The reason it is true of comedy is that when a comedy ends well, that is traditionally the beginning of the real lives of the young people who get married at the end. But in real life, it is silly to say that all's well that ends well. Even in a society as patriarchal as Job's, a man who had lost three beautiful daughters would not be completely consoled by three brand new daughters, no matter how beautiful or how impressively named: it's not a matter of consoling a child for a broken toy by giving him a new toy. The loss of the daughters would be a permanent scar on his existence.

So there are several possibilities here. One is the possibility that if we had seen Job in the middle of his restoration to prosperity, we might not have seen fourteen thousand sheep and a thousand she asses and three beautiful daughters at all. We might have seen nothing but a beggar on a dunghill. And yet that beggar on that dunghill would have seen something that we have not seen, and would know something that we do not know. Of his three new daughters, one of them, Keren-happuch, has a name that means a box of eye shadow. She might not be there at all. And so, the credibility of the restoration of Job would have to involve different levels of existence.

The most ordinary image for two levels of existence comes from waking up in the morning, where we get rid of a dream world simply by abolishing that world. Something of that might be happening here: perhaps Job has wakened up from a nightmare world of loss and boils to find that it was only a dream. But if it were only a dream, then the end of Job is so discontinuous from the main action of the poem that there is hardly any point in the main action of the poem at all. So that's facile; it will hardly do.

I think that when you go back to the speech of Job, you get an impression that some kind of confidential look, almost a wink, seems to have passed between Job and God at that point, and that Job knows something in that instant from which we are excluded. What is it that Job knows that we don't know? The answer is that by definition we don't know, and that's not helpful. Nevertheless, it is something that the statement that he is seeing God, the restoration of all his goods, the re-establishment of his family and community, are all images for.

I've spoken of the form of tragedy, and tragedy is a form that people seem to have a constant itch to wish to explain. Early critics read in

Aristotle the statement that the tragic hero must have *hamartia*, and nobody quite knows what that means, but it's the ordinary word in the New Testament for sin. Consequently, Aristotle has often been interpreted as proposing an extremely moralistic theory of tragedy, that the tragic hero must have done something wrong, so that what he does is morally intelligible. But if you think of the tragedies that you know, you'll see that that won't work. The particular thing called tragedy that happens to a tragic hero does not depend on his moral status. He may be as good a man as Shakespeare's Julius Caesar or as good a woman as Bernard Shaw's Joan of Arc or Shakespeare's Desdemona. Or he may be as bad a person as Shakespeare's Richard III or Macbeth. But the particular thing called tragedy that happens takes no account of that.

I think what Aristotle means partly by *hamartia* is being in a certain place which is especially dangerous or exposed; and very often the qualities that put you in such a place are the qualities of exceptional heroism. Because, after all, an oak tree is much more likely to be struck by lightning than a clump of grass. Cordelia in Shakespeare's *King Lear*, for example, does nothing wrong to deserve her banishment and her eventual hanging. She is just standing in a particular spot, and the lightning strikes that spot.

Similarly, one of the issues raised by the story of Job is the issue connected with the word "property," which in Aristotle means that which is proper to a man, that which is really an extension of himself. And so one of the questions raised by Job's disasters is, How much can a man lose of what he has before it begins to affect the identity of what he is? That question is answered in a rather brusque way, perhaps, by God's remark to Satan that he has to spare Job's life. He can take everything he has, but he must leave what he is. In that situation, the identity of Job is being isolated. It's being cut off from his possessions, because it is still a question raised by Satan as to whether Job is not really a creature of his possessions, of his prosperity and his riches, rather than a creature of God. After he has passed the test, his goods are restored to him, because that question no longer means anything.

The argument of Job and his friends builds to a climax in the beginning of chapter 26. It looks as though an editor, or perhaps even the original author, has cut down the proportions of the dialogue here, because his scheme was originally to have the three friends all speak in turn. But in this round of speeches, the second man, Bildad, has a very curtailed speech, and the third man doesn't speak at all. But Job answers, and his answer carries on until the end of chapter 31, after which it is said that the "three men ceased to answer Job, because he was righteous in his own eyes" [32:1].

Now, as we have already suggested, it's only from the comforters' point of view that he is righteous in his own eyes. The speech of Job himself is really the climax of the whole book as far as Job is concerned. It is his statement as a bewildered but still articulate victim of disaster, and there are insertions in it that make it longer perhaps than it needed to be, such as the hymn in praise of wisdom in chapter 28, which is probably a later interpolation; but Job's speech, from chapters 26 to 31, seems to me the most tremendously noble and impressive statement that I know of in literature of what can only be called the essential dignity and responsibility of human nature. Job does not claim virtue, he does not claim that he must have been unjustly treated: he has stopped all that kind of noise, and says merely that he wishes he knew what the charge against him is, if there is a charge; and he ends, at the end of chapter 31, in the closing verses that begin at verse 35, "Oh that one would hear me! behold, my desire is, that the Almighty would answer me, and that mine adversary had written a book. Surely I would take it upon my shoulder, and bind it as a crown to me. I would declare unto him the number of my steps; as a prince would I go near unto him. If my land cry against me, or that the furrows likewise thereof complain; if I have eaten the fruits thereof without money, or have caused the owners thereof to lose their life: Let thistles grow instead of wheat, and cockle instead of barley. The words of Job are ended" [vv. 35–40].

It is the voice of a responsible ruler, like Oedipus of Thebes: there is a famine in the country; Oedipus is king; therefore he is responsible. So he must consult an oracle to find out why there is a drought. In the case of Oedipus, of course, the outcome is very different. He is told by a prophet that he has murdered his father and slept with his mother, and that the gods are offended. He says, But I didn't know anything about this, and the prophet says, Well, that's just too bad. But in the Book of Job, you have the same willingness to assume responsibility, the same essential dignity which is possible only to a conscious nature. Job is doing what he can with the gifts of consciousness and intelligence. In ending on that tone, he makes it clear that God has won the wager, that Job's integrity is still there and still untouched. After that, you don't need Satan any more.

What follows is the speech of Elihu, which as I say is a later interpolation. Elihu is a young man, and his following the three old men represents a kind of social cycle of moral condemnation which goes on and on. But Job lets Elihu's speech go by without commenting on the fact that he's extremely cocksure. Elihu says things like, "Suffer me a little, and I will shew thee that I have yet to speak on God's behalf" [36:2], as though God had hired him as a lawyer. Job makes no comment on the arguments of Elihu: he's heard it all before, it's all true, and it's all nonsense. He's waiting for a different kind of voice altogether. And eventually, out of the whirlwind, the voice comes.

Then the Lord answered Job out of the Whirlwind
(William Blake, *Illustrations of the Book of Job*, pl. 13)

I have heard thee with the hearing of the Ear but now my Eye seeth thee
(William Blake, *Illustrations of the Book of Job*, pl. 17)

20

Job and Restored Humanity

I was dealing with the question in the Book of Job about the actual tone of the speech of God at the end, and questioning whether he is really the heavy blustering tyrant that he may seem to be on first reading, and that he has often been called by commentators on the book. There does seem to be a hectoring and bullying quality to some of the things he says, as in 40:7: "Gird up thy loins now like a man: I will demand of thee, and declare thou unto me. Wilt thou also disannul my judgment? wilt thou condemn me, that thou mayest be righteous? Hast thou an arm like God? or canst thou thunder with a voice like him?" [vv. 7–9]. This is the kind of thing that puts people off a bit. And yet, if you think of the context, the situation is assumed by Job's friends to be a situation in which God must be justified because he's God, and in which Job therefore must be unjustified.

Throughout the argument there runs the primitive superstition, which at the same time is very difficult to eradicate in the human mind, that if you're unlucky, then you must somehow or other have done something wrong, and that the unlucky are to be avoided, just as people carrying an infectious disease ought to be avoided. In Homer's *Odyssey*, for example, Aeolus, the god of the winds, gives Odysseus a favourable wind, but his treacherous companions let the wind out of the sack and the voyage ends in disaster. So Odysseus goes back to Aeolus and says that through no fault of his own he's run into bad luck. And Aeolus slams the door in his face, and says that an unlucky man is hated by the gods, and he'll have nothing more to do with him [bk. 10].

But I think that one of the things that God is expressing in this speech is the fact that you don't get anywhere in this situation by simply reversing it. If you just turn it inside out, and make it a drama in which

Job is the noble suffering hero, and God is malicious and malignant, you've got a quite comprehensible dramatic situation. It doesn't fit the opening postulates of the poem very well, because a situation like that would identify God with Satan, and that, as I have had occasion to point out in this course already, is something that theologians are perpetually doing, one of their favourite amusements. But in the opening of Job, God and Satan are quite carefully distinguished, and even if Satan disappears from the rest of the action after the second chapter, the distinction is still in the reader's mind.

Around the time of Christ, there were various philosophers known as the Gnostics. There were Christian Gnostics and Jewish Gnostics and pagan Gnostics. We know the Christian ones best of the three, because they were so elaborately refuted by the orthodox, who quoted large passages from their writings to show how wrong they were. They were a large and influential party, just about as old as Christianity itself, and are referred to in the New Testament several times [e.g., 1 Timothy 6:20]. But the Christian Gnostic view was that the creator of the universe and the God of the Old Testament, Jehovah, could only have been an evil God; and it was from that evil God that Jesus had come to deliver us. The Christian Gnostic view, then, would have led to the complete elimination of the Old Testament, and of the Jewish tradition, from the Christian heritage.

That is one element in Christian Gnosticism. What I am even more concerned with, and what I think is even more significant from the point of view of Job, is the pagan Gnostic position, which was really an attack on the order of nature. The Gnostic view in paganism was that the order of nature was a hopeless bungle, that nature is something totally alien to man. Consequently, it could only be, once again, the creation of an evil being; and man has to fight his way out of this alien nature as best he can.

There is a very strong attack made on the pagan Gnostics by the Neoplatonic philosopher Plotinus, who attacked them for holding what seems to us a most utterly obvious point. They said all men are brothers—including the base, as Plotinus adds contemptuously—but that men are not brothers to the stars [*Enneads*, 2.9.18]. In other words, Plotinus' case was that the order of nature must be thought of as created perfect, and that man's destiny is to fit himself into this order, not to break away from it. So the Gnostics are actually raising a pretty important issue and pressing it very hard.

Although this is several centuries later than Job, I am raising the point here because it is something that glints in the background of its whole situation. The same situation turns up many centuries later in Shelley's poem *Prometheus Unbound*. Here, Prometheus bound to the rock is an image of suffering and martyred man; and Jupiter the sky-god is the cruel malevolent being that keeps man in that state of suffering and martyrdom. Some time before the poem opened, Prometheus has pronounced a speech in defiance of Jupiter, including a curse on Jupiter which is repeated soon after the poem begins. At that point, Prometheus says, Well, I'm sorry I made that curse, and recalls it [1.303–5]. Everybody, including Earth, thinks that Prometheus has quit, has given in to the malevolent being, and they think it's all up with everybody forever. But what has happened is the exact opposite. Prometheus has realized that his defiance of Jupiter, his cursing of Jupiter, is in fact the only thing that keeps Jupiter in business; so that when he recalls the curse, Jupiter simply disappears.

Now I'm not sure how clearly I can convey the point in relation to Job, but obviously a continuously defying Job would be keeping a whole Satanic part of Creation in business. Hence, Job's surrender at the end is not a simple surrender. If you look at 42:6, he says, "Wherefore I abhor myself, and repent in dust and ashes." Now, most Western readers of that verse would take it to mean that Job was simply saying that man is always evil, and God is always good, and consequently that the best man can do is to abhor himself, and try to be as much unlike himself as possible. But somebody trained in an Oriental religion might read it very differently. He might read "I abhor myself" more as meaning, I no longer consider what I call 'myself,' an ego, as any reality at all, and I am withdrawing from it.

There is a remark I may have quoted already from Rimbaud. Rimbaud says in one of his letters, "*Je* est un autre": *I* is somebody else.[55] And that may be Job's final discovery—that the person he's been calling Job, the Job ego, is in fact not there; and that you don't see with your eyes, you see through your eyes: your eyes are merely a lens. You don't think with your brain, you think through your brain: your brain is a filter or an amplifier, or something of that kind, for the consciousness. And you don't live as the ego: it's another kind of consciousness altogether that lives through it. It's something of that kind of intuition that comes to Job at the end.

The sense of the subject as the perceiving ego is a kind of perspective we've been born with; and yet there are all kinds of experiences which make us realize that we are not in fact the starting point of our own experiences. For one thing, we are social beings before we are individual ones. We belong to something before we are something. Consequently, our individual egos are rooted in the society we belong to. Whenever we begin to use our consciousness, we find that we can be as objective to ourselves as anything else can be. The central teaching of nearly all higher religions has been precisely that point: man does not discover who he is until he gives up the notion that he is himself.

Thus, consciousness incarnated an individual, but is not confined to the individual. It's the discovery of the realms of consciousness beyond the individual that all the teachings of salvation and enlightenment in all the religions are directed towards. The principle that the ego perceives only what is vague and hazy and general, and that what perceives the specific and particular is something universal in the perceiver, is, I think, an awareness that a great many religions come to focus on.

In Greek tragedy, the hero is very often a god himself, like Prometheus, or a demi-god like Hercules, or is somebody of divine descent, or he is somebody whose nature is somehow half divine and half human. As the action of the Greek tragedy unfolds, its dialectic tends to separate him from anything like a divine destiny. Well, of course that can't happen in a Biblical tradition. You can't have, in the Old Testament at any rate, a human being who is in part divine. Consequently, Job is not in the position of the tragic hero in a Greek tragedy. For one thing, he can't make any noble or heroic gesture: you can't make a heroic gesture if you have to stop and scratch a boil. And the fact that his courage is of the kind that expresses itself in patience and endurance is bound up with the fact that he is not to begin with the typical tragic hero of the Greek kind, who is at least partly divine in nature. So it's a matter of achieving a fully realized humanity; and one of the things that the Book of Job is saying is that a fully realized humanity is redeemable.

I was saying that the shadow of the malevolent or malignant Creator appears in the background of the Job problem; but the postulates of the poem itself really rule that out. There isn't a malignant Creator there, because we have already been shown the distinction between God and Satan. And that, of course, takes us into the heart of the tragic perspective in Job.

If you've read the Shakespearean tragedies with any attention, you must have often noticed how characters in tragedy assume sources for tragedy that are much more mysterious than any that you can actually see. For example, in *Romeo and Juliet*, Romeo speaks of his mind misgiving him that there is some consequence still hanging in the stars [1.4.107].

He speaks as though a kind of tragic fate were being woven for him in the patterns of the stars. When he hears the false news that Juliet is dead he says, "Is it e'en so? Then I defy you stars" [5.1.24], and makes his own resolve to kill himself. But we who look at the play don't feel that we need any astrological explanations for the deaths of the young lovers. They have a perfectly comprehensible cause in the idiotic family feud of the Montagues and the Capulets. Similarly, Gloucester, after he's been blinded, says, "As flies to wanton boys are we to the gods; they kill us for their sport" [4.1.38–9]. And yet Gloucester's miseries have been caused by the treachery of his bastard son Edmund, and by the brutality of Cornwall, who has put his eyes out. Again, the source of Gloucester's tragedy is perfectly human and comprehensible, and there's no need to postulate the existence of malicious gods.

Outside Shakespeare it's the same thing. In *Tess of the D'Urbervilles*, the final paragraph says, "Justice was done and the President of the Immortals had ended his sport with Tess." But that's only a literary flourish which Hardy puts in to show how well-read he was; because actually nothing happens to Tess in the story that does not have a quite specific locatable cause in human malice or arrogance or stupidity.

The general principle to which that leads is that the only mystery is in the existence of evil itself: there's no mystery about its effects. It is that mystery of the origin of evil that Job keeps circling around; and the nearest that we get to it as readers is in the speeches of Satan in the presence of God.

We have there, as we have so often in the Jewish and Christian and Islamic religious traditions, the sense of God as being in charge of the order of nature, but without interfering in it. There's always something of a very human feeling that if we were God, we would work harder to earn our keep; that if we were in charge of what happened, we wouldn't make such appalling bungles as God appears to be making. But all these questions focus on the question of the origin and the existence of evil itself.

So in the foreground, on what I regard as a relatively superficial level of the argument, we have this alleged problem of faith and doubt. Job trusts in God, and his trust is vindicated: whereas, if he had doubted, he would not have been vindicated. But one wonders whether looking at Job as a problem with a solution really gets us very deeply into it. In any case, what appears to be obvious is that Job is vindicated partly because he does protest, and consequently, that doubt is not the enemy of faith. Doubt is the dialectical opposite of faith, and it is an essential part of faith. A faith which never doubts is not worth having. It's in the dialectic of faith and doubt that the reality of faith emerges. The enemy of faith is not doubt, but rather the sheer insensitivity of mind that doesn't see what all the fuss is about.

And so, we have to go from this intellectualized problem of faith and doubt down to the deeper existential problem. Here the virtue is hope rather than faith, and the opposite of hope is not doubt, but despair. Again, despair is not the enemy of hope but the dialectical complement of hope, the thing that hope must fight against if it's to attain its reality. And so, Job goes through the depths of despair. It is because he does so that the hope is sustained at the end.

There's a poem of Emily Dickinson's about hope in which she says, "Could Hope inspect her Basis / Her Craft were done— / Has a fictitious Charter / Or it has none—" [Poem 1283, ll. 1–4]. That is, hope is simply the will to believe the impossible, and without its basis in fiction or illusion, there could be no such virtue. There's a good deal of truth in that, perhaps. What it amounts to is the question of illusion and reality. All through the story of Job, there is the irreducible reality of Job's isolation, his misery, his boils, all the disasters that have happened to him. And at the core, the illusion that there is something on his side, though he doesn't quite know what. At the end of the poem, we have the reversal of these relations of reality and illusion: the miseries all vanish into illusion, and Job's hope, whatever it is, is the one that becomes a reality.

Perhaps I could try to explain that by an analogy; and this might throw a light on what I was saying earlier about withdrawing from the ego as the source of our knowledge of reality. We tend to approach things on the assumption that reality is what is out there, the thing that stares back at us when we stare at it; and that illusions are the subjective things that we have inside ourselves. But now, if we go into a theatre and watch a play, we are at once confronted with an objective illusion. That is, what is on the stage is an illusion, but it's just as much objective as any other datum of sense experience. There's no reality behind that illusion. You can crawl around the dressing rooms and the wings indefinitely without finding any reality behind it. If you ask where the reality is, the nearest you come to an answer is that it is the mood generated in the audience by the play. So that the experience of entering a theatre turns your ordinary experience of reality and illusion inside out by presenting you with an objective illusion and a subjective reality.

The reason that happens in a theatre is that it is part of the human creative world. Thus, you begin to realize that a serious view of the world is impossible until you begin to recognize an element of unreality in what is objectively there, an element of illusion in the unchangeable world around you, and at the same time an element of reality in illusions and wishes and fantasies about what might or could or should or ought to be there instead.

That is where the serious view of the world begins in which human creativity can operate. So that what is restored to Job at the end of the poem is in a considerable measure the world of what Job has recreated by his own endurace.

Herze du wirst mit verlassen die die du sůchest.

djein herz hat sich erfrewt jnn dem herrn.

Dauid + anna

Frewend wurd ich mich frewen jnn dem herrn.

Jn meinem pet durch die nacht wurd ich suchen den da lieb hat mein seel.

ysaias + salomon

Man list jnn dem propheten da niel am xiiij t da er ein gesenckt was jn die lewe grub vn vnuersert blib vor den lewen kam morgens fru der kung zu der selben grub vn schawet wie es stunde bey daniel vn da er jn noch lebendige fand was er nast fro der selb kung bedeut mariam magdalenam die fru kam zu dem grab.

man list an dem lob gesang puch am iij t da der gema hel fand sein spons hat er gesprochen ich han gefunde den der da lieb gehabt hat mein seel ã Der selb gemah el bedeut mariam magdale nam als sy cristum fand vn in bewein wolt ij

Biblia Pauperum 31: CHRIST APPEARS TO MARY MAGDALENE
(John 20:11–18)

Darius finds Daniel living
(Daniel 6:18–23)

The Bride finds the Beloved
(Song of Solomon 3:1–5)

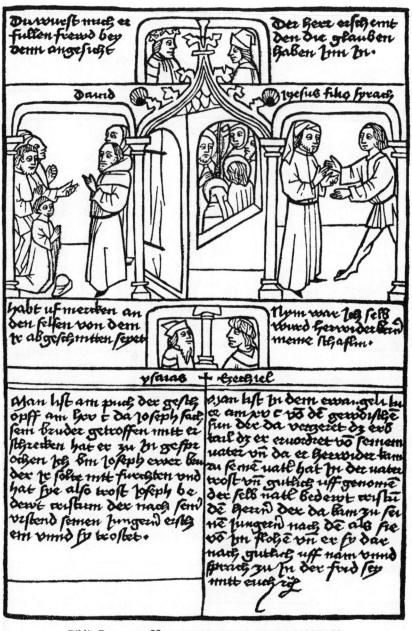

Biblia Pauperum 32: CHRIST APPEARS TO THE DISCIPLES
(Luke 24:36–49)

Joseph revealed to his brothers
(Genesis 45:1–15)

Return of the Prodigal Son
(Luke 15:20–4)

Biblia Pauperum 33: DOUBTING THOMAS
(John 20:24–9)

An angel appears to Gideon
(Judges 6:11–24)

Jacob wrestles with the angel
(Genesis 32:24–32)

21

The Language of Proclamation: Style and Rhythm in the Bible; The Gospel: Rewriting the Commandments

In approaching the part of the Bible that has its centre of gravity in the New Testament, I want first of all to make some observations about the style and rhythm of the Bible. The King James translation has been a great deal praised for its simplicity, and that simplicity certainly exists. But there are two kinds of simplicity. One is the democratic simplicity of one person writing for other people in as lucid a way as he can, so that he is not putting any barriers into his reader's path. But there is another kind of simplicity, a simplicity of authority that is most clearly present in such things as military commands. The officer's orders in an army have to be as straightforward in their syntax as possible—what literary critics call paratactical—and they have to be given in the fewest possible words, because soldiers will not hang themselves on barbed wire in response to a subjunctive mood or a subordinate clause. If there is adjustment or explanation to be done, it is for subordinates to do it.

The simplicity of the Bible throughout is the simplicity of the kind of authority that comes from being unquestionably the boss of the operation. It comes through in the laws, where it is the voice of divine commandment itself. And it comes through in the wisdom literature, because the wise man is speaking with the authority of tradition behind him. It comes through in prophecy, because the prophet's function is to say, "Thus saith the Lord." And of the discourses of Jesus, it is noted that he spoke as one having authority [Matthew 7:29; Mark 1:22]: one notices that quite frequently what he says begins, "Ye have heard that it hath been said unto you ... But I say unto you ... ," and that is that.

So the style of the Bible is a rhetorical style, but it employs a special kind of rhetoric. There are two aspects to rhetoric. On the one hand, it is an orator's attempt to persuade an audience, and on the other hand, it is a study of the figurative use of language, because oratory normally makes use of the standard figures of speech, like metaphor and antithesis, and is continually falling into rhythms like Lincoln's "of the people, by the people, for the people" or Churchill's "We shall fight on the beaches, we shall fight in the hills." The study of figures of speech was part of the school training of Shakespeare and his contemporaries and was the best possible training for poets, as well as for people who were going into the church or the law and who would naturally need to be effective speakers.

But the Bible's rhetoric is of a special kind, and scholars have given it the name *kerygma*, which is a Greek word meaning "proclamation." That proclamation is the core of what the Bible says: that is, it answers the existential question of what one should do to be saved. We notice, again, that this proclamation has the unquestioned authority of a divine origin.

The earliest of the prophets who seem to have recorded their prophecies was Amos, who lived in the eighth century B.C. Amos prophesied in the Northern Kingdom, and as the prophets were very strong supporters of the worship of Jehovah, his criticisms of royal policy were not very popular. So he was approached by an official of the North Israelite court and asked if he please wouldn't go down and prophesy to Judah instead of to Israel, because they were much wickeder in Judah and needed it much more. Also, he then wouldn't be bothering the North Israelite king or the court.

Amos says, in chapter 7, verse[s] 16[–17]: "Now therefore hear thou the word of the Lord: Thou sayest: Prophesy not against Israel, and drop not thy word against the house of Isaac. Therefore thus saith the Lord: Thy wife shall be an harlot in the city, and thy sons and thy daughters shall fall by the sword, and thy land shall be divided by line; and thou shalt die in a polluted land." The prophet may be right or wrong, and he may be reasonable or unreasonable, but the thing he does not do is hedge.

That voice of authority, which is heard constantly through the Bible, is still there in the Pauline epistles, where Paul makes a sharp distinction between what he says which he knows is the voice of God and what he says from himself, which he warns his readers is not to be taken with the same degree of authority.[56]

But we notice that there are different levels on which this authority is expressed. In the Ten Commandments, for example, there are commandments like, "Thou shalt not kill" [Exodus 20:13]: as we say now, period. There is no qualification of any kind. The Hebrew just says, "Kill not." There is no provision to be made for justifiable homicide or killing in self-defence or going to war or executing criminals, although those things are taken care of in other parts of the Mosaic code; because, after all, the commandment is addressed to people who want to kill so desperately that they couldn't even understand an unconditional prohibition of killing, much less obey it. But the point is that it is in that totally unconditional prohibition, "Kill not," that we hear the ring of authority most clearly. Now that means that there may be a difference in level between a law and a commandment, and that the commandment not to kill cannot be a law, because all that it means in the legal sense is, "Private murder is wrong because it's unpredictable and it upsets established social authority but going to war or executing criminals, there's nothing wrong with that. In fact, it's really something quite splendid." That is the legal meaning of the commandment. And yet one is left with a kind of uneasy feeling in the back of his mind that there might possibly be some kind of community or state of being where "Kill not" actually meant "Kill not."

There's a poem of Blake's called *Auguries of Innocence* which consists of aphorisms; and at the opening of the poem, we're told of the various things that befall people who ill-treat animals: "A Robin Red breast in a Cage / Puts all Heaven in a Rage" [ll. 5–6], and later on in the poem, "He who the Ox to wrath has movd / Shall never be by Woman lovd." [ll. 31–2] One's first reaction on reading that is to say that it is nonsense: that possibly it ought to be true that people who abuse animals should be unloved by women, but as a matter of experience, it is not in the least true. They are much more likely to be admired by them. If someone had said that to Blake, he would have said, "I never said that that was true of the state of experience." The poem is called *Auguries of Innocence*: that is, prophecies of an innocent world in which people who abuse and torment animals have no real place in the human community. Possibly the Ten Commandments are different from many of the laws of the Book of Deuteronomy and elsewhere in that they are really auguries of innocence. In other words, they describe a world which is not the world we live in, but which nevertheless is the genuinely human world.

When you turn to the Gospels, you find that Jesus is continually commenting on or quoting the books of the law, the first five books of the Old Testament. He is asked what the greatest commandment is and he quotes from Deuteronomy [Matthew 22:37; Mark 10:30; Deuteronomy 6:5]. The Sermon on the Mount is in very large part a commentary on the Commandments, but is emphasizing a positive element which is grammatically not in the Exodus formulation. The Commandments in Exodus are given a negative form: don't kill, don't commit adultery, don't steal, don't bear false witness. In the Sermon on the Mount, Jesus says in effect, "The commandment says, 'Don't kill'; but what that really means, positively, is a genuine enthusiasm for human life. The law says, 'Don't commit adultery.' But what that really means, positively, is a habitual respect for the dignity of women. And 'Don't steal' really means an enthusiasm for sharing your goods with those who need them more."

What that kind of commentary is doing is bringing out the aspect that I've called the "commandment aspect" as distinct from the aspect of legalism. That is the basis of the distinction in the New Testament between law and gospel, which is not a distinction between one religion and another. As I've said earlier, nowhere in the New Testament is the legalism which it condemns identified with Judaism. Similarly, legalism and what is meant by the gospel are simply two aspects of what may be the same verbal formulation: they are simply different attitudes towards them.

Now, if we drop the question of the Old Testament and just think of law in its ordinary secular sense as the set of rules by which a society orders itself, we notice that in the secular context of law, the crucial difference is between what is done and what is not done: it is the *act* that either observes or breaks the law. From the point of view of the law, therefore, in this secular context, a man is an honest man who has not actually been convicted of stealing. But naturally no society can hold together if it has as vague a sense of morality as all that. There has to be a very much tighter sense of personal integrity even in the secular sphere.

The emphasis in the gospel teaching is at the opposite extreme from that of secular law, because it throws the entire emphasis on the state of mind rather than on the action; and in a sense, a wrong action is only wrong because it manifests a wrong state of mind. That is, the seven deadly sins, the mortal sins that destroy the soul, as they were classified in the Middle Ages, were pride, wrath, sloth, envy, avarice, gluttony, and lechery. Not one of those sins necessarily results in criminal or antisocial actions. Sin is not error or wrongdoing or antisocial behaviour: the word "sin" has no meaning outside of a religious context. Sin is the attempt to block the will of God, and it has no meaning otherwise, no social or moral meaning.

Adultery in the Middle Ages would have been regarded as a subdivision of the deadly sin of lechery; but lechery could take many forms which would hurt nothing except the state of mind of the person himself. It may be immoral, but it is not criminal. Various people have tried to make it criminal, but that is another corollary of the teaching of the gospel: that when you interpret things that the gospel condemns as illegal, and start passing laws against them, then you've got the most fantastic tyranny. That's the situation that Shakespeare sets up in *Measure for Measure*, where the hero is condemned to death because he's betrothed or legally married, but hasn't the public declaration of his marriage, and therefore falls under a remarkably unenlightened law that provides the death penalty for sexual licence. So the distinction is that these conceptions of law in the gospel are rooted in the state of mind of the individual and not in social welfare.

Thus, the emphasis is thrown on the state of mind of the individual, and recurrently throughout the Christian tradition there has been an attempt to incorporate the gospel in legislation: that has resulted, as I say, in the most frightful tyranny. The situation is really the one outlined in Plato's *Republic*, where Socrates erects the pattern of the just state, which would be unmitigated hell to live in, and then, at the end of the ninth book, says, "Do you think any such state could exist?" Those that aren't drunk or asleep by that time simply shudder and say, "Heavens no." Socrates says, "Well, neither do I, but the wise man will always live by its laws, no matter what actual society he may be in" [*Republic*, 592a–b]. That is the conception behind the gospel, the conception of a spiritual kingdom of which we are citizens and follow its laws, but which cannot be incorporated into actual society in the form of legislation. Thus, Paul throws the strongest possible emphasis on the state of mind which he calls justification by faith, as distinct from the person who attempts to add himself up, to calculate his worth, so to speak, in legal terms as a matter of what he does.

You remember the chart that we began with in this course, including first of all the garden of Eden, then the Promised Land, then the city and the temple of Jerusalem and Zion. In the New Testament period, these have become a spiritual kingdom which has dropped its connections with history and a specific society. When I say it has dropped its connections with a history and with a specific society I mean, among other things, that it has disappeared from the world of time and space, and that its conceptions of the ultimate categories of existence take us beyond those normal ultimate categories of time and space.

One of the things that Jesus says about the kingdom of heaven is, "The kingdom of heaven is *within you*": *entos hymon* [Luke 17:21].[57] The New English Bible, which seems to be very unhappy about this remark for some reason, translates it as "among you" and gives four alternatives in the margin which, I daresay, seems to imply, We don't know what the hell it *does* mean. The reason is that, as everywhere in the Bible, we have to remember that the faith of the translator has a great deal to do with the translation he makes; and if you regard psychological truths as the profoundest truths, then you will prefer the word "within": the kingdom of heaven is within you. But if what you want is a social gospel, then you will say, "The kingdom of heaven is among you," and the New English Bible translators obviously had a social conscience, because they prefer to say "among." The Gospel of Thomas, which was not discovered until 1945 but is a collection of sayings of Jesus, says, "The kingdom of heaven is inside you and it is outside you" [v. 3], which makes a good deal of sense, I think. It seems to me that the statement in Luke, "The kingdom of heaven is *entos hymon*," may mean "within you" or it may mean "among you": those are subordinate meanings. The central meaning is, it is *here*, and not *there*. In other words, it transcends our normal sense of space; because everything in our ordinary experience of space is *there*. We live in an alienated world that keeps receding from us, and everything that we point to, even the middle of our own backbones, is still *there*. If we want to arrive at a conception of *here*, we have to draw a circle around ourselves so that *here* is inside it. And yet, *here* is obviously the centre of space. If you apply the same categories to time, you find yourself in the middle of the same paradox of reality and illusion. Time is the fundamental category by which we perceive everything: we perceive nothing that is real except in time. And yet time as we ordinarily experience it consists of three unrealities, a past that doesn't exist any longer, a future that doesn't exist yet, and a present that never quite exists at all. So we get our fundamental reality out of a threefold illusion. And yet, we feel that *now* is the centre of time, just as *here* is the centre of space. But again, as with space, the only way we can get at it is to draw a circle around the very near past and the very near future and say that "now" is somewhere inside it.

It is this sense of the genuineness of here and now that gives us what we might call a real present and a real presence. Now of course that's a rather heavy dose for people to take, so you find over and over again that religious and theological works are shot through with ordinary conceptions of time and space. In religion, there is a use of two words in particular, the word "eternal" and the word "infinite." Now practically whenever everybody uses those words, they mean by "eternal" indefinite time, time that goes on and on and on and on and on and never stops. Similarly, by "infinite" they mean space that just goes on and on and on and never stops. I think what those words actually mean in religion is something more like the sense of the reality of now and the sense of the reality of here. But of course, the notion of a world that went on and on and on in time and never stopped, which would be unending happiness for the virtuous and unending torment for the wicked, was a notion that made something very unpleasant in human nature say "yum-yum." Consequently, you get doctrines of heavens and hells extending indefinitely in time, which were adopted primarily because they were powerful political levers.

Another reason there is so much emphasis on heavens and hells is that in Jesus' teaching, the fundamental reality of things was a division into his spiritual kingdom of heaven and the world of unending torment that man keeps constructing for himself. In his teaching, there are no realities except those of the spiritual kingdom and that which is without, which is outside the spiritual kingdom. But contingent existence as we know it in time is a mixture of the two things, and so there is the parable of the wheat and the tares: that this world is a very badly sown wheat field which is full of weeds [Matthew 13:24–30]. It's no use trying to dig out the weeds and leave the wheat in ordinary existence. That is why there is also an emphasis in the Gospels on the spiritual kingdom as immediate. Again, the general religious tendency was to keep postponing it into the hereafter, into the life after death. But Jesus' emphasis is consistently on its immediacy. That takes one into an area where history can be seen as forming a kind of shape and as having reached a kind of fulfilment. Now in our ordinary experience of history, that never happens: history just keeps on going. That was a great puzzle, we gather, to some of the earliest Christians, who assumed that what Jesus meant was that there was going to be a tremendous fireworks show that would descend on us next Tuesday and would turn the sun into darkness and the moon into blood, and would put an end to history as we've known it. That didn't happen. So it's obvious that that fulfilling of history must go on somewhere else.

The implication, then, is that there are two levels of knowledge, and the thing which is described as knowledge of good and evil entered the world and became the legalism that the New Testament condemns.

This vision of legalism descending from the knowledge of good and evil is the one that engenders the legal metaphor that runs all the way through the Bible, and which thinks in terms of trials and judgments with defenders and accusers. We've seen that even Job is confident that he has a defender, a *go'el*, who will take his part. Then he wishes that his *diabolos*, his accuser, had written a book and stated the case against him. But having read the first two chapters of Job, we can see that while this legal vision is utterly natural and inevitable to Job, it is nevertheless not quite the one that's there.

Biblia Pauperum 34: ASCENSION
(Acts 1:4–12)

Enoch taken up   Elijah's ascent
(Genesis 5:24; Hebrews 11:5)   (2 Kings 2:1–13)

Biblia Pauperum 35: PENTECOST
(Acts 2)

Moses receives the law
(Genesis 24:12–18)

Fire consumes Elijah's sacrifice
(1 Kings 18:17–40)

22

Revelation: Removing the Veil

I've been dealing with various phases of what is traditionally called revelation in the Bible, and it seems to me that what we said at the beginning of the course about the way the Bible is arranged, with its Old Testament providing the types, in the Christian reading, of the antitypes of the New Testament, is a principle that applies here as well.

First of all, the conception of Creation in the Bible provides the sense of an intelligible and controlled order: and the reality to which that points is the redemption of the people of God from a state of tyranny and exploitation. So in that sense, the Exodus is the antitype of the Creation; and in references to bringing Israel up from Egypt, it is spoken of as really the completion of the work of Creation itself, as for example in Isaiah 51[:9–10], where God is addressed as having destroyed the dragon of chaos at the Creation and then destroyed the force of tyranny with the deliverance of Israel out of the sea.

The Exodus gives to the Biblical religions that curiously revolutionary quality which Judaism and Christianity and Islam all have to some degree; and we saw that a nation which has gone through that kind of revolutionary experience becomes a nation with a very strong sense of its own corporate unity because of the experience which its people have shared. Thus, law becomes really the antitype of the birth of Israel at the deliverance from Egypt, or the reality to which it points.

Law, of course, is a social thing, and consequently is approximate and incomplete until it is incorporated in the attitude of the individual; and we saw that wisdom in the Bible was thought of as essentially the individualization of the law.

Then we saw that wisdom is a way of life which looks for continuity and stability, persistence in the same line of conduct, and faces the future with a mental attitude described in the Vulgate as *prudentia*, prudence, the stabilizing of future contingency by past experience. And that, we saw, was something that leads to a much more radical conception, a conception of prophecy, which individualizes the revolutionary feeling just as wisdom does the law, and sees man as at the bottom of a U-curve, between his original state and his final deliverance.

Then again, it is prophecy in particular that is regarded in the Christian Bible as fulfilled by the gospel because, whereas for Judaism the book that Christianity calls the Old Testament is essentially a book of the law, in Christianity the Old Testament is primarily a book of prophecy; and the prophecy is regarded as fulfilled by the gospel, which is the account of God himself in human form going through this U-curve that we described earlier: that is, as descending through the Incarnation into the level of human experience and rising from that again in the Resurrection.

I had to complicate my account of the gospel by talking about the different attitude to time which it seems to me to require. Part of my reason for stressing that is that our notions of time still are apt to persist unchanged; and there's a great deal of advantage in an attitude which keeps its antitypes still in the future. As long as they are as yet unfulfilled, it is in a sense easier to trust to them. That is, Christianity was confronted very early with the dilemma that the redemption of mankind was supposed to have taken place, and yet history seemed to go on very largely unchanged. There is no difficulty about that as long as you remember that two conceptions of time are involved: but if you've only got one conception of time, it is a problem. So concurrently with the conception of the gospel, we have the notion of the gospel itself as being fulfilled in a Second Coming, which puts an end to history as we have known it. Now actually, that is at least metaphorically true of the gospel itself, because one central fact about the conception of Jesus in the New Testament is that he is both master and servant, and symbolically, the dialectic of history ends at the point at which the master and the servant become the same person.

The relation of the first coming to the Second Coming is again portrayed in that image that we found at the end of the Book of Job: "I have heard of thee by the hearing of the ear: but now mine eye seeth thee" [42:5]. That is, the gospel is essentially an oral teaching, and a great deal of emphasis is thrown on the hearing of the Word. The physical appearance of Christ is in curious contrast to the things that he says: his utterances are gathered up and recorded with great care, but the fact that he was bound to resemble some people more closely than others could never have been anything but an embarrassment to the Church, and so we adopted that vaguely Italianate compromise as our visible conception of Christ. But the Apocalypse is essentially an opening of vision, and the phrase that appears very near the beginning of the Book of Revelation is that every eye shall see him [1:7].

Now what they see, of course, is the Word made an object of vision rather than something listened to. I previously remarked, I think, on the fact that the Book of Revelation is a dense mosaic of allusions to the Old Testament [Lecture 3]: Ezekiel and Daniel and Zechariah and Isaiah are made the stuff and texture of the vision that is portrayed in the Book of Revelation itself. The author of Revelation seems to have been closer to the Hebrew text of the Old Testament than most of the New Testament writers, and so when he says that he saw this in a vision on Patmos, the statement is not a contradiction of the fact that his book is a dense mosaic of allusions to Old Testament imagery. In the terms that he was trying to present, there is no difference between what he sees in vision on Patmos and what he sees in the text of Ezekiel or Zechariah, because what he is seeing is primarily for him the meaning of the Word of God. That is why there is such an emphasis on vision in the book, although Revelation is not at all a clearly visualized book. There have been many illustrators that have struggled with its seven-headed and ten-horned dragon, and their testimony is unanimous that the Book of Revelation is not technically visualized. What is thrown into a pattern and more or less projected on a screen is the structure of imagery in the Bible presented as a single unity.

And just as the conception of the relation of the gospel to prophecy relates the present event in the Gospels to the past, so the conception of the Apocalypse relates it to a future. There has always been in what one might call populist Christianity a strong hankering for a dramatic end to history to come at a very short time in the future, which will end time as we have known it.

The popular conception of time in Christianity is perhaps one of its least attractive features. The seventeenth century with Galileo saw mythological space replaced by scientific space, and the Church managed to survive that: we discovered that we could live without the metaphor of God as up there in the sky. The remark of Khrushchev, when the early Russian astronauts started exploring outer space, that they didn't find any trace of God up there,[58] didn't really come with very much of a disastrous impact on any of the Western religions: we're past that particular structure of metaphor and don't need to project it any more.

But at the very time when that revolution in space was occurring, we had Archbishop Ussher in seventeenth-century England explaining that the world was created in 4000 B.C. and would last for six thousand years, when the seventh millennium would begin. Consequently, because there had been an error of four years, the millennium will start in 1996. I think that most of us are resigned to the high probability that the millennium will not start in 1996: in other words, we've gone past the metaphor of time just as we got over the metaphor of space in connection with the existence or activity of God. During the nineteenth century, various millennial sects used to gather on top of a mountain to wait for the end of the world. But the irony of their situation was revealed by the existence of the mountain itself, which had been there for millions of years and had every prospect of staying there for several million years more. So that is why I put the emphasis I do on the necessity of transcending our regular notions of time and space in order to understand what the Bible is talking about. When it talks of time, and says that the *kairos*, the crucial moment of time, is at hand, it is not talking about the ticking of a watch.

The word "apocalypse," the name of the last book of the Bible, is the Greek word for revelation. That is why the book is called Revelation in English translation, and what John at Patmos sees in the book is a panorama of certain things in human experience taking on different forms. The sun is turned into darkness and the moon into blood, there are horses riding across the world, there are huge dragons emerging out of the sea, and the most fantastic events are taking place; but these are the repressed images of a persecuted people coming to the surface, and they are its consciousness of what is occurring. So one wonders if it is possible to go a step further and suggest that man creates what he calls history in order to conceal what is really happening from himself. What applies to the apocalyptic vision in Revelation may also apply to the story of Jesus in the Gospels. The Gospels are a fulfilment of prophecy: therefore they can hardly be history as we understand history. We think of history as trying to put the reader where the events were. History tells the reader what he would have seen if he'd been present, say, at the assassination of Caesar. But what the Gospels tell us is rather something like this: if you had been present on the hills of Bethlehem in the year nothing, you might not have heard a chorus of angels. But what you would have seen and heard would have missed the whole point of what was actually going on. Thus, the antitypes of history and of prophecy as we have them in the gospel and the Apocalypse give you not what you would have seen and heard, or what I would have seen and heard, but what was actually going on, which we don't have the spiritual vision to reach to.

The Bible ends in Revelation 22[:16–17]: "I Jesus have sent mine angel to testify unto you these things in the churches. I am the root and the offspring of David, and the bright and morning star. And the Spirit and the bride say, Come. And let him that heareth say, Come. And let him that is athirst come. And whoever will, let him take the water of life freely." Then we go on to a caution of the type that one often gets in sacred books, saying, you are not to add to or take away from a single word of what is written in this book [v. 19]. Now, the superficial meaning of "this book" is apparently just the Book of Revelation, but the more I study it, the more convinced I am that the author of the Book of Revelation is quite deliberately making his book a coda or conclusion to the entire canon. I don't know how much he knew about the canon in his day, nor do I think it matters, but I think that "this book" has perhaps a much wider reference than the Book of Revelation. He says of "this book" that nothing is to be added or taken away: in other words, this is it. There is no more. This is where the Bible ends. You notice that it is a remarkably open ending.

"The Spirit and the bride say, Come. Let him that heareth say, Come. Let him that is athirst come. And whoever will, let him take the water of life freely." The suggestion seems to be that the Bible reaches in its closing words, not an end, but a beginning. And that beginning is in the mind of the reader. So that the Apocalypse, in its turn, becomes a type. In that case, what is its antitype? If you look over that list,[59] you'll see there's only one thing it can possibly be, and that is where we started, with a new creation: which is how Paul describes the gospel in Romans and elsewhere.

In Milton, for example, you have a great many prose writings and of course all his poetry devoted to the general principle that the Bible must be given an authority independent of the Church, so that the Church does not interpret the Bible, or at least its interpretation is not definitive. Instead, Christianity takes the form of a dialogue between the Word of God and the Church. And yet, while Milton places the authority of the Bible higher than the authority of the Church, he also places the authority of what he calls the "Word of God in the heart,"[60] that is, the reader's comprehension of the Bible, higher than the Bible itself. That sounds as though he were setting up a standard of what is called private judgment over against the whole of history and tradition. But that's not the way Milton was thinking at all. For him, it is in the long run not the ego, not the individual "I," that reads the Bible at all but the Holy Spirit within the reader. And that of course, being a Person of God, has a unity that transcends that of the individual reader.

The important thing is the reversal of perspective which takes place in the reader's mind—or should take place in the reader's mind—when he reaches the end of the Bible, which is also the beginning of his life. Bernard Shaw remarks about the mousetrap play in *Hamlet* that Claudius is enthralled by the play, not because it's a great play, but because it's about him.[61] That is true also of the Bible: that its meaning is *de te fabula*, the story is about you.[62] And the recreation of the book in the reader's mind is the end at which it is directed. Therefore, the Creation spoken of in Genesis is not for us primarily the beginning of nature as such, but rather the beginning of conscious understanding, where the primary defining limits are the beginning and the end, and it winds up with this divine Creation which God made and saw to be good being recreated in the reader's mind.

The new Creation will actually incorporate the whole sequence: it would start certainly as a revolution in the reader's mind, and would also encapsulate the whole sequence down to the Apocalypse itself. It's obvious that if these are all types of antitypes in a single process, they all have to be an essential part of the conclusion. For there can certainly be no sense of a new Creation without a revolutionary expansion of consciousness.

This new Creation is not in the egocentric mind, is not in the individual mind. It's in the mind of the individual reader as a member of a community, and it's in the community as a community within the Holy Spirit, the Person of God. I keep coming back to Milton because he seems to put these things very lucidly: that is how Milton explains in his day why Christianity becomes a revolutionary force in history. It becomes a revolutionary force by trying not to. Society is usually a pyramid of authority with one man at the top. The community, united in the understanding of the word of God, is a four-square community, where everybody is free and equal by their faith. Therefore, every structure of society has to come to terms with this indigestible cube in the middle of it, and eventually has to adapt to it. The gospel begins by dividing spiritual and temporal authority: Jesus says, "Render to Caesar the things that are Caesar's, and to God the things that are God's"

[Mark 12:17]. The trouble is that there comes a point at which Caesar demands what is due only to God, that is, divine worship. As soon as that happens, the four-square community becomes a revolutionary force.

It might not be theoretically true that a counter-revolution is impossible in a new Creation. But when Adam was made a part of the Creation, he was hitched onto an infinite power. He had the free will to break away from that, and consequently, it is the redemption out of bondage that has to be the antitype of Creation. It is that because the Creation included a falling away from Creation, and in the new Creation one is again hitched back on to the eternal, infinite power that began it. It would depend of course on the role that you ascribe to time: if ordinary historical time continues to be the central fact of our experience, there is still the possibility of the falling away again. In fact, we see it happening constantly. But the whole Christian scheme as expounded by Milton and everybody else has a considerable dislike of the closing of the circle which one finds in Oriental religions with the conception of reincarnation. In the Christian odyssey, the one idea is to get back home like Ulysses; but like a baseball player, you have to go around the circle to get there, and when you get home, it isn't quite the same place it was when you left it. And so there is a kind of gap, a kind of spark between the Creation at the beginning and the new Creation at the end. If you close the gap, and make it a completed circle, then you have the Hindu conception of reincarnation as repeating itself at different times through history.

I think that probably every cycle is just a failed spiral, and that history and nature collapse into cycles because they are too lazy to start again at another level. Yet there is the level by which one starts at Genesis and ends in Revelation, and that is followed by what happens in the reader's mind after he does that, which is an experience at a different level, and so on up. But that's something the Bible feels it's not its business to expound.

Biblia Pauperum 36: CORONATION OF THE VIRGIN
(not Biblical—from 12th century; cf. *Biblia Pauperum* 40)

Solomon seats Bathsheba on his
right hand (1 Kings 2:19)

Ahasuerus makes Esther queen
(Esther 2:17)

Der Herr wirt richten den rechten und den unrechten.

Bott wirt richten die und der werlt

Ecclesiastes + Regum

Er wirt richten die haiden und vil völker

Er wiret dich richten nach dem wegen

ysaias + Ezechiel

Man list in iij buch der künig am iii c dz zwo frawen die üppig waren oder dörat et frawen kamen für künig Salomon vn kriegten von ir kinder wegen vor de richter vo des ertenckte sun vn von des lebedige kindes wege rc Bey dem Salomon dem wißen sollent wir versteen ain stum der richten wirt. lebendig vnnd tod nach dem waren gericht rc

Man list in anderd buch der künig j c. dz der künig danid nauch dem tod saul belibe im sileth da kam ainer von dem land amalachitairn vn romet sich er hett de gesalbete des heren getötet rc Danid bode vo woistum der als danid den a malachsvaimgerichtet hett richten wirt alle völker Inn gerechtigkeit vnd wirt be kommen amen ietlichen nach sinen sunden ic

---

Biblia Pauperum 37: DOOMSDAY
(Ecclesiastes 3:17 ; 2 Timothy 4:1)

Judgment of Solomon
(1 Kings 3:16–27)

David condemns the Amalekite
(2 Samuel 1:1–16)

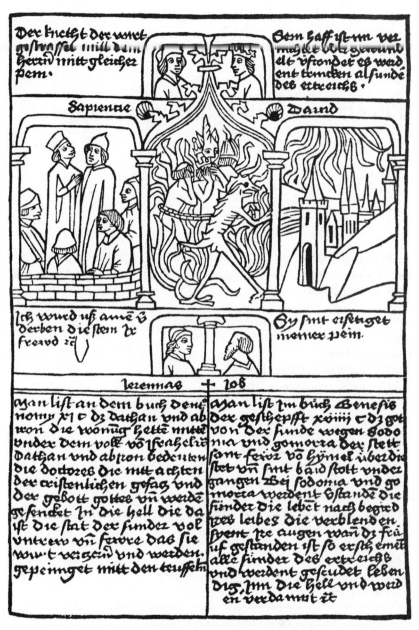

Biblia Pauperum 38: THE DAMNED TAKEN TO HELL
(Matthew 5:29)

Dathan and Abiram (Numbers 16)

Sodom and Gomorrah destroyed (Genesis 19:23–8)

23

Revelation: After the Ego Disappears

I've been distributing an analysis I've made of the Book of Revelation. I don't know whether everybody has a copy or not: I tried to see that there were enough.

[*Revelation Chart*][63]

(Prologue, 1:1–9)
First Epiphany: Son of Man, 1:10–20)
First Commission to Author, 1:11

FIRST SERIES: THE SEVEN CHURCHES AND THE SEVEN REWARDS
1. (Ephesus) Tree of Life, 2:1–7
2. (Smyrna) Crown of Life, 2:8–11
3. (Pergamos) Hidden Manna & Name on White Stone, 2:12–17
4. (Thyatira) Morning Star & Power over Nations, 2:18–29
5. (Sardis) White Garments & Name in Book of Life, 3:1–6
6. (Philadelphia) Pillar in Temple; Name of God Inscribed, 3:7–13
7. (Laodicea) Sitting on Throne, 3:14–22
   Second Epiphany, 4
   First Hymn, 4:8–11
   Third Epiphany: The Lamb Unseals the Book, 5
   Second Hymn, 5:9–14

SECOND SERIES: THE CALAMITIES OF THE SEVEN SEALS
1. Conqueror on White Horse, 6:1–3
2. Red Horse of War, 6:4
3. Black Horse of Famine, 6:5–6

4. Pale Horse of Death 6:7–8
5. Cry of Martyrs & Giving of White Robes, 6:9–11
6. Earthquake, Darkening of Sun, Moon, Stars, 6:12–17
   Fourth Epiphany: Sealing of Israel, 7
   Third Hymn, 7:12
7. Silence & Incense Ritual, 8:1–5

THIRD SERIES: THE CALAMITIES OF THE SEVEN TRUMPETS
1. Hail & Fire: Third of Trees, 8:6–7
2. Mountain in Sea: Third of Sea Blood, 8:8–9
3. Wormwood Star: Third of Waters, Polluted, 8:10–11
4. Sun, Moon & Stars Darkened, 8:12–13
5. Opening of Abyss: Locusts & Scorpions, 9:1–12
6. Loosing of Angels of Euphrates, 9:13–21
   Second Commission, 10
   Third Commission, 11
   Fifth Epiphany: Martyrdom of Witnesses, 11:3–19
   Fourth Hymn, 11:15
7. Opening of Temple: Vision of Ark of Covenant, 11:19

FOURTH SERIES: THE CENTRAL APOCALYPTIC VISIONS
1. Birth of Messiah, 12:1–6
2. Casting out of the Dragon, 12:7–17
3. Rising of the Dragons of Sea & Earth, 13
4. Vision of the Redeemed, 14:1–5
   Fifth Hymn, 14:3–4
5. Messages of Three Angels, 14:6–12
   Fourth Commission, 14:13
6. The Final Harvest, 14:14–16
7. The Final Vintage, 14:17–20
   Sixth Epiphany, 15
   Sixth Hymn (Song of Moses), 15:3–4

FIFTH SERIES: THE PLAGUES OR VIALS
1. Plague of Boils, 16:1–2
2. Sea Turned to Blood, 16:3
3. Rivers Turned to Blood, 16:4–7
4. Heat from Scorched Sun, 16:8–9
5. Darkness from the Seat of the Beast, 16:10–11
6. Drying of the Euphrates; Frogs; Armageddon, 16:12–21

7. Plague of Air; Fall of Babylon; Judgment of Whore, 17–18
   Seventh Epiphany, 19:1–10
   Seventh Hymn, 19:1–4
   Fifth Commission, 19:9

SIXTH SERIES: THE SEVEN LAST THINGS
1. Conqueror on White Horse, 19:11–18
2. Capture of Beasts, 19:19–21
3. Binding of Satan, 20:1–3
4. Millennium, 20:4–6
5. War with Gog, 20:7–10
6. Last Judgment, 20:11–15
7. Descent of Jerusalem, 21–22
   Sixth Commission, 21:5
   Seventh Commission, 22:10
   (Epilogue), 22:18–21

SEVENTH SERIES: THE UNDERLYING SYMBOLIC PATTERN

Category	Apocalyptic Form	Demonic Form (or Form of Wrath)
1. Divine	A. God Enthroned in Heaven	Synagogue of Satan
	B. Everlasting Gospel (14:6)	Mystery (17:5)
2. Spiritual–Angelic	A. Seven Spirits before Throne	Seven Hills of Rome
	B. Morning Star	Wormwood Star
3. Human	A. Son of Man	Divine Caesar
	B. Bride	Great Whore
	C. White Garments	Scarlet & Purple
	D. Cry of Martyrs	Cry of Kings
4. Animal	A. Lamb	Dragon, etc.
	B. Four "Beasts" around Throne	Four Horsemen
5. Vegetable	Tree of Life	Harvest & Vintage
6. Mineral	A. Jerusalem	Babylon, etc.
	B. White Stone	Millstone
7. "Chaos" (Water-World)	A. River of Life	River of Dragon (12:15–16)
	B. Sea of Glass	Lake of Fire (20:15)
	C. Cup of Water of Life	Cup of Blood of Death

Every passage in the Book of Revelation is a dense mosaic of allusions to and echoes from the Old Testament. The author is particularly indebted to the Book of Ezekiel, I think, and in Jewish mysticism there is a whole literature which took off from the opening vision in Ezekiel of the chariot with the four wheels. It was called Merkabah mysticism, and the Book of Revelation is perhaps the only Christian example of it—I don't know. In any case, it presents itself as having been written by someone called John, distinguished from the apostle of that name by the title *theologos*, the Divine, and he is said to have seen this in a vision at Patmos where he was exiled.

I think that if you look at the book in the way that I have tried to do you find that there are recurring sequences arranged in groups of seven, some of which are related to each other. If you look, for example, at the third series, the calamities of the seven trumpets, and compare it with the fifth series, the plagues or vials, you'll see that there are a good many parallels between the two. The parallels between them are partly accounted for by the fact that they are both based on the conception of the plagues of Egypt as something that will recur in the last day. I also try to locate the seven commissions to the author, and the seven hymns and the seven epiphanies, the spread-out visions he has; and if you find my analysis over-schematized, I can only say that I think the Book of Revelation is an over-schematized book, and that its extraordinary insistence on the numbers seven and twelve may have the significance that, by that time, seven was the number both of the planets and of the days of the week, and twelve was the number both of months of the year and of the signs of the zodiac; consequently, seven and twelve represent particularly a world where time and space have become the same thing.

There are, as I see it, six series of seven events, corresponding possibly to the six days of Creation, and being all comprehended in the seventh day of contemplation, which is the characteristic of the world beyond time.

I have previously spoken of the historical passages of the Bible as not being concerned with history as we know it, and as not concerned to adopt the ordinary criteria of history that we should look for in Thucydides or in Gibbon or in somebody who is quite explicitly writing history. That is because the Bible is concerned with another kind of action in human life altogether, and that other kind, which the scholars call *Heilsgeschichte*, sacred history, deals with the repeating events, or at least with the repeating aspects of events, which indicate the universalized meaning of history as distinct from the particular events which are the concern of the historian. For the ordinary historian, of course, everything in history is unique. No action exactly repeats in exactly the same circumstances. But the kind of history that you find for instance in the Book of Judges does show you the same situation recurring with different contexts each time in order to bring out a more universal pattern. So this form of *Heilsgeschichte*, which is also used for presenting the life of Christ in the Gospels, is concerned not with the past, which is dead, but with the past used as material for a present vision.

Now, what applies to the past applies also to the future. We are told by many scholars that everybody in the first generation or so of Christianity expected the end of the world at any time, and interpreted this as a literally future event, something that would happen about next Tuesday and would bring about the end of history as we know it. But it's possible that Biblical prophecy has the same oblique reference to the future that it has to the past, and that the future, like the past, is being assimilated into a present vision.

It is, I think, significant that many people, many great theologians, including John Calvin, have never known what to do with the Book of Revelation: it never struck them as a book they could make any sense out of. One person described it as a book which either finds a man mad or else leaves him so. That is of course quite comprehensible if you struggle with the wrong kind of literalism in reading it. In fact, one might also say the book is designed to drive you mad if you approach it with that kind of literalism in mind.

For many centuries it was accepted as a prophecy of the future troubles of the Church; and that meant that sinister symbols, such as the Great Whore and the dragon and the beast and the Antichrist figure, could be identified in any century by any commentator with whatever he happened to be most afraid of at the time. In Dante's *Purgatorio*, for example, the beast and the whore are identified with the Avignon Papacy and the King of France [canto 32]. In some of the Protestant polemic of the Reformation, they were identified with the Roman Church, considering that body as a continuation of a persecuting Roman Empire, with the Pope as an Antichrist figure, and the Whore of Babylon identified with the Roman Catholic Church. In the eighteenth century, Blake identified the beast and the whore with a new development which he saw taking place in his own time which he called Druidism, and which we should call something more like totalitarianism, the kind of state dictatorship which is designed to crush all freedom and imagination out of human society.

But it is better not to think in terms of relating some kind of future to the author of the book at all. We might take an example from one of the Oriental literatures: there's a very remarkable scripture of Tibetan Buddhism whose English title is *The Tibetan Book of the Dead*. This is founded on a conception of reincarnation: when a man dies, a priest goes and reads this book in his ear. The corpse is supposed to understand what is being read to him, and he is being told that he is going to see a long series of visions or epiphanies of gods, first peaceful ones and then wrathful ones, and that these are his own repressed thoughts coming to the surface, having been released by death. He is not to think of himself as in any way subject to their power: he has created them himself, and if he could only understand that, he would be delivered from them. He is adjured in every paragraph of the book to do the right thing, to become mentally conscious and deliver himself from the wheel of death and rebirth. And then the priest says resignedly, "Well, you probably missed it again, so now you'll have this other vision, and don't miss it this time."

Well, that is in a different context. But the relationship is not so unlike what is being revealed in the Book of Revelation. The Book of Revelation is presenting you the ordinary material of Biblical prophecy, the overturn of society and the tremendous calamities of nature when the sun is turned into darkness and the moon into blood, the great earthquakes and famines and plagues and swarms of locusts and all the rest of it. But these are things which I think the writer is suggesting are going on all the time: it's just that our ordinary processes of sense perception screen them out, and that man creates what he calls history as a means of disguising the Apocalypse from himself. So that Revelation, I think, is intended to mean exactly that this is the revelation of what is underneath what we think we are seeing.

We begin with the address to the seven churches of Asia, and you notice again the emphasis on what I've mentioned in connection with apocalyptic symbolism of the living stone [Lecture 7]. The reward for those who are faithful is a name engraved on a white stone, but the name engraved on the white stone is a symbol of the identity of the person himself: that is, the redeemed are transformed into stones in the temple, and as the temple is the body of Christ, the stones are as much alive as human beings are: in fact, they are themselves human beings. Similarly, later on in the book, an angel comes out, clad in a garment which the King James Bible translates as linen [15:6]. But there is much better textual authority for *lithon*, stone; and so it's clear that the city of gold and jewels that emerges at the end of the vision is intended to represent a city burning in the fire of life, in which the gold and precious burning stones are living and immortal beings. They burn, but they don't burn up, and the fire is not a torturing fire but an expression of their own spiritual energy, like the halo on a saint.

At the end of the third series, we have the opening of the temple, and the vision of the ark of the covenant. The word "ark" is connected with a recurrent image throughout the Bible that is made only by translation. In the Hebrew text, Noah's ark and the ark of the covenant are entirely different words, but the Septuagint uses the same word for both, *kibotos*, and the Vulgate uses *arca* for both, and that is where English gets its "ark."

So there occur sequences of historical cycles—"from ark to ark," to quote Robert Graves's Christmas poem—where you begin and end with a world sunk in water.[64] First of all, there is Noah's ark, which represents the end of one cycle, the antedeluvian civilization, and this seed containing all the forms of new life carried on top of the deluged world. Then we begin the Book of Exodus, where Moses escapes the slaughter of Hebrew firstborn by being concealed in an ark or chest in the bulrushes near the River Nile. Then Israel goes through the Red Sea and brings the ark of the covenant through the desert. And as I explained earlier [Lecture 10], the greatest triumph of David's reign, from the narrator's point of view, comes when he is bringing the ark of the covenant into Jerusalem [2 Samuel 6:1–19], which is symbolically, you remember, the highest point in the world; so that the ark of the covenant in the city of Jerusalem, and later on in the temple, is between heaven and earth, just as Noah's ark resting on Mount Ararat was also on the highest point of the world.

The New Testament begins with Christ born in the manger. In paintings of the Nativity you find an ox and an ass, which come from the opening of Isaiah [1:3], which speaks of the ass knowing his crib, his *phatne*, the same word that is translated as "manger" in the Gospel of Luke. That is a reminiscence of Noah's ark with the animals in it, and it is also the crib enclosing the infant of threatened birth, like the ark of Moses. So the opening of the temple and the vision of the ark of the covenant in the Book of Revelation complete that sequence of cycles built around this conception of the small chest which is the sacred place.

In the fourth series, the central apocalyptic vision, we get first of all an account of the birth of the Messiah. This account is the third one to appear in the New Testament, and as I said earlier [Lecture 5], it's the one that is so frankly and obviously mythical that there is no possibility of our ever getting it on our Christmas cards: it's simply one that has to stay by itself. It presents the birth of the Messiah under the myth of the birth threatened by a dragon that tries to eat the child. Those central visions end with the last harvest and the last vintage, which are the bread and the wine of a demonic Eucharist—that is, demonic in the sense that it is the expression of the wrath of God rather than of the communion with God: man does not eat the bread and the wine; man becomes the bread and the wine and is eaten by the powers of death. The vintage in particular, the identification of wine and blood, has a ready-made association with warfare. The imagery again is derived from Isaiah 63[:1–6], the image of the blood-soaked figure treading the winepress of wrath in the last day. That is a vision which came into the American consciousness through the hymn called the "Battle Hymn of the Republic," and the title of a book like *The Grapes of Wrath* indicates how deeply it has entered American consciousness.

You notice that in the sixth series, there is a prophecy of a millennium, which is nevertheless not the last thing to happen. The view of time in the Bible seems a remarkably childish one. In fact, it seems almost unbelievable that in the century of Galileo and Newton, the seventeenth century, there could still be archbishops working on the chronology of the Bible and deciding that the Creation of the world took place in 4004 B.C., and that consequently the world will come to an end in 1996. The six thousand years of history correspond to the six days of Creation, and the millennium corresponds to the Sabbath, the seventh day. It takes the form of a thousand-year rule of the Messiah. After that, the fun starts, and in 2996 we begin the war with Gog and the Last Judgment.

Now, what that amounts to, I think, is that the author of Revelation is trying to incorporate the whole dimension of time into his vision. So I think that the author of Revelation, in trying to describe the end of things, is also trying to put the entire category of time from Creation to the end of the millennium within a framework which actually transcends it. It is after the millennium that events take place which are in a sense the end of time, because they mark the progression of the human mind from the category of time to the eternal or spiritual world that is something else altogether.

We notice if we turn to the end of Revelation, the end of chapter 22, that when the final separation of things into a world of life and a world of death has been accomplished, and the tree and the water of life given to man in the beginning are now restored to him, there is finally the separation into a world of life and a world of death, and naturally nothing survives in a world of death. And in 22:10: "And he saith unto me, Seal not the sayings of the prophecy of this book: for the time is at hand." Two things in there: one of them is the conception of what might be called—I'm really using the word as a kind of coinage—an *apocryphon*, a secret book, the secretness being symbolized by the seals. There are references in Old Testament prophecy to a book which is sealed, laid up to be read and used when the time comes to read it. And a great deal of the vision of the Book of Revelation has to do with the removal of the seals of revelation, that is, the powers of repression or whatever it is that keeps you from seeing what is going on. The conception is of a book which is secret, not so much because it is kept secret as because the mind of the reader insists on making it a secret.

If you find that difficult to understand, there is a possible example: if you're the type of mentality that wants to censor books because you believe them to be evil, then you try to remove them from people so they can't get hold of them. And if you want something that really does reveal the whole depth and power and horror of evil, you go to something like Shakespeare's *Macbeth*. But the way to censor *Macbeth* is not to remove it from people, but to prescribe it for high schools. There, a self-imposed censorship is turned on it, you see, and makes of it a secret book. Similarly with the visions of the Book of Revelation, where the author symbolizes the fact that he is communicating revelation by the image of the seals being torn off a scroll, one after the other, the powers of repression being removed. Then he is told finally, "Now that you've written your book, don't seal that, because the time is at hand" [cf. 22:10]. The word "time," *kairos*, is a special word for time. It originally meant the notch of an arrow, and now means time in the sense of a special moment, as distinct from *chronos*, which is clock time. *Kairos* is the moment at which there is a passage opened from time into something above time; and that is what is meant by this recurring phrase in the Book of Revelation, "The time is at hand."

And then proceeds the commission to the author. Verse[s] 12[–13]: "Behold, I come quickly; and my reward is with me, to give every man according as his work shall be. I am Alpha and Omega, the beginning and the end, the first and the last." It seems that while Christianity uses the term "Word" in a very special sense when it talks about the "Word of God," nevertheless it is connected with our more ordinary uses of the term "word." Here, God is being described as the Alpha and the Omega, that is, the beginning and the end of all verbal possibilities, the totality of all the things that it is possible to express with words.

And then, verse[s] 16[–17]: "I Jesus have sent mine angel to testify unto you these things in the churches. I am the root and the offspring of David, and the bright and morning star. And the Spirit and the bride say, Come. And let him that heareth say, Come. And let him that is athirst come. And whosoever will, let him take the water of life freely." So that, although this is the end of the Bible, it is a remarkably open end. The implication seems to be that there are two kinds of apocalypse or revelation that he is talking about. One is the panoramic apocalypse, the things which you see in vision as the powers of repression come off your sense perception, and which, because it is panoramic, you see as objective to yourself. Then there is the possessed vision, the vision of the entire Bible that passes into your mind as soon as you have read the last word. That is what Milton calls, in his treatise on Christian doctrine, "the Word of God in the heart":[65] that is, the Bible possessed by the reader. And to that he gives a much higher authority than he gives to the Bible as book.

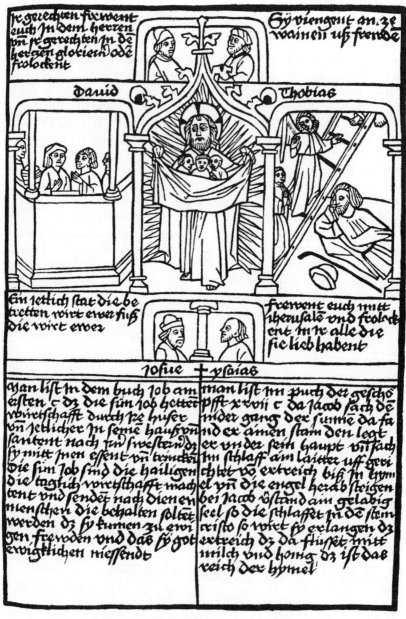

The text within the woodcut illustration (Middle High German):

Top left banner: ir gerechten fröwent euch in dem herzen vn ir gerechten in de hertzen gloriem oder frolockent

Top right banner: Sy vieng an ze wainen uß fröude

Left panel label: David

Right panel label: Thobias

Lower left banner: Ein iettlich stat die betrette wirt erwer fuß die wirt erwer

Lower right banner: fröwent euch mitt iherusale vnd frolockent in ir alle die sie lieb habent

Bottom center labels: Iosue + ysaias

Bottom left text column:
man list in dem buch Job am
ersten c daz die sün Job hetten
wirtschafft durch ire hüser
vn iettlicher in seine haus vnd
santent nach iren swestern dz
sy mitt jnen essent vn truncken
Die sün Job sind die hailigen
die taglich wirtschafft mach
tent vnd sendet nach dien en
menschen die behalten sölter
werden dz sy kumen zu ewi
gen fröuden vnd das sy got
ewigklichen niessendt

Bottom right text column:
man list in puch der geschö
pfst xxvii c da Jacob sach de
nider gang der sunne da fa
md er ainen stain den legt
er vnder sein haupt vn sach
im schlaff ain laitter uß geri
cht vo ertreich biß in hymel
vn die engel herab steigen
bei Jacob vffstand am gelabig
seel so die schlaffet in de stain
cristo so wirt sy erlangen dz
ertreich dz da flußet mitt
milch vnd honig dz ist das
reich der hymel

Biblia Pauperum 39: CHRIST GATHERS THE BLESSED
(Matthew 24:31; Psalm 68:19; Ephesians 4:1–16)

Feast of Job's children · Jacob's dream
(Job 1:4–5) · (Genesis 28:10–15)

Biblia Pauperum 40: REWARD OF THE BLESSED SOUL
(Revelation 2:10)

The Bride is crowned
(Song of Solomon 4:7–8
[Vulgate])

An angel summons John the Evangelist
to the heavenly Jerusalem
(Revelation 21:9–10)

24

The Language of Love

In the traditional use of words, there is a verbal structure, known as A, and a body of phenomena, B. Whenever you read anything, your mind is simultaneously going in two directions, centripetal and centrifugal. In the first place, you're trying to establish a context out of what you read: you're trying to find out what this word means *here*. At the same time you are recognizing the word or words as having conventional or generally agreed-on meanings in a world outside the book. So your mind is simultaneously seeking out what is in effect your memory of what those words mean. Now at a certain point, you may become aware that these meanings, these conventional meanings in the world outside, are forming a structure which is parallel to the structure of what you're reading. When that happens, what you are reading is descriptive in intention: its intention is to set up a verbal counterpart to whatever the words are describing. And in descriptive writing of this sort, the criterion of truth emerges. That is, truth here means truth of correspondence. You have a verbal structure A, you have a body of facts B, which it is describing, and if your verbal counterpart is a satisfactory replica of the body of facts it is describing, then you say it is true.

But sometimes you find that there is no external pattern which the words are describing at all. You are simply establishing a context and reading a structure of words for its own sake, and all the conventional meanings flow back into that verbal structure. That is a sign that what you are reading is literary in intention: and when the intention is literary, the criterion of truth by correspondence does not apply. Aristotle explained that by saying that the poet makes no particular statements, and it is only particular statements that can be true or false. The poet tells you things which are universally true and are therefore self-contained; so that with literary structures there is a barrier between A and B.

Then you find that literary structures can work on the emotions and on the imagination with a very peculiar degree of power. And eventually you realize that words can achieve descriptive truth only to a very limited extent. As long as you have one word, like "iron" or "silver," or any concrete term like that, it may be connected more or less permanently and definitively with something in the outside world which is described. But as soon as you have two or three words, you have started to elaborate a grammatical structure, and a grammatical structure is a fiction. It turns its back on the world outside and sets up its own conceptions of subject, predicate, and object. And so when you are discussing the truth as a verbal structure, you have to allow for the fact that the words conveying this truth are conveying it within their own self-contained structures. You might try to get out of it by saying the subjects and predicates and objects are in fact built into the nature of external reality. But eventually you discover that they are not.

The difference between these two kinds of structures could be illustrated by the difference between the words "story" and "history," which at one time were the same word. A history is a verbal structure which is supposed to be parallel with a body of events in the world outside. The historian makes particular statements, and they are judged as to whether they are true or false. In the story there is no such systematic external reference. The story is told for its own sake. Now applying this principle to the Bible, you find that the traditional view of the Bible is that the Bible is related to a group of phenomena external to it, historical events or concepts or doctrines, and that the Bible is literally true in the sense that it is a definitively accurate verbal counterpart of historical events outside it. That is what is often meant by the word "revelation," which means that something behind the Bible is shining through the Bible on the reader, who is here.

Now that view that the Bible is literally true in the sense of transmitting with definitive accuracy a body of phenomena behind it, was originally intended to exalt the Bible to a uniquely sacrosanct position. But by curious paradox it turned out to do exactly the opposite: that is, it turned the Bible into a servomechanism, into something which is subordinate to something else which is not the Bible. Now what is behind the Bible is not simply a record of historical facts or of doctrines, but ultimately, according to those who have been most deeply concerned with it, the presence of God. And traditionally in Christianity, the phrase "Word of God" is applied both to the Bible and to this thing which the Bible transmits as a revelation, the person of Christ.

At the same time, when you examine the language of the Bible, you begin to suspect that it was never intended to be a replica of facts outside itself, because words can express that kind of truth only vaguely and approximately, as we've just seen. What words do most powerfully and most accurately and most persuasively is to hang together. When we look at the words of the Bible, we find that they do not have the qualities that we would expect from definitively lucid descriptive writing. That is, although nobody would call the Bible a poem, nevertheless it is full of poetic language, of figures like metaphor and simile and metonymy and hyperbole, all the elements of language that relate words to one another instead of to a world outside. Therefore, what the Bible seems to be doing is insisting on its own authority and autonomy as a work. It is cutting us off from anything which is behind itself, and whatever it is presenting, it is presenting as something inside itself. As long as we think of the Word of God as a book transmitting the Word of God as the Person of Christ, as something outside it, then the two aspects of the phrase "Word of God" are simply illogically and ungrammatically related. But if what the Bible transmits is not separable from the Bible, then at least it makes grammatical and logical sense.

Now along with that traditional view of literal meaning came the view that the writers of the Bible were writing essentially from dictation: that they were essentially holy tape recorders who were writing through some kind of external impulse over which they had very limited control. Now if there is one thing that the scholarship of the Bible seems to have established beyond any reasonable doubt, it is that authorship counts for very little in the Bible. We have always traditionally thought, for example, of the author of the third Gospel as Luke; but with the possible exception of the first four verses of Luke, there is not a word in the Gospel of Luke of which Luke is in any modern sense the author. According to what is still the general theory, Luke used Mark and another document of the sayings of Christ which the scholars call Q, which he shared with Matthew, and he also has some material of his own, some of the parables and some of the hymns, like the "Magnificat" and the "Nunc Dimittis," which he is most unlikely to have been the original composer of. So that Luke, like practically all the books in the Bible, is an edited, compiled, composite document.

And so if the Bible is to be regarded as inspired in any sense whatever, sacred or secular, then all the glossing and all the editing and all the redacting and all the splicing and all the editing processes have to be taken as inspired too, because there is no way to distinguish the voice of God from the voice of the Deuteronomic redactor.

This kind of editing and compiling and conflating is a highly conscious and deliberate practice. So whatever the authors of the Gospels were doing, they were certainly not working in a trance. They were working with their minds extremely agile and alert. There isn't a page of the Bible where the editing process is not utterly obvious. In the first five books of the Bible, there are four or five major documents generally distinguished by the different uses they make of the word "God": one of them is called the J account, because it refers to God as Jahweh, and another is called an E account because it refers to God as Elohim: and then there's a Priestly document and so on. And we also notice that certain editorial changes occur. In the book of Samuel we are told that God was angry with David and therefore tempted him to take a census so he would have an excuse for bringing a famine on him [2 Samuel 24:1]. Well, the Chronicler, who was basing his work on Samuel but writing later, is uncomfortable with this, and so changes "God" to "Satan," so that it was Satan who tempted David to take the census [1 Chronicles 21:1]. And in Mark, which is almost always regarded as earlier than Matthew and Luke, Jesus looks around the crowd "with anger" [3:5]. Matthew and Luke transcribe this sentence, but they leave out the words "with anger" [Matthew 12:13; Luke 6:10]. The conception of a God superior to anger is obviously taking shape. There are hundreds and hundreds of signs of editing and glossing in the Bible of that kind.

Then of course there is also what has been forming very largely the bulk of this course, the tremendous amount of self-reference within the Bible, of typological structure, which says the only proof that the gospel story is true is that it fulfils the prophecies of the Old Testament, and the only proof that the prophecies of the Old Testament are true is that they are fulfilled by the gospel, that in other words all evidence is hermetically sealed within the Bible itself. There is no evidence worth anything that Jesus had any historical existence outside the New Testament; and it's obvious that the writers of the New Testament preferred it that way, because they could easily have collected such evidence if they had wanted it. They didn't want it.

What I'm suggesting is that what the Bible means literally is what it says. That is, the answer to the question, What does the Bible literally mean? is always the same. The Bible literally means just what it says.

But there are two ways of applying that answer. One is to make an immediate jump from what the text of the Bible tells you to what you guess about the historical event, or whatever, behind it. The other is simply to accept the Word in the Bible and gain your understanding of its meaning in the way that we gain understanding of all meaning, through its context in the Bible itself. And so the presence of God comes to us not in the form of a history transmitted through a book, but in the form of a story in which the book itself is autonomous and definitive.

The only time you can take the word "literal" seriously is when you read something in the same way that you read a poem, where you accept every word that is given to you without question but do not make any premature association between every word and something in the world outside. That is, your whole attention is directed towards putting the words together. And that is why, as I tried to explain in commenting on the Book of Revelation [Lecture 23], while the Bible does come to an end, and quite a well-marked end, it is nevertheless a remarkably open end. It adds a few verses at the end saying, this is it, there are no more books. Just before that, there is the invitation to drink of the water of life, which means that the reality beyond the Bible is not behind the Bible but in front of it, and starts in the reader's mind.

The reader in his turn is one of a society of readers. The point of view that I'm trying to express has nothing original about it. It's the view, for example, of John Milton, who speaks of the Word of God in the reader's heart as having an authority superior to that of the Bible itself. And if you say to Milton, Well then, how do you avoid the chaos of private judgment, of every individual reader setting himself up as the judge of what the Bible says? Milton would say that the reader is not an ego, he is not a self-contained individual; he is a man with a socially and culturally determined consciousness; and behind that consciousness, according to Milton, there is the real reader of the Bible, who for Milton is the Holy Spirit. Whatever one thinks of that as a doctrine, nevertheless the general principle is I think true, that by eliminating what critics call the referentiality of the Bible, you are at the same time eliminating what is private and egocentric and subjective in the reader's mind. It would take another course to explain that sentence fully, but the point is that when you have a structure of words of this kind, the ordinary gap in experience between the subject, who is here, and the object, which is there, disappears. You have something in the middle that becomes both subjective and objective.

The Bible is a structure of fiction and a structure of syntax, I think, rather than of meanings. When the Bible becomes an instrument of

social authority as it was through the Middle Ages and the Reformation period, then it becomes extremely important to enclose the Bible in
an interpretation which will provide people with the right way of
understanding the Bible. And they understand the Bible through this
interpretation, or else. But the interpretation is really one of the obstacles a society puts in to deflect us from the reality of what it is. It's as
though you had a kernel of a nut and then went around looking for a
shell to put it in, which is an extremely perverse approach to nuts. But
that's what happens when you have an artefact like the Bible and then
look for an interpretation to put around it as a means of imposing
uniformity and authority on society.

The Bible occupies socially and culturally a privileged position among
other books, but the principles don't work when you put the Bible into
a nonprivileged position. They won't work when you put it into a
privileged position either, unless the same essential principles work for
any work which is an artefact. The language of the Bible is fundamentally what the German theologian Rudolf Bultmann calls *kerygma*, which
is a Greek word meaning "proclamation."[66] That is, the language of the
Bible is rhetorical language, and rhetoric always uses the figures of
speech that you find in poetic language. But it's rhetoric of a very
particular and unique kind. It's not the orator's rhetoric which is designed to persuade you of something. The word "proclamation" suggests that within this typical structure there is something which is not
yourself, that you have to fight with the way Jacob fought with the angel.

Now the language in which this proclamation is contained is the
language of myth, and by myth, as we saw, we meant the self-contained
narrative unit, the story, rather than the narrative unit related to something else, or the history. Bultmann decided to talk about demythologizing the Bible, which is like removing the skin and bones from the
body. I don't understand the twentieth-century attraction for these
antiseptic-sounding words beginning with "de." I don't know why
Bultmann speaks of demythologizing the Bible when he means
remythologizing it. And I don't understand in literary criticism why
Derrida speaks of deconstruction when what he means is reconstruction. But that's just original sin.

The *kerygma* or proclamation of the Bible is not the same thing as a
literary story in the way that Homer is a literary story, but it is conveyed
in that language. It is impossible to demythologize the Gospels because
every syllable of the Gospels was written in myth.

It's notable that in the later parts of the New Testament like the
Pastoral Epistles, which are made out of Pauline materials after Paul's

death, the Bible is getting sufficiently self-conscious to talk about itself; and in the New Testament the Word of God is spoken of as though it were a dialectic. That is, Jesus said he came not to bring peace but a sword [Matthew 10:34], and similarly the Word of God is spoken of as a two-edged sword, and as dividing the word of truth [Hebrews 4:12]. But that kind of dialectic seems to be very different in its application from the usual aggressive or thesis dialectic, the argument dialectic which you have in so many philosophers, and there are no true rational arguments in the Bible. There are passages in the Epistle to the Hebrews that look like them, but they all turn out to be various disguises for proclamation. The Bible is not interested in arguing, because if you state a thesis of belief you have already stated its opposite; if you say, I believe in God, you have already suggested the possibility of not believing in him. In that kind of dialectic, every statement is really a half statement which needs its opposite to complete itself. And so that's not what is meant—I don't see how it can be what is meant—by saying that the Word of God is a dividing thing.

What I think it divides are the two elements of reality as they are exhibited in the New Testament, the elements that we call heaven and hell, the kingdom of life, the kingdom of death. It is that which is divided, and divided by an eternal separation. That means that the language of the Bible has to be a language which somehow bypasses argument and refutation. And again, it is very like the language of poetry, because, as Yeats says, you can refute Hegel but not the Song of Sixpence.[67] You can't argue the poetic statement because it is not a particular statement. It is not subject to verification. So that is why, I think, the Bible presents what it has to say within a narrative and within a body of concrete images which present a world for you to grasp, visualize, and understand. The end that it leads you to is in seeing what it means rather than in accepting or rejecting it, because by accepting it you have already defined the possibility of rejecting it.

So the Bible uses the language of symbolism and imagery because the language of symbolism and imagery, which bypasses argument and aggressiveness and at the same time clearly defines the difference between life and death, between freedom and slavery, between happiness and misery, is in short the language of love, and to St. Paul, that is likely to last longer than most other forms of human communication.

That's it. Thank you for your attention.

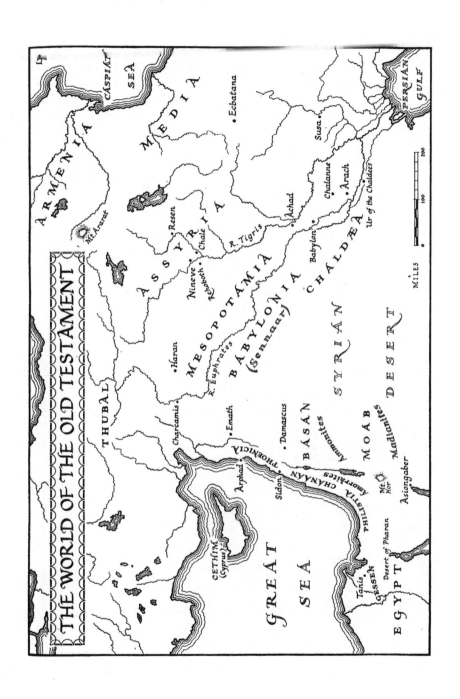

THE WORLD OF THE OLD TESTAMENT

ARMENIA

CASPIAN SEA

MEDIA

• Ecbatana

• Mt.Ararat

ASSYRIA

• Resen
Nineve • • Chale
• Rehoboth
R. Tigris

• Susa

• Achad

Babylon •

• Chalanne
• Arach

Ur of the Chaldees

MESOPOTAMIA

R. Euphrates

• Haran

BABYLONIA
(Sennaar)

CHALDEA

THUBAL

Charcamis •

• Emath

• Damascus

BASAN

SYRIAN

Arphad •

Sidon •

PHOENICIA

CHANAAN

Ammonites

Amorrites

MOAB

DESERT

CETHIM
(Cyprus)

PHILISTIA

Madianites

Mt.
Hor

GREAT

SEA

Desert of Pharan

Asiongaber

Tanis •

GESSEN

EGYPT

PERSIAN GULF

200

100

0
MILES

PALESTINE IN THE OLD TESTAMENT

Sidon
Sarephta
Tyre
Abel-Beth-Maacha
Lais or Dan
Hivites
DAN
Mt. Hermon
Damascus
R. ABANA
R. PHARPHAR
Gessurites

GREAT SEA

PHOENICIA
ASER
NEPHTHALI
Accho (Ptolemais)
Azor
Waters of Merom
MANASSES
Gaulon
Astaroth
LAKE GENERETH
Aphec

Mt. Carmel
ZABULON
Mt. Thabor
Endor
Dor
PLAIN OF ESDRAELON
Jezreel
ISSACHAR
Mt. Gelboe
Mageddo
Ramoth-Galaad

MANASSES
Dothain
Jabes-Galaad
Socoth
R. JABOC

Mt. Ebal
Sichem
Mt. Garizim
EPHRAIM
Silo
GAD
Ammonites

Joppe
Bethel
Hai
Rama
Machmas
Rabba
DAN
Accaron
Gabaon
Gabaa
Maspha
Jericho
Jazer
Jamnia
Cariathiarim
BENJAMIN
Galgal
Azotus
Thamnas
Jerusalem
Mt. Nebo
Eleale
Azeca
Bethlehem
Phasga Mts.
Hesebon
Ascalon
Adullam
Mambre
JUDA
Geth
Eglon
Lachis
Hebron
Bosor
RUBEN
Gaza
Engaddi
Dibon
Aroer
R. ARNON
Hethites
Amorrhites
DEAD SEA

Gerar
Siceleg
Bersabee
Ar
Philistine

SIMEON
MOAB
EDOM
Madianites

Amalekites

MILES
100
50
0

LP

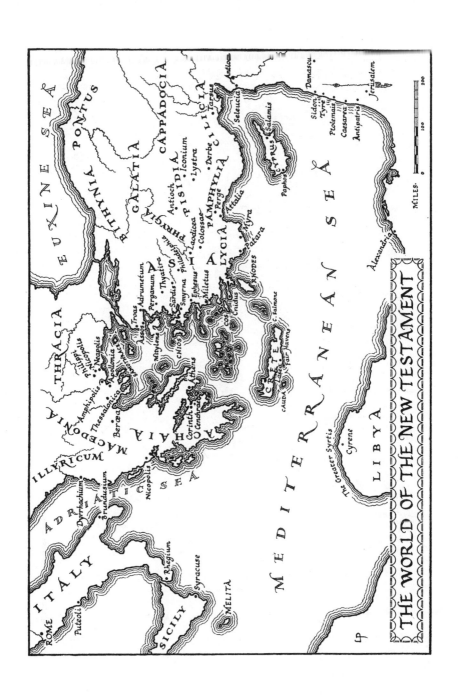

THE WORLD OF THE NEW TESTAMENT

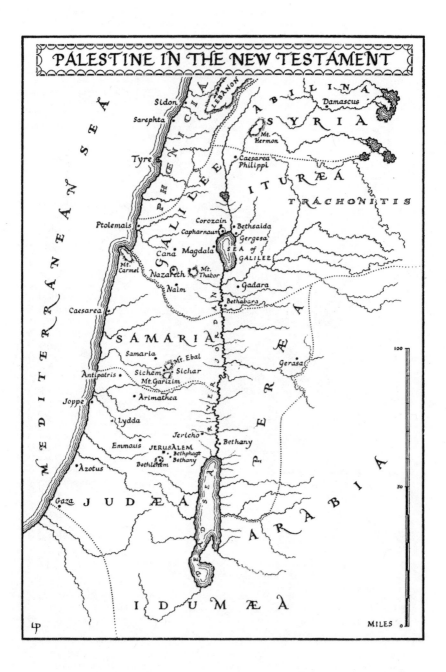

PALESTINE IN THE NEW TESTAMENT

MEDITERRANEAN SEA

Sidon

Sarephta

Tyre

PHŒNICIA

LEBANON

Mt. Hermon

Damascus

SYRIA

ABILINA

ITURÆA

Caesarea Philippi

TRACHONITIS

Ptolemais

Corozain

Capharnaum

Bethsaida

Gergesa

GALILEE

Cana

Magdala

SEA of GALILEE

Mt. Carmel

Nazareth

Mt. Thabor

Naim

Gadara

Bethabara

JORDAN

Caesarea

SAMARIA

Samaria

Mt. Ebal

Sichem

Sichar

Mt. Garizim

PERÆA

Gerasa

Antipatris

Arimathea

Joppe

RIVER

Lydda

Jericho

Bethany

Emmaus

JERUSALEM

Bethphage

Bethany

Azotus

Bethlehem

DEAD SEA

JUDÆA

Gaza

ARABIA

IDUMÆA

100

50

MILES 0

Note on the Illustrations

The *Biblia Pauperum* or "Bible of the Poor" circulated in manuscript during the Middle Ages; like a few other religious works, it began to be published in blockbook form in the Netherlands, especially between 1460 and 1490. As these decades see the end of Gutenberg's career (d. 1468) and the rise of printing from movable type, the blockbook, with each page imprinted from a single carved-out wooden block, looks from the present-day viewpoint like a transitional form between manuscript and modern printing; but for the purpose of the *Biblia Pauperum*, that of drawing out the central and permanent truth of the Bible's mass of stories, this laborious method uniting the sculptural and the simultaneous has its own appropriateness.

As is indicated by another of its titles, *Typos et Antitypos Veteris et Novi Testamenti*, "Type and Antitype of the Old and New Testament," the book lines up the "types" or prefigurative images from Old Testament history with their fulfilments in forty episodes usually from Christ's life and actions in the New Testament. (Frye discusses many of these types: see "Typology" in Index 4, also the chapter "Typology 1" in his *The Great Code*.) Each page offers a framed triptych or three-panel design: centrally an episode from the life of Christ, flanked, usually, by corresponding Old Testament scenes, with, above and below, Old Testament prophets as witness and corroboration. The surrounding text (Latin in most versions but German in this one, printed in Nuremberg in 1471) indicates the relevant passages from the Old Testament story, with verses from the prophets and a few added explanatory lines.

The horned Moses in nos. 6, 18, 25, and 26 requires a note. Where in the AV after Moses spoke with God on Mount Sinai his face shone (or sent forth beams [RV]), the Vulgate translates "his face was horned" (Exodus 34:29–35).

The title—perhaps once a nickname—*Biblia Pauperum* is not to be literally understood, as the books cannot have been cheap and "the poor" could not read; they were perhaps aids to meditation.

This version was reprinted at Weimar in 1906, and is used courtesy of Robarts Library, University of Toronto. Useful books on the *Biblia Pauperum* are:

Henry, Avril. *Biblia Pauperum: A Facsimile Edition.* Ithaca, N.Y.: Cornell University Press, 1987.

Labriola, Albert C. and John W. Smeltz. *The Bible of the Poor: A Facsimile and Edition of the British Library Blockbook C.9 d.2.* Pittsburgh, Penn.: Dusquesne University Press, 1990.

Where there is a choice among Gospel writers, the New Testament passage noted here (except for nos. 31, 32, 34) is the first, not necessarily the fullest, account in the sequence of the four.

1 Eve and the serpent (Genesis 3:1–7); ANNUNCIATION (Luke 1:26–38); Gideon's fleece (Judges 6:36–40)

2 Moses and the burning bush (Exodus 3); NATIVITY (Luke 2); Aaron's rod (Numbers 17)

3 David receives Abner (2 Samuel 3:1–21); EPIPHANY (Matthew 2:1–11); Solomon receives the Queen of Sheba (1 Kings 10:1–13)

4 Purification after childbirth (Leviticus 12); PRESENTATION OF CHRIST IN THE TEMPLE (Luke 2:22–39); Samuel dedicated to temple service (1 Samuel 1:24–8)

5 Rebecca sends Jacob to Laban (Genesis 28:11–46); FLIGHT INTO EGYPT (Matthew 2:13–14); Michal helps David escape (1 Samuel 19:9–17)

6 Moses and the golden calf (Exodus 32); EGYPTIAN IDOLS FALL (apocryphal: cf. Schneelmelcher 1:464–5); Dagon falls before the Ark (1 Samuel 5:1–5)

7 Saul has the priests killed (1 Samuel 22); MASSACRE OF THE INNOCENTS (Matthew 2:16–18); Athalia kills the princes of Judah (2 Kings 11:1)

8 David returns after Saul's death (2 Samuel 2:1 ff.); RETURN FROM EGYPT (Matthew 2:19–23); Return of Jacob (Genesis 32–3)

9 Israel crosses Red Sea (Exodus 14:15–31); BAPTISM OF CHRIST (Matthew 3:13–17); Scouts bring grapes from the brook Eshcol (Numbers 13:17–27)

10 Esau sells birthright (Genesis 25:21–34); TEMPTATION OF CHRIST (Matthew 4:1–11); Fall of Adam and Eve (Genesis 3:1–7)

11 Elijah raises widow's son (1 Kings 17:17–24); RAISING OF LAZARUS (John 11); Elisha revives child (2 Kings 4:8–37)

12 Abraham and the three angels (Genesis 18:1–22); TRANSFIGURATION (Matthew 17:1–13); Three young men in the furnace (Daniel 3)

13 David repents (2 Samuel 12:1–25); REPENTANCE OF MARY MAGDALENE (Matthew 26:7–13; partly legendary); Miriam repents (Numbers 12)

14 Women of Israel greet David (1 Samuel 18:6–9); ENTRY INTO JERUSALEM (Matthew 21:1–11); Sons of prophets honour Elisha (2 Kings 2:1–15)

15 Darius approves rebuilding of Temple (Ezra 5–6); CLEANSING OF THE TEMPLE (Matthew 21:12–13); Judas Maccabaeus cleanses Temple (1 Maccabees 4:36–59)

16 Joseph's brothers deceive Jacob (Genesis 37:12–35); PLOTTING AGAINST JESUS (Matthew 26:1–5); Absalom conspires against David (2 Samuel 15:1–12)

17 Joseph sold to Ishmaelites (Genesis 37:23–8); CHIEF PRIESTS PAY JUDAS (Matthew 26:14–16); Joseph sold to Potiphar (Genesis 37:36)

18 Melchisedek meets Abraham (Genesis 14:17–20; Hebrews 7:1–5); LAST SUPPER (Matthew 26:17–30); Fall of manna (Exodus 16)

19 Ahab sentences Micaiah to prison (2 Kings 22:1–38); CHRIST IN GETHSEMANE LEAVES THE DISCIPLES (Matthew 26:36); Elisha mocked for his prophecy (2 Kings 6:24–7:20)

20 Foolish virgins (Matthew 25:1–13); CHRIST RETURNS TO THE DISCIPLES (Matthew 26:37–45); Fall of rebel angels (Isaiah 14:10–15; Luke 10:18; Revelation 12:9)

21 Joab slays Abner (2 Samuel 3:22–30); BETRAYAL OF CHRIST (Matthew 26:45–52); Tryphon's treachery (1 Maccabees 12:39–52)

22 Jezebel threatens Elijah (1 Kings 19:1–3); CONDEMNATION OF CHRIST (Matthew 27:24); Daniel accused (Daniel 6)

23 Ham mocks Noah's nakedness (Genesis 9:20–7); MOCKING OF CHRIST (Matthew 27–31); Children mock Elisha (2 Kings 2:23–4)

24 Isaac carries wood (Genesis 22:3–9); CHRIST BEARING CROSS (John 19:17); Widow of Zarephath (Sarepta) (1 Kings 17:1–16)

25 Sacrifice of Isaac (Genesis 22:1–14); CRUCIFIXION (Matthew 27:33–54); Brazen serpent (Numbers 21:4–9; John 3:14–15)

26 Creation of Eve (Genesis 2:20–5); CHRIST'S SIDE PIERCED (John 19:34–7); Moses brings water from the rock (Exodus 17:1–7)

27 Joseph put in the well (Genesis 37:18–24); ENTOMBMENT (Matthew 27:57–61); Jonah cast overboard (Jonah 1)

28 David kills Goliath (1 Samuel 17); HARROWING OF HELL (apocryphal,

but cf. Psalm 107:8–16; Hosea 13:14; Ephesians 4:9–10; 1 Peter 3:18–19); Samson kills the lion (Judges 14:5–6)

29 Samson with the gates of Gaza (Judges 16:1–3); RESURRECTION (Matthew 28:1–10); Jonah released from the whale (Jonah 2)

30 Reuben looks for Joseph (Genesis 37:29); WOMEN AT THE SEPULCHRE (Mark 16:1–8); The Bride seeks her beloved (Song of Solomon 5:2–8)

31 Darius finds Daniel living (Daniel 6:18–23); CHRIST APPEARS TO MARY MAGDALENE (John 20:11–18); The Bride finds the Beloved (Song of Solomon 3:1–5)

32 Joseph revealed to his brothers (Genesis 45:1–15); CHRIST APPEARS TO THE DISCIPLES (Luke 24:36–49); Return of the Prodigal Son (Luke 15:20–4)

33 An angel appears to Gideon (Judges 6:11–24); DOUBTING THOMAS (John 20:24–9); Jacob wrestles with the angel (Genesis 32:24–32)

34 Enoch taken up (Genesis 5:24; Hebrews 11:5); ASCENSION (Acts 1:4–12); Elijah's ascent (2 Kings 2:1–13)

35 Moses receives the law (Genesis 24:12–18); PENTECOST (Acts 2); Fire consumes Elijah's sacrifice (1 Kings 18:17–40)

36 Solomon seats Bathsheba on his right hand (1 Kings 2:19); CORONATION OF THE VIRGIN (not Biblical—from 12th century; cf. no. 40, below); Ahasuerus makes Esther queen (Esther 2:17)

37 Judgment of Solomon (1 Kings 3:16–27); DOOMSDAY (Ecclesiastes 3:17; 2 Timothy 4:1); David condemns the Amalekite (2 Samuel 1:1–16)

38 Dathan and Abiram (Numbers 16); THE DAMNED TAKEN TO HELL (Matthew 5:29); Sodom and Gomorrah destroyed (Genesis 19:23–8)

39 Feast of Job's children (Job 1:4–5); CHRIST GATHERS THE BLESSED (Matthew 24:31; Psalm 68:19; Ephesians 4:1–16); Jacob's dream (Genesis 28:10–15)

40 The Bride is crowned (Song of Solomon 4:7–8 [Vulgate]); REWARD OF THE BLESSED SOUL (Revelation 2:10); An angel summons John the Divine to the heavenly Jerusalem (Revelation 21:9–10)

Four plates from Blake's *Illustrations of the Book of Job* (Methuen, 1903), reproduced courtesy of Victoria University Library in the University of Toronto, have been used to accompany Lectures 18–20, on the Book of Job. Blake published the twenty-one plates in spring 1826. They are his last major work, as he died in August 1827. See further:

Frye, Northrop "Blake's Reading of the Book of Job." In *William Blake. Essays for S. Foster Damon.* Ed. Alvin H. Rosenfeld. Providence, R.I.: Brown University Press, 1969. 221–34.

1 Then went Satan forth from the presence of the Lord (pl. 5)
2 Let the Day perish wherein I was born (pl. 8)
3 Then the Lord answered Job out of the Whirlwind (pl. 13)
4 I have heard thee with the hearing of the Ear but now my Eye seeth thee (pl. 17)

The maps on pages 251–4 are reproduced from *The Holy Bible*, translated by R.A. Knox (London: Burns and Oates, 1955).

Notes

1 The first three of these four federated colleges at the University of Toronto were affiliated with religious traditions: Victoria, Methodist (later United Church of Canada); Trinity, Anglican; and St. Michael's, Roman Catholic. University College became the teaching arm of the university when it was secularized in 1849.

2 The American Revised Version was actually published in 1901.

3 Bruce M. Metzger was the editor for the New Testament; Herbert G. May edited the Old Testament.

4 Although Daniel does undergo something of a trial in Bel and the Dragon, he is depicted more as a clever detective than a lawyer.

5 This is recorded in the Book of James, or Protoevangelium, 4–5, and in the Gospel of Pseudo-Matthew 4.

6 The town of St. Anne de Beaupré is northeast of Quebec City on the St. Lawrence.

7 That is, the diagram of a series of connected U-shapes that NF had drawn on the blackboard, similar to the diagram in *GC*, 171.

8 Alexander the Great is alluded to in Daniel's second vision ("the great horn" in 8:8) and explicitly mentioned in 1 Maccabees 1:1–7 and 6:2.

9 More likely a statue to Zeus Olympios, the Greek version of the Syrian Baal Shamen. See 1 Maccabees 1:54, 2 Maccabees 6:2, and Daniel 11:31 and 12:11.

10 See n. 7, above.

11 *On the Trinity*, bk. 7, chap. 5, par. 12.

12 Victoria's comment was inspired by the Hon. Alexander Grantham (Alick) Yorke, one of her grooms-in-waiting, whose job was that of a court wit. He once told a risqué story to a German guest who laughed loudly, moving the queen to ask that the story be repeated. It was, and she wasn't amused.

Her "we" was not really the royal "we," as she was speaking for the affronted ladies of the court (*Notebooks of a Spinster Lady*, 2 January 1900).

13 There is some debate about the location of the Gihon. While Cush (RSV) is generally associated with both Ethiopia (AV) and Arabia, the Gihon may be a local river, the one flowing from Mount Zion in Jerusalem and originating from the Gihon spring, just to the west of Manasseh's Wall in Old Testament times.

14 " ... let thy Holy Spirit lead us in holiness and righteousness all our days; that, when we shall have served thee in our generation, we may be gathered unto our fathers, having the testimony of a good conscience; in the communion of the Catholic Church; in the confidence of a certain faith; in the comfort of a reasonable, religious, and holy hope" ("The Burial of the Dead: Rite 1," from *The Book of Common Prayer*).

15 *AC*, 143.

16 "There's no need for red-hot pokers. HELL IS—OTHER PEOPLE!" Garcin's remark to Inez and Estelle at the conclusion of Jean Paul Sartre's *No Exit*.

17 The reference is to the chart NF put on the blackboard, similar to the one in *GC*, 142.

18 See *Faust*, pt. 1, l. 4119, and George Macdonald, *Lilith* (1895).

19 Reaney's *Rachel* first appeared in his *One-man Masque*, produced in 1960 and published in *The Killdeer and Other Plays* (Toronto: Macmillan of Canada, 1962). *Rachel* was published as a single poem in *Poems: James Reaney*, ed. Germaine Warkentin (Toronto: New Press, 1972).

20 Most commonly the Virgin is balanced by St. John the Evangelist, the other person Christ spoke to from the cross, and who like Mary Magdalene traditionally wears red. After Giotto's Arena Chapel *Crucifixion* of 1300, Mary Magdalene, recognizable by her unveiled streaming hair, most often kneels at the cross's foot. But see, for example, pl. 443 in Gertrud Schiller's *Iconography of Christian Art*, trans. Janet Seligman (Greenwich, Conn.: New York Graphic Society, 1971), vol. 2 (not in colour) and Raphael's *Mond Crucifixion* in the National Gallery, London (where, not exceptionally, the "red" garment is pink).

21 See W.B. Yeats, *A Vision*, rev. ed. (New York: Collier, 1966).

22 That is, the pastoral, agricultural, and urban phases.

23 See Sir James Frazer, *The Golden Bough*, 12 vols. (London: Macmillan, 1907–15). See especially *The Dying God* (pt. 3) and *Adonis, Attis, Osiris* (pt. 4, vols. 1–2)

24 In this quotation NF substitutes "womb" for the AV's "matrix."

25 Although the distinction is not always clear, as a general rule we have

used upper case when "Leviathan" refers to the name of a particular beast and lower case plus article—"the leviathan"—to refer to the beast generically. An exception to this rule occurs in quotations from the AV, where lower case is used; however, the RSV, NRSV (New Revised Standard Version), NIV (New International Version), and NEB (New English Bible) all use upper case in the same passages.

26 The lines from the first hymn are a translation of the opening lines of the *Exsultet*: "Haec sunt enim festa paschalia, / in quibus verus ille Agnus occiditur, / cuius sanguine postes fidelium / consecrantur. / Haec nox est, / in qua primum patres nostros, filios Israel / eductos de Aegypto, Mare Rubrum sicco vestigio transire fecisti." For the second hymn NF has given a prose rendering of the third stanza of *Ad cenam Agni providi*: "Protecti paschae vespero / a devastante angelo, / de Pharaonis aspero / sumus erepti imperio" ("That Paschal Eve God's arm was bared, / the devastating Angel spared: / by strength of hand our hosts went free / from Pharaoh's ruthless tyranny," trans. John Mason Neale, 1851). The first hymn is not by St. Ambrose, though he expresses some of the same ideas in his Epistle 23, and similar themes are found in two Pseudo-Ambrose hymns (see Migne, *Patrologia Latina*, 16, 1179 f., and 1203 f.). The second hymn is also Pseudo-Ambrose.

27 A street on the north side of the Victoria University campus that would have been visible from the windows of the classroom on the third floor of the "Old Vic" building where NF was lecturing.

28 NF's paraphrase of Luke 23:17.

29 The argument is made by Marco Treves in "Two Acrostic Psalms," *Vetus Testamentum* 15 (1965): 86.

30 Hagar was actually a maidservant. Sarah, who was barren, offered her to Abraham in order that they might bear a child (Genesis 16:1–3).

31 See especially Hebrews 11.

32 In fact, as NF himself notes elsewhere (see *CR*, 34, or *NFR*, 55–6, and *GC*, 71), Augustine says precisely the opposite, attributing the remark to somebody else: "See, I answer him that asketh, 'What did God do before he made heaven and earth?' I answer, not as one is said to have done merrily, (eluding the pressure of the question), 'He was preparing a hell, (saith he) for pryers into mysteries.' ... I boldly say, 'that before God made heaven and earth, He did not make anything" (*Confessions*, trans. E.B. Pusey [London: Dent, 1932], 260–1 [bk. 11, chap. 12]).

33 "Then I saw that there was a way to heaven, even from the gates of heaven, as well as from the City of Destruction" (John Bunyan, *The Pilgrim's Progress*, rev. ed. [Harmondsworth, Eng.: Penguin, 1987], 217).

34 See NB 11e, n. 36. For the development of the point about Pynchon, see "Culture as Interpenetration," in *DG*, 17–18, and *DV*, 25–6, or *NFR*, 185–6.

35 Martin Heidegger, *An Introduction to Metaphysics*, trans. Ralph Manheim (New Haven, Conn.: Yale University Press, 1959), chap. 1. See also "The Origin of a Work of Art," in *Existence and Being*, ed. Werner Brock (Chicago: Regnery, 1949), 21–6.

36 NF uses this familiar distinction to refer to the difference between nature as a process of growth and nature as structure, order, or system. The two terms have medieval roots, but their modern usage in Schelling, Coleridge, and others descends from Spinoza's.

37 Bernard Shaw, *Maxims for Revolutionists* (1903), no. 152.

38 See Jacques Lacan, *Écrits: A Selection* (New York: Norton, 1977), 281 ff., and *GC*, 147–8. The phrase "lost phallus" comes from Freud's article "Fetishism" (1927): Lacan made it familiar, as NF notes in *GC*, 242. For Lacan, the phallus is the universal signifier of desire, and its loss or absence is experienced by both sexes.

39 NF's paraphrase of 1 Kings 20:23. He had actually not mentioned this passage earlier in the course.

40 "U" in Greek words that passed through Latin into modern languages regularly became "y" (as in our "dynamic," "hyper-," "tyrant"). Though many literate writers prefer "hubris"—brought in, like "hybris" slightly later, directly from Greek in recent times—the *Oxford English Dictionary* (2nd ed.) marks it, unlike "hybris," as "not naturalized, alien."

41 *The Presocratics*, ed. Philip Wheelwright (New York: Odyssey Press, 1966), 54.

42 Samuel Johnson, *Preface to Shakespeare*, in *Selected Writings*, ed. Patrick Cruttwell (Harmondsworth, Eng.: Penguin, 1986), 268–9.

43 "Art is man's nature," in "An Appeal from the New to the Old Whigs," in *The Writings and Speeches of Edmund Burke*, with introduction by W.G. Falconbridge, 12 vols., Beaconsfield edition (Toronto: Morang, 1901), 4:176.

44 In bk. 7 of the *Odyssey*, after Odysseus tells king Alcinoüs about his seven-year interlude with Calypso, he then reports that he has told the truth but that it has pained him to do so.

45 The references are to the well-known proverbs of Franklin in *Poor Richard's Almanack* (1732–58) and the less well-known maxims of Thomas Chandler Haliburton's Sam Slick papers, observations by a shrewd itinerant clockmaker that were eventually collected into eight volumes (1835–60).

46 James Boswell, *Life of Johnson* (New York: Dell, 1960), 78.

47 "He that spareth his rod hateth his son: but he that loveth him chasteneth him betimes" (Proverbs 13:24).

48 For the story of Ahikar, see *Ancient Near Eastern Texts Relating to the Old Testament*, ed. J.B. Pritchard, 3rd ed. (Princeton, N.J.: Princeton University Press, 1969).

49 Although the idea of playing does not appear in the AV or the RSV, it is explicit in the Douay-Rheims Bible: "I was with him forming all things: and was delighted every day, playing before him at all times; Playing in the world: and my delights were to be with the children of men" (Proverbs 8:30–1). In a slightly different context Johan Huizinga points to this translation in *Homo Ludens: A Study of the Play Element in Culture* (Boston: Beacon Press, 1955), 212.

50 That is, like the funeral panegyrics of the seventeenth-century theologian and orator Jacques-Bénigne Bossuet, known for his balanced, formal, and dignified rhetoric.

51 "The Ready and Easy Way to Establish a Free Commonwealth," in *John Milton: Complete Poems and Major Prose*, ed. Merritt Y. Hughes (New York: Odyssey, 1957), 898–9.

52 Ibid., 895–6.

53 "The pleasure we get from the rhetoric of the book of Job and its tragic picture of a bewildered soul cannot disguise the ignoble irrelevance of the retort of God with which it closes, or supply the need of such modern revelations as Shelley's Prometheus or The Niblung's Ring of Richard Wagner" (G.B. Shaw, "The Bible," in *A Treatise on Parents and Children* [1914], par. 1).

54 The incident is related, in slightly different words, in James R. Mellow, *Charmed Circle: Gertrude Stein and Company* (New York: Praeger, 1974), 468.

55 Arthur Rimbaud, letter to Georges Izambard, 13 May 1971, in *Rimbaud: Complete Works, Selected Letters*, trans. Wallace Fowlie (Chicago: University of Chicago Press, 1966), 304.

56 NF is apparently speaking of the passage in 1 Corinthians 2 where Paul distinguishes between what is known by the natural and the spiritual person, the *soma psychikos* and the *soma pneumatikos*.

57 NF replaces the AV's "God" with "heaven" in this quotation and throughout the following discussion.

58 Actually Yuri Gagarin, responding to a questioner on his return from the first manned space flight, 12 April 1962.

59 That is, the list of the phases of revelation.

60 "There is no power but of God, saith Paul, Rom. 13, as much as to say, God put it into man's heart to find out that way at first for common peace and preservation, approving the exercise therof" (*The Tenure of Kings and Magistrates*, Hughes, 758–9). Cf. *Paradise Regained*, bk. 1, ll. 460–4: "God

hath now sent his living Oracle / Into the World, to teach his final will, / And sends his Spirit of Truth henceforth to dwell / In pious Hearts, an inward Oracle / To all truth requisite for men to know." The Biblical source of the idea is in Psalm 119:11, in the parable of the sower in Luke 8:5–18, and elsewhere. See *GC*, 138.

61 G.B. Shaw, *The Quintessence of Ibsenism*, in *Major Critical Essays* (London: Constable, 1930), 155.

62 *Quid rides? Mutato nomine de te fabula narratur* (Why are you laughing? Change the name and the story is about you) (Horace, *Satires*, 1.1.69).

63 The analysis was not a part of the printed lectures but was included with the study guide for the twenty-ninth program (Lecture 23).

64 "Water to water, ark again to ark, / From woman back to woman" (*To Juan at the Winter Solstice*, ll. 13–14).

65 See n. 59, above.

66 See, e.g., Rudolf Bultmann, "New Testament and Mythology," in *Kerygma and Myth*, ed. Hans Werner Bartsch (New York: Harper and Row, 1961), 1–44.

67 "You can refute Hegel but not the Saint or the Song of Sixpence." William Butler Yeats in a letter to Lady Elizabeth Pelham, dated 4 January 1939—the last letter Yeats wrote; quoted in Richard Ellmann, *Yeats: The Man and the Masks* (New York: Dutton, 1948), 285.

The Bible and Further Readings

KJV   King James Bible (1611 with some later emendations)
AV   Authorized Version (same thing)
RV   Revised Version (OT 1884, NT 1881, Apocrypha 1895)
ASV   American Standard Version (1901)
RSV   Revised Standard Version (U.S.—OT 1952, NT 1946, Apocrypha 1957)
NEB   New English Bible (British 1970, with Apocrypha)
NIV   New International Version (U.S. 1973)
NRSV   New Revised Standard Version (U.S. 1989, with apocrypha)

See Stephen M. Sheeley and Robert N. Nash, Jr., *The Bible in English Translation: An Essential Guide* (Nashville: Abingdon Press, 1997).

The Bible: Authorized King James Version. Edited with introduction and notes by Robert Carroll and Stephen Prickett. Oxford: Oxford University Press, 1996 (World's Classics). Includes "The Translators to the Reader," "The Epistle Dedicatory," and the Apocrypha. Introduction and very compressed commentary, with a reach into cultural history, are broadly based, non-theological, and richly illuminating.

    Other recent Bible editions with valuable extras are the Oxford Annotated RSV (ed. May and Metzger) and NRSV (ed. Coogan et al.) and the NIV Study Bible (Zondervan).

Bible Atlases. Many available (amazon.com at time of writing lists 120): most are historically arranged, supplied with illustrations and charts, and packed with information. Very full and detailed is *Harper Atlas of the Bible*, ed. J.B. Pritchard (New York: Harper, 1987). Good but less elaborate are *Macmillan Bible Atlas* (rev. ed., 1977), closely tied to the Bible narrative up to the second century A.D.; *Holman Bible Atlas* (1998); *Oxford Bible Atlas*, with section on "Archaeology and the Bible" (1985); and *Atlas of the Bible and Christianity*, ed. Tim Dowley, with chapters on the early and the modern Church (1997). An outline version, adequate for most non-scholarly purposes and taking in "The Hellenistic World," "The New Testament," and "Modern Times," is *The Illustrated Bible Atlas*, with historical notes by F.F. Bruce (Jerusalem: Carta, 1994).

Charles, R.H. *The Apocrypha and Pseudepigrapha of the Old Testament in English.* 1913. Oxford: Clarendon Press, 1968. 2 vols.

Cruden, Alexander. *Cruden's Complete Concordance [to the Old and New Testaments].* 1737. London: Lutterworth Press, 2003. The ancestor of modern Bible concordances. Its late-nineteenth-century successors, notably those by Robert Young and James Strong (both likewise based on the AV), append the original Hebrew, Aramaic (Strong's "Chaldee"), and Greek vocabularies. Many concordances (cf. Zondervan's to the NIV) come in a range of modern editions.

James, Montague Rhodes, ed. and trans. *The Apocryphal New Testament, being the Apocryphal Gospels, Acts, Epistles, and Apocalypses.* Oxford: Clarendon Press, 1924.

Schneemelcher, Wilhelm, ed. *New Testament Apocrypha.* Eng. trans. ed. R. McL. Wilson. Louisville: John Knox, 1991. 2 vols.

Bobrick, Benson. *Wide as the Waters: The Story of the English Bible and the Revolution It Inspired.* New York: Simon and Schuster, 2001. From Wycliffe and the early struggles for an English Bible to the Revolution of 1689.

Cornfeld, Gaalya. *Archaeology of the Bible: Book by Book.* New York: Harper, 1976.

Daniell, David. *The Bible in English: Its History and Influence.* New Haven: Yale UP, 2003. 900-page coverage of the significnt translations through to the twentieth century with broad cultural range; discusses, e.g., Handel's *Messiah*, Blake, Holman Hunt, U.S. slavery, and U.S. "Jesus fiction" to *Ben Hur* (1880). Unusually informative illustrations and captions.

Finkelstein, Israel, and Neil Asher Silberman. *The Bible Unearthed: Archaeology's New Vision of Ancient Israel and the Origin of Its Sacred Texts.* New York: Free Press, 2001. Authors find Biblical narrative to be less history than "a brilliant product of the human imagination" and thus of universal import.

Friedman, Richard Elliott. *Who Wrote the Bible?* New York: Summit, 1987. An examination of how the earlier historical books, Genesis to 2 Chronicles, were put together and with what effect.

Gordon, Cyrus, and Gary A. Rendsburg. *The Bible and the Ancient Near East.* 1953. New York: Norton, 1997. Largely running comment on the historical books.

Mazar, Amihay. *Archaeology of the Land of the Bible, 10,000–586 BCE.* New York: Doubleday, 1992. (Anchor Bible Reference Library.)

McGrath, Alister E. *In the Beginning: The Story of the King James Bible and How It Changed a Nation, a Language and a Culture.* New York: Doubleday, 2001. Story of the KJV's creation, production, and dissemination, from the invention of the printing press and "the rise of English as a national language"; brief coverage thereafter to nineteenth century.

Nicolson, Adam. *God's Secretaries: The Making of the King James Bible.* New York: Harper Collins, 2003. [British title: *Power and Glory.*] Personalities and power politics, 1603–11.

Pearlman, Moshe. *Digging Up the Bible: The Stories behind the Great Archaeological Discoveries in the Holy Land.* London: Weidenfeld and Nicolson, 1980.

Dalley. Stephanie, ed. and trans. *Myths from Mesopotamia: The Creation, the Flood, Gilgamesh, and Others.* Oxford: Oxford University Press, 1999. (World's Classics.)

Frymer-Kensky, Tikva. *In the Wake of the Goddesses: Women, Culture, and the Biblical Transformation of Pagan Myth.* New York: Free Press, 1992.

Gray, John. *Near Eastern Mythology: Mesopotamia, Syria, Palestine.* London: Hamlyn, 1969. Text complemented by particularly splendid illustrations.

Jonas, Hans. *The Gnostic Religion: The Message of the Alien God and the Beginnings of Christianity.* 1958. Boston: Beacon Press, 2001.

Josephus. *Jewish Antiquities*, in *The New Complete Works of Josephus*, trans. William Whiston with commentary by Paul L. Maier. Grand Rapids, Mich.: Kregel Press, 1999. 47–663.

McCall, Henrietta. *Mesopotamian Myths.* Austin: University of Texas Press, 1990.

Pagels, Elaine. *The Gnostic Gospels.* New York: Random House, 1979.

Philo Judaeus (or "Philo of Alexandria"). *The Works of Philo, Complete and Unabridged*, trans. C.D. Yonge. Peabody, Mass.: Hendrickson, 1993.

Pritchard, J.B., ed. *Ancient Near Eastern Texts Relating to the Old Testament.* 1954. Princeton, N.J.: Princeton University Press, 1969.

Alter, Robert, and Frank Kermode, eds. *The Literary Guide to the Bible.* Cambridge, Mass.: Harvard University Press, 1987. Literary-critical exposition, in both book-by-book and general essays.

Caird, George. *Language and Imagery of the Bible.* London: Duckworth, 1980.

Frye, Northrop. *The Great Code: The Bible and Literature*. New York: Harcourt, Brace, Jovanovich, 1982. In effect an expanded and more structured version of these lectures.

Frye, Northrop. *Words with Power: Being a Second Study of the Bible and Literature*. San Diego: Harcourt, Brace, Jovanovich, 1992.

Frymer-Kensky, Tikva. *Reading the Women of the Bible*. New York: Schocken, 2002. A work of Jewish scholarship, so that in AV terms "Bible" means the Old Testament and some names have different forms, notably "Rivka" for Rebekah. Reads stories of Biblical women as "elastic, complex, ambiguous."

Josipovici, Gabriel. *The Book of God: A Response to the Bible*. New Haven, Conn.: Yale University Press, 1988. "... fresh and energetic, casting insights in all directions ..." N. Frye.

Norton, David. *A History of the English Bible as Literature*. Cambridge: Cambridge University Press, 2000. Compressed version of his 2-vol. 1993 *History of the Bible as Literature*. Study of the KJ and Revised versions with their background and influence: "an examination of the shifting relationships between religion and culture": engagingly written.

Prickett, Stephen. *Words and the Word: Language, Poetics, and Biblical Interpretation*. Cambridge: Cambridge University Press, 1986. Examines the historical and continuing "debate on the relationship of poetry to religious language."

Four Ages:
The Classical Myths

Jay Macpherson

I'll tell ye, 'tis not vain, nor fabulous
(Though so esteem'd by shallow ignorance),
What the sage Poets taught by the heav'nly Muse
Storied of old in high immortal verse
Of dire Chimaeras and enchanted Isles,
And rifted Rocks whose entrance leads to hell,
For such there be, but unbelief is blind.

Milton

Foreword

This book is organized chronologically, in four phases: creation and the coming of the gods; pastoral life and the ordering of the seasons; the adventures and the labours of the heroes; war, tragic tales, and decline into history. This scheme corresponds very roughly to that of the Classical Four Ages—hence the title. The title is intended to suggest that myths are ordinarily told in a sequence which, though not strictly historical, has some analogy to history. Some of the details of this analogy are indicated in a chart at the end.

Grateful acknowledgment for permission to reproduce the illustrations which appear on the pages indicated is made to the following: the executors of the late Sir Arthur Evans (for the illustrations on pages 343 and 347, from *The Palace of Minos* by Sir Arthur Evans); the Museum of Fine Arts, Boston (page 305); the Metropolitan Museum of Art, Rogers Fund, 1910 (page 363); the *Journal of Hellenic Studies* (pages 377 and 380); the *Journal of Hellenic Studies* and the British Museum (page 285); the Syndics of the Cambridge University Press (page 348, from *Zeus* by A.B. Cook; and pages 326, 352, 355, 361 from *Prolegomena to the Study of Greek Religion* by J.E. Harrison).

My warmest thanks are due to Kildare Dobbs, who suggested it; to Hope Arnott Lee, who encouraged and advised; to Clive Parsons, who dispelled difficulties and made it presentable; and to Northrop Frye, whose guidance supplied, among other things, and in much the words used above, the book's general shape. As of 2003, I am grateful also to Alvin Lee, general editor of the Collected Works of Northrop Frye, for suggesting the publication of this new edition; to Margaret Burgess, editorial assistant for the Collected Works, for her truly dedicated editing; to Emmet Robbins, for needed corrections; and to Constance Boldt, for updating the artwork.

J.M.

Sea-god

Introduction

"Myth" is a Greek word meaning story, especially a story about gods or heroes. We do not know exactly when and how these stories began to be told, but they come into literature first of all in the works of the early Greek poets Homer and Hesiod. The Greeks had no Bible, or single collection of sacred writings. Their sacred stories are not fixed in a single written version like those of the Jews, but are continually re-shaped by later poets and dramatists. Disputes arise about what the stories mean, whether they are "true" and if so in what sense; but they keep on being told, whatever different hearers may make of them.

Some generations later than Homer, when people began not just to tell the stories but also to ask what they "really" meant, the answers they found were of different kinds. Some thought that the gods and heroes were mortal men remembered after their death for remarkable deeds and gradually coming to be thought of as more than human—in other words, that the myths were really history. Others thought they were a kind of natural science: that Zeus the father-god did not just live in the sky but was the sky itself, and his wife Hera the air. Another kind of interpretation is moral, making the stories into examples of how the good man should behave. Here the hero's enemies all represent vices and temptations.

We have to remember that the myths are not all of the same kind, or even of the same age, and no one explanation will fit them all. Some do seem to refer to historical events. For example, though most of the Greek myths are about Zeus and his family, all the Greek writers know that before these "younger gods" arrived there were older generations of gods. When we are told that Zeus seized the throne of Heaven from his father Cronus, or that Apollo took over the shrine at Delphi from the earth-goddess, the stories suggest vague memories of how an older religion was displaced by a new one. Myths in which Greek heroes perform great actions in Troy, Crete, and Egypt remind us of those rich and powerful Mediterranean empires that were already in decline before Greek civilization arose.

Another view of the myths as history, which we might call anthropological, sees in some often-repeated incidents facts of primitive social life and ritual, perhaps glossed over or not understood by the storyteller. The Classical Greeks sacrificed animals to the gods, but certainly not human beings. But stories in which a youth or maiden connected with the fruitfulness of the earth dies or is carried away suggest that possibly the Greeks' remote ancestors put young human victims to death to ensure the yearly harvest. Again, the reader will be struck by the number of kings, in heaven as on earth, who try to make away with their children for fear of being supplanted by them. In many prehistoric societies, and very likely in early Greece as well, an ageing king would be killed by his successor before his strength began to decline, for the good of his people and the land.

We shall find also in the myths some explanations of natural events. Mount Etna in Sicily is a volcano because the dreadful monster Typhon is buried under it; his anger shakes the ground, and he vomits forth fire and molten rock. The Great Bear never sets into the western sea because the god of Ocean is angry with her. The earth is barren for half the year because the corn-mother Demeter is mourning for her daughter, the spring-maiden Persephone, hidden beneath the ground.

As for moral explanations, they are much harder to prove. A few of the myths can be told so as to bring out examples of virtue or the truths of religion, but it is doubtful that their first tellers thought of them in that way. Many of them, especially those in which the gods cheat, lie, kidnap, and seek vengeance, could hardly offer worse models of conduct. At the same time, we frequently meet figures who bear the names of moral or spiritual qualities: Metis (Counsel), Prometheus and Epimetheus (Forethought and Afterthought), Cupid and Psyche (Love and the Soul), and whose stories suggest allegorical or "deeper" meanings.

It was not until late in the Classical age that the most remarkable thing about the myths began to be discovered. By then the altars of the Greek and Roman gods were cold: Christianity had replaced their worship. Readers of the Bible and of other eastern literatures began to see striking resemblances between the myths of the Greeks and those of other peoples: a discovery both exciting and perplexing. Christian readers recognized familiar themes in the garden of the Hesperides, where a serpent twines about a marvellous tree; the destruction done to mankind by an apple and a woman, or by that other "all-gifted" woman with her fatal curiosity; Deucalion's flood; the dividing up of the world among three brothers; a maiden sacrificed by her father; a hero, born of a god and a mortal woman, who triumphs over death. Many explanations for such similarities were offered. Some thought that these were stories of the devils who ruled the world before Christ came into it and overthrew their power; others, that they were parodies of the truth put about by demons to lead the faithful astray. A more charitable view made them fragmentary and shadowy accounts of the truths that God revealed fully only in the Bible: thus Christians might read these fables of the heathen poets without harm and perhaps even with some profit.

In our own day explanations are still being sought for the similarities that exist among the myths of all peoples. Did all cultures take their rise from a single source—some Mesopotamian or ancient Indian valley? an Atlantis long gone under the western sea? perhaps the dark continent of Africa, or the still mysterious North? It may be a question for psychology: does the human imagination work by laws that are the same everywhere, producing the same stories again and again from the common materials of life—day and night, seed-time and harvest, fear, desire, and rest?

Whatever explanations we may give for their continuing power, these stories, among the oldest in the world, are still among the best. They have been so important to writers from Homer right down to the present that we can no more study literature without them than we can without the Bible, the fountain-head of Jewish and Christian tradition. Their meaning has been transformed from generation to generation and from writer to writer, but the old patterns and characters survive.

Myth is the most ancient kind of story-telling; and these tales from ancient Greece and Rome, along with those of the Bible and the later European folk tales like those collected in Germany by the brothers Grimm, remain the basis of our fiction. There are really very few stories, as we must all have thought at the movies. Or rather, there are any number of stories, but they are all based on a few kinds of plot: narratives of creation, transformation, and destruction, of love, loss, revenge, of friendship and conflict, of quest and disappointment and success.

There are also only a few basic settings: the heavenly world above the clouds, the underworld, and between them our own earth, whether paradisal and unspoiled or ravaged by greed, pride, and war. Myth makes far more use than modern fiction does of celestial and infernal settings, and its characters are mainly either gods or heroes with lesser but still superhuman powers. Apart from science fiction, which often seems startlingly close to fairy tale and myth, most modern novels and films are set firmly in the ordinary world and deal with characters whose powers are limited like our own. Nevertheless, in many the old patterns can still be traced out. The cruel father, the helpless princess, the brave rescuer, the child of mysterious origin, the wise old prophet, the curse, the quest, the fatal treasure—these may take as many forms as the shape-changing Old Man of the Sea, but like him they are indestructible, and like him they can tell the one who holds them fast something of where he is going and what he is.

Eros

I. In the Beginning

The Creation

In the beginning how the heavens and earth
Rose out of Chaos ...

Milton

In the beginning, before the heavens and the earth, all there was was Chaos, the dark and formless void. And after ages of time had passed, there appeared two tremendous beings, the most ancient goddess Night and her brother Erebus, the Depth. And from these two was born Eros, who is Love, the most powerful of all the gods.[1] After him arose Gaia, the great Earth-Mother, who brought forth from herself first the world we live on and then Uranus, the starry sky, that lies above and around her and is the eternal home of the blessed gods. Then subtle Eros brought the Earth-Mother and the Sky-Father together in love, and from them in the course of time were born a series of strange and monstrous creatures, the early births of time. First came the three brothers Gyes, Cottus, and Briareos, huger than mountains, fifty-headed and hundred-handed, terrifying to look upon. So at least thought their father Uranus, and he took them from their mother and shut them up in the dark places under the earth. Gaia next bore the three Cyclopes, the Wheel-Eyed ones, smaller than the Hundred-Handed but still giants, and each having a single round eye in the centre of his forehead. These too their father shut away in the earth, afraid less of their size and strength than of their skill at forging metal weapons, for they were the first smiths.

The last children of Gaia were the twelve Titans, six sons and six daughters, larger than mortal men but not monstrous, endowed with beauty and majesty. Then Gaia, weary of Uranus' cruel treatment of her other children, appealed to her Titan sons to avenge their sufferings. She offered them a sharp sickle of adamant,[2] the hardest of stones, with which to wound their father and drive him away. Only Cronus,[3] the youngest and bravest, dared attempt such a deed. He waited until night fell and Uranus came down to embrace Gaia; then he took the sickle and maimed his father, severing the embrace of Earth and Sky. Then Cronus ruled in his father's place over the whole world; but he would not release his monstrous elder brothers from their captivity under the earth.

The six Titan brothers took their six sisters for wives, and their progeny were the gods that fill the land and sea and air. To his oldest brother Oceanus,[4] Cronus gave the stream that girdles the earth, and his children were the deities of the water. His innumerable sons were the Rivers of the earth, and his daughters were the Nymphs of fountain, lake, and stream, as well as of the sea.[5] The Nymphs are a gentle and kindly race, beloved by gods and men; but one of them, whose name is Styx, the Hateful, is unlike the others. Her stream rises in a sunless underground cavern and her waters are chill and numbing to the heart. Even the gods if they swear by Styx fear to break their oath.

The most beautiful of Uranus' Titan children were the light-god Hyperion and his sister-wife Thea, who lived in a palace of clouds in the eastern sky and whose children were Helios the Sun, Selene the Moon, and Eos the Dawn. Eos became the mother of Phosphorus the Morning Star, Hesperus the Evening Star,[6] and the Planets, the wandering stars.[7] Her other children are Eurus, Zephyrus, Notus, and Boreas, the Four Winds that blow from east, west, south, and north.

The Golden Age

For during Saturn's ancient reign it's said
That all the world with goodness did abound:
All lovèd virtue, no man was afraid
Of force, ne fraud in wight was to be found:
No war was known, no dreadful trumpet's sound,

Peace universal reigned mongst men and beasts,
And all things freely grew out of the ground:
Justice sate high adored with solemn feasts,
And to all people did divide her dread behests.

Spenser

The long reign of Cronus, whom the Romans called Saturn,[8] was the happy time that the poets call the Golden Age.[9] It was then that men came into being, formed from earth mixed with rain-water by Prometheus, the wise son of the Titan Iapetus. He made them in the image of the gods, unlike the animals, standing erect and looking up to heaven. In those days the whole earth was a paradise, a land of eternal spring like the dwellings of the gods. The earth brought forth its produce without man's labour and unwounded by his sharp ploughshares; the rivers ran with milk and nectar, and honeydew dripped from the bitter oak. The animals lived at peace with one another and with man, and man was at peace with his neighbour. Metals and precious stones slept undisturbed in the ground; there was no war, no commerce, and no need for courts of law.

The men of the Golden Age lived innocently, honouring the gods, and they died peacefully without sickness or creeping age. There were as yet no women on the earth, and so the good race passed away without leaving children; but their spirits inhabit the middle air between earth and heaven and watch in love and benevolence over the righteous, blessing their flocks and fields. After they had gone, loss and change began to enter the world, which now endured progressively worse ages, the Silver, the Brazen, and the harsh Age of Iron. In the Silver Age began the four seasons as we know them, with their succession of heat and cold. In those days men began to build shelters and to sow corn in the ground, harnessing bullocks to the yoke. The men of the Silver Age were foolish and impious, and Zeus, Cronus' successor, destroyed them because they would not honour the gods. Then he created a third race, the men of bronze, who cared for nothing but warfare and died by their own violence. Last came the present race, the men of iron; these too in their turn shall Zeus destroy, say the poets.

War in Heaven

Who stands secure? Are even Gods so safe?
Jupiter that just now is dominant—
Are there not ancient dismal tales how once

A predecessor reigned ere Saturn came,
And who can say if Jupiter be last?
                                        Browning

When Cronus drove away his father, Uranus had cursed him, saying that he should in turn be overthrown by his own children. Through all the long years of his happy reign, this remembrance troubled Cronus and disturbed his peace. Every time his wife Rhea bore him a child, he took it from her and swallowed it, in order to defeat the prophecy. After he had swallowed in this way her first five children, Hestia, Demeter, Hera, Hades, and Poseidon, Rhea resolved that the sixth child should escape the fate of the others, and she went for counsel to her mother Earth. On Earth's advice she hid herself from Cronus in a cave of Mount Ida on the island of Crete, where she was delivered of a male child, whom she called Zeus. She left him with the Nymphs of the mountains to be nursed, and returned to Cronus. With her she brought a large smooth stone from the mountain-side, and this she wrapped in swaddling clothes and gave to Cronus, telling him that this was the latest born of her sons. Cronus, suspecting nothing, swallowed the stone as he had done his children.

Meanwhile the infant Zeus grew and flourished, nursed by the kind Nymphs and by a stranger foster-mother, the silky-white she-goat Amalthea, who gave him milk and played with him. There is a story that one day the little god grasped her horn too roughly and broke it off. He immediately made a new one grow in its place, and the old horn he gave to the Nymphs in thanks for their care, promising that they should always find it full of whatever foods they most wished for, fruit and grain and honey and every other good thing. The Nymphs treasured the gift of Zeus, which was called the Horn of Plenty (Latin, *cornucopia*).

The other friends of Zeus in the Cretan cave were a band of armed youths called the Curetes, warriors born from the earth who entertained him with leaping dances, clashing their spears against their shields when necessary to drown the noise of his crying, for fear Cronus should hear it from his high palace.

When Zeus had come to manhood, Gaia sent to him Metis, "Counsel," one of the daughters of Oceanus, who told him the time had come for him to avenge the wrongs done by his father. Acting on her instructions, he came to Cronus' golden palace and introduced himself as a stranger. When Cronus was far gone in wine, Zeus slipped into his cup a powerful herb that Metis had given him from Earth. No sooner had Cronus swallowed it than he vomited up first Rhea's stone, then his five elder children, all now full-grown. His brothers Hades and Poseidon joined to help Zeus bind their father in chains; but Cronus called aloud for his Titan brothers, who came running to attack the young intruders. The younger gods, seeing the Titans advancing on them, fled out of heaven to the top of Mount Olympus above the clouds, where they gathered their forces for the war that must follow.

For ten years war was waged between the younger gods and the Titans, and still the issue hung undecided. Finally Zeus, weary of the useless struggle, set out to consult the wisdom of Mother Earth at her mysterious oracle in the Pythonian cave. The words that came to him were clear, but their meaning was obscure: "Let him who would conquer in the war first set free those imprisoned in Tartarus." Zeus knew nothing of the events that had taken place in heaven before he was born, nor did he know that Gaia still hated Cronus for leaving her elder children in captivity, so he was puzzled by her message.

It happened that among the Titans there was one, the wise Prometheus, who would not fight on the side of the elder gods. He of all the living saw deepest into the secrets of time, and he knew that the reign of Cronus was running out and would soon give place to that of the Olympians. First he tried unsuccessfully to persuade his father and brothers to lay down their arms. Then, rather than fight against them himself, he came to Zeus and offered to interpret to him the oracle of Earth. When Zeus understood all that had gone before, he descended with Prometheus to the underworld, soon reaching the gate of brass-walled Tartarus, the dreadful place where Gaia's monstrous children lay imprisoned. The entrance was guarded by a she-serpent, which Zeus killed. He brought the Cyclopes back to the upper world to help him against the Titans, and the Hundred-Handed with them, but only after he had made them swear to go and live beyond the farthest bounds of the ocean, so terrifying was their destructive power.

The Cyclopes immediately set up a smithy in the depths of Etna the Sicilian volcano; and the sky above soon flared red as they hammered out gifts for their friend Zeus and his brothers. To the eldest, Poseidon, they gave a trident[10] with three sharp prongs of adamant; to the second, Hades,[11] a helmet of invisibility; and to Zeus himself, the thunderbolts that tear through all resistance and make him dreaded by gods and men. It is on this tremendous weapon that his power mainly rests, and he alone has the secret and the use of it.

Armed with their three gifts, the Olympians once more advanced to the assault on heaven. This time they were crushingly successful: the Titans could not stand against the new weapons, but fled thunder-scarred out over the battlements and plunged into the depths below. The Olympians pursued them, giving all they captured into the charge of the Hundred-Handed, who stowed them away in those very under-world caverns from which they themselves had just been released. A remnant of the Titanic forces, Cronus and a few followers, got away to a high mountain in Northern Greece, where they held out for a time, sheltering in caves from the dreaded thunderbolts; but at last they were routed out of this stronghold and fled away over the sea, finding a haven, some say, in sunny Italy before the Romans were ever thought of. Others say that the hunted king came to rest only among the mists and glooms of Britain, far on the ocean's remotest verge. No stories tell his end.

In the last flight one prisoner was taken: Atlas, a brother of Prometheus, a giant of great strength. Zeus ordained as his punishment that he should stand at the western edge of the world bearing on his shoulders the weight of the sky. No wonder his name is thought to mean "he who suffers."

The Reign of Zeus

> At Heaven's door
> Look in, and see each blissful deity
> How he before the thunderous throne doth lie,
> Listening to what unshorn Apollo sings
> To the touch of golden wires, while Hebe brings
> Immortal nectar to her kingly sire.
>
> Milton

Zeus and his brothers ruled earth and Mount Olympus together, and they cast lots for the rest of the world. Zeus won for his share the air and sky, from which he takes his title of Cloud-gatherer. Poseidon the Earth-shaker rules the sea, and Hades the dark realms under the earth. Besides being the sky-god, Zeus was the guardian of law and order on earth, upholding fatherly and kingly authority and protecting travel-lers and guests. Of his sisters, the most famous is his queen Hera, the patron of marriage. Another, Hestia, was the guardian of the sacred fire in heaven and of the hearth, the centre of family worship, in homes on earth.

Most of the other Olympian gods[12] were children of Zeus. An earlier wife of his was his adviser, the goddess Metis. Fearing the prophecy that one of his children would one day overthrow him in his turn, he took the precaution of swallowing Metis, whose daughter Athene when she was ready to be born sprang out through the top of her father's head. Some say she was wearing full armour at the time. Athene was a warrior-maiden, the patroness of Athens, and she inherited her mother's wisdom.

Throned Zeus

Jealous of Zeus' having apparently produced a child all by himself, Hera, calling on Earth to help her, brought forth a son without a father, the smith-god Hephaestus. But Hephaestus was born lame, and his mother in disgust threw him out of heaven. Or, as another story has it, he took his mother's side in a quarrel with Zeus, who threw him over the heavenly threshold. All day from morning to night he fell, until he struck earth on the island of Lemnos,[13] where after he recovered he built an underground forge. Later he was gladly welcomed back into heaven, on account of his marvellous skill. Another of Hera's children was the goddess Hebe, the cup-bearer at the celestial feasts.

Phoebus Apollo and the huntress Artemis were Zeus' children by the Titaness Leto, who before their birth fled all over the Mediterranean looking for a place where she could escape the jealous anger of Hera. The island of Delos offered her shelter, but even then Hera would not let the birth-goddess Eileithyia go and attend her until all the other

goddesses insisted. Then at last her twins were born, and Apollo built a
temple on Delos as a reward for its kindness.

Hermes the swift messenger, the son of Zeus by the nymph Maia,
was a tricky and precocious child. On the day of his birth he invented
the lyre[14] by stretching sinews on a frame whose base was a tortoise
shell.[15] Then he went for a stroll in the country and drove off fifty cattle
that belonged to Apollo, making them walk backwards to deceive any
pursuer. Having shut them up safely, he tucked himself back into his
cradle, where Apollo found him. Accused of the theft, he pretended to
be too young even to know what cattle were. But Apollo was not taken
in, and he would have punished the guileful baby severely if Hermes
had not given him the lyre as payment for the cows. This was the first
act of barter, and it established Hermes as the god of merchants as well
as of thieves.

Aphrodite, the goddess of love delighting in laughter, was born from
the foam of the sea near the island of Cythera and came ashore at
Cyprus. Both islands remained sacred to her. She was the wife of

Aphrodite attended by the Loves

Hephaestus, but preferred the war-god Ares, the turbulent son of Zeus and Hera.

These twelve great Olympian gods were not the only dwellers in heaven. Zeus had a third sister, the corn-mother Demeter, who watched over the fruitfulness of the earth. A son of Zeus was the vine-god Dionysus, a graceful young man attended by a drunken old fellow, Silenus, who called himself his tutor. Hermes' goat-footed, goat-horned son Pan chose to live on earth rather than in the halls of the gods. His home was in the woods and fields of Arcadia, where he played on his pipes to the nymphs and satyrs[16] and was worshipped at rural altars as the god of shepherds and goatherds.

Prometheus

Or, like the thief of fire from heaven,
Wilt thou withstand the shock?
And share with him—the unforgiven—
His vulture[17] and his rock?

Byron

For a long time after the earth appeared, its hills and valleys and broad meadows lay untenanted, except for the nymphs and the satyrs, godlings of the countryside, who danced and played and chased one another in forest and field. We have seen already how Prometheus at last created man. A different story tells how the gods charged with the task not only Prometheus but also his brother Epimetheus. Since the name of Prometheus means "he who thinks before" and that of his brother, "he who thinks afterwards," it seems that Epimetheus did not have all his brother's wisdom. He began with the creation of the animals; and he was so lavish with the gifts he gave them—gifts of strength and speed and cunning, strong claws and sharp teeth, warm coverings of feathers and fur—that there was nothing left over for man, his poor shivering last creation. So Epimetheus called upon his wise brother to repair the mistake. Prometheus not only made man upright and beautiful, but he decided to use his craft to win extra advantages for man from Zeus, the king of the gods. Once when gods and men had met together, Prometheus cut up a great ox for them all to feast on. Dividing the body into two portions, he wrapped all the good meat up in the skin so that it looked very unappetizing, but the bones he set apart, covering them over with fat. Then he asked Zeus which portion he would take for himself and his fellow-gods. Zeus, deceived by the rich look of the glistening fat, chose with it the heap of bones that it concealed; and from then on when men killed cattle to eat, it was the bones that they sacrificed to the gods, keeping the meat for themselves.

When Zeus saw that he had been outwitted, he was angry, and in revenge he refused to give mankind the gift Prometheus wanted for them, the precious blessing of fire, but jealously guarded it in his heavenly halls. The friend of man, undaunted, went up to Olympus and stole away a flickering flame in a hollow stalk of fennel to give to the helpless race of mortals in place of the animals' strength and speed, sharp teeth, and warm skins.

Then Zeus looked down from Olympus and saw everywhere on the broad earth the far-shining fires, and his anger against Prometheus knew no bounds. He sent two of his strong servants to bind him to a rock in the Caucasus Mountains, where he lay for long ages stretched out, held down by his chains, exposed alike to hot sun and fierce winds and piercing cold. To increase his torments, Zeus sent an eagle to tear continually at his liver; and because the Titan was immortal like Zeus himself, his sufferings were to be without end.

There was a third reason for Zeus' cruelty besides Prometheus' two victories over him. When Prometheus had helped Zeus against Cronus and the other Titans, it was not because he thought Zeus' reign would be any more just than the reigns of Cronus and Uranus before him, but because he alone of all the dwellers in heaven knew the secrets of Fate, and he saw that it was of no use to struggle against what was to come. The Fates are three sisters, Clotho, Lachesis, and Atropos, the daughters of Night, who sit in a cave spinning the thread of man's life. The first sister spins the thread, the second draws it out, and the third, the most dreaded, is she who cuts it off. Prometheus, who was admitted to their counsels, knew not only that Zeus was destined to hold the supreme power, but also that another was to come after him and seize the power in his turn. This successor was to be one of Zeus' many sons—Zeus himself knew that much: it was Prometheus who kept the crucial secret of who would be the child's mother—her name, and whether she was goddess, nymph, or mortal woman. Like his father and his grandfather, Zeus lived in fear of his eventual overthrow and would have done anything to prevent it or put it off. Underestimating his old friend as he had done before, and forgetting that without Prometheus' help it would have taken him much longer to become lord of Olympus, he thought he could torture Prometheus into telling what he knew. But Prometheus with his superhuman endurance remained steadfast.

Most stories agree that at last Prometheus was released from his mountain-top. The deed is ascribed to the greatest of the heroes, Zeus' son Heracles, who sailed to his rescue in a golden cup lent to him by the Sun. Prometheus never told Zeus who was to be the mother of his destroyer, but he did warn him not to marry the sea-nymph Thetis, as his heart was set on doing, because she was destined to bear a son who would be greater than his father. Zeus prudently changed his mind and bestowed the lady on a minor hero named Peleus.

Thetis, however, had all the tricky character of her native element, and Peleus did not win her easily. He seized her one day as she slept on the seashore, whereupon she awoke in a fright and changed herself into all kinds of creatures—a bird, a tree, a tigress, a raging fire—in her struggle to escape him. But the hero held her fast, and at length she returned to her proper form and agreed to become his wife. Zeus gave the couple a famous wedding which was attended by a great throng of gods and men. Their son was Achilles, the hero of the Trojan war, a greater man than his father Peleus but a mortal like other men, not a contender for the throne of heaven.

Pandora's Box

> More lovely than Pandora, whom the gods
> Endowed with all their gifts, and O too like
> In sad event, when to the unwiser son
> Of Japhet[18] brought by Hermes, she ensnared
> Mankind with her fair looks, to be avenged
> On him who had stole Jove's authentic fire.
>
> Milton

Zeus' revenge did not stop with the punishment of Prometheus. Though he could not take the gift of fire away from men once it had been kindled in a thousand places on the earth, he was determined they should suffer for their possession of it.

This story agrees with the story of the Golden Age: at first the life of man on earth was happier than it is now, and then miseries and discontents gradually crept in. It seems that Prometheus and Epimetheus created men only, not women. When Zeus was angry with mankind, he devised the worst punishment he could think of, and invented Woman. Hephaestus, the smith of the gods, was instructed to form her from the earth and make her irresistibly beautiful. Each of the gods gave her his own special gift or skill, and from this she was called Pandora, "all-gifted."[19] When she was perfected with every gift and arrayed in all her loveliness, this treacherous treasure was taken down to earth by Hermes, the messenger-god who wears winged helmet and sandals to speed his flight, and given to Prometheus' foolish brother Epimetheus. Now Prometheus had warned his brother not to accept anything from Zeus, even if it looked like a gift sent in friendship; but Epimetheus as usual acted first and thought afterwards. He accepted the maiden from Hermes and led her into his house, and with her a great jar—some say a box or chest—which the gods had sent with her, telling her to keep it safely but never never think of opening it. This was too much for a lively girl like Pandora, who among her gifts was endowed with the first feminine curiosity. After restraining it for a little while, she at last gave in and lifted the lid from the jar, and from that moment began the sorrows of mankind. For each of the gods had stored in it the worst thing he was able to give, and wonderful as had been the gifts with which they endowed her, just as dreadful were the evils that rushed eagerly from the jar in a black stinking cloud like pestilent insects—sickness and suffering, hatred and jealousy and greed, and all the other cruel things that freeze the heart and bring on old age. Pandora tried to clap the lid on the jar again, but it was too late. The happy childhood of mankind had gone for ever, and with it the Golden Age when life was easy. From then on man had to wrest a hard living by his own labour from the unfriendly ground. Only one good thing came to man in the jar and remains to comfort him in his distress, and that is the spirit of Hope.

Deucalion's Flood

... the ancient pair ...
Deucalion and chaste Pyrrha, to restore
The race of mankind drowned, before the shrine
Of Themis stood devout.

Milton

One more story is told of the early ages of the world. As time went on mankind became less and less noble, and evil and crime walked in open daylight on the face of the earth. When Cronus wounded his father Uranus, two new kinds of creature sprang from the blood where it had dripped down on the earth. One group was the three sisters called the Erinyes or Furies, terrible to look at, who track down and punish the wicked, especially those who murder their own kin. The other was the race of Giants, cruel and bloody-natured, who at last grew so arrogant that they resolved to conquer the stronghold of the gods. To do this they piled Mount Pelion on top of Mount Ossa as a base from which to reach Olympus, whereupon Zeus hurled at them one of his thunderbolts: the mountains came crashing down, over-whelming the Giants in their fall, and the Earth received the blood of her sons in torrents. So that they should not be forgotten, she breathed life into the blood where it had mixed with the ground, and formed a new race of men, violent and cruel in their turn. These intermarried with the race already on the earth and further corrupted their nature; and so it was that evil and crime walked abroad, while Shame and the maiden Justice departed from mankind.

The gods seeing this became greatly perturbed, and Zeus resolved to visit the earth in disguise and take a closer look. Asking here and there for hospitality as a weary traveller, he was so unkindly received that he lost patience, and hastening back to Olympus he called a council of the gods. Before all the assembled divinities of earth and sky and sea, he announced his decision to destroy mankind and replace them with a better race who would honour the gods. At first his intention was to launch a flight of thunderbolts against the earth; but remembering an old prophecy that the whole universe would eventually be consumed by fire, he laid his thunderbolts aside and chose instead to let the heavens open and destroy man with a flood. Accordingly he sent forth Notus the south wind to drive the rain out of the clouds onto the earth. At Zeus' request Poseidon called together the rivers and sent them out to break down their banks and spread themselves over the land; then he struck the earth with his trident, and torrents of water gushed up from under the ground. The floods rushed triumphantly towards the sea, carrying before them crops and orchards, cattle and men, houses and temples, even the sacred images of the gods. Those buildings that did not collapse under their fury were overwhelmed by the high waves, and fish swam through their doorways and gazed at the rooms with their cold eyes. Soon the waters had covered everything: the whole world was sea, and sea without a shore.

At first some tried to escape by climbing the tops of hills, but the floods soon swept them away. Others took to boats, the curved keels gliding for a time above what had been homesteads and ploughed land. Beside them, for as long as they could keep up, swam all kinds of animals, wolves and sheep jostling together in their efforts to escape. Birds took to the air, and wandered long in search of somewhere to rest;

at last their wings grew weary and they dropped into the sea. Most of mankind was swallowed up by the waves. Even those in the boats soon died, succumbing to famine and to the sicknesses brought on by the universal stench of corruption.

In the whole world only one spot of land still showed above the waves: the double peak of cloud-piercing Parnassus in the north of Greece. To this place after many days came floating a huge wooden chest,[20] from which there stepped out on the dry land one man and one woman, Deucalion and his wife Pyrrha, the children respectively of Prometheus and of Epimetheus. The wisdom of Prometheus was responsible for their preservation. Knowing of Zeus' intention to destroy mankind before even Zeus himself knew it, he instructed his son and his niece and daughter-in-law to build the chest and stock it with all the provisions they would need.

Being pious people, Deucalion and Pyrrha made it their first action to give thanks to the gods for their escape. When he saw this, Zeus in pity drove back the waters with the help of Boreas the north wind, whom all this time he had kept imprisoned, and Poseidon called in all the floods he had sent out before. It was fitting that mankind should be restored from this pair, now sitting discouraged on the mountain-top; for they had kept their hands clean from the general guilt, and besides being gentle and upright they honoured the gods. Coming down from the mountain as the floods ebbed, they could see no signs of life, and felt all the horror of being the only living creatures on an empty and desolated earth. As they wandered along they came to a temple of the goddess Themis, one of Uranus' Titan daughters, who now had a place on Olympus and was worshipped beside the younger gods. Deucalion and Pyrrha, disregarding the water-weeds that slimed the steps and hung in festoons from the discoloured roof, entered the temple and implored the goddess's help and advice. After they had stood praying for a while, the voice of the goddess came to them, as if from a great distance but clearly. "Depart from my temple," it said, "veil your heads, loosen the girdles of your garments, and cast behind you the bones of your great mother." This command greatly terrified the man and his wife. Even if both their mothers were not buried far away, how could they do anything so inhumane and disrespectful? Deucalion first understood what the goddess meant. "It is Earth that is the great mother of us all, and her bones are these stones that lie on the ground." They walked away from the temple, veiled their heads, loosened their garments, and began to throw stones behind them as they walked. The stones falling to the ground lost their stiffness and hardness and began to take the form of human beings. Those Deucalion threw became men, and those Pyrrha threw became women. Ovid, the Roman poet who tells the story, explains, "So it comes about that we are a hard race, accustomed to labour, still bearing the mark of our stony origin."

Phaëthon

The brotherless Heliades
Melt in such amber tears as these.
Marvell

Many years after these events, the great sun-god Helios,[21] the son of the Titans Hyperion and Thea, came down to earth to visit a mortal woman named Clymene, the Queen of Ethiopia, a country especially dear to him; and when he went back to his palace in the sky he left her with a child. Clymene called him Phaëthon,[22] "Shining." When he was still a young boy, being teased by his friends about having no father, Phaëthon persuaded Clymene to tell him the secret of his birth. "I swear to you," she said, "by the light above that sees me, that you are the child of that sun which you see, the sun that guides the world."

Phaëthon was eager to go immediately and seek out his great father, and Clymene instructed him how to get there. The way was not far, as the Sun's palace stood at the eastern edge of the world. By passing first through his own land of Ethiopia and then through the land of the Indians, Phaëthon was able to get there quite easily.

The palace of Helios was a wonderful structure, glittering from far off with gold and bronze that shone like fire. Inside Phaëthon discovered the great Sun sitting on his throne, in a blaze of light that made it hard to look at him. Phaëthon stood trembling and shielding his face until the Sun turned on him those eyes that see everything, and said, "My son—for I am proud to call such a young hero my child—tell me why you have come all this way to find me." Phaëthon boldly asked for some proof that he was indeed the child of Helios, and the god replied: "Ask for any gift you desire, and I shall bestow it on you. Let that hidden underground river which alone of all things my eyes have never seen, and by which the gods take their unbreakable oaths, be witness to my promise."

Then Phaëthon's pride was kindled, and he asked to be allowed for one day to drive the chariot of the Sun.

No sooner had these words been spoken than Helios repented of his oath. "My son," he said, "there is nothing I would not give to be released from my promise. You do not know what you are asking. Not one of the gods besides myself, not even mighty Zeus who hurls the thunderbolts from Mount Olympus, has the strength and skill to manage my chariot. Its fire-breathing horses are impetuous and wild, and hard enough even for me to control. Be warned in time and ask a different gift."

Burning with eager ambition, Phaëthon stood firm; and his father, sad at heart, led him out to the chariot, the work of the smith-god Hephaestus. While he was still admiring it, the moment came: Eos the dawn-goddess opened the doors of her rosy house, the stars departed, led by their shepherd the Morning Star, and the fire-breathing immortal horses of the Sun stamped in their harness. There could be no delay. Setting his son in his place, and advising him to be sure to keep to the broad middle path across the heavens, Helios let him go. Phaëthon seized the reins, gave them a shake, and was off.

As soon as they felt that an unskilled hand was guiding them and that the chariot carried less than its usual weight, the winged horses whinnied, tossed their heads, and plunged wildly about, forsaking the broad track and racing towards the highest heavens. The wretched Phaëthon was terrified when he saw how far the earth lay beneath him, and the cold stars of the northern constellations shuddered to feel the unaccustomed heat as the chariot hurtled past. Meanwhile those on earth missed the sun's friendly warmth, usually so constant, and wondered what could have happened to cause such upheaval in the heavens. The great beasts of the upper sky, the Scorpion and Crab[23] and the rest, scared the frantic driver right out of his wits; in his fright he let the reins fall from his hands, and the horses now sped entirely without control. Shying away from the highest stars, they began to dash towards the earth. Their speed scorched even the cool clouds, and the Moon as they passed was astonished to see her brother's chariot dive lower than her own.

The earth began to catch fire, starting at the mountain-tops. Where all moisture was dried out the ground split open, riven with great cracks and fissures. Meadows, crops, and forests were blasted; wooded hills flamed like torches. In the fierce conflagration the skins of the Ethiopians were scorched black and Libya became a desert. Many rivers plunged underground to escape, and some have not reappeared yet: the Nile fled to the ends of the earth to hide his head, which is still hidden, leaving empty the seven channels through which he used to meet the sea.

Beholding this universal destruction, Zeus called together all the gods. With one voice they agreed, even sorrowful Helios, that if the whole earth were not to perish the desperate charioteer must be stopped. Then, mounting to the highest point of heaven, Zeus launched one of his powerful thunderbolts that always reach their mark. Cleaving the skies it struck Phaëthon and tumbled him from the chariot. With his hair on fire he fell like a comet, leaving a trail of light; at last the waters of the Italian river Po received him, far from his native land. The nymphs of Italy buried his body beside the river-shore.

There was great lamentation in the palace of Ethiopia when Phaëthon's fate was known. His sisters, also children of the Sun and called after him Heliades,[24] were especially wild in their sorrow, until the gods pitying their distress changed them into weeping trees—poplars, from whose bark drip tears of amber to this day.

Demeter, Triptolemus, Persephone[1]

II. Spring and Winter

Demeter and Persephone

> . . . that fair field
> Of Enna, where Proserpin gathering flowers,
> Herself a fairer flower, by gloomy Dis
> Was gathered, which cost Ceres all that pain
> To seek her through the world.
>
> Milton

There was a time when the corn-mother Demeter, the sister and at the same time one of the wives of Zeus, poured out her blessings on the earth in the same abundance all the year round. That was before her griefs estranged her from the councils of the gods.

Demeter bore a child to Zeus, the slender-ankled maiden Persephone, who grew up in surpassing beauty. When Zeus' brother Hades, the dark ruler of the underworld, asked for her in marriage, Zeus swore that he should have her, whatever her mother might say. The two brothers called in Earth to help them, and the three of them together laid a plot.

One day Persephone went to play with the daughters of Ocean in the meadows of Enna in Sicily, away from her mother, and wandered here and there with her companions gathering the flowers of all the seasons that were blooming there together. At the will of Zeus Earth sent up from her lap a new flower, a wonderful sight for mortal men or deathless gods, a bright narcissus[2] with a hundred blooms growing from its single stalk. The sweetness of its perfume delighted the heavens and the earth and made the sea laugh for joy. Persephone stood amazed at the flower's beauty; then as she stretched out her hand to pick it, suddenly the earth gaped, a wide chasm opened at her feet, and out of it sprang Hades in his golden chariot, drawn by deathless coal-black horses. Seizing her before she could find the power to move, he set her in his chariot and drove the horses forward.

As long as Persephone could still see the earth and the broad sky and the sea with its crowding fish, she was calm and quiet. But when the tall gates of Hades' realm came in sight and earth seemed to be lost behind her, she gave a shrill cry, so that the heights of the mountains and the depths of the sea rang with her immortal voice. Her father Zeus heard her, sitting in his temple receiving the offerings of men, and rejoiced that his design had been carried out. Her mother Demeter heard her, and the cry filled her heart with grief and fear. She rent her headdress apart with her hands, and casting over her shoulders a dark blue cloak, she hastened like a wild bird in search of her child, over the firm ground and the unstable sea. But there was no one who was willing to tell her the truth, even among those who knew it. For nine days and nights majestic Demeter searched over the earth, with flaming torches in her hands, so grieved that she would neither partake of the food of the gods nor refresh her body with water.

On the tenth day the dark goddess Hecate approached her, with a torch in her hand, saying: "Lady Demeter, who brings on the season and bestows good gifts, who of heavenly gods or mortal men has stolen away Persephone and pierced your heart with sorrow? For I heard her voice as she cried out, but I did not see the event."

Together Hecate and Demeter approached the sun-god Helios, who watches the doings of both gods and men. Standing before his horses, Demeter asked him whether he had seen the theft of her child. Helios replied to her: "Queen Demeter, daughter of Rhea, I pity you in your grief for your slim-ankled daughter. One alone of all the deathless gods is to blame, and that is cloud-gathering Zeus, who gave her to his brother to wife; and Hades it was who seized her, and took her in his chariot despite her loud cries down to his kingdom of mist and gloom. But, goddess, cease your lamenting: the divine ruler of a third part of the world is not an unfitting husband for your child." So saying, he hastened on with his horses, urging them forward to make up for the time he had lost.

At Helios' words the grief in Demeter's heart became more terrible and savage, and she was so angry with Zeus that she forsook the assemblies of the gods and the high places of Olympus, wandering unknown among the cities and fields of men; and during the whole time of her mourning, the seed remained hidden in the ground and the new leaves and sprouts remained closed in the plants, so that no new crop came in response to men's labours.

At last Demeter came to Eleusis,[3] ruled over by King Celeus, and she sat down in her distress by a well outside the town, looking like an old and weary woman. There the four daughters of Celeus met her when they came out to draw water. Not recognizing the goddess, they asked her who she was and why she did not come into the town in search of hospitality. Then Demeter, to explain why she had come alone to a strange city, told them that she had been carried away by pirates from her native Crete and had only now escaped. "But take pity on me, maidens, and tell me to what house I may go to find work suitable to my age. I can nurse a newborn child, and keep house, and supervise the women in their work."

The eldest of the daughters of Celeus replied: "None of the women who run the households of our town would send you away if you came to them, but rather they would welcome you; for there is something gracious in your appearance. But if you will, stay here, and we will go home and tell our mother, the lady Metaneira, all your story, so that you may come to our house rather than any other. She nurses in the hall her infant son, late-born, long prayed for, and welcome; and if you brought him up to the age of young manhood, our mother would hasten to reward you in gratitude."

The goddess agreed, and the maidens hurried home with their pitchers. When they found their mother and told her what had passed, she told them to bring the stranger back with them with all the speed they could. Catching up the folds of their garments, they hastened back to the goddess as she waited by the roadside, and led her back to their father's house. They hastened ahead like young deer in the springtime, while Demeter in the grief of her heart walked behind, with her head veiled, draped in the dark blue cloak that floated around her slender feet.

Soon they came to the house of the just Celeus, and passed through the gateway to where the stately Metaneira sat, leaning against a pillar, with her little son in her arms. As the goddess passed through the entrance, she seemed taller than before, and a divine light glowed around her. Metaneira greeted her with reverence and kindness; but for all that she could do, Demeter would neither sit in a comfortable place nor take food or drink nor smile, so great was her grief.

At Metaneira's request, Demeter undertook to nurse her young son Demophoön, and the child throve under her care, growing like one of the gods. By day Demeter gave him ambrosia, the food of the gods, and at night, when all the house was asleep, she would hold him in the heart of the fire to burn away what was mortal from his nature. By her power she would have made him ageless and deathless forever, if Metaneira had not one wakeful night stood at the door of her scented chamber and seen her, and cried out in fear, "Demophoön, my little son, is the stranger woman burying you in the fire?" Demeter in anger snatched the child from the flames and let him fall onto the palace floor, exclaiming to Metaneira: "You mortals are blind to your destiny, whether good or evil, and never see aright what comes upon you. Your folly has undone my work. I would have made your son ageless and deathless forever, and bestowed eternal honour upon him, but now he cannot escape death and the fate of men. But he shall have honour all his life, because he was the nursling of the goddess Demeter and lay on my knees and slept in my arms."

So saying, she cast off her old age and weakness: beauty spread round her, and sweet fragrance drifted from her robes, and the house was filled with a brightness like lightning. And she went out from the palace.

When she had gone, for a long time Metaneira was unable to speak or move, or even to pick up her son from the floor. But his sisters heard his pitiful wailing, and sprang out of their comfortable beds; they gathered around him as he struggled, and picked him up and caressed him; but they were less skilful than the divine nurse he had lost, and his heart was not comforted.

When Demeter had travelled far from Eleusis, she sat down and continued to grieve for her daughter. It was a very cruel year for all mankind, since Demeter kept the seed hidden in the ground and the oxen ploughed the fields in vain. Fearing that she would destroy the whole race of men, and that the gods on Olympus would be without their customary honours and sacrifices, Zeus sent Iris, the rainbow-goddess who carries messages for the gods, to speak to Demeter where she sat veiled in her dark blue cloak in one of her temples.

"Demeter, Father Zeus the all-wise calls you to come back to the councils of the eternal gods; come with me, then, and do not disregard his message."

So said Iris; but her words did not soften the heart of Demeter. Zeus then sent all the eternal and blessed gods to persuade her, offering her gifts and anything else she might wish. But she was still so angry that she swore she would never set foot in Olympus nor let the crops grow until her own fair daughter was restored to her sight.

And when great Zeus saw that she would not relent, he sent swift-footed Hermes down to the underworld, to win over Hades with soft persuasions and bring back Persephone to the light, so that her mother might see her and give up her anger. Hermes descended to the underworld, where he found Hades in his house seated on a couch, with his sad bride beside him. Approaching, he addressed the dark-haired ruler: "King Hades, lord of the dead, Zeus has commanded me to bring the lovely Persephone up to the realm of the gods, so that her mother may see her and cease to be angry with the immortal gods. For now she sits in her temple apart from the gods, brooding a plan to keep the seed hidden forever in the earth, and so to destroy the feeble tribes of men and the honours of the deathless gods."

So he spoke. And Hades, lord of the dead, smiled a grim smile and obeyed the command of Zeus, urging Persephone to return with the messenger. But when she joyfully sprang up to prepare for her return, he took her aside and secretly gave her to eat the seeds of the sweet pomegranate, so that she might not remain forever with her lady mother. Then he harnessed his immortal horses to the golden chariot, and she mounted, and strong Hermes took the reins and whip in his hands and drove swiftly upwards from the dark realm of Hades. And they travelled over land and sea, stopping for nothing until they came to the place where Demeter brooded in her temple.

When Demeter saw them she hastened out to meet them, while Persephone leaped from the chariot and ran and embraced her. But while Demeter still held her dear daughter in her arms, suddenly she began to fear some deception, and she stopped caressing her and asked: "Tell me, my child, surely you did not taste food while you were in the underworld? For if you did not, you can leave the hateful king of the dead forever and live with me and your father, Zeus of the dark clouds; but if you have tasted food, you must go back again to the secret places of the earth for a third part of every year."

Then Persephone wept, and told how she had been persuaded to eat of the pomegranate before her long journey to the upper world. And having taken food in the country of the dead, she could not leave it altogether and be with her mother and honoured by the immortal gods. But Demeter promised her, "Yet when the earth shall blossom with all the flowers of spring, you shall come up from the land of gloom and darkness to gladden the sight of gods and mortal men."

So Persephone was restored to her mother, and Demeter's sorrow was healed and her anger left her; soon the bare fields and plains waved with long ears of wheat, and the rich land was busy with preparations for harvest. But for a third part of every year, Persephone descends to the grave country of Hades, returning in the spring to gladden gods and men.

Adonis

... Beds of hyacinth and roses
Where young Adonis oft reposes
Waxing well of his deep wound
In slumber soft, and on the ground
Sadly sits the Assyrian queen.

Milton

Another young person whose coming is said to bring with it the fruitfulness of the earth, though this time a mortal, is the beautiful Adonis, born from a myrrh tree in Sabaea, the land of spices.[4] His mother Myrrha was turned into a tree after offending Aphrodite, the laughter-loving sea-born goddess, and the drops of precious gum that flow from its bark are the tears she still sheds for her fault.

When he was still a very young man, Adonis' beauty struck the heart of Aphrodite, who used to accompany him on the hunting expeditions in which he delighted. But on one sad day, when she had just left him in her swan-drawn chariot, a wild boar rushed out of a thicket and gored Adonis in the thigh. The boar is said to have been sent by the war-god Ares, jealous of Aphrodite's attentions to the young huntsman, or to have been Ares himself in disguise. Adonis sank to the ground, blood pouring from his wound, and Aphrodite, who heard from far off his cries of pain and astonishment, arrived only in time to take him in her arms and see him die. Overcome with grief, she leaned over his body and washed away the blood; as it touched the ground, from every drop there sprang a flower the colour of blood. Beautiful and frail, its petals are loosened by the wind that stirs it and from which it takes its name: wind-flower, anemone.

But there are some who say that Adonis returns every year from the dwelling of the dark queen Persephone, and every year he is slain by the rough boar his enemy and mourned by the great goddess who loves him, while the river Adonis in Lebanon runs red with his blood. In the country festivals held in his honour, baskets of flowers were thrown into the rivers and springs to commemorate his short life, and the mourners would say, "Farewell, dear Adonis, and may you find us all happy when you come again another year."

Hyacinthus

> For so Apollo, with unweeting hand,
> Whilom did slay his dearly-lovèd mate,
> Young Hyacinth, born on Eurotas' strand,
> Young Hyacinth, the pride of Spartan land;
> But then transformed him to a purple flower.
>
> Milton

The Spartan Hyacinthus, the friend of Apollo, also had a life that was pleasant but short. For his sake the god left his oracle and temple at Delphi, and they spent their time together in sports in the open air. Once when they were tired from hunting, they took to throwing the discus in turn to see who could throw it farther; and then it was that Apollo with an unlucky cast struck his companion on the forehead. All Apollo's famous skill in healing was in vain, and Hyacinthus died from the injury. Since he could do nothing to save his friend, Apollo found a way of keeping his memory alive: from Hyacinthus' blood sprang the hyacinth flower, lily-shaped, purple-hued, and marked on its leaves with the Greek letters αιαι, the syllables of grief.

Narcissus

> Foolish Narcisse, that likes the wat'ry shore.
>
> Spenser

As beautiful as Adonis was the ill-fated Narcissus, who from his childhood was loved by all who saw him but whose pride would let him love no one in return. At last one of those who had hopelessly courted him turned and cursed him, exclaiming: "May he suffer as we have suffered! May he too love in vain!" The avenging goddess Nemesis heard and approved this prayer.

There was nearby a clear pool, with shining silvery waters. No shepherd had ever come there, nor beast nor bird nor falling branch marred its surface; the grass grew fresh and green around it, and the sheltering woods kept it always cool from the midday sun.

Here once came Narcissus, heated and tired from hunting, and lay down by the pool to drink. As he bent over the water, his eyes met the eyes of another young man, gazing up at him from the depths of the pool. Deluded by his reflection, Narcissus fell in love with the beauty that was his own. Without thought of food or rest he lay beside the pool addressing cries and pleas to the image, whose lips moved as he spoke but whose reply he could never catch. Echo came by, the most constant of his disdained lovers. She was a nymph who had once angered Hera, the wife of Zeus, by talking too much, and in consequence was deprived of the use of her tongue for ordinary conversation: all she could do was repeat the last words of others. Seeing Narcissus lying there, she pleaded with him in his own words. "I will die unless you pity me," cried Narcissus to his beloved. "Pity me," cried Echo as vainly to hers. Narcissus never raised his eyes to her at all, though she remained day after day beside him on the bank, pleading as well as she was able. At last she pined away, withering and wasting with unrequited love, till nothing was left of her but her voice, which the traveller still hears calling in woods and waste places.

As for the cruel Narcissus, he fared no better. The face that looked back at him from the water became pale, thin, and haggard, till at last poor Echo caught and repeated his last "Farewell!" But when she came with the other nymphs to lament over his body, it was nowhere to be found. Instead, over the pool bent a new flower, white with a yellow centre, which they called by his name. From this flower the Furies, the avengers of guilt, twist garlands to bind their hateful brows.

Orpheus

Orpheus with his lute[5] made trees
And the mountain tops that freeze
Bow themselves when he did sing;
To his music plants and flowers

Ever sprung; as sun and showers
There had made a lasting Spring.

Everything that heard him play,
Even the billows of the sea,
Hung their heads, and then lay by.
In sweet music is such art,
Killing care and griefs of heart
Fall asleep, or hearing die.

Shakespeare

Orpheus the Thracian is the magical musician and divine poet of Greek story. Shortly after his marriage to the nymph Eurydice, the young bride while wandering through the meadows was fatally bitten by a snake that had been lurking among the flowers. The grieving Orpheus resolved to take the terrible journey to the underworld in search of her. Singing of his loss to the music of his lyre, he passed Cerberus, the three-headed hell-hound who guards the gate of Hades' sad realm, crossed the river Styx in the boat of Charon the ferryman of the dead, and stood at last in the grim presence of Hades and Persephone, the only man in all that vast court with breath in his body. So irresistibly touching was his song of lost love that the thin shades wept in sympathy and the torments of the great sufferers, Ixion stretched on his wheel and Sisyphus straining against his rock,[6] for a few moments ceased. Hades himself, the dark king of shades, relented, and told Orpheus that Eurydice might follow him back to the upper world, on one condition: he must not turn back to look at her before they had both reached the light.

Orpheus rejoiced as he began the long journey back, trusting that his wife was behind him. Just as he was approaching the borders of the light, his trust in Hades failed, and in an instant of doubt he turned his head: he saw Eurydice, but at once her form began to fade. As he embraced her the shades of night pressed round her again and she was gone, leaving him to clasp the empty air.

At this second loss, Orpheus was plunged into grief even more overwhelming. In vain he tried a second time to cross the river of death, pleading to be taken with the waiting shades: the ferryman turned his back. At last he went home to Thrace, where he wandered about the wintry mountains, singing of the happy past and the desolated present. At his sad music the animals forgot to prey on one another and lay peaceably side by side as never since the Golden Age, and trees and stubborn rocks were moved by his song.

Once as he was singing to this audience, a group of Maenads, frenzied women who worshipped the god Dionysus, came by in a wild dance. They saw the musician and called out to him to play something cheerful for their revels. When he paid no attention to them but continued his sad strains, they became enraged and fell on him as an enemy of their god, and finally tore him to pieces. His limbs were scattered about the countryside; his head was thrown into the nearby Hebrus river flowing down from the mountains, and as it was borne towards the sea it never ceased to sing. At last the head came ashore at the island of Lesbos, and with it came the gift of song that was to make the island famous for its poets, Arion, Sappho and Alcaeus.[7] Apollo in pity set up a shrine for the head in a grove where the nightingales ever afterwards have sung more beautifully than anywhere else in the world. Some say that when the head was brought ashore it became silent; others, that the sweet voice of Orpheus can still be heard there, uttering oracles and stories of the gods.

Boar

III. Loves of the Gods and Metamorphoses

Loves of Zeus: Callisto, Io

> The gods themselves,
> Humbling their deities to love, have taken
> The shapes of beasts upon them: Jupiter
> Became a bull, and bellow'd; the green Neptune
> A ram, and bleated; and the fire-rob'd god,
> Golden Apollo, a poor humble swain.
>
> Shakespeare

Apparently in the earliest times the forms of things were more fluid than they are now, seeing that the Greeks have many tales of shape-shifting, or metamorphosis, most of them in connection with the love affairs of the gods.

The god who most regularly fell in love with mortal women was Father Zeus himself. He courted Europa in the form of a bull, Danaë in a shower of gold, and the virtuous Alcmena in the shape of her husband. Leda, whom he visited as a swan, later hatched from an egg her two daughters Clytemnestra and Helen, and also Castor and Polydeuces, the Heavenly Twins.

The main hindrance to Zeus' activities was the jealousy of his wife Hera, who did her best to punish him and his conquests. One of them, Callisto, whom Zeus lured away from hunting with Artemis and her band of nymphs, Hera turned into a bear. After Callisto's son Arcas[1] had grown up and become a huntsman himself, Hera brought him to his mother's den. But as he fitted an arrow to his bow, Zeus carried Callisto up to heaven, where she shines as the Great Bear, later joined by the star Arcturus,[2] her son. In a fury Hera made Poseidon refuse to admit them to his waters, so that they alone of all the constellations never dip below the horizon.

Another unfortunate maiden loved by Zeus was Io, daughter of the river Inachus. When one day Hera saw that the earth was shrouded in clouds and dense darkness, she suspected her wandering husband; piercing through the clouds, she found him standing beside a fine white cow, into which he had quickly transformed his beloved. Hera, pretending to be struck with the cow's beauty, asked Zeus to give it to her as a present, and for fear of worse he dared not refuse. She immediately gave poor Io into the keeping of Argus, the hundred-eyed watchman, who spied on her day and night, never closing all his eyes at once.

Zeus called his son Hermes and commanded him to kill Argus. Adopting the disguise of a herdsman, the messenger-god came down to the mountain-top where Argus sat, and began to charm him with stories and with tunes played on a pipe of reeds. Argus became drowsy,

Maiden with deer

and at length closed every one of his hundred eyes: then Hermes sprang up and struck off his head with a single sword-blow.

Hera took the eyes of her faithful servant and placed them in the tail of her own bird, the peacock. She continued her persecution of Io, tormenting her with a gadfly that drove her all over the known world. At length when Io reached the stream of Nile, Hera relented and allowed her to return to her proper form. The Egyptians built temples to her and worshipped her as a goddess.[3]

Pan and Syrinx

> Pan's Syrinx was a girl indeed,
> Though now she's turned into a reed;
> From that dear reed Pan's pipe doth come,
> A pipe that strikes Apollo dumb;
> Nor flute, nor lute, nor gittern can
> So chant it as the pipe of Pan.
>
> John Lyly

The reed-pipes with which Hermes lulled Argus to sleep have a story of their own. Syrinx, an Arcadian nymph who like Callisto used to hunt on the mountains in Artemis' train, attracted the attention of the goat-footed forest-god Pan, who pursued her over hill and over dale till she reached the shallow river Ladon. Here she stopped and prayed to the nymphs of the stream to help her; and when Pan thought he had caught her, he found himself grasping a handful of marsh reeds. As he stood there sighing, the wind blew through the reeds and drew from them a thin, melancholy music. This almost consoled Pan for the loss of Syrinx: he took reeds of different lengths and fastened them together with wax, producing the first reed-pipes, or Pan-pipes as they are still called after him.

Apollo and Daphne

> The gods, that mortal beauty chase,
> Still in a tree did end their race:
> Apollo hunted Daphne so,
> Only that she might laurel grow;
> And Pan did after Syrinx speed,
> Not as a nymph, but for a reed.
>
> Marvell

A similar story is told of Apollo and Daphne, daughter of the river Peneus. Apollo was incautious enough one day to tease the boy Eros[4] for being a child and carrying toy weapons: Eros thereupon drew two arrows from his quiver and fitted them to his bow. The first, gold-tipped and sharp, flew straight to the heart of Apollo, kindling there the flames of raging love. The other, blunt and leaden, pierced Daphne, making her hate and fear the very name of love. When the two met, in spite of all that Apollo could say she turned and fled from him. Coming in her flight to her father's river, she begged him to take away the beauty that was so troublesome to her; and at once she became a shining, trembling tree. Since the maiden had escaped him, Apollo swore henceforward to love and honour the laurel, which ever afterwards crowned his head and is the token of poet's or conqueror's fame.[5]

Clytie

The heart that has truly loved never forgets,
    But as truly loves on to the close;
As the sunflower turns on her god when he sets
    The same look that she turned when he rose.

Thomas Moore

A maiden who loved a god without return was Clytie, whose affections were fixed on the sun-god Helios. Day after day she stood still and gazed at him in his passage across the sky, turning her face to catch the last glimpse as he dropped below the horizon. At last she became fixed in her place, where she now stands as a sunflower, rooted in the ground but still straining to watch the disdainful beloved.

Endymion

Peace, ho! the moon sleeps with Endymion,
And would not be awak'd.

Shakespeare

Not only gods but also goddesses were sometimes attracted to mortals. One such was the moon-goddess Selene, who fell in love with the shepherd Endymion as he tended his flocks on Mount Latmos in Caria; she cast him into an eternal sleep so that she could visit him when she liked, and when the night sky is dark, it is because she has descended to the cave where her shepherd sleeps.

Arachne

> The most fine-fingered workwoman on ground,
> Arachne.
>
> Spenser

The spider was once a young woman, Arachne,[6] who presumptuously challenged Athene to a contest in weaving. The goddess sat down at the loom and very quickly produced a tapestry that showed the rivalry between herself and Poseidon for the guardianship of Athens, not yet bearing her name. Poseidon struck the rocks with his trident, and out sprang a horse, his gift to the people of Attica; but Athene gave them the olive-tree, with its fruit and rich oil and finely-grained hard wood, which was adjudged the better gift. In the corners around this scene, the divine artist worked four little pictures of punishments sent by the gods upon presumptuous mortals. Arachne, unabashed at the goddess's success, worked on her web pictures of the gods in the various disguises they had worn to deceive mortal women: Zeus as a bull, as a swan, and as a shower of gold, Apollo and Poseidon and the others in various unworthy shapes. Athene was angered both by the brilliance of the weaving and by the insult to the gods. Tearing Arachne's tapestry to pieces, she beat her about the head with her shuttle. Arachne in shame tried to hang herself; but Athene immediately transformed her as she dangled from the rope, with the curse that she should not die but remain suspended in the air for all time, both herself and her descendants, shrivelled and eight-legged and eternally spinning thread from her belly.

Procne and Philomela

> Ah! thought I, thou mourn'st in vain,
> None takes pity on thy pain:
> Senseless trees they cannot hear thee,
> Ruthless beasts they will not cheer thee.
> King Pandion he is dead,
> All thy friends are lapp'd in lead,

All thy fellow birds do sing
Careless of thy sorrowing.
Even so, poor bird, like thee,
None alive will pity me.
                              Richard Barnefield

King Pandion of Athens had two daughters, named Procne and
Philomela. Procne, the elder, was married to King Tereus of Thrace, and
after five years of marriage she asked her husband to let her sister come
to visit her. Tereus, agreeing, himself set out by sea to fetch her. But
when the lovely Philomela had come aboard the ship, Tereus conceived

Dionysus

a wicked passion for her, and instead of taking her to her sister, he landed on the rocky coast and dragged her deep into the forest, where he kept her in an ancient tower as his captive. So that she should not tell her story, the barbarous king cut out her tongue. Then he returned to the Thracian court, where he told Procne that her sister had died on the journey.

For a whole year Philomela grieved in the dark forest. Then, setting up a rough loom, she wove on it a tapestry in which her story was shown, and by signs instructed a servant to take it to the Thracian queen. Unrolling the tapestry, Procne read the dreadful tale. At once she hastened to the forest, released her sister, and brought her secretly back to the palace, where the two plotted revenge. Seizing Procne's little son, they killed him and cut up his body, cooking the meat in a dish which Procne set before her husband. Not until he had eaten did she tell him what was in it, while Philomela, still dabbled in the child's blood, came out and stood before him. When he understood all, Tereus grasped his sword and pursued the sisters. To prevent more bloodshed the gods at once transformed all three of them: Tereus to a hoopoe wearing a crest of feathers and Procne to a chattering home-dwelling swallow, while Philomela, her voice at last restored, became the nightingale who tells her sorrows all night to the silent woods.

Midas' Touch

Thou gaudy gold,
Hard food for Midas, I will none of thee.
Shakespeare

Another story of transformation concerns the wine-god Dionysus, whose fat drunken old tutor Silenus one day fell asleep in the garden of King Midas of Phrygia, where he was found by the servants and brought into the palace. Midas recognized Silenus and made much of him, feasting him merrily for ten days, after which Dionysus came to fetch his friend away. In gratitude to Midas, he promised him whatever gift he should ask as a reward, and Midas hastily demanded: "Grant that whatever I touch shall be turned into gold." The god would rather have given him something better, but Midas had made his choice; so he left him to find out about it.

At first Midas was delighted with his boon, touching twigs and stones and flowers and seeing them turn to the finest gold in his hands;

but when he sat down to eat and his food and wine became solid metal the moment they touched his mouth, he began to complain bitterly and to implore Dionysus to take back the cruel gift. Seeing him repent of his rashness, Dionysus told him to wash in the nearby river Pactolus: the river took the touch from him, and ever afterwards has had golden sands.

Midas' thoughtlessness was to bring him trouble again. He was once present at a contest in music between the rustic god Pan with his pipes and Apollo with the lyre, when the judge, the wise old mountain Tmolus, decided in favour of the leader of the Muses. Immediately Midas cried out that the decision was unjust and Pan's music the sweeter. The insulted Apollo forced Midas to bear the sign of his foolish judgment, turning his ears to the long grey twitchers of an ass.

Midas, ashamed of this stigma, tried to conceal it by keeping his head wrapped in a purple turban, which only his barber was ever allowed to disturb. Afraid to tell the king's secret and yet longing to share it, the man one day dug a hole in the earth into which he murmured what he had seen, and went his way with a quiet mind. But some reeds grew up out of the earth he had filled in, and they began to whisper among themselves, and when the south wind blew they spoke so that all could hear them: "King Midas has ass's ears."

Ceyx and Alcyone

> The winds with wonder whist
> Smoothly the waters kissed,
> Whispering new joys to the mild oceän,
> Who now hath quite forgot to rave,
> While birds of calm sit brooding on the charmèd wave.
>
> Milton

The Thessalian king Ceyx once parted from his wife Alcyone, a daughter of Aeolus, to go on a long voyage by sea. The first night after he left her a storm blew up and wrecked his ship: he and all his men were drowned. Meanwhile Alcyone waited at home without news of her husband, and constantly offered to the gods prayers for his safe return, above all to Hera, the protectress of married love. Wearied with prayers for one already dead, Hera sent Iris to the drowsy house of Sleep to ask the god to let Alcyone know the truth in a dream. The home of Sleep is a cave where the sun never enters, in a dark and silent countryside.

Poppies grow in abundance before the doors, and from the cave flows the slumbrous murmuring river of forgetfulness. Within on a high dark couch lies the god sleeping, and here Iris spoke her message.

From among his many sons Sleep sent Morpheus, the dream-god, to stand at Alcyone's bed-side in the form of her drowned husband, naked and streaming with water. "My poor wife," he said, "do you not know your husband, or has death changed my face? Your prayers did not save me from shipwreck and drowning. Rise up, put on mourning garments, carry out the rites for the dead lest I descend unwept to the land of shades."

As the figure slipped away, the force of Alcyone's grief woke her, and she hastened down to the shore, where the waves rolled in the body of Ceyx to her feet. Flinging herself in distraction into the water, she was changed by the pitying gods into a kingfisher, and her husband with her. Now every winter for seven calm days Alcyone broods upon the sea, with wings outstretched to cover her floating nest, while her father Aeolus keeps the winds locked up until the little birds are hatched. This period we call the halcyon days.

Nisus and Scylla

> Ah cease, rash youth! desist ere 'tis too late,
> Fear the just gods, and think of Scylla's fate!
> Chang'd to a bird, and sent to flit in air,
> She dearly pays for Nisus' injur'd hair!
>
> Pope

The city of Megara on the Isthmus of Corinth was ruled by King Nisus, who among his white hairs had a single purple lock, on which the city's fortune depended. The powerful King Minos of Crete once besieged Megara, and Nisus' daughter Scylla, watching the struggle from a tower in the city wall, soon got to know all the warriors by sight. Among them she was most struck by Minos himself: in fact, she fell violently in love with him and would shortly have done anything to win his favour. She stole one night to her father's bedroom and, as he slept, cut off the charmed lock; then she made her way through the ranks of the enemy to Minos' tent, carrying the lock in her hand. When she came before Minos, she offered it to him as a pledge of her love.

Minos, horrified by Scylla's betrayal of her father, shrank away from the gift and sent her with scorn back to the city. Soon, its ruler's luck being gone, Megara fell into Minos' hands. The Cretans plundered it freely and then set sail for home. Scylla fled down the beach after Minos and seized the rudder of his ship; but she was beaten back by a huge sea-eagle—her father, transformed by the gods. Just as she fell into the water, she too was changed into a sea-bird: the *ciris*, or "shearer," called after her act. And wherever she is seen there too is the sea-eagle, pursuing her with his cries.

Philemon and Baucis

> I saw myself the garlands on their boughs,
> And tablets hung for gifts of granted vows;
> And offering fresher up, with pious prayer,
> The good, said I, are God's peculiar care,
> And such as honour heaven, shall heavenly honour share.
> Ovid, translated by Dryden

In the countryside of Phrygia an oak and a linden tree stood side by side, always hung with fresh garlands by those who lived near by. Round about lay a stagnant, marshy lake, the haunt of croaking birds. Once, it is said, Zeus and Hermes, disguised as ordinary travellers, came down to this spot of earth and wandered from house to house seeking hospitality. Everywhere they were refused and turned away, at great houses and small, until Zeus, the special protector of travellers far from home, began to get angry. At last they came to a little cottage, poorly thatched with reeds, whose owners opened the door to them and made them warmly welcome. The old couple, Philemon and his wife Baucis, hastened to offer such comforts as they had. Philemon drew up rickety chairs and invited them to rest themselves, while Baucis put the stew-pot on the fire, feeding the flames with twigs and chips of bark. Bustling about, she soon had a meal spread for the gods—cottagers' fare, smoked bacon cut down from the rafters, vegetables out of the garden, eggs baked among the ashes, served on clay and wooden dishes with a little sour wine. Nuts and fruit, figs, plums, apples, and grapes made up the dessert, with honeycomb besides.

Busy caring for their guests, the old couple did not at first notice that however many times they filled the cups with wine, the pitcher remained full. When this sign of the gods' presence struck them, Baucis and Philemon were alarmed. They begged forgiveness for the humble meal, offering to kill their single goose if only they could catch it. This the gods would not permit. Revealing themselves, they declared that the neighbourhood would be punished for its meanness towards strangers, Philemon and Baucis only excepted. These they invited to come with them to the top of a hill overlooking the district.

When Philemon and Baucis turned on the hill-top to look down, they saw the whole countryside drowned in marshy waters, their cottage alone left standing. As they watched, grieving for the fate of their neighbours, the cottage was changed into a temple, gold-roofed and gleaming with white marble. Then Zeus asked the old man and his wife what gift they would like from him. After a moment's consultation they replied, "To be your priests while we live, and to die at the same instant so that neither of us outlives the other."

Zeus established them in the temple, which they tended for several years. Then when Baucis and Philemon had grown very old, one day as they were reminiscing about the events that had brought them there, each saw the other begin to put forth leaves. "Goodbye, dear friend!" they cried out together. As they spoke, bark closed over their bodies and they were changed into an oak and a linden. The trees were long honoured for the sake of Baucis and Philemon, and as a memorial of the acts of the gods.

Gorgon shield[1]

IV. The Heroes

Perseus

Danaë in a brazen tower
Where no love was, loved a shower.
John Fletcher

"You will have no sons of your own, and your daughter's son will be your death." So ran the answer of the oracle to King Acrisius of Argos, who had come to ask about his future. Acrisius went home in a fury, and promptly shut up his beautiful daughter Danaë in a tower of bronze where no man could see her, but all to no purpose; for Zeus poured himself in at an opening in the roof as a shower of gold, and gave her a son, whom she called Perseus. Resisting the will of the gods, but still reluctant to kill his own flesh and blood, Acrisius set Danaë and her child afloat in a wooden chest, expecting that the raging sea would soon finish them off. But their ark at length was carried to the island of Seriphos, where a fisherman named Dictys cast his net around it and drew it ashore.

Welcomed by the fisherman and his wife, Danaë and Perseus lived with them for several years. Dictys' brother Polydectes, as harsh as Dictys was kind, was king of the island, and he in time demanded the

marriage. He was greatly astonished when Danaë
fully grown, resisted him, and he resolved that
ot rid of forthwith. To this end, he gave out that he
˷ᴄad to marry a neighbouring princess and invited the
˷ᴏ men of the island, Perseus among them, to a celebration. Each of
the guests brought a present: only Perseus in his poverty had none.
Taunted for it by Polydectes, he flung back proudly that he was prepared to go out and win by his own efforts a rarer gift than any—"even
the head of the Gorgon Medusa herself." That was just what Polydectes
had hoped to hear. "Very well," he said, "we will see no more of you till
you have it."

> What was that snaky-headed Gorgon shield
> That wise Minerva wore, unconquered virgin,
> Wherewith she freezed her foes to congealed stone?
>
> Milton

The original Gorgons were two monstrous sisters, bird-winged, snake-
haired, and plain-faced enough to scare off anything, living on a solitary rock at the edge of the western sea. These two were divinely born
and immortal, but a mortal woman had been sent to join them as
punishment for a crime against the gods. She, Medusa, was the most
terrible of the three, with a face so appalling in its ugliness and hatred
that whoever looked at it was turned into stone.

Perseus' task would have been impossible had he not been helped by
Pallas Athene and by Hermes, the messenger of the gods. Giving him a
brightly-polished shield of bronze, Athene warned him never to look
directly at the face of the Gorgon but only at its reflection in the mirror-
like surface. Hermes lent him his own winged sandals to shorten the
long journey and a sickle of adamant with which to cut off the Gorgon's
head. They both gave him advice about the beings he must seek out for
the remaining information and equipment he needed.

The first place to which Perseus' winged sandals carried him was the
home of the Gorgons' three sisters, the white-haired Graeae, dwelling
in the farthest west. These had only one eye and one tooth among them,
and Perseus easily got control over them by snatching the eye as they
were passing it from hand to hand, and threatening to throw it into the
sea. They were quickly persuaded to direct him to the Gorgons' rock
and to give him the things he asked for: a helmet of invisibility to wear
when he was about to strike, and a leather wallet in which the head
could safely be carried.

Arriving at the Gorgons' rock, he found the three horrors asleep. This gave him time to decide which was Medusa, the only one who could be killed: to attack either of the others would have been fatal. Hovering over her in his winged sandals, he struck off her head with one blow and dropped it into the leather wallet. The sister Gorgons woke at the noise and howled in fury at the murder, but Perseus sprang into the air, concealed by the helmet of darkness. As he flew back towards the east, drops of the Gorgon's blood fell from the wallet onto the Libyan sands, where they became all manner of snakes: that is why to this day the Sahara desert swarms with deadly serpents.

> ... that starred Ethiop queen that strove
> To set her beauty's praise above
> The Sea Nymphs, and their powers offended.
>
> Milton

On his way back to the court of Polydectes, Perseus met with another adventure. He was flying over the land of Ethiopia when he saw a maiden on the seashore, chained to a rock, her arms outstretched against it. Hastening down, he learned her story from her. She was the unfortunate Andromeda, whose mother Queen Cassiopeia, glorying in her beauty, had boasted that she excelled all the daughters of the sea-god Nereus.[2] To avenge the insult Nereus had sent a sea-monster, whose ravages of crops and men could be checked only by the sacrifice of the princess. While they were still speaking, the monster appeared out to sea, swimming towards the shore. Perseus, standing in front of Andromeda, snatched the head from its pouch and held it aloft, making his first trial of its powers. Instantly the great serpent stopped; its coils congealed; it was no longer a living creature, but an immense black rock, stretching far out into the waves. Before putting the head away again, Perseus laid it for a moment on some seaweed, which stiffened and became the first coral.

Andromeda's grateful parents gave her to Perseus in marriage, and she accompanied him on his return to Seriphos. They found on arrival that far from marrying a princess from the mainland, as he had said he meant to do, Polydectes was still pursuing Danaë with his attentions, and that she and her protector Dictys had taken refuge in a nearby temple. Perseus went straight to the palace, where the king and his nobles were banqueting just as they were when he saw them last. "Here is the promised gift, O King"; and with that he showed them all the head. Visitors to the island are still shown the circle of stones he left behind him. Then, having no more use for the Gorgon's head, Perseus gave it to his protectress Athene, who attached it to the shield that she carries in battle.

Leaving the kingdom to Dictys, Perseus with his wife and his mother crossed the sea to Argos, hoping that Acrisius would by now have forgotten his fears and be prepared to receive them. Far from it: Acrisius fled to a neighbouring kingdom. Perseus, unaware of this, happened to come there shortly afterwards to compete in the funeral games held for the king's old father. When Perseus threw the discus, the wind carried it aside so that it struck Acrisius as he stood in the crowd and killed him. Perseus buried his grandfather with due honour, recognizing in the accident the will of the gods, and returned to inherit the kingdom of Argos. There he and his family lived long and happily, and to him was born a son whose child in turn was Alcmena, the mother of Heracles, the greatest of the heroes of Greece.

The Labours of Heracles

> Great Hercules is presented by this imp,
> Whose club kill'd Cerberus, that three-headed *canis*;
> And when he was a babe, a child, a shrimp,
> Thus did he strangle serpents in his *manus*.
>
> Shakespeare

Of all the heroes of the Greeks, Heracles was the strongest and the bravest. He and his twin brother Iphicles, a very ordinary person, were born at Thebes to a mortal woman, Alcmena, after Zeus visited her disguised as her husband. Zeus intended his son to be a great king, but he reckoned without the jealousy of Hera, who was enraged at his unfaithfulness. On the day when Heracles was supposed to be born, Hera heard Zeus declare: "He that is born today of my blood shall rule over all his neighbours." She immediately hastened to Thebes and sat down by the door of Alcmena's room, cross-legged and with her arms and fingers crossed.[3] Not only did she design thus to hinder the birth, she also prevented Eileithyia the birth-goddess from entering the room for seven days and seven nights. On the first day a boy of Zeus' blood was born at Mycenae, Eurystheus, another descendant of Perseus, so that Heracles was robbed of his royal birthright. But the jealous Hera might never have let him be born at all if she had not been tricked in her turni one of Alcmena's maids, suspecting magic, raised a cry of rejoic-ing as if her mistress had been delivered, and when Hera in astonish-ment sprang to her feet, Eileithyia slipped into the room and the twins were born.

Before Alcmena's babies were a year old, Hera sent two serpents into the nursery to kill them. The shrieks of Iphicles brought the whole household running; when they got there, Heracles was laughing in his cradle, a strangled snake drooping in each small fist. From that night it was clear that the child was marked out for a special destiny.

> Like that great champion of the antique world
> Whom famous poets' verse so much doth vaunt
> And hath for twelve huge labours high extolled ...
>
> Spenser

When he came to manhood, Heracles earned the gratitude of his fellow-Thebans by driving off a neighbouring king who had long been troubling them, and in reward he was given the hand of the princess, by whom he had three sons. After he had enjoyed several years of happy marriage, Hera sent upon him a fit of madness, in which he killed his wife and children. In his remorse after he returned to his senses, he was not satisfied with the formal rite of purification from blood-guilt,[4] but demanded a suitable penance of Apollo's oracle at Delphi. There the priestess counselled him to seek his kinsman King Eurystheus and serve him for twelve years in whatever way he should command. In the penance set by Eurystheus consist the famous Twelve Labours of Heracles. The oracle said further that at the conclusion of his labours he would become one of the immortals.

The first of Heracles' labours was to kill the Nemean Lion, a huge animal whose skin was proof against all weapons. After trying in vain to subdue it with arrows, sword, and the heavy olive-wood club he always carried, Heracles seized it in his arms and choked it to death. Henceforward he wore its skin round his shoulders as a cloak. His second labour was to kill the Hydra, the serpent offspring of a pair of monsters, that lived in the swamp of Lerna. It had nine heads, each of which sprouted anew if cut off. Heracles dealt with this hazard by cutting off the heads and then searing the stumps before they could grow again. The third, fourth, and fifth labours were the killing or capturing of the Erymanthian Boar, the golden-horned Hind of Ceryneia, and the man-eating Stymphalian Birds, which shot their sharp metallic feathers like darts at all who came near them. Sixth, Heracles had to clean out in a single day the stables of King Augeas, where dung had been accumulating year after year: this he did by diverting the course of a river and letting it carry the filth away. The seventh labour was the capture of a wild bull that was laying waste the crops of Crete. The eighth was capture of four mares that the cruel king Diomedes regularly fed with the flesh of guests visiting the palace: Heracles flung them the body of their master, whereupon they became tame. The ninth labour was the acquisition of the golden girdle belonging to Hippolyta, the queen of the Amazons, which Heracles carried off partly by bravery and partly by charm. The tenth was to fetch the cattle of Geryon, a king with three bodies and three heads who kept his herds on a western island towards the sunset. Heracles sailed there in a golden cup that he borrowed from the Sun,[5] setting up on the way two famous pillars at the far end of the Mediterranean,[6] at the points of rock now called Ceuta and Gibraltar. He then had to kill first Geryon's dog, next his herdsman, last Geryon himself, before he could load the cattle into the cup and carry them back to Mycenae.

Heracles in the Cup of the Sun[7]

Before thee stands this fair Hesperides
With golden fruit, but dangerous to be touch'd,
For death-like dragons here affright thee hard.
                                        Shakespeare

Heracles' eleventh and twelfth labours were the hardest of all. First he had to take the steep road down to the underworld and bring up Cerberus, the three-headed watchdog of the infernal gate. It was on this expedition that he released his cousin Theseus from the Chair of Forgetfulness. Last of all, he was to journey to the western end of the world and bring back some fruit from the golden apple-tree guarded by the serpent Ladon and three nymphs called the Hesperides. Not knowing how to proceed with this task, Heracles set out in search of the wise old sea-god Nereus. Finding him asleep beside the river Po, he seized him and began to ask him what to do. To escape him, Nereus changed his form rapidly into a whole series of creatures, as some sea-gods had the power of doing; but Heracles held him fast until Nereus gave his advice: to persuade the giant Atlas to get the apples for him.

When Heracles reached the Garden of the Hesperides, he saw Atlas standing there, bent under the burden of the sky, and asked him for help. Now Atlas was reluctant to see the garden robbed, as he was its guardian; but an oracle had told him many years before that some day a son of Zeus would come and strip the tree, and moreover, he saw a chance of escaping from his burden. So he agreed to fetch the apples if Heracles would take the weight of the sky for a few minutes; and soon he came back, smiling and tossing the apples from hand to hand. "Hero, you can stand there a little longer, and I'll take these to Eurystheus myself." "Very well, comrade, if you'll just take the sky a minute while I roll my lion-skin into a pad for my shoulders." The foolish Atlas bent under the sky again, and Heracles snatched up the apples and walked off.

> Earth's son Antaeus ... in Irassa strove
> With Jove's Alcides,[8] and oft foiled still rose,
> Receiving from his mother Earth new strength,
> Fresh from his fall, and fiercer grapple joined,
> Throttled at length in the air, expired and fell.
>
> Milton

On his way back to Eurystheus, Heracles met and defeated the Libyan giant Antaeus, who wrestled with all comers and used their skulls to roof a temple he was building. He was the more terrible an opponent because every time he touched the ground his mother Earth renewed his strength, however weary he might be: Heracles overcame him by holding him high in the air until he became as weak as a child and was easily crushed. Before leaving Africa Heracles killed the blood-thirsty Egyptian king Busiris, who used to sacrifice all strangers to Zeus. Making his way to Troy, he arrived just in time to rescue a maiden called Hesione who was about to be sacrificed by her father to a sea-monster. Heracles leapt into the open mouth of the creature and struggled for three days in its belly, slashing about with club and sword until at last it was mortally struck and he cut his way out. It was on this journey too that Heracles travelled to the Caucasus Mountains and released Prometheus from his long sufferings.

Less glorious than these exploits was Heracles' action when in a fit of anger he killed a young man who was a guest under his roof: Zeus, who always upholds the laws of hospitality, decreed as punishment that he must be sold into slavery for a year. The divine messenger Hermes led him into Asia Minor and sold him to Queen Omphale of Lydia, who completed his disgrace by making him sit dressed as a woman among her maiden attendants, turning his clumsy fingers to spinning and weaving, while she draped herself in his lion-skin and played at wielding his club.

> Methought I saw my late espousèd saint
> Brought to me like Alcestis from the grave,
> Whom Jove's great son to her glad husband gave,
> Rescued from death by force though pale and faint.
>
> Milton

Besides harrowing the underworld and capturing the apples of immortality, Heracles had another contest with death. When Zeus, as we shall see, struck down the presumptuous healer Asclepius, his father Apollo, not daring to take a direct revenge on the ruler of the gods, murdered the Cyclopes who had made the fatal thunderbolt in their underworld smithy. In punishment Zeus bound Apollo in servitude to a mortal man, King Admetus of Pherae, whose shepherd and herdsman he became. Admetus and his wife Alcestis treated him with great kindness, and in return he obtained from the three Fates (some say by making them drunk) the promise that Admetus' approaching death-day could be postponed if another would consent to die in his place. Admetus went to everyone he could think of, including his old father and mother, imploring them to give up their lives for him: all refused but Alcestis his wife. When the day came, Alcestis quietly died and the household went into mourning for her. At this point Heracles came by on his way to Thrace to tackle the mares of Diomedes, and Admetus thought it right to welcome him without mentioning his cause for sorrow. However, Heracles found out from the servants about Alcestis' sacrifice, and immediately resolved to fight Death himself for her. He lay in wait beside her tomb until the messenger from the underworld appeared, and then challenged him to a wrestling match, in which the hero was soon the winner. Then taking the restored Alcestis by the hand, he led her to her husband in thanks for the hospitality he had received.

> The shirt of Nessus is upon me; teach me,
> Alcides thou mine ancestor, thy rage;
> Let me lodge Lichas on the horns o' the moon;
> And with those hands that grasp'd the heaviest club
> Subdue my worthiest self.
>
> Shakespeare

After the death of his wife Heracles married a maiden named Deianeira. As he was bringing his bride home, they were stopped by a river in flood. Heracles was able to get over by himself, and the centaur Nessus, who was the local ferryman, offered to carry Deianeira. In midstream he turned and attempted to run off with her, whereupon Heracles shot him with his bow. As Nessus lay dying, he murmured to Deianeira that she should take some of his blood and keep it as a charm: if a time should ever come when Heracles ceased to love her, she could win him back by smearing some of it on a garment for him to wear. Deianeira kept the blood for several years, until she heard a rumour that Heracles was enamoured of a captive princess whom he was bringing home with him from the successful siege of a city. Deianeira sent a messenger to meet him with presents, among them a newly-woven shirt dyed in the blood of Nessus, thus unwittingly bringing to pass the prophecy of an old oracle: "No living man shall be the death of Heracles: by a dead enemy shall he be brought low." Heracles put on the shirt to offer sacrifices to the gods, and immediately he felt his flesh burn in consuming pain. He tried to tear the garment from his back, but the magic substance made it stick fast. Yelling with agony, he seized the unfortunate messenger and flung him into the sea. Then he called aloud to the gods for death; but because of his divine birth, the poison that tormented him could not kill him. To end his suffering, he asked his friends and servants to build him a great pyre on Mount Oeta and place him on it: there among the flames his mortal part was burned away, while his immortal part was carried up to Olympus in the chariot of Zeus. Hera at last relented from her long enmity and married him to her daughter Hebe, the gods' cup-bearer, and in the halls of the gods Heracles enjoys a merry afterlife, feasting and recalling the heroic deeds that raised him above the common fate of men.

Sons of Boreas pursuing the Harpies

Jason and the Golden Fleece

Her name is Portia . . . and her sunny locks
Hang on her temples like a golden fleece,
Which makes her seat of Belmont Colchis' strand,
And many Jasons come in quest of her.
Shakespeare

Aeson, the king of Iolcos in Thessaly, was deposed from his throne by his envious half-brother Pelias. Fearing for the life of his young son Jason, Aeson brought him to Cheiron, the wise Centaur who lived in a cave in the side of Mount Pelion. Endowed with prodigious strength and nobility, half man, half horse, Cheiron was entrusted with many of the sons of the heroes to be trained in all the heroic arts, as well as the gentler ones of healing and song. When Jason had learned all that Cheiron could teach him, he set out for Iolcos to claim his father's kingdom.

On his way to the seashore city he had to cross on foot the tumultuous river Anauros, without ferry, bridge, or ford. There he met a poor old woman, who begged him to carry her across. This he did with some difficulty, but with no more mishap than the loss of one of his sandals; and when he set her down on the further bank, the old woman revealed herself as the goddess Hera, henceforward his protectress.

When Jason reached Iolcos, he enquired his way to the palace of Pelias and soon stood before the usurper. Pelias trembled to see him, recognizing the man by whom he should be overthrown; for he had long ago been warned by an oracle: "Beware of the man with one sandal." However, he dissembled his fears, and when Jason said who he was and what he had come for, Pelias welcomed him with smooth words. "But, nephew, perhaps you can give me a word of advice. What would you do with a man from whom your life was in danger?" "I would send him to fetch the Golden Fleece." "Nephew, you are that man."

A generation before Jason's own time, King Athamas of Boeotia married trouble in the form of his second wife, Ino the daughter of Cadmus. Athamas had two children by a former marriage, Phrixus and his sister Helle. Their stepmother Ino hated them, and conceived a plot to get rid of them. One year she secretly roasted the country's entire supply of seed-corn, so that the countrymen, though they sowed as usual, waited in vain for the harvest. When, as Ino expected, her husband sent messengers to enquire of the oracle at Delphi why the land was so afflicted, she bribed them to bring back a false report that the god was angry and demanded the deaths of Phrixus and Helle. Athamas, to save his people from famine, sorrowfully consented to the sacrifice. But just as the priest stood over the children with his knife, Zeus in pity sent a golden ram, that miraculously appeared before the altar. It took the children on its back and fled away with them through the air, over the unknown eastern sea. As they were passing the narrow strait that separates Europe from Asia, Helle slipped from the ram's back and was drowned in the waters that are called after her the Hellespont, or Helle's Sea. Her brother Phrixus hung on until the ram set him down in distant Colchis at the far end of the stormy Euxine Sea.[9] There Phrixus in gratitude sacrificed the ram to Zeus, and its fleece was hung on a tree in a sacred grove and guarded by a dragon. There too in time he married Chalciope, the daughter of Helios' son King Aeetes, and there while still quite young he died.

And now, Pelias told Jason, the ghost of his kinsman Phrixus came to him night after night in dreams, begging him to recover the fleece and take it back to his old homeland, so that his troubled spirit might find rest. If Jason could carry out the task, Pelias would gladly restore to him his father's kingdom. But in his heart he hoped the young man would never return.

> But silent sat the heroes by the oar,
> Hearkening the sounds borne from the lessening shore;
> The lowing of the doomed and flower-crowned beasts,

The plaintive singing of the ancient priests,
Mingled with blare of trumpets, and the sound
Of all the many folk that stood around
The altar and the temple by the sea.
So sat they pondering much and silently,
Till all the landward noises died away,
And, midmost now of the green sunny bay,
They heard no sound but washing of the seas
And piping of the following western breeze,
And heavy measured beating of the oars;
So left the Argo the Thessalian shores.

> William Morris

The first thing Jason did was to send messengers to all the cities of Greece to summon the heroes to the quest; and Hera, his friend, kindled in their hearts the love of glory. One of the first who came was the shipwright Argus, and to him Jason entrusted the building of their vessel, the first large ship ever to put out on the sea, called after her maker the Argo. Fixed in her bow was a piece of wood from the talking oak of Dodona which gave advice when asked, and she had places for fifty oarsmen. Among the Argonauts, the fifty heroes who sailed in her, were many of the noblest of Greece: Heracles the strong man with his armour-bearer Hylas, Castor and Polydeuces the twin sons of Zeus,[10] Peleus the father of Achilles, Mopsus the soothsayer who knew the language of the birds, Orpheus the sweet singer, Zetes and Calaïs the sons of the North Wind, and many more.

The Argo first sailed northwards along the eastern shore of Greece, and then struck east through the Hellespont into the Propontine Sea. At Cius they stopped while Heracles, who had broken his oar, looked for wood for a new one. After uprooting a large fir tree, which he dragged behind him, Heracles came back to his companions to find that his young armour-bearer was not with them. He began to crash about in the forest, roaring "Hylas! Hylas!" at the top of his great voice. But Hylas was out of hearing. Having set off on his own to look for water, he had come to a deep pool and leaned over it with his pitcher; and the nymph of the spring, seeing the charming boy, caught him by the arms and drew him down to her underwater world. So Heracles never found him again, but wandered the whole night up and down, calling "Hylas! Hylas!" till all the shore resounded. And the Argo sailed on without him.

Their next adventure occurred shortly after they entered the Euxine

Sea, in the realm of King Phineus. Phineus was one of the sons of Agenor sent out in search of their sister Europa, carried off by Zeus, and he had come thus far in his wanderings and never returned home. But that was long ago, and now he was an old and wretched man. His one gift, that of prophecy, had proved no blessing to him, for by it he had angered the gods, who sent blindness upon him and moreover plagued him with a pair of Harpies. These were flying monsters with the bodies of women and the wings of hawks, who every time the table was spread before him burst into the palace with a terrible clatter, swooped down on the food, and fled away with it shrieking, spattering dirt on any they left behind. Because they were messengers of the gods' vengeance, they were known as "the hounds of Zeus." No sooner had the poor old king laid a banquet to welcome the heroes than the loathsome creatures appeared. Immediately Calaïs and Zetes, the winged sons of Boreas, sprang into the air in pursuit; and some say they are chasing them yet, in the squalls and black airs that vex the Euxine Sea. But the Harpies never troubled King Phineus again; and in return for this service, he gave Jason good advice about the further conduct of his voyage.

One of the dangers about which Phineus warned the Argonauts was the Symplegades, the clashing blue rocks that barred their way, grinding against each other with fearsome noises. Here Jason let loose a dove, which sped only just in time through a narrow passageway, losing a few tail-feathers as the rocks crashed together behind. As soon as they drew apart again, the Argonauts heaved powerfully on their oars and drove the ship through before the passage could close, as Phineus had told them they must do.

After many long days of rowing eastward along the shore, the heroes sighted the snow-covered Caucasus Mountains that mark the eastern limit of the Euxine Sea. On the highest lay stretched out the Titan Prometheus, with the eagle of vengeful Zeus tearing at his liver: at the foot of the range lay the land of Colchis, the goal of their journey. Entering the mouth of the river Phasis, the Argonauts rowed up it to the grove of Ares and the city of Aeetes, child of the Sun, where in a shady backwater they cast anchor and passed the night in consultation.

> As that brave son of Aeson, which by charms
> Achiev'd the golden fleece in Colchid land,
> Out of the earth engendered men of arms
> Of dragon's teeth, sown in the sacred sand ...
>   Spenser

When dawn broke, Jason with a few chosen comrades set out for the palace of Aeetes, built for him by the divine smith Hephaestus. With the king lived his queen, their daughters Chalciope the widow of Phrixus and Medea the witch-maiden, priestess of the dark goddess Hecate, and their young son Absyrtus. Jason came boldly into the presence of Aeetes and declared his errand. Now Aeetes valued the Golden Fleece as the treasure of his realm, and had no intention of parting lightly with it to any stranger; but he disguised the anger in his heart and proposed to Jason a trial of strength.

"If you are indeed a descendant of the gods and as worthy a man as I myself, then I will give you the Fleece to carry back with you. But first you must prove your merit by accomplishing a prodigious feat, though one within my own powers. Hephaestus made for me two brazen bulls, breathing fire from their jaws: these I yoke on the field of Ares and with them do a full day's ploughing, casting into the furrows teeth from the serpent Cadmus slew. Immediately there springs up a strange harvest of armed men, and as they rise I cut them down into the ploughed earth until none is left. No man who fails to carry out this task as I can shall bear away the Fleece."

When Jason heard this challenge, his courage almost failed him; but now that he had brought his companions so far into foreign lands, he had no choice but to accept. His face was troubled as he turned to go back to the ship. But the goddesses who befriended him, Hera and Athene, shed grace and beauty on him as he walked, so that he shone out from among the crowd. And the heart of Aeetes' daughter Medea was stirred in his favour, so that she put away the veil from her face and followed him with her eyes. All night she lay wakeful, troubled with love for Jason and fears for his safety, and then again with shame at her disloyalty to her father who saw this stranger as an enemy.

In the morning Medea's mind was made up. She sent a messenger to ask Jason to meet her at the shrine of Hecate, and then calling her maids she set out for the appointed place. When she met the hero, she was so overcome by her conflicting feelings that she could scarcely speak, and Jason had to strain to catch her words.

"When night comes, go apart from your companions and offer sacrifice[11] to the powerful goddess Hecate, patroness of magic and sorcery: then turn away, and do not let anything you hear, whether the baying of hounds or the trampling of feet, make you look back, if you ever want to return to your companions. At dawn, steep in water this charm I give you and anoint your body all over with it, also your weapons: then for a single day you will be invulnerable, so that neither the breath of the fiery bulls nor the clashing of the earth-born men can harm you. When the dragon's crop springs up, cast among the armed men a great stone, and they will turn against one another and shorten your labour. Then the king will give you the Fleece, and you will sail away to your dear native land; but what will become of me, poor maiden, who have betrayed my father to save a stranger's life?" Moved by her grief, Jason swore to the princess that if with her help he succeeded, she should return with him to Iolcos, where he would marry her. So Medea returned comforted with her maids to her father's palace.

When Jason came back to his companions at the Argo and told them all that had passed, the heroes rejoiced that he had found help against the wicked schemes of Aeetes: all but one, who bitterly reproached him. "Son of Aeson, is it now come to this, that we who are men, skilled in the deeds of war, rely on the arts of Aphrodite, on magic, and on the wiles of young girls? Shame, I say, shame and empty folly." But all the others approved Jason's agreement with the fair-haired witch-maiden.

Now night was falling, and Jason took his way to a lonely place, a meadow under the open sky, where he dug a pit, killed a sheep and kindled a fire under it, letting the blood soak into the ground and pouring libations of honey, all the while calling on dark Hecate, goddess of enchantments. And from the depths of the earth the dread goddess heard him, and came herself to the sacrifice offered by Aeson's son; and with her approach serpents twined in the nearby oak boughs, torches shone in the darkness, and about her howled the hounds of hell. Jason saw and heard these things, and felt the ground tremble under him; but he remembered Medea's words, and quickly sought the ship without looking back.

When dawn came, Aeetes arrayed himself in his armour, placing on his head a golden helmet that gleamed like the rising sun; then mounting his swift-drawn chariot he drove out of the city to the field of Ares, attended by a great multitude of the Colchians. Meanwhile Jason had bathed himself in the water in which he had steeped Medea's charm, and also bathed his weapons; and godlike strength entered into him, and great courage, so that he longed for the contest. The heroes stood around him shouting with joy and hope. When all were assembled, the bulls came charging out from their underground stable, wrapped in black smoke and breathing forth flames of fire, so that all who saw them were afraid. But Jason stood firm before their onset, warding off their sharp horns with his shield, protected from the withering heat by

Medea's charm. Then, grasping the horn of one of the bulls, he brought it to its knees, and next the other, and fastened to their necks the adamantine yoke fashioned for King Aeetes by Hephaestus, the divine smith. Taking in his hand a bronze helmet filled with the dragon's teeth, he began his day's ploughing of Ares' field, moving steadily along the dark furrows, undaunted by the angry plunging of the bulls.

At evening Jason loosed the bulls from the yoke and drove them from the field. Already the strange harvest began to cleave the earth, first the gleam of helmets showing above the surface, then whole bodies of fully-armed men springing into view; and each one as he rose turned on Jason as his fated enemy. But Jason quickly threw into their midst a great boulder, and immediately they began to fight among themselves, destroying one another in merciless slaughter, while Jason rushed in and out of the combat dealing fearful blows. The furrows of the field were filled with blood as the last of the earth-born died. And bitterness filled the heart of King Aeetes, who turned away from the contest and went back to the city, plotting the destruction of Jason and his comrades.

When Medea heard all that had happened, she felt sure that her father did not mean to honour his promise. Taking her last look at the home of her childhood, she passed out through the gates in the dark, veiling her face and speeding past the watchmen. As she fled, the rising moon caught sight of her and murmured in triumph: "Then I am not the only maiden betrayed by love, when I hasten down the sky to the cave on Mount Latmos where the shepherd Endymion sleeps! Many times you have driven me away and darkened me with your spells, and now you too suffer; for some god has given you Jason to be your grief." But Medea fled on till she came to the shore where the Argo lay at anchor, and called to the sailors to take her aboard.

"Aeetes knows all and is plotting some treachery: save yourselves before day breaks and he mounts his chariot in pursuit. And I myself will lull to sleep the fierce dragon and give you the fleece of gold: but, stranger, son of Aeson, swear before the gods the oath you swore to me alone, and now that I have forsaken my country and my friends, do not leave me to shame and dishonour." And Jason swore once more, calling Zeus and Hera to witness, that when they came home to Iolcos he would make her his wife.

> Meet I an infant of the house of York,
> Into as many gobbets will I cut it
> As wild Medea young Absyrtus did.
> Shakespeare

Then they rowed the ship up the river to the grove of Ares, and Jason and Medea landed opposite the oak tree where the Golden Fleece hung, dazzling to the eye and reflecting the beams of the sun just rising. But in front of it stirred the unsleeping dragon, moving his head from side to side and hissing so that the river-bank echoed and mothers still sleeping in the town held their children closer. And Medea stepped up to him, calling on Hecate and on Hypnos the god of sleep to help her, and singing lullabies, so that his cruel head sank to the ground in harmless slumber, and his numberless coils lay spread about the grove. Then Jason snatched the Golden Fleece and held it tightly to him, and he and Medea returned to the Argo, where the heroes had watched the approach of the treasure, gleaming through the trees. And Jason placed Medea in the stern, and the Argonauts shouted and pulled on the oars to carry the ship down to the mouth of the river. By now Medea's part in aiding the heroes was known to King Aeetes and all the people of Colchis, and countless as the leaves that fall in autumn they armed themselves and thronged clamouring along the river-bank, while above them all shone the king in his well-made chariot. But already the Argo, borne on by the swift Phasis and the strength of her oarsmen, had reached the open sea. And the king in anger and grief lifted his hands to Helios his father and Zeus the ruler of the gods to witness the wrongs done against him; and against his own people he uttered threats of vengeance unless they would pursue the strangers and bring back the witch-maiden Medea.

So he spoke; and the whole nation of the Colchians put to sea in pursuit. But the cunning Medea had brought with her the young prince, her brother Absyrtus. And with treacherous hand she struck him down on the decks, so that his blood stained her silver robe as she shrank from his fall; and she cut his body into pieces and threw them overboard to delay the pursuers, who stopped and gathered them aboard the Colchian ships for burial. By this cruel means they were able to outstrip the fleet of Aeetes; and cheered by the songs of Orpheus, they sped before a favouring wind along the Euxine Sea.

> So sung he joyously, nor knew that they
> Must wander yet for many an evil day
> Or ever the dread Gods should let them come
> Back to the white walls of their long-left home.
> William Morris

The slaying of Absyrtus brought upon the heroes the grievous wrath of Zeus, king of the gods, who stirred up storm winds to block their way on the sea. And now they must all have perished on the wide sea and never come again to their dear native land; but as they were tossing hither and thither a voice called to them, speaking from the beam of their hollow ship that Athene had set in the prow from the sacred wood of Dodona. And fear seized upon them as it told of the anger of Zeus, declaring that they should not escape alive from the endless roads of the sea and the deadly tempests unless the enchantress Circe purified them from the blood-guilt of Absyrtus' murder. So spoke the ship in the dark night.

And they left the Euxine Sea and passed by the great mainland rivers of the north to the Italian shore and the famous island of Aeaea, the home of bright-haired Circe, child of the Sun. And they found her bathing her head in the salt sea-spray, sorely troubled by visions of the night. For she dreamed that the walls and chambers of her palace ran with blood; and now she was bathing her hair and her garments for a purification. And strange beasts surrounded her, as flocks follow their shepherd, beasts of mixed and uncertain forms. While the heroes gazed in wonder, Jason and Medea followed Circe to her palace. There they refused the seats she offered them, sitting as suppliants in the dust of the hearth,[12] with downcast faces; and Jason fixed in the ground the great sword with which Absyrtus was slain. Then Circe understood her dream, and that they had come to her for purification from guilt of blood. And she offered sacrifice and burned cakes for an atonement, praying that the avenging Furies might relent and Zeus show them favour.

When the rites were done, Circe raised them and seated them, and began to question them concerning their country and their journey; and when Medea raised her eyes, Circe knew her for her kinswoman. For those of the race of Helios are recognized by the gold gleam that flashes from their eyes. So the daughter of sorrowful Aeetes told her all she asked, speaking softly in the Colchian tongue, of the quest and the wanderings of the heroes, and the trials set Jason, and her own sin and sorrow in aiding him; but of the murder of Absyrtus she did not tell. Nevertheless the enchantress knew all, and said to her, "Wicked are the ways that you have devised, and shameful shall be your homecoming. But since you have come to me as a suppliant and kinswoman, I shall do you no harm: go on your way with this unknown man you have chosen, the enemy of your kin." And Medea veiled her face and wept, trembling as Jason led her from Circe's halls.

... the Sirens three
Amid'st the flowery-kirtled Naiades
Culling their potent herbs and baleful drugs,
Who as they sung would take the prisoned soul
And lap it in Elysium. Scylla wept
And chid her barking waves into attention,
And fell Charybdis murmured soft applause.

Milton

When Hera saw that they were resuming their journey, she called to the rainbow-goddess Iris to seek out Thetis, the silver-footed sea-nymph Zeus had given in marriage to the hero Peleus. Thetis came to her from the chambers of the sea, and Hera said: "The Argonauts, who are under my protection, are about to pass the twin perils, Scylla and Charybdis. Now in the name of our old friendship and the many favours we have done each other, lend your aid to the heroes, among whom is your husband Peleus, so that neither shall Charybdis on one side draw them down into her whirlpool, nor deadly Scylla on the other snatch them up in her horrible jaws."[13] And Thetis consenting set out on the paths of the sea in search of her sisters.

But before the Argo reached Scylla and Charybdis she had to pass the flowering island of the clear-voiced Sirens, whose forms were partly like birds and partly like maidens, who beguiled passing sailors with their sweet songs and lured them ashore to destroy them.[14] There Orpheus took up his lyre, singing and playing so that the songs of the Sirens were quite drowned out. Only one of the heroes still listened, his soul melted by their ringing voices, and he leapt up from his rowing-bench and sprang into the sea. Swimming through the dark waters, he climbed up on to the beach; and that would have been the end of him if laughter-loving Aphrodite had not pitied his youth and soft heart and carried him away to dwell with her in one of her sacred places. Grieving for the loss of their companion, the heroes went on their way.

And now to one side rose the steep rock of Scylla, and on the other Charybdis boiled and sputtered; but Thetis and her nymphs caught up the ship and tossed it from one to the next along the waves, as young girls play with a ball, and so they came safely through. And the nymphs dived back like seabirds to their homes under the water, while Scylla gnashed her ugly jaws at them.

Next they came to Scheria, the island of the good king Alcinoüs, ruler of the Phaeacians. There they met a great host of Colchians, still searching for Medea and afraid to go home without her; these demanded that Jason either give her up or prepare for battle. But Alcinoüs tried to pacify them, hoping the issue could be settled without bloodshed. And Medea sat at the feet of his queen Arete and implored her not to let her be given up; she implored the heroes too, for fear that in their weariness and longing for home they might forget their promises to her, stained with crime as she was. And each man among the Argonauts swore to protect her against an unjust judgment.

At night, when Alcinoüs lay on his couch thinking the matter over, his wife Arete pleaded with him for Medea: "for the maiden in the greatness of her suffering has broken my heart with her prayers." Alcinoüs' heart was softened by the words of his wife, and he said to her: "Arete, you know I could drive the host of the Colchians from the island and defend the maiden with force; but I fear to do an injustice in the eyes of almighty Zeus. Hear, then, what I have decided. If Medea is still unmarried, then she is rightly under the authority of her father King Aeetes, and to him she must return; but if on the journey Jason has already wedded her, then she shall go with him, for I will not separate a wife from her husband." So he spoke, and afterwards he fell asleep. Then Arete rose and sent a messenger to Jason, telling him Alcinoüs' judgment and advising him to marry Medea without delay. The messenger hastened to the heroes, and rejoicing they offered sacrifices and decked the bridal couch with the Golden Fleece, while Orpheus sang the marriage-song. And thus the marriage of Jason and Medea was accomplished, in fear as much as love, and not in the halls of Jason's father at home but hastily and in a foreign land. In the morning Alcinoüs gave his judgment, and the Phaeacians came thronging to the ship bearing gifts for the new-wedded bride. As for the Colchians, they gave up their pursuit of Medea and never returned to face the anger of Aeetes, but settled in the island.

Great labours were still in store for the heroes. Leaving Scheria, they were seized by the winds and carried into the gulf of Syrtis on the Libyan coast, where they were stranded among the shoals. For twelve days and twelve nights they carried the ship overland on their shoulders, and at last with the help of the gods they struck the open sea again. And now between them and the mainland of Hellas lay the island of Crete, guarded by Talos, the man of bronze.

There are two stories about Talos' origin. According to one, he was one of the many wonders created by the master-smith Hephaestus, like Aeetes' brazen bulls and yoke of adamant. The other says that Talos was a survivor from the brazen race of men.

Whatever his origin, he was presented by Zeus to Europa to be the guardian of her Cretan island, and three times every day he walked all the way round it on his brazen feet, keeping watch. When he saw the Argo, he tore great handfuls of rocks out of the cliffside to cast at her. But Medea had a plan to overcome him. She knew the secret of his life: that while his whole body was bronze and invulnerable, all his blood was carried in a single vein that was plugged with a pin at the ankle. Calling to him sweetly, she told him that she was sent by the gods to reward his long service by drawing out the pin and replacing his blood with a magic ichor that would make him ageless and deathless for ever. The simple-minded giant let her approach and lull him to sleep; but once she had drawn out the pin and let all his blood run into the sand, she left him and he died. And so the Argonauts were able to take fresh water on board and continue on their way.

> O, for Medea's wondrous alchemy,
> Which wheresoe'er it fell made the earth gleam
> With bright flowers, and the wintry boughs exhale
> From vernal blooms fresh fragrance!
>
> Shelley

At last Jason and his shipmates arrived back in Iolcos, where they were welcomed by Jason's ancient father Aeson. Pitying his father's age and weakness, Jason asked Medea if she knew any witchcraft powerful enough to restore his lost youth, and Medea agreed to try. That night, after offering prayers and sacrifices to her goddess Hecate, she brewed magic herbs in a cauldron, drained out the old man's blood, and filled his veins with her potion. Immediately his hair regained its colour and his flesh filled out, and he appeared before Jason as a young man again.

With this success behind her, Medea went to the palace of Pelias, claiming that she had quarrelled with her husband, and was kindly received by Pelias' daughters. Once she had their attention, she told them what she had been able to do for Jason's father, and offered to demonstrate her powers. She took an old ram, cut its throat, and threw its body into a cauldron together with the magical herbs, and in a moment a young lamb sprang out and ran away bleating.

Pelias' daughters were convinced, and they implored Medea to do the same for their old father. Medea consented, with some show of reluctance, and when the old man was sleeping, she directed them to cut up his body and drain out the blood. She then flung the pieces into the cauldron, but neglected to pronounce the proper spells over them, running instead to the palace tower to signal to Jason that he could now enter the city and seize the throne.

With Pelias' murder now added to their crimes, Jason and Medea were not allowed to rule very long in Iolcos before Pelias' son gathered a force together and drove them out. Exiled, they wandered to Corinth, whose king took them in. And now Jason, weary of a wife so stained with guilt, cast off Medea and made preparations to marry the young daughter of his host. Medea sent the maiden for a wedding gift a poisoned robe: when she put it on it burned her to the bone, and her father, trying to help her, was consumed with her. To complete her vengeance, Medea then stabbed to death the children she had had by Jason, and fled away in a dragon-borne chariot sent by her dark protectress Hecate.

Jason's faith to Medea had long ago been sworn on the names of the gods, and from the day he broke it he was never lucky again. His later life was spent in wandering, without home or friends, until in old age he found himself once more at Corinth, sitting on the shore in the shadow of the Argo. As he sat there remembering the past, a piece from the stern crashed down, killing him in its fall. Afterwards the old ship disappeared from the harbour: Poseidon, the god of the sea, had carried it up and placed it among the stars.

Bellerophon and Pegasus

> Up led by thee
> Into the heaven of heavens I have presumed,
> An earthly guest, and drawn empyreal air,
> Thy temp'ring; with like safety guided down
> Return me to my native element:
> Lest from this flying steed unreined (as once
> Bellerophon, though from a lower clime)
> Dismounted, on the Aleian field I fall,
> Erroneous there to wander and forlorn.
>
> Milton

The Corinthian prince Bellerophon, a grandson of the impious Sisyphus, had the misfortune to accidentally kill his brother. Fleeing to Proetus, the king of Tiryns, for purification, Bellerophon was kindly received there. But Proetus' wife fell in love with him, and when he would not

Man and Winged Horse[15]

listen, she accused him privately to Proetus of having wronged her. As Bellerophon was his guest, Proetus was reluctant to commit any violent act against him; so he sent him to Iobates, the king of distant Lycia in the east, with a sealed letter of introduction. Iobates feasted Bellerophon royally for nine days, and on the tenth he asked to see the letter. There he read that Proetus wanted the young man killed.

No more anxious than Proetus to court Zeus' anger by treachery to a guest, Iobates thought of a way to accomplish the same end. He asked Bellerophon to kill for him a monster that was troubling the land: the Chimaera, which had a goat's body and a serpent for a tail and breathed forth flames from a lion's head. Bellerophon could not refuse. Consulting a seer, he was advised to catch the winged horse Pegasus, who had

Chimaera

never been ridden or bridled. In fact the only work Pegasus had ever done was to strike a rock on the Muses' mountain Helicon with his hoof, from whose imprint flowed a clear spring ever afterwards called Hippocrene, the Horse's Well.

With a magic bridle, the gift of Athene, Bellerophon was able to catch and tame the marvellous horse. That made his task easy: from Pegasus' back he shot the Chimaera without once coming close to its fiery breath. When he returned, Iobates sent him on other difficult missions, against a warrior tribe called the Solymi and then against the Amazons. These he accomplished successfully, with Pegasus' help. At last Iobates, convinced by Bellerophon's good fortune that he had been unjustly accused, gave up trying to kill him and married him to one of his daughters.

Bellerophon might have remained happily in Lycia and inherited the throne of Iobates, had it not been for his excessive ambition. Confident in the powers of Pegasus, he tried to ride him up Mount Olympus to the halls of the gods; but Zeus sent a gadfly that stung Pegasus, so that he reared and threw his rider back to earth. Pegasus finished the journey, and was received and stabled among the immortal horses of Zeus. Bellerophon, hated by the gods, wandered alone on the Aleian plain, gnawing at his own heart and shunning the paths of men until he died.

Theseus

> Whilom, as oldë stories tellen us,
> There was a duke that hightë Theseus.
> Of Athens he was lord and governour,
> And in his timë swich a conquerour
> That greater was there none under the sonnë.
>
> Chaucer

When Medea fled from Corinth to escape the wrath of Jason, her dragon-borne chariot carried her to Athens, ruled at the time by King Aegeus, who not only offered her hospitality but made her his wife.

Shortly afterwards, a stranger made his way to the court. Medea, suspecting him to be a pretender to the throne, mixed a poisonous cup of aconite[16] and persuaded Aegeus to hand it to him. Just as the stranger was about to drink, Aegeus recognized the sword at his side and struck the cup out of his hand. This sword was one which he himself had left many years ago, together with a pair of sandals, under a large rock in Argolian Troezen across the Saronic Gulf, saying to the princess Aethra,

"When your child becomes a man able to lift the rock, send him to me in Athens with these tokens and I shall acknowledge him as my son."

This stranger was indeed Aegeus' son Theseus. Leaving his mother Aethra, he had set out for Athens overland, by the long way round, hoping to meet adventures along the road. The land route to Athens was infested with robbers and murderers who preyed on all who travelled it, and Theseus meant to clear the way of them.

The first he met was Corynetes, the Cudgeller, who used to knock travellers' brains out with a huge brazen club: Theseus snatched it from him and served him the same way. The next was Sinis, nicknamed Pityocamptes, the Pine-bender, who tied all he caught to two pine-trees bent down to the ground, and then released them so that his victim was torn apart: he too was done by as he did. Next came Sciron, who forced passing travellers to wash his feet for him and then as they bent over kicked them over the cliff's edge into the sea, where lived a man-eating turtle who finished them off. Him Theseus presented to his old dependent the turtle. The last bandit Theseus met was one Procrustes, who invited all travellers to pass the night at his house. He had a remarkable bed, which his guests always found either too long or too short. Procrustes would force them to lie down, and then either stretch them or trim them till they fitted it exactly, the treatment being always fatal. Now at last the maker of the murderous bed was made to lie on it, and that was the end of him.

When Theseus was welcomed to Aegeus' palace, he learned of the troubles of the kingdom. The first was that Aegeus' brother and his fifty sons, who had always disputed Aegeus' right to reign in Athens, were just now plotting to overthrow him. Theseus led his father's forces against them in battle, and compelled them to sue for peace. The second evil had its origin in an event of some years before, when Minos, son of Europa and king of the ancient kingdom of Crete, had sent his son Androgeus to the Panathenaic games. Androgeus won every trophy that was offered, and Aegeus, fearing the friendship of this powerful prince with his conspiring nephews, had him ambushed and killed. Minos demanded that the Athenians in reparation should annually send to Crete seven youths and seven maidens to be delivered to the Minotaur.[17]

Now the Minotaur was a monster, having the body of a man and the head of a bull, that had been born to Minos' queen in punishment for an offence committed by Minos against the gods. Wanting to hide the shame of such a child, Minos had commanded the cunning craftsman

Daedalus[18] to design a mysterious building, full of winding passages and known as the labyrinth,[19] in the middle of which the Minotaur had his den. The labyrinth was built in such a way that the single entrance, once passed, was impossible to find again, so that even if one of the young victims managed to escape the monster he would certainly die of hunger and exhaustion before he could find his way back to the light.

> His waxen wings did mount above his reach,
> And melting heavens conspired his overthrow.
>   Christopher Marlowe

Daedalus, the master-craftsman who built the labyrinth, learned his skills from Athene, the patroness of handwork of all kinds. Born in Athens, he was banished from his native city for murdering one of his apprentices, a young craftsman whose skill threatened to rival his own. Daedalus sought refuge at the court of Minos, who welcomed him for his wonderful abilities. After he had made for Minos not only the labyrinth but many other marvels, Daedalus wanted to leave Crete; but Minos refused to let him go, some say locking him up in the labyrinth he had designed. Daedalus' ingenuity showed him a way of escape. He fashioned two pairs of great wings, one for himself and one for his son Icarus. As he fastened the wings to his son's shoulders, he warned him not to rise too high, for fear the sun would melt the wax holding the pinions together. But Icarus, enraptured with the new experience of flying, disobeyed and mounted up towards the sun, whereupon his wings fell apart and he plunged into the sea and was drowned. His father sorrowfully carried his body for burial to a nearby island, since called Icaria.

Daedalus was kindly received by King Cocalus of Sicily. Meanwhile Minos, determined not to lose the most valuable of his servants, travelled all over the Mediterranean in search of him. He took with him a spiral shell, offering a large reward to anyone who could pass a linen thread through it, there being only one man in the world equal to such a problem. Cocalus undertook to get the shell threaded, and handed it to Daedalus. Drilling the shell at the top, Daedalus tied a strand of gossamer to the leg of an ant, which he induced up through the whorls by smearing honey around the drilled hole. Then he joined the linen thread to the end of the gossamer and drew it through. Cocalus returned the shell and claimed the reward: Minos replied that Cocalus was certainly sheltering his runaway servant and must give him up.

The daughters of Cocalus, for whom Daedalus had made ingenious toys, contrived at this point to boil Minos to death in his bath, so that Daedalus was able to stay in Sicily for the rest of his life. Minos and his brother Rhadamanthus, as Zeus' sons by Europa, were honoured in the underworld by being made the judges of the dead.

Minotaur

Thou mayst not wander in that labyrinth;
There Minotaurs and ugly treasons lurk.
Shakespeare

Soon after Theseus' arrival in Athens, and before Minos set off again in search of Daedalus, the tribute again fell due, and the fourteen youths and maidens were chosen by lot. In spite of his father's pleading, Theseus resolved to go as one of their number. When the ship carrying the victims was crossing over to Crete, King Minos, who had come along to supervise, boasted to Theseus of being a son of Zeus. "Prove it!" said Theseus; whereupon Minos raised his hands and prayed to Zeus, who answered with a roll of thunder out of a clear sky. Minos then challenged Theseus' own powers by throwing his gold signet-ring into the sea and ordering the young man to retrieve it. Theseus dived over the side, was escorted to the bottom by a school of dolphins, and received the ring back from Amphitrite, the wife of Poseidon, god of the sea; then he swam back up and returned it to King Minos.

Having arrived in Crete, Theseus gained the love of Minos' daughter Ariadne, who offered to help him overcome her beast-formed brother if he would take her back to Athens and marry her. The help she gave him was a ball of twine and the knowledge of how to use it. When he entered the labyrinth, he tied the end of the thread to the doorpost, unwinding it as he walked on, so that at any time he could find his way back by rolling up the clew.[20] Deeper and deeper he went into the mysterious network of paths, until scattered bones and a smell of filth and decay warned him that he was near the Minotaur's den. Suddenly from the central darkness the monster came charging at him. Theseus drew a short sword, the gift of Ariadne, and stepping aside, struck at him as he passed. Wounded and bellowing, the monster turned on him. This time Theseus was able to despatch him, driving the sword through his body and then cutting off his head.

With the Minotaur dead, Theseus still had to escape from the labyrinth. Winding up the thread in his hand, he soon retraced the path to the entrance where Ariadne was waiting for him. Meanwhile she had overpowered the guards with drugged wine and released the other prisoners; and together they all fled to the ship and set sail for Athens.

> Paint me a cavernous waste shore
> Cast in the unstilled Cyclades,
> Paint me the bold anfractuous rocks
> Faced by the snarled and yelping seas.
> Display me Aeolus above
> Reviewing the insurgent gales
> Which tangle Ariadne's hair
> And swell with haste the perjured sails.
>
> T.S. Eliot

On the way up the eastern coast of Greece, the company disembarked for a day or two on the island of Naxos; and when Theseus sailed away, he left Ariadne sleeping on the shore. Why this treachery to her, no one knows. She awoke just in time to see the ship departing over the horizon, and began to shriek aloud in grief and terror. At that moment it happily chanced that the wine-god Dionysus came by, with his laughing and singing companions, and took the forsaken maiden to be his bride, setting on her head a marvellous crown. His bridal gift to her can be seen now among the stars: we call it the constellation Corona Borealis, the Northern Crown.

When the ship with the fourteen victims had set out all those weeks ago from Athens, it carried a black sail in token of mourning. Aegeus gave his son on leaving a white sail to hoist, if he ever returned, as a signal of his success. In the haste and excitement of the return, Theseus forgot to hoist the white sail and entered the harbour at Athens under the black one. His old father was watching for the ship on Cape Sunium, the southernmost point of Attica, and seeing it enter the Saronic Gulf under the signal of mourning, he lost all hope and threw himself into the sea, which to this day is called the Aegean after him.

Theseus' heroic career did not end with his becoming king of Athens in his father's place. He is honoured by the Athenians as the first man to bring all the people of Attica together under one strong rule, and as having then dissolved the kingdom and established a commonwealth. During his reign at Athens, the district of Attica was invaded by the Amazons, a tribe of warrior-women from the east. Theseus defeated them and married their queen Hippolyta, who bore him a son, Hippolytus.

> Like as the cursèd son of Theseus,
> That following his chase in dewy morn,
> To fly his stepdame's love outrageous,
> Of his own steeds was all to pieces torn,
> And his fair limbs left in the woods forlorn;
> That for his sake Diana did lament,
> And all the woody Nymphs did wail and mourn.
>
> Spenser

After some years Hippolyta died and Theseus married Phaedra, another daughter of Minos. Meanwhile his son Hippolytus was growing up into a fine young man, devoted to hunting and to Artemis, the maiden goddess of the chase. Because Hippolytus had no use for her and her ways, the love-goddess Aphrodite swore vengeance, which she accomplished by making his stepmother Phaedra fall in love with him. Hippolytus would have nothing to do with her, and her love soon turned to hatred. She hanged herself in despair in her royal apartment, leaving a letter that falsely declared her death was due to the shame of being secretly wooed by her husband's son. Now it was Theseus' turn to swear revenge against Hippolytus, and he uttered a curse on him and sent him into banishment. As Hippolytus was driving away from Athens, dashing in his chariot along the shore, Poseidon sent to meet him a huge sea-monster, which so terrified his horses that they bolted, and he was thrown from his chariot and killed. His friend Artemis then told the truth to Theseus, who would have given all he possessed to turn against himself the hasty curse: but in vain.

The Romans have a tradition about the fate of Hippolytus. Artemis, deeply grieved at the death of her favourite, appealed to the divinely gifted healer Asclepius, the son of Apollo and trained by Cheiron. He

allowed himself to be persuaded, and restored Hippolytus to life. But
Hades and the three Fates, alarmed at what might happen if a mortal
healer could go on snatching their subjects from them, made Zeus
destroy Asclepius with a thunderbolt. Artemis, however, had got what
she wanted. Wrapping Hippolytus in a thick cloud, she transported
him to her sacred grove of Nemi[21] at Aricia in Italy, a mysterious place
beside a dark, cliff-surrounded lake, where he went on living under the
Latin name of Virbius, married to the nymph Egeria.

This Arician grove of Artemis, or Diana, as the Romans called her,
was ruled by a curious custom. Besides the immortal Virbius and his
divine consort, the grove was inhabited by a solitary mortal, its priest,
who was known as "the king of the wood." This man was always one
who had first come there as a runaway slave, seeking sanctuary. In the
grove, which was of oak trees, there was one tree among whose dark
foliage shone a single bough of gold.[22] This the fugitive had to break off
as a ritual act of challenge: he would then fight for the priesthood with
whoever was the priest at the time. The fight was always to the death:
the winner held the priesthood as his right until challenged and killed
in his turn.

> Facilis descensus Averno ...
> Sed revocare gradum superasque evadere ad auras,
> Hoc opus, hic labor est.
>
> Virgil

(The descent to Avernus is easy; but to retrace your way and
escape to the upper world, that is the difficulty.)

Besides the Amazons, other invaders of Attica were the tribe of the
Lapiths under King Peirithoüs. Trying to drive off a herd of cattle, these
were indignantly pursued by Theseus. When he caught up with
Peirithoüs, who turned to face him, each was so impressed with the
other's strength and courage that they forthwith swore to be friends
whatever might happen.

After the death of Phaedra, Peirithoüs being also without a wife, the
two friends agreed to make an expedition together to Sparta and carry
off the little princess Helen, the daughter of the Spartan queen Leda by
Zeus, who had visited her in the form of a swan. Though still a very
young girl, Helen already gave promise of becoming the most beautiful
woman in the world. The agreement was that after capturing her they

would draw lots for her, and the winner would help the loser to carry off as his bride some other one of Zeus' daughters. Theseus having won Helen, he and Peirithoüs descended to Tartarus in an effort to steal away Persephone, the queen of the underworld. Hades welcomed the pair as his guests and invited them to be seated, but the seat he offered them was a very odd one called the Chair of Forgetfulness, and it held them fast. There they sat on and on, until many years later Heracles came down to the lower world to fetch up Cerberus: Theseus he pulled free by main force, but the chair would not release Peirithoüs, the leader of the raid, who is sitting there still.

While Theseus was held a prisoner in the house of Hades, Helen's brothers, the twins Castor and Polydeuces, rescued her and took her home to Sparta, and with her they took Theseus' mother Aethra to be Helen's slave. On Theseus' return to Athens he found not only his mother and his bride gone but many things changed and the kingdom in disorder; and, weakened as he was by his sufferings, he decided to leave rather than reclaim his throne. His travels brought him to the island of Scyros, where the reigning king, the friend of an old enemy, murdered Theseus by pushing him over a cliff.

Many generations after the death of Theseus, the Athenians fought a critical battle against the Persians on the field of Marathon; and the ghost of Theseus came up out of the ground in the thick of the fight, swinging the brazen club that the hero in his first adventure took from the bandit Corynetes. Years later on the island of Scyros was found a stone coffin containing the skeleton of a giant man along with some weapons of bronze. Revered as those of Theseus, the bones were carried back with rejoicing to Athens. There they were housed in a temple newly built, to honour both his exploits and the wise institutions he gave to Attica.

Labyrinth

Europa and the Bull

V. The Royal House of Thebes

The Children of Agenor

... Or sweet Europa's mantle blew unclasp'd,
From off her shoulder backward borne:
From one hand droop'd a crocus: one hand grasp'd
The mild bull's golden horn.

Tennyson

King Agenor of Tyre[1] had among his children a daughter called Europa
and a son called Cadmus[2]. Europa was so charming a maiden that she
won the heart of Zeus himself. Happening to see her once when looking down to earth, he laid a plan to carry her off. While she was playing
with other young girls beside the seashore, he turned himself into a
milk-white bull with golden horns, so gentle and playful that the princess came fearlessly up to him and decked him with the flowers she
was gathering. She put out her hands and patted his neck, and even
mounted on his back: whereupon he immediately sprang up from the
grass, dashed out over the yellow sands and plunged into the sea,
swimming far out of sight of the maidens left shrieking on the shore.
The terrified princess dropped her flowers and clung to him, crying for
help all the time. On they rushed through the sea, with Europa's veil
blowing out behind her. At last Zeus brought her ashore in the meadows of Crete, where he calmed her fears and promised her that the

whole continent should be called Europe after her, and her children should be kings.

Meanwhile Europa's family were greatly distressed. King Agenor sent his son Cadmus out to find her, warning him not to come home if he failed. In his wanderings Cadmus crossed the sea and came to Apollo's oracle at Delphi, where he asked for advice. Apollo told him: "Travel till you meet a heifer that has never been harnessed to the plough. Follow wherever she leads you, and note the first place where she lies down: there build yourself a city, and call the district Boeotia (Cow-land)."

Cadmus and his friends kept on until they met the heifer, who led them on for some time before she at length lay down to rest. Cadmus gave thanks and sent his companions into the woods to fetch water to pour out with offerings to the gods. Deep in the wood they found a spring with a cave beside it. As soon as they began to draw water, a vast serpent crawled out of the cave and attacked them: some it poisoned, some it crushed, until none was left alive. Tired of waiting, Cadmus came in search of them, only to see the serpent crawling over the bodies of the dead and drinking blood from their wounds. Furiously he threw his javelin at it and pierced its throat. It struggled and thrashed wildly about, but finally grew weak and sank to the ground.

While Cadmus watched its dying struggles, a voice came out of the wood announcing that he had grievously offended the war-god Ares by killing the serpent that was under his protection. Immediately Cadmus' protectress Athene appeared, commanding him to plough up the earth and sow in the furrows the serpent's teeth. As soon as he did so there sprang up a crop of armed men, who began to quarrel and fight desperately among themselves until all but five lay dead; with the help of these five men Cadmus founded his city of Thebes. In time he married Harmonia, a daughter of Ares, whose anger was somewhat appeased by the death of the earth-born men.

Zeus and Semele

Brighter art thou than flaming Jupiter
When he appeared to hapless Semele.
Christopher Marlowe

Whether or not because of Ares' displeasure, many misfortunes befell the house of Cadmus. He and Harmonia had four daughters and a son, all of whose families felt the anger of the gods.

One of the daughters, Semele, was beloved and visited by Zeus, who left her pregnant with a divine child. Before the child was to be born, Zeus' jealous wife Hera, disguised as an old woman, tempted the princess by playing on her curiosity. "If your lover really is the father of gods and men, why does he not appear to you in his full glory, as he does to his divine consort?" Semele then began to tease her lover, until Zeus, wearied, came to her brandishing his thunderbolts and in the full blaze of his majesty, so that she was instantly burnt up. Zeus snatched the child from the ashes and sewed him in his thigh until he was ready to be born. For this reason the young god Dionysus was known as "the twice-born," or "he of the double door." One of his deeds in later life was to descend to the underworld and rescue his mother Semele, whom he introduced with divine honours into Olympus.

Ino and Athamas

By Leucothea's lovely hands,
And her son that rules the strands . . .

Milton

Cadmus' second daughter Ino married King Athamas of Boeotia and plotted the death of Phrixus and Helle, his children by a former wife. When he found out her wickedness, Athamas turned against her and the children she had borne him, stabbing the elder in a fit of madness. Ino seized her younger son and fled, finally leaping into the sea with him to escape Athamas' rage. Zeus turned them both into divinities of the sea, under the changed names of Leucothea and Palaemon.

Pentheus

Bacchus that first from out the purple grape
Crushed the sweet poison of misusèd wine . . .

Milton

The third daughter, Agave, had a son named Pentheus who ruled over Thebes in his grandfather's place. During his reign the god Dionysus returned to Thebes from his long journeyings in the east. Now Dionysus had for his province the vine with its fruits and their products, and he was worshipped appropriately with ecstatic singing and dancing. The people of Thebes rushed out of doors to join the throngs of Maenads, his frenzied women worshippers who roamed about the hills dressed in fawn-skins and carrying the thyrsus[3] in his honour. Pentheus, though warned not to meddle by the old blind prophet Teiresias,[4] spoke out strongly against these practices and even tried to capture the god. Dionysus sent madness on Agave, who was roaming about with the rest, so that she thought her son a wild beast and tore him apart with her bare hands, helped by the other women.

Actaeon

I would I were Actaeon, whom Diana did disguise,
To walk the woods unknown whereas my lady lies:
A hart of pleasant hue I wish that I were so,
So that my lady knew alone me and no mo.

The shaling nuts and mast that falleth from the tree
Should serve for my repast, might I my lady see;
Sometime that I might say when I saw her alone,
"Behold thy slave, alone, that walks these woods unknown!"

                                                          Anon.

Cadmus' remaining daughter was the mother of Actaeon, a young huntsman who had the misfortune one day while hunting to come upon a pool which was a favourite retreat of the huntress-goddess Artemis. The goddess was just then bathing there, surrounded by her nymphs, who had laid aside their bows and quivers and were refreshing themselves in the heat of the day. As soon as they saw the startled intruder, they all drew together to protect their mistress, while she stood up in the midst of them and uttered a few angry words, at the same time splashing him with water. Immediately the rash Actaeon felt a change come over him. His limbs lengthened and were covered with a brown coat, and horns began to sprout from his forehead: in no time he had become a fine stag, like the very ones he had taken such pleasure in hunting. As soon as his hounds saw him, they started off in fierce pursuit. Their master tried to call out to them, but his voice was no longer his own: all that could be heard among the barking of the hounds was the panting of an exhausted stag. The chase lasted only a short time. Actaeon was pulled down by his own hounds, in fearful punishment for disturbing the retreat of the goddess Artemis.

Oedipus

Although a subtler Sphinx renew
Riddles of death Thebes never knew.
Shelley

The only son of Cadmus had a grandson, Laius, who became king of Thebes and married his cousin Jocasta. Laius was warned by the Delphic oracle that the son he longed for would be his murderer. When the baby was born, Laius bound his feet tightly together and commanded a shepherd to leave him on the mountain-side to die. Instead, the shepherd gave him to a herdsman from Corinth, telling him to take the baby far away. The herdsman carried him to the Corinthian court, where the king and queen, having no children of their own, adopted him. They called him Oedipus, from his bruised and swollen feet.

When he reached manhood, Oedipus asked the Delphic oracle what the future held for him, and learned to his horror that he was fated to kill his father and marry his mother. Turning his face from Corinth and his supposed parents, he took the road east towards Thebes. In a narrow mountain pass he met an old man in a chariot, driving furiously towards Delphi. Ordered to stand aside, Oedipus kept straight on: when the old man struck at him, Oedipus knocked him into the roadway to be trampled by the horses. Then he fought and killed all his attendants but one, who fled back to Thebes with the news that King Laius was dead.

Oedipus and the Sphinx

Thebes at this time was troubled by a ravaging monster, the Sphinx,[5] whose body was that of a winged lion with the head and breast of a woman. Lying in wait for travellers, she put to all she caught the following riddle: "What is it that goes in the morning on four feet, at noonday on two, on three in the evening?" None being able to answer, she throttled and devoured them all. It was to consult the god about this pest that Laius had set out for Delphi.

Continuing along the way to Thebes, Oedipus was met by the Sphinx, who posed him her riddle. Without hesitating he replied, "Man: in the morning of life he goes on all fours, in maturity on his two feet, in old age leaning on a staff." The Sphinx in her mortification flung herself off a cliff. Rid of her hateful presence, the Thebans rewarded Oedipus with the kingdom[6] and the hand of its widowed queen Jocasta.

For several years Oedipus lived happily with Jocasta, who bore him two sons and two daughters. But the people suffered for the unknown guilt of their king, being visited with famine and plague. The Delphic oracle, consulted, ordered the Thebans to cast out from their gates the murderer of Laius. When search failed to find the man, Oedipus pronounced on him, whoever he might be, a dreadful curse; then he sent for Teiresias, by now very old, to ask what he knew of the matter. Teiresias, seeing that the truth could only cause more suffering, refused to answer: Oedipus in his own blindness sent him away with insults and threats.

When in spite of such a warning Oedipus continued the search, the truth began to be uncovered. From all the accounts of Laius' death, he realized that this was the old man he had killed near Delphi, and that he had thus pronounced the curse against himself. Worse was to follow. The king of Corinth died, and Oedipus in the midst of his grief rejoiced that he had not brought about his father's death. The Corinthian messenger checked him: "But you were his adopted child: it was I myself who brought you to him, a helpless baby given to me by a shepherd of King Laius."

Then at last it was clear that Oedipus was indeed the murderer of his father and the husband of his own mother, the man whose guilt polluted the city. Jocasta in horror hanged herself from a beam of the palace, while Oedipus put out his eyes and wandered in exile from Thebes, leaning on his faithful daughter Antigone. After long journeyings he came to the grove of Colonus in Attica, where the gods forgave him and he died. Thebes meanwhile was ruled by Jocasta's brother Creon.

When Oedipus' two sons Eteocles and Polynices reached manhood, they arranged that they would rule for alternate years. Eteocles began, and at the end of his first term showed no intention of ever giving up the kingdom; whereupon his brother gathered six powerful friends with their armies and the seven contingents marched against Thebes. In the battle each of the brothers gave the other his death-wound, so that sad Creon was once more left in power. He decreed that the body of Eteocles should be buried with funeral honours, while that of Polynices should be left outside the gate for carrion beasts and birds. This was more than an insult, because while a body lay unburied the ghost could not cross the river of death but wandered miserably up and down the shore. Antigone dared to cover her brother's body with earth, and Creon, afraid of disorder in the state if her action went unpunished, had her walled up alive in a tomb. "Life for life," Teiresias had warned him; and now Creon's son Haemon, who was to have married Antigone, died by his own hand. Thus all the children of Oedipus perished through family dissension, except for the younger daughter, who refused to help her sister. The story does not tell what became of her.

Eris

VI. The Tale of Troy

The Apple of Discord

The Abominable, that uninvited came
Into the fair Peleian banquet-hall,
And cast the golden fruit upon the board,
And bred this change ...

Tennyson

The story of the ten-years' struggle at Troy[1] begins a generation before the war broke out, with the wedding of Peleus and Thetis, the destined parents of the hero Achilles. All the Olympians and the lesser gods came to do them honour, all but Eris, the hateful goddess of discord, who was not invited. But Eris stole in unnoticed, and she threw down on the long banqueting-table a golden apple inscribed "For the fairest."

Three of the lady goddesses, Hera, Athene, and Aphrodite, immediately began wrangling over it, and Father Zeus, who deals justice to gods and men, was appealed to for a decision. Zeus, fearing the ill will of the losers, commanded Hermes the divine messenger to lead the three to Mount Ida in Phrygia where the shepherd Paris was tending his flocks, and there let him decide.

Now Paris was the son of King Priam of Troy and his wife Hecabe, and at his birth his mother had a dream in which she brought forth a firebrand, interpreted by the seers to mean that the young prince was to be his country's downfall. Priam in alarm gave him to his chief herdsman to take away and kill; but the man brought back false proofs of the child's death and brought him up unknown as his own son. Paris lived the life of a simple shepherd, happy in the love of the fountain-nymph Oenone.

Into this pastoral solitude came Hermes and the rival goddesses. Seeing that Paris was abashed and bewildered at the sight of so much divine beauty being paraded before him, each offered him a gift if he would award the prize to her. Hera promised power and honour, Athene victory in war, and Aphrodite the hand of Helen of Sparta, the daughter of Zeus and the loveliest of mortal women. At the mention of Helen's name, Paris immediately forgot about everything else, even his sweetheart Oenone, and he gave Aphrodite the apple, thus making Hera and Athene his eternal enemies.

Shortly after this, public games were to be held at Priam's court, and Paris persuaded his foster-father to accompany him there. Once arrived at Troy, Paris insisted on competing. He won all the events, defeating among others Priam's other sons, whose jealousy was so great that they resolved to kill him. They blocked off the exits from the arena and all attacked him at once with their swords. Priam's herdsman, to save Paris' life, sprang forward and declared to the king who the young man was. Priam received his son with great rejoicing, the fatal oracle never once entering his mind.

Paris, remembering the love-goddess's promise to him, soon found a pretext to go and visit King Menelaus of Sparta, to whom the beautiful Helen was married. He repaid Menelaus' hospitality by carrying off his wife and many treasures from the palace and sailing with his booty straight back to Troy. There Helen was warmly welcomed for her exquisite grace and charm, and amid public celebrations Paris married her.

Helen's husband Menelaus had been one of many suitors to ask for her hand. For fear that strife would break out when she made her choice, Tyndareus, the husband of her mother Leda, had required all the suitors to swear to accept her decision and to defend the man she chose against anyone who might try to take her from him. Now Menelaus, finding Helen gone, hastened to Mycenae[2] to his brother Agamemnon, and the two of them sent messengers to all the princes of Greece who had been her suitors and had taken the oath. Menelaus went himself to Ithaca to appeal to its king Odysseus, famous for his cunning.

Now Odysseus had been warned by an oracle that if he went to Troy he would be away twenty years and then return a poor man and friendless; and he resolved to feign madness rather than go. Menelaus found him in the fields, in a peasant's cap, furiously ploughing with an ox and an ass yoked together and sowing the furrows with salt. Snatching Odysseus' little son from his mother's arms, Menelaus laid him down just in front of the team, so that Odysseus had to rein them back quickly to avoid trampling him. "Aha!" exclaimed Menelaus, "there's a man with his wits about him!" Having been found out, Odysseus could not in honour refuse; so he sadly left his wife Penelope and the young Telemachus to join the expedition.

The other hero whose services the brothers were most anxious to secure was Achilles, the son of the mortal Peleus and the sea-goddess Thetis. Not only was he destined to be a great champion, but an oracle had declared that Troy could never be taken without his help.

When Achilles was born, Thetis had resolved to make him immortal like herself. According to one story, she dipped him in the deadly underground river Styx to make his body invulnerable, so that the only place that could still be wounded was the spot at the heel by which she held him. The other story is that Peleus caught her trying to burn away Achilles' mortal nature in the fire, as Demeter did with the child of Celeus. When Peleus interfered, Thetis was so angry that she left him forever and went back to her home in the sea; but she continued to watch over the fortunes of her son.

Peleus took his motherless child to the cave of Cheiron to be educated, and there Achilles quickly surpassed all the sons of the heroes in running, wrestling, and hunting. Thetis, watching from her far-off home, was grieved to see him excel. She knew that he was destined either to live a most glorious life and die young or to live long but obscurely; and naturally she wanted to lengthen his life. For this reason she disguised him as a girl and sent him to live among the maidens at the court of a friendly king. Here Odysseus now came to seek him out. Arrived at the palace, he displayed a huge chest of gifts, most of them dresses and jewels, from which the ladies were invited to choose for themselves. When one among them gave a loud cry and seized a shield and spear from the heap, Odysseus recognized his man, who was easily persuaded to take up a warrior's life and join Agamemnon's force. With Achilles went his friend Patroclus.

Other famous leaders of the army were the brave but foolhardy Ajax, Diomedes the Argive, and the old king Nestor of Pylus, renowned for his wisdom and his gift of persuasive speech, who had ruled over three generations of men. With them also went Calchas the seer, a Trojan priest of Apollo who had forsaken his own people to help the Greek cause.

The War

> Was this the face that launched a thousand ships
> And burnt the topless towers of Ilium?
>
> Christopher Marlowe

The Greek fleet gathered at Aulis in Boeotia, where for several days contrary winds forced them to remain in harbour. Calchas, who had already prophesied to the army that they would spend nine years besieging Troy and take it only in the tenth, now declared that the goddess Artemis was angry and could be appeased only by the death of Agamemnon's daughter Iphigeneia. To this Agamemnon sorrowfully consented. To get the girl away from her mother Clytemnestra, he sent a message that the princess was to come to Aulis to be married to Achilles, and Clytemnestra sent her gladly, decked in her wedding garments. There she was sacrificed, the gale dropped, and the fleet set out on its northeast course across the Aegean. But some say that Artemis accepted the maiden's dutifulness instead of her life and, before the knife could fall, carried her away wrapped in a cloud to Tauris to serve as her priestess.

The fleet put ashore briefly at Tenedos, where the famous archer Philoctetes was bitten in the foot by a serpent so venomous that the wound could not be cured, but festered and stank intolerably. Since no one could bear to be near him, his companions left him on a small rocky island, where he kept himself miserably alive on what he could shoot.

Arriving at Troy, the Greeks drew their ships up onto the shore, set up their camp, and proceeded to lay siege to the city.[3] And there for weeks and months and years they remained. The struggle dragged out to nine years: King Priam and the Trojans would not surrender, and Agamemnon with his forces would not go away. The army was weary and homesick, and in the tenth year Apollo became angered and took up his stand beside the ships, shooting arrows of pestilence day after day into the Greek camp. At the same time Achilles quarrelled with Agamemnon over a woman captive, awarded to him in token of his prowess. He withdrew from the fighting to his tent, where he sat brooding. The Trojans, seeing division in the enemy camp, attacked with such spirit that Agamemnon quickly arranged a truce, during which Paris and Menelaus were to fight it out, man to man, for fair Helen. But nothing was to be decided by this means; for Aphrodite, when she saw that Menelaus was winning, wrapped a cloud around her favourite Paris and bore him away from the field, back to his house in Troy.

Agamemnon, Odysseus, and their friends did their best to placate the wrathful Achilles, but to no avail. Meanwhile his friend Patroclus day after day went out to battle in Achilles' armour and fought brilliantly, until Apollo himself disabled him, and he was then easily killed by the bravest of Troy's defenders, Priam's son Hector, who stripped him of the armour as his rightful prize. When the news was brought to Achilles, he almost went mad with grief: he forgot his anger against the Greek leaders and swore to re-enter the conflict and avenge his friend. His mother Thetis and her attendant sea-nymphs came up out of the sea to comfort him, walking in a long line across the sands to his tent. Hearing him swear to kill Hector, she warned him that Hector's death must soon be followed by his own; but he thought little of that, and she went sadly away, promising to bring him new armour, which she would persuade the smith-god Hephaestus to forge. Meanwhile Achilles, unarmed as he was, hastened to help the Greeks defend the body of Patroclus, which the exulting Trojans were trying to drag back to the city, to dishonour it and expose it on the city wall. Standing at the trench that bounded the camp, he shouted aloud three times, with such a trumpet-sound that the Trojan horses wheeled round in confusion. Twelve of the Trojan nobles were thrown and crushed by their own chariot-wheels, while the rest scattered in flight and Achilles bore away the body of his friend.

On high Olympus, Hephaestus sponged the workshop grime from his face and arms and received the goddess Thetis into his house of marvels. Here she was always honoured and welcome; for many years ago she had taken him in and sheltered him after his fall from heaven. Glad that she now called on his skill, he promised her what she asked; "and would that I could keep your son from death's sight in the evil day, as easily as I can make him armour that will amaze the eyes of men."

> The wrath
> Of stern Achilles on his foe pursued
> Thrice fugitive about Troy wall.
>   Milton

The finished armour that Thetis brought to Achilles was of the finest craftsmanship, in copper and tin and silver and gold. Most splendid of the pieces was the shield, on which the divine smith had pictured the stars of heaven and scenes of earthly life, of peace and war, city and country, the whole encircled by the stream of Oceanus that girdles the world. Achilles rejoiced when he saw the armour. Calling the leaders of the army together, he made up his quarrel with them; then he armed himself and went furiously out to battle. As his charioteer guided them along, Achilles spoke to his horses, saying, "When we finish this day's fighting, mind you bring me safely back to the camp, not leave me dead on the plain as you did Patroclus." His horse Xanthus bowed his head and spoke: "Mighty Achilles, today we shall bring you back safe, but your evil day is near, brought on by heaven and stern Fate, and not by any fault of ours." The Fates would not let him say more, and Achilles grieving replied: "Xanthus, why do you foretell my death? I know that I shall fall here, far from my dear father and mother; but I will not leave the field till I have given the Trojans their fill of fighting." And he urged the horses forward with a shout.

Achilles made havoc among the Trojan host till the river Scamander was choked with corpses and red with blood. In anger the river-god spoke from his channel and asked him at least to do his killing on land; and when Achilles was slow to comply, Scamander rose from his banks and chased him along the plain, roaring to Simois his brother flood to join him. Hera, to help Achilles, sent her son Hephaestus to drive Scamander back with fire. When the river rushed boiling down into his bed she called out, "Now hold back your flames: it is not fitting for us to use such violence against a god for the sake of mortal men."

King Priam, watching from the city wall, saw how the Trojans were falling before Achilles, and he commanded that the gates should be opened to give them refuge. They came crowding through in panic, flying like a herd of deer before Achilles, who was half mad with vengeful battle-lust and the thirst of glory. Soon all the Trojans were safe in the city, all but Hector, who, heedless of his friends' entreaties to come inside, waited for Achilles before the gates.

When Achilles bore down on him, his armour flashing, raging like the war-god Ares himself, Hector's courage failed him and he fled in dismay, three times circling the city walls with Achilles after him. So evenly matched were the runners that it was like a pursuit in a dream, where one cannot escape nor the other overtake; for neither could Achilles catch up with Hector nor Hector break away from Achilles.

Even so, Hector might yet have saved his life by his speed if Fate had not decided otherwise. On the summit of Olympus, Zeus took up his golden scales. He placed a doom[4] on each side, one for Achilles and one for Hector, and Hector's fell down towards the realm of Hades while that of Achilles flew up and kicked the beam. When he saw that, Hector's protector Apollo, who had hitherto kept up his strength and nerved his running, left him.

Now for the fourth time they were passing the twin springs of the Scamander and the stone troughs where in peacetime the Trojan women brought their washing, when Athene, always friendly to Achilles, resolved to make Hector fight. She assumed the form of his favourite

The weighing of dooms[5]

brother Deïphobus and hastened up to him, saying: "I have stayed outside the wall for your sake: now let us make a stand together against the fierce Achilles." With these words she persuaded him to turn and face Achilles; but when the two met, Hector, looking round for his brother, saw how he had been tricked. "Oh, shame!" he cried out, "the gods have betrayed me to my doom: then let me not die without a struggle, but fight so that those who come after may remember me."

Hector then charged down on Achilles with all his force, while Achilles watched closely for a place to strike. As he came on, Achilles drove his spear through the base of his throat, where the armour taken from Patroclus did not protect him. Hector fell, and as his strength flowed from him he implored Achilles to accept whatever ransom the Trojans would offer for his body, so that it might be buried at home with due rites: this Achilles refused. Then Hector said with his last breath: "I know what you are, iron-hearted man whom prayers cannot soften. But see that your treatment of me does not move the gods to vengeance, in the day when Paris and Apollo shall cut you down beside the Scaean

Gate." As he spoke, the shades of death enfolded him, and his soul went down lamenting to the house of Hades. And Achilles replied to the dead body: "It is over for you; as for me, I will accept my fate whenever the gods see fit to send it." Then he attached the body by the ankles to the back of his chariot and dragged it through the dust towards the ships, while all the Trojans watching from the wall bewailed the death of their champion. They mourned for Hector, but it was for themselves that they lamented; for they saw approaching their own evil day.

Having killed Hector, Achilles now held Patroclus' funeral, burning his body on a pyre along with dogs, horses and Trojan captives slaughtered in his honour, and raising a tomb over the remains. Round the tomb he daily dragged the body of Hector, as an added revenge. Yet in spite of this dishonour Apollo kept the body fresh and free from corruption, and drove away the dogs that would have eaten it. At last the gods became angry at this shameful treatment of a dead enemy, and Hermes himself led old Priam, the Trojan king, to Achilles' tent at night, bearing gifts, to try to ransom the body of his son. Hermes cast a deep sleep on the sentries, so that Priam with his attendant and the mule-cart laden with treasure passed unnoticed through the body of the host.

Priam found Achilles seated in his tent, and going up to him he clasped his knees in a gesture of supplication and kissed the dreadful hands that had killed so many of his sons. Achilles marvelled to see him, and Priam besought him: "Think of your own father, godlike Achilles, who is an old man as I am. Perhaps he too is helpless, at the mercy of his neighbours; even so his son still lives, and he looks forward with rejoicing to his dear son's return from Troy. But I who had many sons now have lost almost all, and last the bravest, Hector, the strong tower of our city. On his account I have come to you, to offer a great ransom for his body. Remember your own father and show pity to me, who have done what no man ever yet forced himself to do, kissed the hands that slew my son."

Achilles wept at Priam's words, thinking now of his father Peleus and now of his friend Patroclus, and Priam at his feet wept for Hector, so that the tent was filled with lamentation. At last Achilles raised Priam to his feet, saying: "Unhappy man, how could you have the courage to come alone to the ships as a suppliant to the slayer of your sons? Surely your heart must be of iron. But sit beside me, and we will hide our griefs in our hearts, for weeping cannot help us. This is the lot the gods have spun for miserable men, to live in pain; yet they them-

Mourning women

selves are sorrowless. So it is with my father Peleus, the hero, blessed in his marriage with a goddess: for he has no child but only me, who am fated to an early death; and I cannot stay with him in his age, since it is my destiny here at Troy to trouble you and your sons." Then Achilles called aloud on his dead friend Patroclus to forgive him for leaving his revenge unfinished; for he had meant to throw Hector's body to the dogs rather than let his family bury it. He took the gifts and gave Priam the body, and Priam returned with it to Troy, the Greeks holding back their forces from the city until the funeral rites were accomplished.

The Fall of the City

Set where the upper streams of Simois flow
Was the Palladium, high 'mid rock and wood;
And Hector was in Ilium far below,
And fought, and saw it not—but there it stood!

It stood; and sun and moonshine rained their light
On the pure columns of its glen-built hall.
Backward and forward rolled the waves of fight
Round Troy; but while this stood, Troy could not fall.
                                        Matthew Arnold

Not long after the death of Hector, Achilles too met his end. Hidden in a cloud, the archer-god Apollo met Paris in the thick of battle beside the Scaean Gate and guided his hand, so that his arrow struck Achilles in his vulnerable heel. His cousin Ajax carried his body through the host back to the Greek camp, while Odysseus fought off all who tried to stop him.

Funeral games were held in Achilles' honour, as for all the great heroes killed in the war. His mother Thetis offered his divinely-wrought armour as a prize to the most valiant of the Greeks left alive. Ajax and Odysseus both claimed this recognition, which the common vote adjudged to Odysseus. The mortified Ajax went into a mad battle-rage, striking out in the dark at harmless cattle that Athene, the friend of Odysseus, made him mistake for his enemies until his frenzy was exhausted. When in the morning he came to his senses and saw the havoc he had made, he threw himself on his sword.

Calchas the prophet now declared that Troy could not be taken without the help of Heracles' bow and arrows. These had been given many years before by the dying hero to Philoctetes, as a reward for his lighting the pyre on Mount Oeta; but Philoctetes had been left alone on an Aegean island because of his offensive wound. Odysseus and one companion now sailed back to find him. Philoctetes, whose distrust was soon overcome by their kind words and promises, returned with them to the Greek camp. Here a surgeon successfully treated the wound, and on his recovery Philoctetes went out to the field of battle and shot Paris mortally with the fatal bow. The Trojans carried their dying prince to Mount Ida, where he implored the help of his forsaken nymph Oenone, who was skilled in healing drugs. But she remembered his desertion of her, and refused, and he was borne back to Troy to die.

One more condition remained to be fulfilled before the city could fall. The Trojans guarded in a rich shrine an ancient and famous image of Pallas Athene, known as the Palladion, with which the city's fortunes were bound up. This Odysseus stole away, creeping under the cover of night.

After Philoctetes and his weapons had been fetched and the Palladion carried off, Athene put into the minds of the Greeks a plan whereby the city could be taken. They built an enormous horse of wooden planks,

Odysseus carrying off the Palladion

large enough to hold a small company of armed men in its belly, and carved on its flank a dedication to the goddess Athene. Leaving it on the shore, they broke up their camp, burned the more permanent structures in it, and took to their fleet and sailed out of sight. The Trojans, amazed and delighted to see them go, held earnest debate about the wooden horse. Some were for burning it where it stood, fearing a trap. Others, afraid of desecrating the goddess's property and hoping to win her to their side, counselled bringing it with all honour to the city. While they were still arguing, a portent occurred that settled the matter.

Foremost among those who suspected the horse was the priest Laocoön, who declared, "I mistrust the Greeks even when they bring gifts." Having done his best to persuade his fellow-citizens, he went down to the shore with his two sons to offer sacrifice to Poseidon. Apollo happened to see them go, and remembering that this man had once grievously offended him, he sent two monstrous serpents up out of the sea, which coiled about the father and the two boys and despite their struggles crushed them wretchedly to death. The Trojans interpreted this as a punishment from the gods for Laocoön's opposition to the horse, and were all the more determined to bring it into their city. The only one still to oppose it was Priam's daughter Cassandra, a priestess with the gift of prophecy, who could get nobody to listen to her tale of the griefs that would follow.

As the Trojans were preparing to drag the horse in, a lone Greek soldier, who had been left behind, appeared at the gates and begged Priam to give him shelter. His story was that Odysseus and some of the other Greek leaders had plotted against his life, so that he had escaped to Troy rather than go with them. Questioned about the horse, he replied eagerly that it had been built as an offering to Athene, who after having befriended the Greeks for so long was now angry with them for stealing her sacred image from its Trojan shrine. "But why then was the horse made so large?" "For fear that you should take it into the city and gain Athene's favour for your side." Nothing more was needed to convince the Trojans: they immediately laid down rollers over a carpet of flowers and dragged the horse in with shouts of rejoicing, though they had to break down part of the city wall to do so. They might not have been so hasty if they had known their guest to be Sinon, a cousin of the wily Odysseus.

When darkness fell and found the Trojans celebrating their enemies' departure with feasting and drinking, the Greek fleet, which had merely rounded the nearest cape, turned rapidly back towards Troy. Tired from their revelling, the Trojans were all in a deep sleep when thirty armed men, Odysseus among them, slipped down a rope-ladder from the belly of the horse and signalled to their comrades outside the walls. The whole Greek army was soon crowding the streets and ransacking the houses, slaughtering their unarmed defenders.

Priam died on the palace steps, the last of his sons falling around him, and his body was cast unburied on the tomb of Achilles. His queen Hecabe, with Hector's widow Andromache and other high-born Trojan women, was led off into captivity. Hector's little son Astyanax was thrown from the battlements, for fear he should avenge his city when he grew to be a man. The wronged Menelaus went straight to the apartment of Helen, intending to avenge on her all the sorrows of the long war; but her god-born beauty still shone in her worn face, and his heart relenting, he cast away his sword and led her gently to the ships.

Having massacred its betrayed defenders, the Greeks sacked and burned the city, dividing up as plunder everything they could carry away with them, both goods and captives.

The Returns[6]

The Return of Menelaus

Dear is the memory of our wedded lives,
And dear the last embraces of our wives
And their warm tears: but all hath suffer'd change:

For surely now our household hearths are cold,
Our sons inherit us: our looks are strange:
And we should come like ghosts to trouble joy.
Or else the island princes over-bold
Have eat our substance, and the minstrel sings
Before them of the ten years' war in Troy,
And our great deeds, as half-forgotten things.

Tennyson

The victorious Greeks looted and destroyed without restraint; and their ferocity brought on them retribution from the gods, especially from Athene. On the night of Troy's fall the prophetess Cassandra took refuge in Athene's temple, where the Greeks who broke in found her clinging to a wooden statue that now replaced the Palladion. By dragging her forcibly away, they flouted Athene's protection and violated her sanctuary. The man chiefly responsible for this was one Ajax—not the great Ajax, who died before the war ended, but a lesser man. The injured goddess persuaded Poseidon to help her take vengeance, by stirring up the seas and snatching from many their hope of return. Thus two powerful divinities who had been on the side of the Greeks now became their bitter enemies.

Poseidon himself took care of the lesser Ajax, wrecking his ship on a rocky shore. Ajax would have escaped with a wetting if he had not boasted as he scrambled up the rocks that the gods couldn't drown him if they tried: the angry Poseidon split the rock Ajax stood on with his trident and made him a liar.

The first to suffer from Athene's wrath was Menelaus, who lost most of his fleet in a violent storm. Then he was held up with the remaining five ships in Egypt, waiting for favourable winds. Just as his men were running out of provisions and had taken to fishing with improvised tackle, a sea-nymph, taking pity on Menelaus, came up to him as he was sitting by himself and advised him to seek out her father Proteus, an old immortal living under the sea off the Egyptian coast. He, if Menelaus could only hold him fast, would advise him about his journey. Giving him precise instructions as to how Proteus could be captured, she then dived back under the sea.

Menelaus set off for the island of Pharos, three of his men with him, and there on the shore they lay in wait under four fresh sealskins provided by the nymph, who gave them also some divine ambrosia[8] to ward off the stench. For a long morning they watched while the seals

Athene and Poseidon[7]

came up to bask on the shore, until at noon up came the old man of the sea himself, who counted over the seals like a shepherd his flock before lying down to sleep in the midst of them. Then the four rushed on him with a shout and seized him; whereupon he began to change his shape, becoming a lion, a dragon, all manner of wild beasts, then running water, then a tree; but Menelaus and the sailors still held fast. At last Proteus gave in, admitting that he recognized Menelaus and knew why he had come. He advised Menelaus if he wanted to break the calm, to return to the mainland and offer generous sacrifices to Zeus and the other gods, who would then let him finish his voyage.

When Menelaus asked Proteus how his friends were faring on their way home, the old prophet had many sad tales to tell him, of shipwreck on the sea and forgetfulness or worse at home. He ended by telling Menelaus of his own further fate. "You shall not die in Sparta, but the gods will take you to the Elysian fields[9] at the world's end. There life is pleasanter than anywhere else, for there falls no rain, nor hail, nor snow, but always a fresh singing breeze blows from the sea and renews the spirits of men. You shall enter this happy place because you are married to fair Helen and thus are the son-in-law of Zeus." Then he slipped back into the sea, and Menelaus with a heavy heart returned to the ships on the Egyptian shore, arriving not long afterwards with Helen at his palace in Sparta.

The Return of Agamemnon

Sometime let gorgeous Tragedy[10]
In sceptr'd pall come sweeping by,
Presenting Thebes, or Pelops' line.
Milton

For Menelaus' brother Agamemnon a worse fate was reserved. Unlike so many of the others, he reached his palace in Mycenae with very little trouble, bringing with him as part of his spoils Priam's daughter, the prophetess Cassandra. He was royally welcomed home by his queen Clytemnestra, the sister of Helen, who spread a feast for him and first of all led him to the bath to wash off the dust of his travels. As he stepped out of the bath, she held out a robe; but instead of helping him into it, she threw it over his head, so that he could not stir. Then she and Agamemnon's cousin Aegisthus, with whom she had been plotting during the long years of the war, stabbed him to death. Cassandra, who knew already what was to happen, fell next by Clytemnestra's hand.

This was only one in a long series of crimes committed in that ill-fated family. For Agamemnon's great-grandfather was Tantalus, who feasted at the tables of the gods as their friend until he offended them by betraying their confidence and by a still worse outrage: once when they were paying him a return visit, he killed and served up to them in a stew his young son Pelops,[11] to test their powers of detection. They all rose in horror from the board, excepting Demeter, who, still grieving for her daughter, had eaten some flesh from the shoulder without noticing what it was she ate. First the gods tumbled Tantalus down to the underworld, where he is condemned to stand forever thirsting in a stream that flees when he tries to drink of it, and hungering under a fruit tree that continually snatches its laden branches away from him. Then they assembled the pieces of Pelops out of the stew-pot and brought him back to life, replacing the missing shoulder with one made of ivory.

Pelops' two sons, Atreus and Thyestes, quarrelled over the throne of Mycenae, which by the expressed will of Zeus fell to Atreus. Discovering meanwhile that Thyestes had insulted his young bride, Atreus sent him a friendly invitation to come and share the city with him, and spread a banquet before him in welcome. When Thyestes had eaten heartily, Atreus made a servant carry in to him on a dish all that was left of the bloody banquet, the remains of Thyestes' murdered sons. Thyestes rose from the table, choking on the unnatural meat, and before he left Mycenae he turned and pronounced a curse on the house of Atreus.

Both these warring brothers had sons who reached manhood. The revengeful Atreus was the father of Agamemnon and Menelaus, who married sisters, the Spartan princesses Clytemnestra and Helen: two unlucky marriages. Menelaus escaped the worst effects of the curse, but Agamemnon felt its full force in his death. Thyestes' surviving son Aegisthus murdered his uncle Atreus, and lived to assist Agamemnon's wife in his destruction. Agamemnon was murdered in revenge not only for his father's crime but also for his consenting to the sacrifice of his daughter Iphigeneia.

Such a chain of crimes could not go unnoticed by the gods, who at last intervened. Apollo with Zeus' consent encouraged Agamemnon's son Orestes, now grown to manhood, to avenge his father's death by killing his mother Clytemnestra and her guilty friend. This Orestes carried out, with the willing help of his sister Electra.

The act brought on Orestes the hatred of the Erinyes, the three horrible hags who smell out the blood of those who die by the hand of their kin and demand punishment: they are so ancient that they despise the Olympian gods as newcomers and upstarts. The Erinyes pursued Orestes over land and sea, driving him to madness and delusion. After a year of exile he came to Athens, with the avengers still on his heels. They dragged him before the Areopagus,[12] the Athenian court of judgment. Here the Erinyes were his chief accusers, while Apollo himself came forward in his defence. The question at issue was whether his father's murder justified a son in killing his mother. Apollo in his speech declared that the mother who bore a child was not so essentially his parent as the father: she merely nurtured the seed.[13] The twelve judges then cast their votes, which were found to be evenly divided; so Athene as the city's patron goddess was called upon to decide. Athene, who not only never became a wife or mother herself but moreover was born from the head of Zeus, took an anti-feminine view. "I am for the father," she announced, giving judgment in Orestes' favour. This done, she pacified the Erinyes, who, baulked of their victim, were gnashing their long tusks. She promised them a gloomy shrine under the Athenian

Acropolis,[14] where henceforward they should receive offerings and perpetual worship under the new name of the "Eumenides"—no longer the Furies but the Kindly Ones.

The Return of Aeneas

Golden branch amid the shadows,
    kings and realms that pass to rise no more.

Tennyson

Another story of the aftermath of Troy, though not exactly a "return," is that of the wanderings of one of the Trojan princes,[15] Aeneas, the son of the goddess Aphrodite and a mortal man, Anchises, with whom she fell in love while he was tending his flock on the slopes of Mount Ida. Her passion for him was sent by Zeus, in revenge for the many humiliations that she and her prankish son Eros had inflicted on him and the other gods. Anchises later was so foolish as to boast of his conquest, and Zeus, seeing that the joke was getting out of hand, loosed a thunderbolt at him. Aphrodite interposed her marvellous girdle and saved his life, but he was never able to walk again.

Protected by his divine mother, Aeneas escaped from the flames of Troy, bearing his old father on his back and the figures of his household gods in his arms, accompanied by a few friends and his little son Ascanius. He had been told in a dream that it was his destiny to found a nation in a country lying far to the west, Italy, to which divine guidance would eventually bring them. A prophet advised them how to direct their journey: they must take a roundabout way in order to avoid certain perils they would not be strong enough to overcome. Many years of wandering lay before them, at the end of which they would reach their new home.

Passing Sicily, where lived the monster Polyphemus, who shouted terrible threats after them from the shore, they were met by a fearful storm sent by Hera, who hated all the Trojans but especially Aeneas, and had resolved that he should never reach Italy. He with his small fleet came safely through the storm, however, and landed near the city of Carthage[16] in North Africa. Carthage was under the protection of Hera, who knew that the city the Trojans were destined to found would in later times go to war against Carthage, raze it to the ground, and lay waste all the surrounding territory; so she devised a plan to divert Aeneas from his course. The hero was to fall in love with Dido, the beautiful early-widowed Carthaginian queen, and settle quietly down as her consort. His mother Aphrodite was willing to help entangle Aeneas in this love affair, knowing what Hera did not know, that Zeus had sworn her son should fulfil his destiny as the founder of a new Troy to become the greatest empire on earth.

For a time Aeneas lived at Carthage, happy in Dido's love. But when he and his men were thoroughly rested and refreshed from the long campaign at Troy and their wanderings since, the gods decided to end this trifling. Hermes, sent from Zeus, arrived one day to remind Aeneas of his duty. Ashamed of his luxurious idleness, Aeneas immediately ordered his men to prepare for departure, heedless of Dido's pleading and laments. That very night the ships set sail, and that same night Dido had raised a high funeral pyre, on which she stabbed herself to death, calling on the gods to avenge her fate. From this harsh return for her generosity is supposed to have sprung the enmity between Carthage and the race of Aeneas, later the Roman people.

Leaving Carthage behind, Aeneas held his course towards Italy. The fleet had again left Sicily behind when he lost his valued and experienced pilot, Palinurus, who one night fell asleep at the helm and slid into the sea. Aeneas, awake while his men slept, saw that the ship had lost its pilot and was drifting. He took the helm himself and guided the ship all that night, grieving for his friend: "Alas, Palinurus, you trusted too much in the sky and the quiet sea: now you will lie unburied on an unknown shore."

Passing the Sirens' rock, Aeneas landed on the west coast of Italy. There he sought out the Sibyl of Cumae, the prophetic priestess of Apollo, to enquire the will of the gods about his journey. She gave him no advice herself, but promised to guide him to the underworld where he could consult the ghost of his old father Anchises, who had died on the way in Sicily. The path to the lower world was hard and dangerous, and to undertake it in safety Aeneas must carry in his hand the mysterious golden bough, sacred to Persephone, the queen of the dead. Guided by two doves[17] sent by his mother, Aeneas saw the golden bough glimmering in the dark grove surrounding Lake Avernus, where the underworld pathway began, and breaking it off he carried it back to the Sibyl. She, after sacrificing to Hecate, led him in the night down the steep road to Tartarus.[18]

> Four infernal rivers, that disgorge
> Into the burning lake their baleful streams:
> Abhorrèd Styx, the flood of deadly hate;

Sad Acheron of sorrow, black and deep;
Cocytus, named of lamentation loud
Heard on the rueful stream; fierce Phlegeton,
Whose waves of torrent fire inflame with rage.
Far off from these a slow and silent stream,
Lethe the river of oblivion rolls
Her wat'ry labyrinth, whereof who drinks
Forthwith his former state and being forgets,
Forgets both joy and grief, pleasure and pain.

Milton

Five rivers encircle and wind through the abode of the dead: Styx or the Hateful, the river by which Zeus swears, Acheron the Sorrowful, Phlegethon the Fiery, Cocytus or Lamentation, and Lethe, the river of Forgetfulness. Their banks are crowded with pitiful wailing souls, waiting for Charon the infernal ferryman to row them over in his creaky boat. The golden bough was sufficient passport for Aeneas and his guide, who quickly reached the farther shore, where they placated the three-headed watchdog Cerberus by throwing him small cakes brought for the purpose. Among the fields of the dead they met the pale shade of Dido, who passed them without a look or word, pale with anger and bleeding from her mortal wound. At last they found Anchises, who greeted his son affectionately, instructed him where he should settle and how he should proceed, and prophesied to him the future glory of Rome.

Back on the Italian shore, Aeneas with his men made his way to Latium, the district around the mouth of the Tiber where Rome was eventually to be founded. There Hera stirred up trouble for them among the inhabitants. Coming in peace and asking only for a place to settle, they met armed resistance and had to make war for the right to stay. At length Aeneas put down all his enemies, and he married Lavinia, the daughter of Latinus the friendly king of Latium; and from them sprang the Roman people.

The Return of Odysseus

That long wand'ring Greek
That for his love refusèd deity.

Spenser

The longest tale of wanderings on the return from Troy is that of Odysseus, the wily king of the rocky island of Ithaca in the Ionian Sea, who after the ten years' siege took ten years more to get home. One of the first places where his fleet put in was the land of the Lotus-Eaters, gentle people whose main food was the lotus-fruit, which they offered to the sailors. Those who ate immediately forgot about the long war behind them and their homes ahead, and thought of nothing but staying here contentedly forever. Odysseus needed all his presence of mind to contend with this peril: he had the men carried back on board immediately, and kept them tied up until the effect wore off.

Next they came to the island of Sicily, inhabited by the dangerous Cyclopes, giants with a single eye in the middle of their foreheads. They lived as shepherds, sleeping with their flocks in solitary caves among the rocks. Odysseus and some of his men entered one of these caves during the day while its owner Polyphemus was out. They knew it belonged to someone, as there were kids and lambs penned at the back and around the walls were bowls, milk pails and newly-made cheeses. The Greeks made themselves comfortable, lighting a fire and helping themselves to the goat's-milk cheeses. In the evening Polyphemus came home, drove his flock into the cave, and afterwards blocked the entrance with a huge stone. Then he caught sight of the travellers, who politely requested his hospitality, Odysseus acting as spokesman. The answer they received was a rough one: "Stranger, you are a fool, or you don't know where you are. Why talk about Zeus and his protection of suppliants? We Cyclopes are stronger than he is, and care nothing for his laws." So saying, he snatched up two of Odysseus' comrades, dashed their brains out on the cavern floor, and gobbled them down for his evening meal. The others watched horror-struck as he swilled down the last morsels with milk and then stretched himself out on the ground to sleep. Odysseus thought of killing him with his sword, but what good would that have done them? they could never have moved away the stone from the cavern's mouth.

After a night passed in fear and lamentation, they watched the monster dispose of two more men for his breakfast; then having milked the she-goats he shoved away the stone and drove out his flock, blocking the cave mouth again immediately. In his absence they worked out a plan. At night, after Polyphemus had again supped off two of their fellows, Odysseus approached him with a bowlful of some wine he had with him, pretending that he hoped with this offering to soften the giant's heart. Polyphemus greedily gulped it down and demanded more. After three bowlfuls, he asked Odysseus' name and promised to give him a present. "My name is Outis (No one): now what will you give me?" "Outis shall be eaten last of his companions: that is his present;" and with that the Cyclops fell into a drunken sleep. Immediately Odysseus jumped up and seized a huge pole of fresh-cut olive-wood that was lying in the cave, and when he had sharpened one end, the men thrust it into the embers of the fire to heat. When the sap began to hiss and run out, they drew it from the fire and thrust the point into the Cyclops' single eye as he lay sleeping with his head flung back. Polyphemus screamed till the cave re-echoed, and staggered to his feet blinded and bellowing. The other Cyclopes living near by came running to find out the cause of the disturbance; but when they heard Polyphemus roaring, "No one has blinded me! No one is murdering me!" they went grumbling back to their caves to finish their night's sleep.

While the giant groaned and stumbled about the cave, Odysseus was carrying out a stratagem whereby he and his men might escape. He noiselessly seized the rams of the flock and bound them together in threes, strapping a man under each of the middle ones. For himself he took the largest of all the rams, clinging to the thick wool under the belly. When morning came, Polyphemus let out his flock, passing his hand over each of the animals' backs as they went by but missing the men underneath. When Odysseus' own ram had got safely outside he let go and ran to untie all the others. Reaching their ships and silencing their friends' cries of wonderment and welcome, they took their places at the oars and began to row away. Then Odysseus stood up and shouted back at Polyphemus: "You brute, would you eat up harmless travellers? The gods did well to punish you for such wickedness." Polyphemus in a rage threw half a mountain at them, so violently that they were driven back towards the shore. When by hard rowing they were once more well out to sea, Odysseus began to taunt him again, though his companions begged him not to: "If anyone asks who spoiled that handsome eye of yours, tell him it was Odysseus of Ithaca who did it." Then the Cyclops lifted up his hands to heaven and prayed to his father Poseidon. "Hear me, great god of the sea: if I am indeed your son, see to it that Odysseus never gets home alive, or if he does, may he suffer the loss of his ships, his men and all he has, and return friendless and destitute to a troubled house." Poseidon heard his prayer, and the Greeks rowed on sorrowful for their friends and fearful of what was to come.

They came next to the floating island of Aeolus the god of the winds, where he lived with his six sons who were married to their six sisters.

There they were kindly entertained, and when Odysseus left, Aeolus gave him as a parting present a skin bag in which were shut up all the winds unfavourable to the homeward journey—all the winds, that is, but the west wind which helped them along. For nine days and nine nights they sped forward, until on the tenth day they could make out their homeland rising out of the sea, and see the fires burning the autumn stubble. Then Odysseus, weary with watching, fell into a light sleep. His men began to talk among themselves, saying that he was bringing home treasure in that sack, and that they who had shared his troubles and labours should have a share in his rewards as well. One of them untied the cord round the mouth; whereupon all the winds burst out howling together in a storm that carried ships and weeping men far from their native land. Driven back to the Aeolian island, Odysseus entered the god's house and sat down by the hearth as a suppliant, explaining the misfortune that had brought him back and asking a second time for help. For all that he could say, the god was angry at the misuse of his gift and declared that a man so unlucky must be one deservedly hated by heaven. Odysseus sadly returned to the ships, having gained nothing by his visit, and they set off once more.

After long rowing, they arrived at the country where lived the Laestrygonians, man-eating giants, who waited till most of the fleet had moored in their land-locked harbour and then began to cast huge rocks down on the ships and spear the men like fish. All caught within the harbour died a cruel death, while Odysseus, who had prudently made fast his own ship just outside, cut the cable with his sword and shouted to the men to row for their lives. So they sailed on, glad to have escaped death but sorrowful for the loss of their friends.

> Who knows not Circe,
> The daughter of the Sun, whose charmèd cup
> Whoever tasted lost his upright shape,
> And downward fell into a grovelling swine?
>
> Milton

In time they came to the island of Aeaea, the home of the great and cunning goddess Circe, sister to the magician Aeetes and child of the Sun. There they beached their ship in a safe harbour, and for two days and nights they lay on the shore, worn out with their troubles. On the third day Odysseus, having no idea of their whereabouts, sent off some of his men under his lieutenant Eurylochus in the direction where he had seen the smoke of a house rising among the trees.

Circe[19]

As the band approached the house, they were met by all kinds of wild beasts, wolves and mountain lions among them, which to their amazement were not fierce at all but fawned on them like dogs on their master. Standing at the house gates, they could hear the goddess working at her loom within, and all the house rang with her singing. As soon as they called to her, she opened the gates and invited them in with kind words, setting food and wine before them—all but the cautious Eurylochus, who stayed mistrustfully outside. And the event proved him right, for the moment the men had swallowed Circe's drugged wine, she touched them on the shoulder with her wand and they were transformed into pigs, hairy and grunting, and shut up in her pigsties. Then, too late, they understood the nature of the strange animals in the wood.

When his comrades failed to return, Eurylochus hastened back in terror and distress to Odysseus, who immediately set out to find them. In the enchanted grove surrounding the house he met the god Hermes, in the likeness of a young man, recognizable by the golden herald's staff[20] he always carried. Hermes greeted Odysseus kindly, explained the fate of his companions, and gave him a magical herb called moly that would protect him against Circe's enchantments. The root of moly is black, it has a milk-white flower, and only the gods can uproot it from the earth.

Welcomed by Circe, Odysseus drank her wine without becoming stupefied by it; and when she struck him with her wand, crying, "Be off to the pigsty with your friends!" he rushed at her with his sword and made her fall at his feet in supplication. "Who are you, that you can withstand my enchantments? You can only be Odysseus, who was destined to come here: put up your sword and let us be friends." Odysseus relented only after she had promised to release not only his comrades but all her other captives as well. Thereafter she entertained them all so royally that they stayed with her for a whole year without once thinking of their homes.

At length Odysseus' men began to press him to continue the journey, and he asked the goddess for her advice. "Before you can reach your homeland, you must go to the house of Hades and his queen Persephone to consult the ghost of Teiresias, the blind prophet of Thebes. He alone of all the dead preserves his understanding, while the other ghosts flit mindlessly about. Enter your ship, set the sails, and the wind will carry you straight to the shore of Persephone's country,[21] where the sun never shines, where black poplars stand in groves and the willows drop their fruit before it ripens. Where the rivers Phlegethon and Cocytus flow into Acheron, there you must dig a trench and pour a drink-offering to the dead. Then sacrifice a ram and a black ewe with your face turned away, and let their blood run into the trench. The ghosts of the dead[22] will crowd about it and try to drink, but you must keep them off with your sword until Teiresias has drunk of the blood and answered all your questions. He will direct you over the sea and tell you how you will reach home."

All happened as the goddess had promised. When Odysseus poured out the blood of the sheep, the ghosts came trooping up from the ground, eager to drink it, flitting with faint screams around the trench. Odysseus held them all back till the shade of Teiresias had lapped its fill and gathered strength enough to speak. "You will have a hard journey home, pursued by the anger of Poseidon; but you may still get there if you can keep your men when they get to Sicily from driving off the oxen of the Sun, who hears and sees everything. Even then, you are destined to lose all your men and to arrive in wretchedness in another man's ship: then you will find trouble in your house, strangers devouring your property and humiliating your patient wife Penelope. You will get rid of them, but then you must undertake another journey to placate Poseidon, carrying an oar over your shoulder until you reach a land where men do not salt their food, have never heard of the sea, and mistake the oar for a winnowing fan. There you will set up the oar in the ground and sacrifice to Poseidon; afterwards you may go home and live to a quiet old age, but death shall come to you from the sea at last."

Teiresias then told Odysseus that if he wished to speak with any more of the ghosts, particularly that of his mother, he should let them drink of the blood, and then their memory and speech would return. Odysseus' mother confirmed Teiresias' words about the trouble in Ithaca, telling him how the chief men of the town, supposing him dead, had moved into his house under pretext of courting his wife, while his old father was reduced to poverty and his son Telemachus, now a grown man, was running the estate as best he could.

When she had finished speaking, Odysseus tried to embrace his mother; but though he stretched out his arms to her three times, each time she flitted from him like a phantom or a dream. At last he cried out, "Does Persephone want to torment me, troubled as I am, by mocking me with an empty shadow?" "My son," she replied, "most unfortunate of men, it is not that Persephone deludes you, but we are all like this when we are dead. Our sinews no longer hold our flesh and bones together, and nothing is left but a fleeting ghost."

Lastly there came to the trench the shades of some of Odysseus' companions in the war. Among them was Achilles, who asked him weeping, "Why have you ventured to this miserable realm, among the empty ghosts of the dead?" Odysseus tried to cheer him, saying: "Surely you should be contented. No man was ever blessed as you have been, for living you were honoured among us like the gods, and now you lord it mightily among the dead. Is that so evil a fate?" "Do not try to praise death to me," Achilles replied. "I would rather serve as a bondsman to a poor farmer, if only I might be above the earth, than be king of kings over all the host of the dead."

> And the Sirens, taught to kill
> With their sweet voice,
> Make every echoing rock reply
> Unto their gentle murmuring noise.
> Thomas Campion

Leaving the dark grove of Persephone, Odysseus resumed the homeward voyage. Now they approached the island of the Sirens, the fatal singers who sit in a green meadow heaped with the rotting bones of those they have decoyed. Circe had warned him of them, advising him to stop his men's ears with wax, which he did; but he left his own ears free, having himself bound to the mast instead so that he could not leap out to destruction. Next they had to pass between the rock of the six-

Odysseus and the Sirens

headed yelping monster Scylla and the terrible whirlpool Charybdis; by keeping to Scylla's side of the channel they got by without being sucked down, but they paid for their escape: as they passed, each of her six heads scooped up one man.

Circe as well as Teiresias had warned Odysseus about the herds of the Sun on the island of Sicily, and the peril attendant on the theft of a single beast. He was very careful to warn his men that they must content themselves while there with the food Circe had sent along in the ship. At first his counsels prevailed. But the anger of the gods still pursued them: first Zeus sent a storm, and then a contrary wind blew steadily for a month, so that they exhausted their provisions and still could not leave the island. At last they took to fishing and setting traps for small birds, with no luck at all. Then one day when Odysseus was sleeping a little way off, his lieutenant Eurylochus gathered the others around him and declared they would starve if they went on obeying the order. Hunger overcame prudence, and Odysseus when he returned to the ship smelt roast beef and cursed his fate. The Sun in a rage went to Zeus and swore he would go down to the house of Hades and shine among the dead if the loss of his beloved cattle was not made up to him. Zeus could appease him only by promising to shatter the ship into little bits with a thunderbolt. Portents of disaster began immediately: the hides of the dead cattle crawled about, and the meat as it was being roasted and eaten lowed like living cows.

When at last the wind dropped, the ship put out to sea. Immediately the sky darkened, a terrific squall blew up, and Zeus let fly with his thunderbolts. The ship went whirling round and round: all the men were swept from the decks and were either drowned or struck by the lightning. Odysseus managed to hang on to some pieces of wreckage from which he improvised a raft, and being carried along all night by the waves, in the morning he found himself back on the brink of Charybdis. He only just escaped alive, by clinging to a solitary tree growing on a rock until his raft, sucked in by the whirlpool, was disgorged again.

Eventually the raft brought him to the island of Ogygia, where the nymph Calypso received him kindly, promising him eternal youth like her own if he would only stay with her. She was in a position to enforce her wishes, as Odysseus for all his longing for home had no means of getting away. At last after seven years Athene, concerned for the troubles of his wife and son as well as his own, persuaded Zeus to send Hermes to Calypso with a message that she had kept Odysseus long enough and must let him go. Calypso was angry, but could not move the gods; so she went to Odysseus where he was sitting homesick on the beach looking at the sea, and told him that if he persisted in his preference for a troubled house and a wife neither immortal nor divinely beautiful, she would help him to build and equip a raft strong enough to take him home. Wondering at her willingness, he set gladly to work. In five days the raft was completed and fully stocked with provisions, and Odysseus set out on it, keeping the Bear on his left as Calypso had instructed him, and guiding his raft with a rudder. He had almost reached the land of the Phaeacians when Poseidon caught sight of him sailing along and flew into a rage. "The gods have been favouring this fellow: well, they forgot about me." He blew up the worst storm he could muster, commanding the winds of all the four quarters to fall upon Odysseus and his makeshift vessel, sweeping him into the roaring water and snatching the raft out of his grasp. Just as Odysseus was giving up hope, the sea-goddess Ino appeared and lent him her veil, which held him up until after great efforts he was able to reach the shore. There he struggled into the mouth of a river and scrambled up on the bank, casting the veil back into the water. He lay there until morning, worn out with his troubles.

When dawn broke, Nausicaa, the beautiful daughter of King Alcinoüs and Queen Arete, came down to the river-mouth with her women to do the palace washing.[23] After it was done and the linen dried in the sun and folded to be carried back in the wagon, the princess threw a ball to one of the girls, who missed it, letting it drop into the water. Their cry awoke the hero, who came out from the bushes that had sheltered him and walked forward, naked, wild-eyed with hunger, and bruised from his struggle with the sea. Nausicaa, moved by his evident distress, had him bathed and clothed and brought him back to the town; but being a princess of remarkable discretion, she left it to him to present himself at the palace. "So that no scandal will be caused by my taking a strange man under my protection, you must wait at the outskirts of the town to allow us to get home before you ask your way to the house of my father Alcinoüs. When you come into the building, walk straight through the inner court till you come to my mother Arete, sitting by the fire and spinning her purple wool with her maids around her. Close to her sits my father, drinking like the immortal gods; but pay no attention to him, go up to my mother and lay your hands on her knees in supplication if you want to see your home again."

Guided by Athene, Odysseus reached the palace, splendid like the sun or the moon and surrounded by a walled garden in which grew every kind of fruit tree, whose fruit never failed the whole year round, a new crop ripening as the old was gathered. On either side of the gateway sat dogs of gold and silver, made by Hephaestus to guard the house, ageless and deathless for ever: within were golden statues with torches in their hands, to light the banqueters by night.

Entering, Odysseus went straight to Queen Arete as he had been told. All went well and he was kindly welcomed. Alcinoüs summoned the chief citizens of Phaeacia to a feast, where they were entertained by the bard Demodocus, whom the Muse dearly loved but rewarded with both good and evil, bringing him the divine gift of song but taking away his sight. Demodocus began to sing of the events at Troy, whereupon Odysseus, who was still unknown to the court, drew his cloak over his face and wept. Alcinoüs, noting his grief, began to suspect who his guest was, and he questioned him until Odysseus consented to tell the whole story of his travels.

Afterwards Alcinoüs sent off Odysseus loaded with gifts in one of the intelligent ships of the Phaeacians, that know where they are going without rudder or pilot. Then was fulfilled an old prophecy: Poseidon, from whom were descended both Alcinoüs and his wife Arete, had always threatened that one day, if the Phaeacians continued to send escorts with everyone who asked for them, he would wreck one of their ships on its way home from such a mission and bury their city under a high mountain. When Poseidon saw the Phaeacian ship reach Ithaca and Odysseus set ashore by the sailors, he was angry, and waiting till the ship had almost reached home, he struck it with the flat of his hand just offshore, turning it into a rock. Then Alcinoüs, remembering the prophecy, hastened with all the people to sacrifice to Poseidon, for fear he should carry out his threat and bury their city under a mountain; and there the story leaves them.

> Homer doth tell in his abundant verse
> The long laborious travels of the man,
> And of his lady too he doth rehearse
> How she eludes with all the art she can
> The ungrateful love which other lords began;
> For of her lord false fame long since had sworn
> That Neptune's monsters had his carcass torn.
> Sir John Davies

Odysseus arriving on his native shore was greeted by Athene, who warned him of the dangers he must face at home, gave him the appearance of an old and wretched man, and brought him secretly to the hut of Eumaeus, his old swineherd. During his twenty years' absence, a group of princes from Ithaca and the neighbouring islands had been demanding the hand of his faithful wife Penelope, and with it the kingdom. She put them off by all the shifts she could, trusting in Odysseus' eventual return; and when at last she was compelled to name a day when she would choose among them, she promised to do it when she had finished the work she had at that moment on the loom—a shroud for her old father-in-law. The shroud was never finished, however, for she secretly unravelled every night almost as much as she had woven in the day. Meanwhile the unruly suitors had moved into the palace and were feasting themselves liberally on Odysseus' flocks, herds, and store of wine. Their insolence and impatience increased daily, especially since just before this time one of Penelope's maids had told them why the web was taking so long. Penelope was now living all but imprisoned in the upper rooms, while her son Telemachus had travelled to Sparta to ask if Menelaus had any news of Odysseus.

Now that Odysseus had returned, Athene fetched Telemachus back from Sparta and brought him to Eumaeus' hut, where father and son greeted each other affectionately. Then they laid their plans to get rid of the troublesome suitors.

The next morning Telemachus went home to the palace, Odysseus coming after dressed as a poor old beggar. As he reached the gate his old hound Argus, lying in the path, recognized him and feebly wagged his tail. Odysseus dared not bend down and caress him, and as he walked away the old dog died.

When Odysseus appeared as a beggar in the hall, the suitors mocked at him and ill-treated him, one of them throwing a footstool that bruised his shoulder. Penelope, hearing of this, was angry, and sent for the beggar to ask if he knew anything of Odysseus. Coming into her presence, he told a long tale of having met her husband and heartened her with promises that he would soon be home; and all the time he spoke Penelope looked at her husband but did not know him. Odysseus pitied her and longed to reveal himself, but he was afraid she might accidentally betray him before his revenge was accomplished.

When she had heard the story, Penelope called an old servant, Eurycleia, who had been Odysseus' nurse, to come and bathe her guest's feet. No sooner did she bend over the tub than she recognized an old scar on his thigh that he had got hunting on Mount Parnassus many years ago with his grandfather Autolycus, the famous thief and liar. In her shock she dropped his foot so that the tub overturned, spilling the water out: immediately Odysseus caught her by the throat and commanded her to hold her tongue. "Child," she said, "what are you thinking of? You know that nothing can bend or break me: I will be as dumb as a stone or a lump of iron."

When Odysseus took leave of Penelope, who had noticed nothing, she told him that after all she feared her husband might be dead, that she was afraid to hold off the suitors any longer and was considering some trial of strength or skill by which she might make her choice. Yet still she hesitated: she had lately dreamed of a great eagle that descended from the sky and destroyed a flock of geese as they fed at the trough: might not this be an omen that Odysseus would return and destroy the unwelcome suitors? "Stranger, I do not know what to think. There are two gates through which dreams come to us from the underworld, one of horn and one of ivory.[24] Those that come by the gate of ivory are empty and vain, but true dreams pass the gate of horn: for my son's sake and my own, I trust my dream was one of those." So saying, she went upstairs to her couch, where Athene shed sweet sleep on her eyes.

When day came, the suitors all arrived at the house and began their usual feasting, heaping insults on Odysseus, who held his peace. After they had eaten, Penelope brought from the storeroom a great bow, with its quiver of arrows, left behind twenty years ago by Odysseus when he went to the war. She stood before the suitors and told them that she would marry whichever one of them could string Odysseus' bow and with it shoot an arrow through a series of twelve iron rings set up in a row. All the suitors tried in turn to string the bow; while they were trying, Odysseus went out to the courtyard and made himself known to two old servants of whose fidelity he was sure, the swineherd Eumaeus who had sheltered him unknowing, and another herdsman. These he directed to close off the door to the women's apartment and the other exits of the house. When he went back into the hall, the last of the suitors had just given up. Odysseus asked if he might try, to see what strength remained to him in his old age; the others were angry, but Telemachus rebuked them and had it passed to where he sat. After examining it a moment, Odysseus strung it as easily as a bard fits a new string to his lyre, and shot an arrow straight through the line of rings that had been set up. Then he threw off his rags, signalled to Telemachus, who sprang armed to his side, and began to shoot his quiverful of arrows at the suitors, who, helpless with amazement, fell one by one. When his arrows ran out, Eumaeus and the herdsman, who had provided themselves with armour from the storeroom, came to his aid, and the goddess Athene stood by and encouraged them in the slaughter. Finally only two were left, wretches who had been compelled by the suitors to serve them, a priest who performed their sacrifices and a bard who sang for their entertainment. The priest begged for his life, but Odysseus would not hear him. "Many a time have you prayed to the gods to delay my homecoming," he said, and struck off the man's head as he knelt. Then the bard came forward: "You will be sorry if you kill a bard like me who can sing before both gods and men." Him Odysseus spared.

When at last Odysseus paused and looked about him, the hall was crowded with dead men, lying like fish hauled out of the sea and left on the bank to gasp their lives away. Then he opened the door of the women's apartment and called down the old nurse Eurycleia. When she saw that sight, she opened her mouth to cry out in triumph; but Odysseus checked her, saying: "Rejoice in silence: it is an unholy thing to triumph in the death of men. The anger of the gods and their own evil deeds have destroyed them." Under his direction the maids set to work thoroughly to cleanse the hall; meanwhile Eurycleia went upstairs with the light step of a young woman to tell Penelope that her husband had come home and made an end of the insolent suitors who had troubled his house. Penelope at first would not believe it, supposing her old servant to have gone mad. "Odysseus has met his death far from Ithaca," she said, "he will never return to his homeland." But she was persuaded at least to go down and see for herself.

Coming down into the hall, she seated herself by the fire opposite Odysseus and looked at him for a long time without speaking, so long that Telemachus began to reproach her with hard-heartedness. Still full of amazement, she would not believe until Odysseus had spoken to her

Hermes

of things that only he could know about; then at last she went to him and embraced him. Meanwhile Hermes the guide of souls called together the ghosts of the suitors, rousing them with his golden staff and drawing them whining and gibbering after him. As bats fly about squeaking in the depths of a great cavern when one has fallen from the mass in which they cling, so the ghosts moaned and squealed as Hermes the healer of sorrows led them down into the gloomy dwellings of death.[25] When they had passed the streams of Ocean and the Leucadian Rock, they came to the Gates of the Sun and the land of dreams, and then to the meadows of asphodel where live the shades of those whose labours are finished.

And Odysseus and his family made their peace with the relatives of the suitors, and Odysseus after his long wanderings was once more master in his own house.

Dragon[1]

VII. Cupid and Psyche

O latest born and loveliest vision far
Of all Olympus' faded hierarchy!
                                        Keats

There was once a king living in a certain city who had three daughters, Psyche, the youngest, being so beautiful that citizens and strangers joined in paying her divine honours, half believing her to be a new birth of the love-goddess Venus who once rose from the foaming sea. The people pressed about Psyche as she walked through the town, calling her by the goddess's name and titles and offering her flowery garlands. As her fame spread, travellers came from farther and farther away to see her, until the shrines of Venus, even that at Cythera itself, lay neglected and her altars stood untended and covered with old ashes.

Venus became angry at this, and swore to be avenged. "What, shall I who am the kindling spirit of all the world share my worship with a mortal girl who must one day die?" She called to her aid her winged son Cupid, who does all kinds of mischief without caring for anyone, and pointed out Psyche to him where she sat in her father's house. "My dear son, I adjure you by a mother's love, punish this disobedient beauty that offends me. Make the girl fall into a desperate passion for the most wretched creature living, something so foul and sick and deformed that nothing can compare with it." So saying, she embraced her son and set off towards the sea, attended by nymphs singing and playing about her.

Psyche meantime, loved by all, nevertheless pined in her unfortunate beauty; for Venus' displeasure kept suitors away from her. She was praised and admired like some painted image rather than sought as a young woman of flesh and blood. Her two elder sisters were splendidly married to kings, while she sat lonely at home and hated the sad chance that set her apart from the ordinary fate of women. Her father, fearing that some god was the cause of her misfortune, made a journey to an oracle of Apollo, which gave this alarming reply:

> King, lead your daughter to the mountain-side
> Apparelled for her harsh fate like a bride.
> He who shall claim her is no mortal brood,
> But horrid dragon furious and rude
> Who beats the upper air with iron wings,
> Who wearies and breaks down the strongest things.
> He frights great Jove and gods on high that dwell,
> Rivers, and rugged rocks, and shades of Hell.

When they heard the god's answer, the unhappy family spent several days in mourning as the time of the funereal marriage approached. The torches burned with feebly flickering light, the wedding music was broken by lamentations, the bride wiped away the tears with her veil; the whole city mourned with her parents. Psyche reproached them: "When all the people paid me divine honours, calling me the new Venus, then you should have wept and grieved for me; now dry your useless tears and lead me to the place." The people accompanied her to the top of the mountain where she was to meet her strange fate, and there they left her. Then when she was left alone, weeping and trembling on the rock, gentle Zephyr caught her up with her robes and carried her through the air, setting her down after some time in a deep valley on a bed of softest flowers.

Looking about her, Psyche found herself beside a crystal stream and a green wood, and in the heart of the wood rose a stately palace, more finely wrought and decorated than the work of man, shining with precious stones like the light of the sun. At the pleasant sight Psyche took heart and entered; and as she walked through the courts and rooms, which all lay open without lock or bar, she saw many delightful things but no person at all. When she had seen everything, she heard a voice that said: "Lady, why do you marvel at these treasures? All that you see is at your command, and we who speak are here to serve you; take therefore some rest, and bathe and refresh yourself, and whatever dishes you care for shall be set before you when you please." Then Psyche thanked the gods who watched over her, and refreshed herself as the voice had said. At table she was served by invisible hands and entertained by invisible musicians, and all was done for her that she could desire.

At night Psyche went to the chamber prepared for her and lay down to sleep; and there after a while someone came to her, known only by his voice and touch in the darkness. This was the master of the palace and its treasures, and he greeted her with great kindness. Night after night he came to her room, always leaving her again before the morning light.

In this way and with this strange companionship, which became very dear to her, Psyche lived in happiness for many weeks. One night her lover told her that her sisters were searching for her, but that if she heard their lamentations she must pay no attention unless she wished to bring great sorrow on herself and him. Then Psyche remembered her home and family, and suddenly her fine palace seemed to her a prison if she could not speak to her sisters; so she begged and implored him to have them carried to the valley to visit her. At last he gave in to her pleading, but warned her again about taking them into her confidence.

When gentle Zephyr set her dear sisters down in the valley, Psyche made them welcome with great joy, entertaining them with the best the palace could afford. When they saw her happiness and how splendidly she was served, envy took hold in their hearts, and they pressed her for an account of her husband; but she put them off with a tale of his being a fair young man who passed the days hunting on the hills. Then filling their laps with jewels and golden ornaments, she commanded Zephyr to carry them home again.

Away from her their envy at her good fortune increased beyond all measure, and they complained to each other that she was giving herself airs like the consort of a god. Once more Psyche's husband warned her against them, and told her, moreover, that as a testimony of their love she was now carrying his child, who was destined to become one of the immortal gods if only she concealed his secret. Then Psyche was more joyful than before, and loved her husband more dearly than ever.

But those wicked sisters commanded Zephyr to bring them back to the valley, and after congratulating Psycho on the child she would soon bear, they pretended to be concerned for her safety: "for we have learned that he who comes to you every night is a monstrous serpent, who watches over you and caresses you only until your child is born, when he means to devour you both together." Forgetting all the tenderness of her husband, his admonitions and her promises, poor Psyche was very much frightened, and she begged her sisters to advise her in her extremity. Their counsel was to hide a sharp knife and a burning lamp in her room, and at night, after her unknown lover had fallen asleep, to bring out the lamp and strike him by its light. Then having done their work they went away.

At night Psyche made her preparations, trembling still with fear for herself and her unborn child. When her lover slept, she brought out the lamp and carried it towards the bed: and there she saw lying the fair body of her husband, Cupid the god of love himself, still ignorant of her treachery. Now it was with shame and fondness that she trembled, and in her haste to hide the lamp she let a drop of burning oil fall on his shoulder, waking him with the pain. Without a word he caught up his bow and quiver and rose into the air on his white-plumaged wings, flying in a moment far out of sight.

Cupid made his way straight to his mother's chamber, where he lay uneasily waiting for his burned shoulder to heal, enduring Venus' reproaches for flouting her commands. Meanwhile faithful Psyche wandered about searching for him, often weary with her burden but taking no rest. From altar to altar of the lady goddesses she travelled, performing humble services in their temples and imploring their help. Juno, Ceres, all, pitied her repentance and her condition, but none would advise her for fear of the anger of Venus, who of all the divine powers is best able to avenge a slight.

In her distress, Psyche resolved to approach the offended goddess herself, whom she might yet placate by her humility and tears. As she came within sight of the house of Venus, one of the servants ran out and seized her, dragging her by the hair into the presence of the goddess, who beat and struck her and reviled her as a shameless wench. Then she spilled out on the floor a great quantity of wheat, barley, lentils, and other grains and ordered her to sort them before night. Psyche did not even begin, but as soon as she was left alone sat down and wept. Immediately an ant, pitying the sorrows of the woman married to a god, called to all her sisters, daughters of the ground that is mother of all, to sort the seeds into separate piles. When the task was done they slipped out of the house and disappeared. But Venus when she came in was furious: "No mortal could have accomplished the task: that scapegrace son of mine must have helped you." She threw her a crust of bread and let her sleep in a corner, while she devised another trial.

In the morning Venus sent Psyche into a thick forest to bring back some golden wool from the fierce sheep that fed there. When Psyche reached the forest, her first thought was to throw herself into the river that ran by and end her griefs; but a green reed on the river-bank, stirred into murmuring music by the wind, whispered to her that this task was an easy one, if only she waited till the heat of the day was past and the sheep came down to the water to drink, leaving tufts of their fleece caught on the bushes. This she could gather and carry back to Venus' house.

Still, when she had done so, Venus accused her of using trickery, and now she set her a harder task yet. From a black rock on top of a high mountain there flowed down a freezing stream whose flow became the dreary Stygian shallows and Cocytus' angry river: with that water she was to fill a crystal vial. The rock proved impossible to climb, and was moreover guarded by crawling dragons that rolled their sleepless bloodshot eyes. As Psyche stood there, cold and rigid like any stone, Jupiter's royal bird the eagle, who had an old obligation to Cupid, swept down on his broad wings and offered to fill her flask as required with the dreadful water of Styx of which the gods themselves are afraid. When Psyche carried it back to Venus, she was received with worse insults than ever. "You must be a black sorceress, to carry out these tasks and return safely: let us see you perform one more. Take this box and descend to Hell and the house of shadows, and ask Proserpina to send me a little of her beauty, and come back with it as quickly as you can."

At this command Psyche was in the deepest despair. Without pausing even to think of how to carry it out, she hastened up to the top of a high tower intending to throw herself down. Then the tower gave forth a voice and spoke to her: "Wretched woman, do not take the shortest way to Pluto's house and give up your hope of return; but enquire along the roads the path to Taenarus in the waste, where you will find a pit, the breathing-place of Hell.[2] There you can enter, taking in your hands two honey-cakes and in your mouth two pieces of money.[3] On the downward path you will meet people who ask you for help: those you must ignore. At the deadly river, let Charon the ferryman take a coin from your mouth, and he will then carry you over in his rickety boat. As you cross, an old man swimming in the river will hold out to you his rotting hands and cry to you to take him into the boat; but do not heed his crying. When you meet the dog Cerberus that guards the desolate house of death, cast him a honey-cake, and the other one on your return. Proserpina when you enter will make you welcome and offer you a soft seat and delicate foods: be sure that you sit down on the hard ground and accept nothing but a crust of bread.[4] When you have obtained what you came for, go back to the upper world by the way you came. But above all, be careful not to look into the box that Proserpina has filled, nor be too curious about the treasure of the divine beauty."

Psyche immediately made ready for the descent, following the tower's instructions. She passed by in silence all those who would detain her, paid Charon's fee, refused the dead old man in the river, stopped Cerberus' mouth with a honey-cake, and so came into the presence of Proserpina, where she sat down on the hard ground and contented herself with a crust of bread. On her way back, when she had almost reached the house of Venus, she was overcome with a great desire,[5] saying to herself, "Am I not a fool, knowing that I carry the divine beauty, not to take a little of it so that I may please my lover?" And thereupon she opened the box, which seemed to be empty, but a deadly sleep came stealing out of it and covered her face, so that she fell down in the pathway like one dead.

Meanwhile Cupid had recovered from his burn and flown out by the window from the room where Venus thought to keep him shut up, and was now searching to find what had become of his Psyche. When he saw her lying in the path, he wiped the dreadful sleep from her face and put it back in the box, waking her with gentle words. Then he sprang into the air, while Psyche carried to Venus the present of Proserpina.

Won over at last by the long patience of his wife, Cupid flew straight to his father Jupiter to declare his cause. When he had heard all, Jupiter replied with some severity: "My son, you have never treated me so dutifully as you ought, seeing that I am both your father and the lawgiver of the universe: it is your fault that my reputation has been stained by wicked intrigues, to say nothing of transformations at various times into the lowly forms of beasts and birds. However, I will do for you what I can." So saying, he called a council of all the dwellers on high Olympus. He reminded the gods of the wrongs they had suffered at Cupid's hands and from the painful prick of his arrows: now, he said, it was time that the mischievous boy should settle down to a man's responsibilities, and to that end they were gathered together to celebrate his marriage with a virtuous young woman of tried fidelity.

Even Venus could not cross the will of great Jove, who pacified her with gracious speeches. Then calling Psyche before him, he gave her to drink the divine nectar, so that she might remain forever with her husband Cupid, ageless and deathless like the immortal gods and honoured like them in the temples and hearts of men.

Now the great marriage feast was prepared, and Cupid sat at the head of the table with his dear bride in his arms. The Hours[6] had decked all the house with garlands of roses, the Graces[7] perfumed it, the Muses[8] sang sweetly in time to the harping of Apollo their leader, and Venus danced in the midst of them. And when in due time her child was born into happiness and the bright looks of his parents, Psyche named him Pleasure.

VIII. The Passing and Afterlife of the Gods

The oracles are dumb,
No voice or hideous hum
Runs through the archèd roof in
           words deceiving.
Apollo from his shrine
Can no more divine,
With hollow shriek the steep of
           Delphos leaving.
No nightly trance or breathèd spell
Inspires the pale-eyed priest from
           the prophetic cell.
           Milton

The gods of the Greeks and Romans had many ways of making their will known to men. Before any great undertaking, animals were sacrificed and the priests noted their behaviour and searched their bodies for omens. Sometimes the gods sent signs in the form of unexpected natural happenings, as once when Zeus signalled his approval to Odysseus by thundering out of a clear sky. Or a god might send a message in a dream, true or deluding as suited his purpose. Most important, however, certain of the gods had oracles or consulting-places, shrines where people could put questions to the god and obtain answers. At some the questioner slept a night within the holy precinct, expecting a significant dream. In the sacred oak grove of Zeus at Dodona, the priests translated the rustling of the leaves into messages. At the oracle of Trophonius, named after a mortal man favoured by Apollo, the suppliant after rigorous purification descended into a dark and gloomy cave, where he received his answer in a state of trance.

The most famous of all oracles was that of Apollo at Delphi, called the centre or navel of the earth.[1] In earlier times it had belonged not to him but to Gaia, for whom it was guarded by a huge serpent known as the Python. When scarcely more than a child, Apollo killed the Python with his arrows and seized the shrine, whereupon Earth went to Zeus and demanded justice. She was pacified when Apollo established the Pythian Games[2] in the Python's honour, and when he called the priestess of the shrine the Pythoness after it. When questioned, the Pythoness would seat herself on the tripod[3] and breathe in the vapours that rose from a cleft in the earth. She would then fall into a trance and begin to utter frenzied words, which the priests arranged into rough verses.

Apollo, the god of music and poetry, was also the god of prophecy,

Delphic priestess on tripod

which he could pass on as a gift to one whom he especially favoured, as he did to the Trojan princess Cassandra. However, when Cassandra later lost his affection he added the penalty that no one should believe what she said. Thus, though she foresaw the whole fate of Troy and its royal house, she could do nothing to avert it.

The angry northern wind
Will blow these sands like Sibyl's leaves abroad.
Shakespeare

To the Cumaean Sibyl, another woman whom Apollo loved, he promised whatever she might ask. Taking up a handful of dust from the ground, she asked to live as many years as there were grains in her hand; but she forgot to ask for perpetual youth. Apollo offered her this as well if she would grant him her love, and when she refused, he swore that what she had desired should be her punishment. Her destiny was to live for a thousand years in old age and weakness. At last, long after the visit of Aeneas, she shrank to a pitiful heap of skin and bone, and was hung in a bottle from the temple roof. Nothing but her voice was left to her by the Fates. Children playing near the shrine would call out, "Sibyl, what do you want?" and from the bottle a faint chirping voice would answer, "I want to die." Her oracles, in the days when she still gave them, were confused answers written on leaves and tossed up into the wind that swirled about her cave.

When an old woman, this Sibyl came before an early king of Rome named Tarquin the Proud with nine ancient and tattered books of prophecies, which she offered him at a great price. When he refused, she burned three of them in his presence and offered him the remaining six at the same price. He again refused, and now she burned all but three, which she offered him still at the same price. This time Tarquin took the offer. Known as the Sibylline Books, they were kept in the temple of Jupiter on the Capitoline Hill[4] and consulted in national emergencies.

The lonely mountains o'er,
And the resounding shore,
A voice of weeping heard, and loud lament.
Milton

After many generations the oracles began to decline, and stories were told of how the gods had deserted their holy places. One story, indeed, records the death of a god. A ship on its way from Greece to Italy was passing the island of Paxi when a voice was heard calling the pilot by name: "Thamus!" The first and second times Thamus was too astonished to reply, but the third time he called back. Then the voice cried out, "When you come opposite to Palodes, announce there that Great Pan is dead." Thamus half wanted to ignore the mysterious command;

but when, opposite Palodes, the wind dropped and all was still, he raised his voice and called towards the land, "Great Pan is dead." Immediately the people on board heard a loud cry of lamentation, as if from a crowd of mourners.

As this took place at about the time when Christ was born, Christian writers made much of the story, because it meant to them the death or overthrow of the old gods at the birth of the new. But the gods did not altogether die; they survived in altered shapes in the stories and traditions of Europe.

> Canst thou bind the sweet influences of Pleiades,
> or loose the bands of Orion?[5]
>
> The Book of Job

One place in people's minds where the gods lingered on was in the theory of astrology, or the influence of the stars on human life, now regarded as superstition but once a scientific study. The gods of the Greeks and Romans had originally very little connection with sun, moon, stars, and other natural forces. However, long before the Greeks, the Babylonians had worshipped the sun and moon and the five planets under the names of their great gods, among them the creator-god Marduk and the love-goddess Ishtar. In later times astrological belief spread to Greece and Rome, and the planets began to be called after the Olympian gods who most resembled the Babylonian planetary gods. The names of "the seven stars in the sky" are recalled in those of the days of the week all over Europe, though not always in the same order. Sunday and Monday are called after the sun and moon, and Saturday is Saturn's day. The Latin names of the gods are still to be seen in the French names for the remaining four days: Tuesday is *mardi*, Mars' day; Wednesday *mercredi*, Mercury's day; Thursday *jeudi*, Jove's day; Friday *vendredi*, Venus' day. Our names for these days result from later identification of the Classical gods with the gods of the Norsemen. Tuesday belongs to their war-god Tyr, Wednesday to Woden or Odin, the father-god who rules the sky, Thursday to the thunder-god Thor, and Friday to the love-goddess Freya. The correspondence with the Classical gods is close but not complete. The Norsemen have no god who resembles Mercury, and they divide Jove's offices of All-Father and thunder-god between Odin and Thor. In German Thursday is not called by a god's name but is *Donnerstag*, the thunder's day.

Each planet ruled on the day called by its name. The planetary powers were supposed to bestow their own characteristics on children born on their own days. That is where we get some adjectives for different kinds of people: "sunny," "lunatic," "martial," "mercurial," "jovial," "venerean" (amorous), "saturnine" (gloomy and sluggish). Some people who regarded the old gods as evil blamed their planets for burdening man with seven deadly sins, respectively: gluttony, envy, wrath, avarice, pride, lust, and sloth.

In the familiar rhyme, "Monday's child is fair of face," the old characteristics can hardly be recognized. But an older version recalls that Monday is the moon's day and Mercury, the patron of merchants, is also the god of thieves. Here he has even stolen the place of his father Jove; for we know from the French day-names that his planet's day is Wednesday.

> Sunday's child is full of grace,
> Monday's child is full in the face,
> Tuesday's child is solemn and sad,
> Wednesday's child is merry and glad,
> Thursday's child is inclined to thieving,
> Friday's child is free in giving,
> And Saturday's child works hard for a living.

A line that most of us know better, "Friday's child is loving and giving," looks back not only to Venus but also to the Christian associations of the day.

Our names for the months of the year are Roman, and four of them come from the names of divinities. March, May, and June are called respectively after Mars, Maia the mother of Mercury, and Juno. January is from a Roman god, Janus the guardian of doorways (Latin *ianua*, door), the "opener" of the year. He is always represented with two faces, so that he can look both ways at once.

> Lo, this is she that was the world's delight.
> Swinburne

Long after the decline of Classical religion, Venus the love-goddess was said to hold her court in northeastern Germany under a hill which was called after her the Venusberg or mountain of Venus. Travellers passing after dark would see gleams of torchlight and hear far-off revelry. The goddess herself appeared before the minstrel Tannhäuser and beguiled him into the heart of the hill, where she entertained him splendidly for seven years. At last he sickened of her court with its uninterrupted round of pleasures, and prayed for help to the Virgin Mary; whereupon the side of the hill opened and he came out into the fresh night air. He first took his way to the nearby village church, where he made his confession to the priest and begged to be absolved of the guilt of his seven-years' dallying with the powers of Hell. Horrified by the story, the priest sent him to ask absolution from a higher authority, who also refused him and sent him on. At last he came with his tale before Pope Urban IV, a man renowned for his severity, who drove Tannhäuser away with the words, "Sooner shall the staff in my hand grow green and put out flowers, than God shall pardon thee!" At that Tannhäuser fell into despair, and he made his way back to the Venusberg, the only place left for a man shut out from Christendom. When he had been gone three days, the Pope's staff grew green and broke into flower. Then Urban sent messengers in search of the minstrel, but as they came up he stepped into the mountain-side, which closed forever behind him.

Such tales show how the gods of the old religion did not die but became the fiends and demons of the new. In goat-horned and goat-footed Satan we may recognize the great god Pan, once the kindly protector of flocks, but now the prince of bogeys. Satan's limp and his connection with subterranean fires probably come to him from Vulcan, the Latin form of Hephaestus, the lame smith of the gods. Vulcan's mysterious craft in story often seems somewhat demonic, and like Lucifer he was once thrown out of heaven.

About the fifth century B.C., Zeus' daughter Artemis, the virgin huntress, began to be thought of as the moon. The Romans, who called her Diana,[6] took up this view of her, sometimes depicting her with a crescent moon on her forehead; her brother Phoebus Apollo, the bright-haired archer-god, they explained as the sun. They associated Diana especially with the clear moonlight, and her cousin Hecate[7] and her half-sister Proserpina (Persephone) with the moon's dark or sinister aspects. In European folklore these powers still rule the night: the fairies dance under the protection of Diana, the fairy queen is called Titania (a name of Diana) or Proserpina, and Hecate is the goddess of the witches.

Some of the figures of myth have had a pleasanter afterlife. Apart from her role as a sorceress, Venus lived on as the Queen of Love in the poetry of the Renaissance, and the poets had still more to say about the mischief caused by her arrow-shooting son Cupid. The four sons of Eos, Boreas, Notus, Eurus, and Zephyr, can be seen puffing out their cheeks in the corners of old maps. Triton, the fish-tailed conch-blowing son of Neptune (Poseidon), becomes the merman of travellers' tales. The mermaid's origin is more complex. Her dangerously sweet voice recalls the Sirens, while her looking-glass and the

> golden comb
> Wherewith she sits on diamond rocks
> Sleeking her soft alluring locks
> Milton

perhaps connect her with Venus and other Mediterranean love-goddesses who rose from the sea. Saint George's rescue of a princess from a dragon looks very like Perseus' rescue of Andromeda, or Hercules' rescue of Hesione. The Pied Piper who can draw rats by his piping is only one of many magical musicians whose gifts recall those of Orpheus. Psyche's task of sorting a heap of seeds occurs in many familiar stories, and she herself and her mysterious lover meet us again in the tale of

The sleeping shepherd[8]

Beauty and the Beast. And where was it that we first met Endymion, the sleeping shepherd?

> Little boy blue, come blow your horn,
> The sheep's in the meadow, the cow's in the corn.
> Where is the boy who looks after the sheep?
> He's under the haystack, fast asleep.
> Will you wake him? No, not I;
> For if I do, he's sure to cry.

LINES

Here often, when a child, I lay reclined,
I took delight in this locality.
Here stood the infant Ilion of the mind,
And here the Grecian ships did seem to be.
And here again I come, and only find
The drain-cut levels of the marshy lea, —
Grey sandbanks, and pale sunsets, —dreary wind,
Dim shores, dense rains, and heavy-clouded sea.

Tennyson

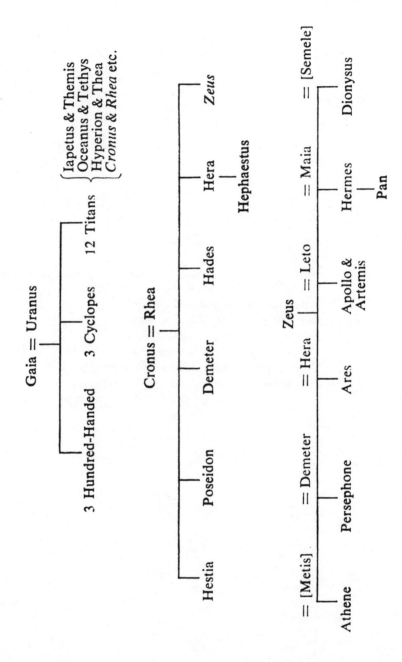

FAMILY TREE OF THE OLYMPIANS

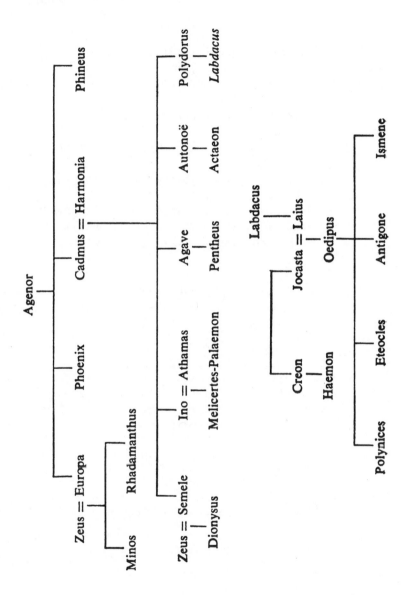

FAMILY TREE OF THE ROYAL HOUSE OF THEBES

MYTHOLOGY

CREATION

Reign of Uranus (Sky) and Gaia (Earth)

GOLDEN AGE   Reign of Cronus and Titans

SILVER AGE   Reign of Zeus and Olympians ....

Birth of younger Olympians

BRONZE AGE

Age of ancestors (Europa, Cadmus, Tantalus, etc.) ....

Age of heroes (Jason, Theseus, Heracles, etc.) ....

Fall of Troy to Greeks under Mycenaean king Agamemnon ......

IRON AGE   Return of exiled sons of Heracles from the north ....

Dido receives Aeneas at Carthage ....

Romulus and Remus found Rome ....

> *The Greek myths are told in a sequence which has some relation to the historical sequence of events in the right-hand column. Many of the myths were suggested by the historical events, and where this is the case the two are connected on the chart.*

Decline of the oracles and death of Pan...

HISTORY

	OLD STONE AGE
	NEW STONE AGE
	BRONZE AGE
Great Pyramid and Great Sphinx built in Egypt	B.C. 2500?
... Achaean invasions from the north, bringing Olympian religion to Greece	2000–1300
... Great age of Mycenaean civilization: founding of Greek city-states	1600–1200
... Fall of Minoan empire, destruction of Cnossus; Achaean raids on Crete, Egypt, shores of Black Sea	1400?
... Fall of Troy	1184?
... Dorian invasion from the north, bringing iron	IRON AGE
... Founding of Carthage	814?
Homer, author of *Iliad* and *Odyssey*; Hesiod, author of *Works and Days* and *Theogony*	8th cent.
... Founding of Rome	753?
Fall of Jerusalem to Nebuchadnezzar	586
Great age of Athens: tragic dramatists Aeschylus, Sophocles, Euripides	5th cent.
Greeks defeat Persians at Marathon	490
Death of Athenian philosopher Socrates	399
Alexander the Great carries conquests into India	326
Apollonius Rhodius, author of *Argonautica*; Apollodorus, author of *Bibliotheca*	3rd cent.
Beginning of Rome's wars with Carthage	264
Destruction of Carthage by Rome	146
Birth of Virgil, author of *Aeneid* (Latin)	70
Invasion of Britain by Julius Caesar	54
Birth of Ovid, author of *Metamorphoses* (Latin)	43
Probable date of birth of Christ	4
Death of Augustus, first Roman Emperor	A.D. 14
Birth of Apuleius, author of *The Golden Ass* (Latin)	123
Conversion of Constantine, first Christian Roman Emperor	312

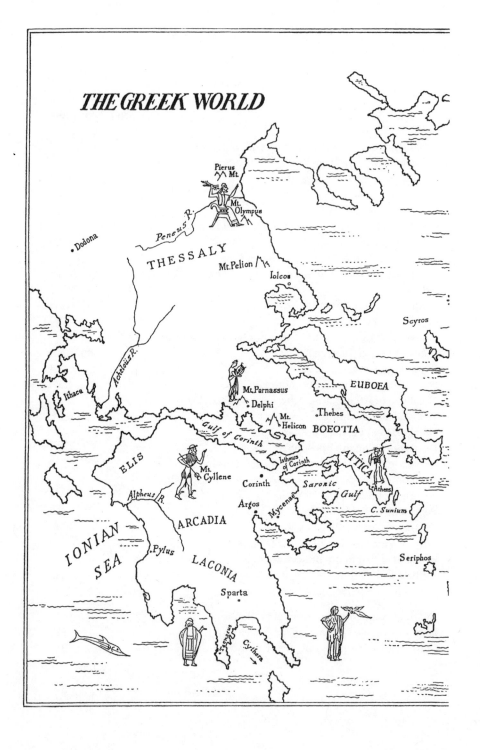

THE GREEK WORLD

Pierus Mt.

Mt. Olympus

Peneus R.

Dodona

THESSALY

Mt. Pelion

Iolcos

Scyros

Achelous R.

Ithaca

Mt. Parnassus

Delphi

Mt. Helicon

EUBOEA

Thebes

BOEOTIA

Gulf of Corinth

ELIS

Mt. Cyllene

Isthmus of Corinth

ATTICA

Athens

Corinth

Saronic

Gulf

Alpheus R.

ARCADIA

Argos

Mycenae

C. Sunium

IONIAN

SEA

Pylus

LACONIA

Seriphos

Sparta

Cythera

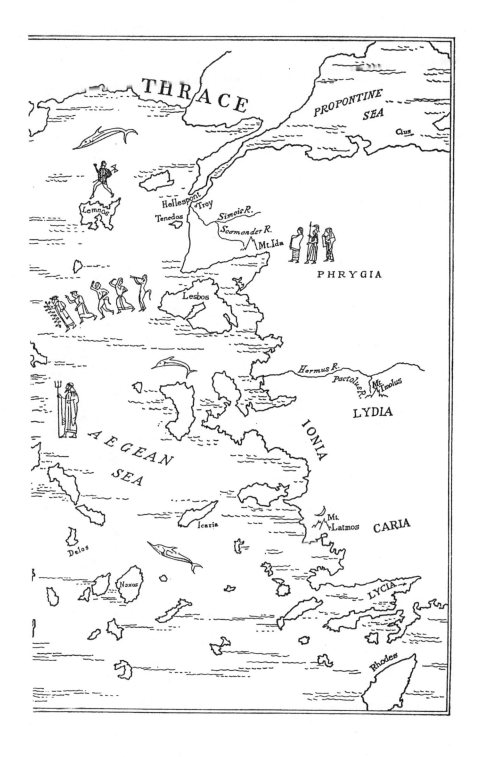

THRACE

PROPONTINE SEA

Cius

Lemnos

Hellespont

Troy

Tenedos

Simois R.

Scamander R.

Mt. Ida

PHRYGIA

Lesbos

Hermus R.

Pactolus R.

Mt. Tmolus

LYDIA

AEGEAN

SEA

IONIA

Mt. Latmos

CARIA

Icaria

Delos

Naxos

LYCIA

Rhodes

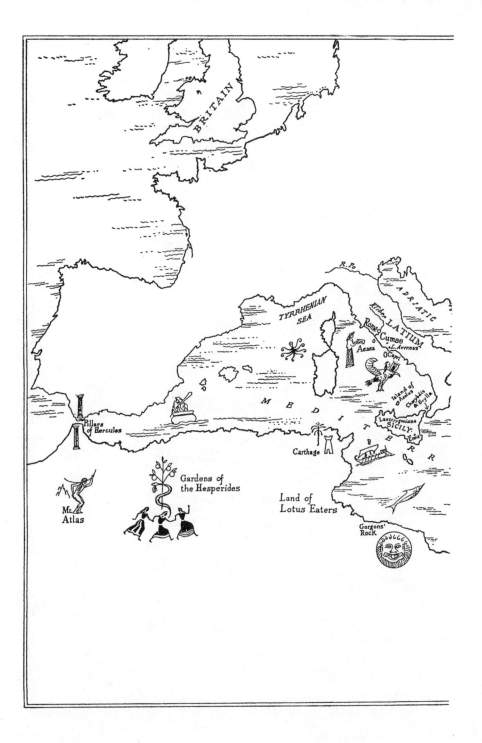

BRITAIN

R. Po

ADRIATIC

TYRRHENIAN SEA

Kirke. LATIUM
Rome Cumae
Aeaea L. Avernus
Capri

Island of
Aeolus
Charybdis
& Scylla

Laestrygonians
SICILY
Etna

M E D I T E R R

Pillars
of Hercules

Carthage

Mt.
Atlas

Gardens of
the Hesperides

Land of
Lotus Eaters

Gorgons'
Rock

THE MEDITERRANEAN WORLD

Sources of Quotations

52   Alexander Pope, *The Rape of the Lock*, bk. 3, ll.121–4.
50   Ovid, *Metamorphoses*, bk. 8, ll. 722–4 (trans. John Dryden).
55   John Fletcher, *Hear, ye ladies*.
56   John Milton, *Comus*, ll. 447–9.
57   John Milton, *Il Penseroso*, ll. 19–21.
59   William Shakespeare, *Love's Labour's Lost*, 5.2.589–92.
60   Edmund Spenser, *The Faerie Queene*, bk. 1, canto 11, st. 27, ll. 1–3.
62   William Shakespeare, *Pericles*, 1.1.26–8.
63   John Milton, *Paradise Regained*, bk. 4, ll. 563–8.
64   John Milton, *On His Deceased Wife*.
65   William Shakespeare, *Antony and Cleopatra*, 4.10.56–60.
67   William Shakespeare, *The Merchant of Venice*, 1.1.166–73.
69   William Morris, *The Life and Death of Jason*, bk. 4, ll. 83–96.
71   Edmund Spenser, *The Ruines of Rome*, Sonnet 10, ll. 1–4.
76   William Shakespeare, *II Henry VI*, 5.2.57–9.
77   William Morris, *The Life and Death of Jason*, bk. 9, ll. 327–30.
78   John Milton, *Comus*, ll. 253–9.
82   Percy Bysshe Shelley, *Alastor*, ll. 672–5.
83   John Milton, *Paradise Lost*, bk. 7, ll. 12–20.
86   Geoffrey Chaucer, *The Canterbury Tales: The Knight's Tale*, ll. 861–5.
88   Christopher Marlowe, *Doctor Faustus*, Prologue, ll. 21–2.
89   William Shakespeare, *Henry V1, Part I*, 5.3.188–9.
91   T.S. Eliot, *Sweeney Erect*.
92   Edmund Spenser, *The Faerie Queene*, bk. 5, canto 8, st. 43, ll. 1–7.
93   Virgil, *Aeneid*, bk. 6, ll. 126–9.
96   Alfred, Lord Tennyson, *The Palace of Art*, ll. 117–20.
98   Christopher Marlowe, *Doctor Faustus*, sc. 12, ll. 107–8.
99   John Milton, *Comus*, ll. 875–6.
99   John Milton, *Comus*, ll. 46–7.
100 Anonymous Elizabethan song.
101 Percy Bysshe Shelley, Chorus from *Hellas*.
105 Alfred, Lord Tennyson, *Oenone*, ll. 220–3.
109 Christopher Marlowe, *Doctor Faustus*, sc. 12, ll. 81–2.
111 John Milton, *Paradise Lost*, bk. 9, ll. 14–16.
116 Matthew Arnold, *Palladium*.
120 Alfred, Lord Tennyson, *The Lotos-Eaters*, ll. 114–23.
123 John Milton, *II Penseroso*, 97–9.
126 Alfred, Lord Tennyson, *To Virgil*.
128 John Milton, *Paradise Lost*, bk. 2, ll. 575–86.

129   Edmund Spenser, *The Faerie Queene*, bk. 1, canto 3, st. 21, ll. 5–6.
133   John Milton, *Comus*, ll. 50–3.
137   Thomas Campion, *A Hymn in Praise of Neptune*.
142   Sir John Davies, *Orchestra*, ll. 15–21.
148   John Keats, *Ode to Psyche*.
157   John Milton, *On the Morning of Christ's Nativity*, ll. 173–80.
159   William Shakespeare, *Titus Andronicus*, 4.1.104–5.
160   John Milton, *On the Morning of Christ's Nativity*, ll. 181–3.
161   Job 38:31.
163   Algernon Charles Swinburne, *Laus Veneris* (*The Praise of Venus*), l. 9.
164   John Milton, *Comus*, ll. 880–2.

Note on the Illustrations

All the illustrations, with three exceptions, are taken from Greek pottery; for of all the various materials on which the Greeks painted or drew only their baked clay has come down to us in any quantity. It is durable in itself, yet is not so apt to be broken up or melted down for reuse as such stronger substances as marble or bronze.

The earlier or "archaic" vases have their designs painted in black glaze on the reddish Greek clay, giving a silhouette or "black-figured" effect. Page **115** shows a very early example. Often the faces and hands of women are filled in with white, as in the later example by the painter Amasis on page **121**; details are scratched into the glaze so that the clay of the vase shows through. Amasis and Exekias are two outstanding Athenian masters of this style, known to us because they signed their work.

Towards the end of the sixth century B.C. a new technique was introduced, the "red-figured," which gradually replaced the black-figured. Figures were now drawn in outline on the clay surface against a background painted out in black. Red-figured work demanded a finer skill in drawing than black-figured; but it allowed greater freedom of line, as details within the outlines could be applied with pen or brush rather than incised. From the work of Macron, the painter who collaborated with the Athenian potter Hiero, we have taken the red-figured designs on pages 286, 296, and 365.

The three exceptions occur on pages 343, 347, and 401. The first shows a Cretan coin, the second an Egyptian seal. The third is not ancient, but is taken from a medieval manuscript copy of Ovid's *Metamorphoses*; the artist has never seen Classical painting, and so he draws the gods and goddesses like men and women of his own time.

Further comment on certain illustrations (those on pages 296, 317, 322, 339, 361, 368, 377, 388, and 401) will be found in the notes following.

Note on Classical Names

Most of the Classical myths arose in Greece some centuries before the birth of Christ. In the second century B.C. Greece fell under the power of Rome, and Roman writers began to retell the Greek stories, altering the names to suit Latin spelling and sometimes changing them to those of their own less colourful gods. Thus Heracles became Hercules, and the sky-god Zeus became Jove or Jupiter. The name "Greece" itself is Latin: the Greeks themselves have always called their country Hellas and its people Hellenes.

It was the Romans who civilized most of Europe, sending in armies, building roads and towns, establishing the rule of law. When the Roman Empire crumbled away, it left in its place the Roman Catholic Church, which continued to use Latin in its services and its books. Roman Catholicism was the religion of the whole of Western Europe until the Protestant Reformation took place in the sixteenth century. Thus Latin remained for centuries the international language of educated Europe, and Greek books and writers were known only in Latin versions. So it comes about that the Latin names of gods and heroes are still often more familiar to us than the original Greek ones.

In this book Greek names are used, except in stories in the last two chapters told only by Latin authors. However, Latin spellings have been preferred when these were more familiar: Phoebus and Oedipus instead of Phoibos and Oidipous, Jocasta instead of Iokaste, Circe instead of Kirke. A list of Greek names with their Latin equivalents follows:

Zeus – Jupiter, Jove
Poseidon – Neptune

Pan – Faunus
satyrs – fauns

Hades – Pluto, Dis
Hera – Juno
Demeter – Ceres
Persephone – Proserpina
Dionysus – Bacchus
Ares – Mars
Athene – Minerva
Artemis – Diana
Hephaestus – Vulcan, Mulciber
Hermes – Mercury
Aphrodite – Venus
Eros – Cupid
Hestia – Vesta

Cronus – Saturn
Rhea – Ops
Uranus – Coelus
Gaia – Tellus
Helios – Sol
Selene – Luna
Eos – Aurora
Phosphorus – Lucifer
Hesperus – Vesper
Heracles – Hercules
Asclepius – Aesculapius
Hecabe – Hecuba
Polydeuces – Pollux

Notes

I. In the Beginning

These stories are told by several Greek writers, most fully by the early poet Hesiod in his *Theogony*, or Births of the Gods. Hesiod lived, probably in the eighth century B.C., on the slopes of Mount Helicon, where he claimed the Muses taught him his songs as he was tending his sheep. The story of Deucalion and Pyrrha, like that of Phaethon following, is taken from the Latin poet Ovid. His *Metamorphoses* or Transformations is an elaborate retelling of nearly all the Greek myths and some Roman ones for a sophisticated Roman audience. The poem is bound together by its grand theme of transformation, which the poet sees as the essential process of the universe. Born in 43 B.C., Ovid was a contemporary of the Emperor Augustus.

1 The powers of Eros include the physical force of attraction in matter.
2 Adamant, meaning "invincible," was a name given in Classical times to the hardest iron and steel, or to diamond.
3 Roman writers explained Cronus as meaning Time, which devours the years as Cronus did his children. This happened through confusion with Greek *chronos*, "time"; and it explains why pictures of Father Time show him carrying Cronus' sickle.
4 Oceanus is thought of as a great river flowing in a circle round the flat disk of the earth.
5 Nymphs are properly maiden spirits of waters and springs. Similar spirits are dryads and oreads, attached to trees and mountains. "Nymphs" is frequently used as a general name for any of these.
6 Morning Star and Evening Star are both names of the planet Venus.

7 It is later in the Classical age, under Babylonian influence, that the planets are given the names of Ares, Hermes, Zeus, Aphrodite, and Cronus (our Mars, Mercury, Jupiter, Venus, and Saturn), and star-worship enters Greek religion. See p. 398.

8 During the Roman feast of Saturnalia held every year in honour of Saturn, slaves were waited on by their masters. This reversal of the social order commemorated Saturn's reign when everyone was equal.

9 Archaeology also divides the early history of man into four periods, named after the materials he used in each—the Old Stone, the New Stone, the Bronze, and the Iron Ages. ("Archaeology" comes from two Greek words meaning "ancient things" and "word," that is, body of knowledge.) History sees man as working his way up from primitive origins, while mythology usually sees him as progressively falling away from an early happy state. The historical and mythological Bronze and Iron Ages correspond. Homer, living in the Iron Age, knows that his twelfth-century B.C. heroes did not have the use of iron, and carefully describes their armour, weapons, and chariots as bronze.

10 A "three-toothed" fishing spear. Britannia on the British penny grasps the trident, symbolizing her rule over the waves.

11 Hades, like "the Hesperides," was in Classical times always a personal name, never that of a place.

12 Once Zeus is established, the names "Mount Olympus" and "heaven" mean the same thing to Greek writers—the abode of the gods.

13 Like other places pointed out as subterranean workshops of Hephaestus, Lemnos was volcanic. "Volcano" comes from Hephaestus' Latin name, Vulcan.

14 All peoples have stories about the invention of things. In Genesis Jubal and Tubal-Cain are the first musician and the first smith.

15 The tortoise-shell is the base, which works as a sound-box. It supports two upright wooden arms, one on each side, connected at the top with a cross-bar. Seven strings of equal length are stretched between the cross-bar and the shell. These are struck with a plectrum, often as an accompaniment to singing or recitation. A "lyric" poem originally meant one that could be chanted to the accompaniment of the lyre.

16 Associated with Pan in art and legend are wild men with animal parts like goats' legs and horns or horses' tails, living among woods and hills. The Latin name for Pan is Faunus, for the satyrs *fauni*. From the names of Faunus' wife and the Roman goddess of flowers we get our words "fauna" and "flora."

17 Byron in this poem on the career of Napoleon is thinking not of the royal bird of Zeus but of the two vultures who tear at the liver of Tityus, another ambitious giant punished by Zeus. The ancient authors themselves quite often combine two stories in this way.

18 Milton, writing in the mid-seventeenth century, is following the historians of his day in identifying figures of Classical mythology with those of the Bible, here the Titan Iapetus and the third son of Noah. The person he is comparing to Pandora is Eve.

19 The name at first meant "All-Giver," showing Pandora to be a form of the earth-goddess; Hesiod has deliberately misread it in his fable of woman as man's undoing. Her older identity may play some part in Ovid's account of Deucalion and Pyrrha, seeing that several earlier sources make her the mother of one or both.

20 Another floating box appears in the story of Perseus (p. 55). The Latin word for "chest" is *arca*: hence our word "ark" for the vessel in which Noah survived the Flood.

21 The sun-god gives his name to a chemical element, helium, besides such adjectives as heliocentric, heliotropic (of plants, "turning towards the sun").

22 The phaeton, a four-wheeled light carriage drawn by two horses, was named after him. This story is one of many dealing with a rash promise or repented wish or curse: compare Theseus' curse on Hippolytus (p. 345). The theme reflects the belief of primitive peoples in the magically binding power of words. The god who broke an oath sworn by Styx forthwith lay unconscious for a year and for the next nine years was banished from heaven.

23 Scorpio and Cancer, two of the twelve constellations making up the Zodiac or path of the sun through the sky. "Zodiac," like "zoölogy," is related to Greek *zoös*, "living."

24 Heliades means "children of Helios," here the daughters of Helios. Similarly, the Hesperides are the daughters of Hesperus; Alcides, a name of Heracles, means "grandson of Alcaeus"; and Agamemnon is sometimes called Atreides after his father Atreus. Names like these indicating parentage or ancestry are called "patronymics."

II. Spring and Winter

The story of Demeter and Persephone is told best in an early Greek poem known as the *Homeric Hymn to Demeter*, though no longer thought of as Homer's work. The tale of the wandering goddess is older still than Greek mythology, going back to Egypt and the search of Isis for her lost husband

Osiris. Ovid tells the stories of Adonis, Hyacinthus, Narcissus, and Orpheus in his *Metamorphoses*.

1 Triptolemus (another name for Demophoön), is said to have been sent forth in a chariot by Demeter to carry seed-corn and the art of its cultivation to distant countries.
2 Probably the yellow daffodil. A sinister flower in mythology, its name is connected with *narke*, "numbness," from which we get "narcotic."
3 A town near Athens where an elaborate festival called the Eleusinian Mysteries was celebrated every autumn in honour of Demeter and her daughter. Probably one of the intentions of this story was to explain Demeter's connection with Eleusis.
4 The Biblical Sheba, whose Queen brought gold and spices to Solomon.
5 A guitar-like stringed instrument of Shakespeare's time, replacing in the poem the Classical lyre.
6 Ixion and Sisyphus were impious men condemned to endless suffering in Tartarus, the underworld place of punishment. Ixion, a friend of the gods and a guest at their table, repaid their hospitality by attempting to carry off Hera, and was punished by being bound to a fiery wheel. Sisyphus, who betrayed a secret of Zeus, had forever to keep pushing a heavy stone uphill, which never reached the top but always kept rolling down again. Other sufferers in Tartarus were Tantalus (p. 369); Tityus (p. 420); the fifty Danaids (daughters of Danaus), who for murdering their husbands were forced incessantly to try to carry water in sieves, or jars with holes in the bottom.
7 Arion, Sappho, and Alcaeus were the earliest Greek lyric poets whose names, and of the last two also some writings, have survived. We know almost nothing about their lives, but legends grew up around all three. Sappho, a woman, was sometimes called "the tenth Muse." Arion is said to have been thrown overboard by sailors and carried triumphantly ashore by dolphins, who appreciated his skill with the lyre.

III. Loves of the Gods and Metamorphoses

All the stories told in this chapter are from Ovid's *Metamorphoses* and are best known in his versions.

1 Arcas was the supposed ancestor of the Arcadians, as Phoenix was of the Phoenicians and Romulus of the Romans. A man who gives his name to a race, or more likely is invented to explain its name, is called its " eponym."

2 "The bear-guard," a star in the constellation Boötes, next to the Great Bear. In other accounts Arcas became the constellation of the Little Bear, whose tail contains the Pole Star by which early sailors steered. The sailors' name for the Pole Star and its constellation, Cynosure, literally "dog's tail," comes to mean in English "a focus of attention."

3 The Greeks, who unlike the Egyptians did not worship animal-formed or animal-headed deities, explained the Egyptian cow-goddess Hathor, a form of the great goddess Isis, as the transformed maiden Io.

4 In the story of the creation told by Hesiod, Eros ("Love," Latin Cupid) was brought forth in the beginning by Night and Erebus, and thus is almost the oldest of the gods. Later writers, though, make him the youngest, the child of Aphrodite, an eternally mischievous little boy wounding men and gods alike with his arrows. In the Roman story of Cupid and Psyche, told near the end of this book, Love begins to grow up.

5 Only much later, by a Renaissance pun that transformed Latin "baccalarius," bachelor, into "baccalaureatus," "[crowned] with the laurel berry," did Apollo's plant come to honour also university graduates taking their first degree.

6 This story, like some that follow, is "aetiological": that is, it is told to give the "cause" of something, here the spider's nature. Modern examples would be some of Kipling's *Just-So Stories*, like "How the Leopard got his Spots." Sometimes aetiological stories explain ritual, like Hesiod's tale of why men burn bones for the gods (pp. 287–8).

IV. The Heroes

These tales of the heroes before the Trojan War are all told briefly by Ovid in the *Metamorphoses*, and at greater length by a late Greek writer, Apollodorus, born about 180 B.C., in his *Bibliotheca*, or Library, a survey of Greek mythology. The fifth-century B.C. tragic dramatists Sophocles and Euripides used incidents from the lives of Heracles, Jason, and Theseus in their plays. The history of Jason is told most fully by the Alexandrian poet Apollonius Rhodius in his epic *The Argonautica*, written in Greek in the third century B.C.

1 Greek shields were decorated, often with Gorgon faces to frighten enemies. Gorgon masks were attached also to ovens, foundries, and house-chimneys to scare off evil spirits.

2 The stories do not agree as to whether it was of her own or her daughter's beauty that Cassiopeia boasted. Milton calls her "starred" because the adventure is recorded in the names of a group of northern constellations:

Cassiopeia, Andromeda, Cepheus (Andromeda's father), Perseus, Cetus ("Sea monster"), and Pegasus, the winged horse said to have sprung from Medusa's body at her death.

3 This is "sympathetic magic," the attempt to produce a certain effect by imitating it—bring rain by scattering water, injure an enemy by wounding an image of him. In some places the belief still lingers that a baby cannot be born or a soul part from its body in a house where there are doors locked or knots tied.

4 A murderer, whether man or god, had to undergo a ritual of purification, sometimes with a penalty of exile, before he could return to society. Apollo, who saw to this law's being carried out, himself submitted to purification and exile twice: for the deaths of the Python (p. 396) and of the Cyclopes (p. 324). The ritual required the sacrifice of a ram or pig, probably as a substitute for the blood of the murderer.

5 The cup of the Sun was the vessel in which the sleeping Sun was carried over the sea every night from west to east.

6 Our dollar sign $ may come from the symbol on old Spanish dollars of the Pillars of Hercules decked with garlands by sailors setting out across the unknown western sea, or rejoicing in their return.

7 The hero carries his club and bow, and wears the head of his lion-skin as a helmet.

8 "Alcides" is a patronymic (see p. 420, n. 24, above).

9 "Friendly to strangers," now more suitably called the Black Sea. Like the "Eumenides" (p. 371) and the "Pacific" Ocean, the "Euxine" is a complimentary, not a descriptive, title.

10 Castor and Polydeuces (Latin Pollux) were later changed into the constellation Gemini, the Heavenly Twins. Perhaps because of their voyage in the Argo, they were the protectors of sailors. Another name for them is the Dioscuri, or "sons of Zeus."

11 For the Olympians, a white victim, usually an ox, was killed on an altar with its throat upward. The inedible parts were burned for the gods, while the worshippers ate the meat (see pp. 287–8 for an explanation of this custom). For the powers of earth or the underworld the victim, usually a black ram or pig, was killed with its throat downwards, bleeding or falling into a pit. The worshipper took none of the meat, the carcass being usually destroyed in a "holocaust" or wholesale burning. This type of sacrifice, performed also at funerals to honour the dead, was carried out at night.

12 An exile or stranger claiming shelter or asylum at a temple sat down by the altar. In a private house he sat by the hearth, the centre of family life

and worship. Suppliants like other strangers were under the special protection of Zeus.

13 Charybdis was a whirlpool, Scylla a dangerous rock, the home of a dog-headed, man-eating hag.

14 Two or three in number, like the Harpies the Sirens had the heads of maidens and the bodies of birds. In later times they were thought of as fish-tailed, like our mermaids.

15 The figure is actually Hades.

16 A poison extracted from the plant monkshood or wolfsbane.

17 Literally, "Minos-bull." This is probably a story told to explain some features of Cretan religious ritual, in which, to judge from excavated seals, vase-paintings, and murals, both bulls and labyrinths had a central place.

18 The supposed inventor of carpentry, and of several devices including the saw, the axe, the plumb-line, the augur, and glue, also life-sized automata, or robots. His name means "skilful," and from it comes English "daedal," meaning manifold or mysterious.

19 A Greek word meaning "maze." The original labyrinth of the story may have been the immense and complicated palace at Cnossus in Crete, already in ruins when Greek civilization began, and excavated in the early twentieth century by Sir Arthur Evans. The ancient Cretan Bronze Age culture, which collapsed from unknown causes in about 1400 B.C., is called after its legendary king "Minoan."

20 Literally, a ball of thread. From its use in this tale comes the meaning usually attached to its other spelling, "clue."

21 So called from the grove, Latin *nemus*.

22 This reappears in the story of Aeneas (p. 372). One of the most influential books of modern times, Sir James G. Frazer's *The Golden Bough*, explains the bough as mistletoe with its yellow berries growing on the oak. Surveying the whole field of European folklore, Frazer attempts to account for the strange custom of Nemi.

V. The Royal House of Thebes

These stories are told by several Greek writers, and by Ovid in the *Metamorphoses*. Euripides in the fifth century B.C. told the story of Pentheus in his tragedy *The Bacchae*—"women followers of Bacchus," or Dionysus. Sophocles composed a series of four plays about the later troubles of Thebes: *Oedipus the King*, *Oedipus at Colonus*, *The Seven Against Thebes*, and *Antigone*.

1 With Sidon and Byblus, Tyre was one of the great seacoast cities of Phoenicia, already a powerful trading nation before the rise of Greece. Its valuable export was the purple dye from the *murex*, a shellfish, which became a sign of rank throughout the Mediterranean world.

2 Cadmus was said to have carried the alphabet to Greece. His father Agenor, a great-grandson of Io (pp. 307–8), came to Tyre from Egypt, and Cadmus' brother Phoenix became the ancestor of the Phoenicians. Though historians do not now believe that Thebes, which Cadmus was said to have founded, was a Phoenician colony, it is certain that the Greek alphabet is descended from the Phoenician, and possible that Phoenician script itself came from Egypt.

3 Staff tipped with a pine-cone, an emblem of Dionysus. From it comes the pine-cone design we sometimes see in lacework patterns or in the stonework on buildings. Artists who forget its origin make it look like a pineapple.

4 Like most poets and prophets of Greek myth, a blind man gifted with inner sight. Compare Phineus (p. 329) and Demodocus (p. 382). As a punishment for offending the gods Teiresias spent some years as a woman, and had thus gained complete human experience.

5 Most of the hybrid monsters of Greek mythology come originally from the East. The best-known sphinx is the immense stone one, lion-bodied and human-headed (but without wings), that guards the Nile Valley at Gizeh in Egypt. The Great Sphinx, as it is called, is one of the earliest works of Egyptian civilization, which began at least two thousand years before that of Greece. "Sphinx," related to "sphincter," originally a band or drawstring, means throttler.

6 The Greek hero who wins a kingdom, even if he is the true heir, regularly comes to it after long wanderings and the withstanding of some great ordeal. As in fairy tales, he often receives with the kingdom the hand of a princess. This has suggested to some that in early European societies the ruling power was inherited by the women of the royal house, not the men, who acquired it only by marriage to one of them. This institution, where a king rules less in his own right than as the queen's consort, is called "matriarchy." One might compare the position of Arete (p. 382).

VI. The Tale of Troy

The histories of the Trojan War and the return of Odysseus are told by the earliest and most famous of Greek poets, Homer, in the two great Greek epics, the *Iliad*—"the matter of Ilion," or Troy, and the *Odyssey*—"the matter of Odysseus." Nothing definite is known of Homer's life. He lived some time before 700 B.C.: his name means "hostage," suggesting a prisoner or slave, and tradition makes him a blind bard like his own Demodocus (p. 382), singing his lays at the courts of princes. Homer does not tell the stories of the apple of discord and the homecoming of Agamemnon: these are taken respectively from *The Trojan Women* by the fifth-century B.C. dramatist Euripides, and the *Oresteia* by his older contemporary Aeschylus, a cycle of three plays about the house of Atreus: *Agamemnon*, *The Libation-Bearers*, and *The Eumenides*. The wanderings of Aeneas, the ancestor of the Romans, are the subject of the greatest of Latin poems, Virgil's *Aeneid* (unfinished at his death in 19 B.C.), the epic of the founding and destiny of Rome. Virgil and Apollonius Rhodius drew largely on Homer in their epics: this is one reason why the adventures of Aeneas and Jason often closely resemble those of Odysseus.

1 Troy was situated in Phrygia in Asia Minor beside the entrance of the Hellespont (modern Dardanelles) from the Aegean. Heinrich Schliemann, excavating in 1873 on the site of the modern Turkish village of Hissarlik, unearthed not just Homer's Troy but a series of nine cities built each on the ruins of its predecessor, stretching in time from before 2500 B.C. to after the reign of the Roman Emperor Constantine (died A.D. 337). Homer's Troy was the seventh of these cities: Troy VII had a strong wall with watchtowers and three gates, and was destroyed by fire at about the date traditionally assigned to Troy's overthrow by the Greeks—1184 B.C.

2 Agamemnon was the overlord of the Argive district of the Peloponnesus; its principal cities were Argos, Mycenae, and Tiryns. These last two were among the oldest of Greek cities, being centres of Minoan civilization (see p. 424, n. 88). Mycenae, excavated by Schliemann in 1875, is famous for its Lion Gate, its nine "beehive" tombs—Schliemann called the largest "the Treasury of Atreus"—and the immense hoard of finely-worked gold articles buried with its princes.

3 Not a siege in the modern sense, with the city surrounded and its defenders starving. The Trojans were able to keep up their trade with the hinterland, while the Greeks bought supplies along the seacoast and from the islands. Consequently the war could go on indefinitely.

4 What Zeus weighs are two *keres thanatoio*, "dooms of death," one for each of the heroes. A *ker* is a small winged sprite, the bearer sometimes of good but usually of evil. The ills that flew out of Pandora's box—griefs, diseases, old age, and death—were a swarm of *keres*, and Hope too was a *ker*. The *ker* that Zeus weighs for each of the heroes is that hero's own impend-

ing death, and Hector's sinks down because his fate is upon him. Zeus is using his scales to ascertain what outcome the Fates have decreed: he is not using them to decide the contest itself, as our expression "his fate hangs in the balance" might suggest.

5 The artist has shown Hermes holding the scales in place of Zeus, probably because he thinks of Hermes as revealing to men on earth what takes place in heaven.

6 *Nostoi*, the name the Greeks themselves gave to these tales of the aftermath of Troy. Hence English "nostalgia," homesickness or longing for the past, from *nostos*, homecoming, and *algos*, pain.

7 Athene's upper garment is her *aegis* or short "goat-skin" cloak. It is edged sometimes with curly tufts of goat's-hair, sometimes as here with curling snakes.

8 Meaning "immortal," "divine," ambrosia is the food of the gods as nectar is their drink.

9 A happy place, sometimes called the Isles of the Blessed, where certain especially favoured heroes enjoy an immortal life after death. It was sometimes thought of as in the far west, otherwise as part of the underworld realm of Hades.

10 The Greek tragic dramatists, Aeschylus, Sophocles, and Euripides, took the subjects of their greatest plays from the histories of Thebes (Oedipus and his children) and the house of Atreus or Pelops (Agamemnon's family).

11 He gives his name to the Peloponnesus, "Isle of Pelops," the peninsular southern half of Greece, joined to the mainland by the Isthmus of Corinth.

12 "The hill of Ares," just outside Athens, where the court of justice was held. It is called after Ares because he committed a murder and became the first to be tried there. This is "Mars' Hill" where St. Paul preached to the Athenians (Acts 17:22).

13 Apollo is here the spokesman of a new principle. In early times the Greeks like other peoples traced descent through the female line, which was easier to establish than the male. Thus a son's first responsibility would be to his mother as his nearest kin. The Furies' accusation of Orestes rests on this old order of things. At some time a switch to emphasis on the male line—"patriliny" rather than "matriliny"—took place, probably under the influence of the new Olympian religion if not exactly by a god's decree. Greek religion as we know it, dominated by Zeus the All-Father, is male-centred. But before an invading people brought in the worship of the Olympians, the Greeks seem to have been much more concerned, like most of their Mediterranean neighbours, with female powers such as Mother Earth.

14 "High point of the city," citadel. Ancient cities usually began as fortified hill-tops and spread outwards: temples and palaces would later occupy the central height. The Athenian Acropolis is crowned with a group of buildings that is still one of the wonders of Europe, constructed in the fifth century B.C. from the local white marble. Chief among these is the Parthenon, the temple of "the virgin" (Athene).

15 Trojan princes were numerous. King Priam, an oriental-style monarch with a harem, had fifty sons; Hecabe, his chief wife, was the mother of Hector. Aeneas belonged to the younger branch of the Trojan royal house: his great-great-grandfather Tros—hence "Troy"—was also Hector's. Not only the Romans were anxious to trace their ancestry to Troy. The English in the Middle Ages believed that their island was settled by Aeneas' descendant Brutus and took from him its name of Britain.

16 A colony of the great trading city of Tyre in Phoenicia, founded about 814 B.C. in North Africa—nearly four hundred years too late to shelter Aeneas as he fled from Troy. Virgil, who tells the story, is not pretending to write history when he suggests a background for the later troubles between Carthage and Rome.

17 Doves were sacred to Aphrodite and were said to draw her chariot through the air. The eagle was sacred to Zeus and the peacock to Hera. Through its association with Athene, the owl, figured on the coins of her city, became the traditional bird of wisdom.

18 Sometimes used for the whole realm of Hades, but properly the under-world place of punishment inhabited by the great sinners, Tantalus, Sisyphus, and the rest.

19 The Greeks always mixed their wine with water in a bowl before drinking it.

20 The caduceus, carried by Greek heralds and ambassadors as a mark of their office. That of Hermes had two serpents twined round it, their heads meeting at the top, and in late Classical art was surmounted by a small pair of wings as a symbol of his speed. It is not to be confused with the staff of Asclepius, the patron of medicine, about which twines a single snake. Hermes' staff had magical powers: it could lull people to sleep, and also controlled the souls of the dead, which it was Hermes' duty as "psychopomp" to lead to the underworld. Hermes is recognized also by winged boots and a traveller's broad-brimmed hat, sometimes also winged.

21 The early Greeks had two conceptions of the abode of the dead: that it was underground, and that it was a country in the farthest west, the direction of the setting sun. In the *Odyssey* these traditions are combined: the en-

trance to the house of Hades is in "Persephone's country" in the west, where the ghosts come up when they are summoned.

22 The afterlife imagined by the Greeks was a joyless, shadowy affair. The ghosts were the merest phantoms, without strength and without understanding, lacking the blood that is the vigour of living men. They were objects of pity, but hardly of fear. Homer speaks with respect in this passage of "the glorious tribes of the dead," but again in almost the same breath he calls them "the weak heads of the dead."

23 Most Homeric kings, with a few exceptions like Agamemnon, were very petty rulers indeed—the chief men of their districts, comparable to English squires. Conditions of life in that age did not allow even royalty to be idle: princesses washed, princes like Anchises tended cattle, queens spun and wove. Mediterranean women in remote places still trample their wash in stone cisterns built in the paths of streams.

24 While horn cut thin enough is transparent, ivory is opaque, therefore perhaps deluding. The Greeks, like the Egyptians, from very early times brought ivory in from Ethiopia.

25 The Leucadian Rock (not to be confused with the cape on the Ionian island of Leucas, north of Ithaca) was a mythical landmark beyond the western sea. The Gates of the Sun were those by which the sun-god Helios descended every night to commence his journey under the earth back to his eastern point of rising. The land of dreams was said to be either a part of the underworld or situated beside its entrance. The realm of the dead, ruled by Hades and Persephone, was a dreary plain covered with asphodel, a greyish-leaved lily common in Greece. Our word "daffodil" comes from "asphodel," though the narcissi are a different family.

VII. Cupid and Psyche

Only one author gives this story: Apuleius, in the course of his Latin prose novel, *The Golden Ass*, written late in the second century A.D. There it is told by an old woman in a robbers' den to a kidnapped maiden to pass the time. We have no way of knowing whether Apuleius found the story or invented it. In many ways it is more like the fairy tales of medieval Europe than like the older Classical myths. The names of its hero and heroine are suggestive: Cupid, in Greek Eros, is the god of Love, and *psyche*, the Greek word for "butterfly," also means "soul."

1 The monster depicted is Typhon (p. 276).
2 In the later Classical age many barren or dreary regions, not necessarily in

the far west, were thought of as entrances to the underworld. In Taenarus in the Peloponnesus was the cave through which Heracles was said to have dragged up Hades' watchdog Cerberus. Lake Avernus (p. 372) had another such entrance-cavern, through which Aeneas descended with the Sibyl. Poisonous vapours pouring from its mouth helped its infernal reputation: Virgil derives its name from Greek *a-ornos*, "birdless."

3 The Greeks buried their dead with an obol (a small coin) in the mouth as Charon's fee. Psyche takes two coins, as she will make the crossing twice.

4 Just as Psyche would have put herself in danger had she stopped to help those who asked her, so by accepting from Proserpina more than was strictly necessary she would have given Proserpina power over her. Proserpina herself became bound to the underworld by accepting the pomegranate offered her there by Pluto, Greek Hades (p. 301).

5 What helps to make this story so like a fairy tale is its insistence on magical prohibitions: the lover who must not be looked at, the box that must not be opened. Examples in other stories are Pandora's box (p. 290), the bag of the winds (p. 376), and Hades' command to Orpheus not to look back at his wife (p. 304). Like Adam and Eve, heroes and heroines always break these conditions: otherwise there would be no story.

6 Goddesses of the seasons, concerned with the fertility of the earth. They were sometimes three, sometimes four, and had different names in different places.

7 The three daughters of Zeus and Eurynome, called Charites by the Greeks, embodying qualities of grace, beauty, and charm. They do little in mythology but wait on the love-goddess. Names: Aglaia, Euphrosyne, Thalia.

8 Daughters of Zeus and Mnemosyne (Memory), patronesses of poetry and of music, which takes its name from them. "Music" is "that which belongs to the Muses," and a "museum" is a "place of the Muses." They are nine in number, and their haunts are all mountains—Boeotian Mount Helicon, where they appeared to Hesiod, with its sacred spring Hippocrene; Mount Pierus in Pieria, where they were born; and Phocian Mount Parnassus, at whose foot was Apollo's oracle of Delphi. Apollo, the god of poetry, is their leader and plays for their dances on his lyre. The Romans assigned specific functions to the Muses according to their traditional names: Calliope was the Muse of epic poetry, Clio of history, Euterpe of flute-music, Terpsichore of the dance, Erato of lyric poetry, Melpomene of tragedy, Thalia of comedy, Polyhymnia of rhetoric, and Urania of astronomy.

VIII. The Passing and Afterlife of the Gods

1 The story was that Zeus had released two eagles, one from the eastern edge of the world and one from the western, and that they met at Delphi. The oracle possessed a sacred rock known as the *omphalos* or navel.

2 A festival held regularly at Delphi, consisting of athletic contests but more importantly of "musical" competitions, in instrumental music, singing, drama, and verse and prose recitations. These events were held in honour of Apollo, and were second in importance only to the Olympic Games, celebrating Olympian Zeus, held at Olympia in the western district of Elis and consisting entirely of athletic events. Victors in the Pythian Games were crowned with wreaths of bay leaves (also called laurel) cut in the nearby Vale of Tempe; Olympic victors, with wild olive.

3 "Three-legged," the stool on which the priestess sat.

4 One of the seven hills on which Rome was built. Its name is said to mean Hill of the Head, from a bleeding human head found by workmen laying the temple's foundations.

5 The English Bible uses the Greek names of these constellations. The Pleiades were the seven daughters of Atlas, taking their name from their mother, Pleione. Orion, the great hunter, pursued them for five years; and the chase never ended, but was translated by the gods to the heavens. Orion became a constellation and the sisters a cluster of seven stars near by. One of the seven was Maia, the mother by Zeus of Hermes.

6 Other names the poets give to Diana as moon-goddess are Luna, Latin "moon"; Phoebe, the feminine of Phoebus; Titania, the feminine of Titan, a title of the sun; Cynthia, from her birthplace, Mount Cynthus in Delos. Early Greek mythology had a moon-goddess, Selene, and a sun-god, Helios, though never very important. Most later writers retelling their stories make Diana, and not Selene, the goddess who loved Endymion, and make Apollo the father of Phaethon in place of Helios.

7 One of the ancient female powers of older Greek mythology. She may have once been very important: Hesiod says that Zeus gave her power "in earth and sea and sky." In historical times she was a minor goddess, associated with darkness, magic, and the underworld. To her belonged crossroads, places where a road was joined by a side-path, where her image might be set up with three faces to look in all three directions. The Romans called her Hecate Trivia, "of three ways," and thus she became known as a "triple goddess." When she was later identified with the dark of the moon,

and writers had forgotten why she was triple in the first place, they connected her with Diana and Proserpina to make up the three phases of the moon.

8 This is actually a French medieval illustration to the tale of Hermes and Argus. Both are dressed as peasants, and Hermes plays, instead of the Classical shepherd's pipe, a simple form of bagpipe.

Suggestions for Further Reading

Carpenter, Thomas H. *Art and Myth in Ancient Greece: A Handbook*. London: Thames and Hudson, 1991.

Dowden, Ken. *The Uses of Greek Mythology*. London, New York: Routledge, 1988. Uses to the Greeks themselves; that is, a valuable, unstuffy exposition of backgrounds and contexts.

Edmunds, Lowell, ed. *Approaches to Greek Myth*. Baltimore: Johns Hopkins University Press, 1990. Essays on such modern approaches as the psychoanalytic, the structural, etc.

Gantz, Timothy. *Early Greek Myth: A Guide to Literary and Artistic Sources*. Baltimore: Johns Hopkins University Press, 1993.

Grant, Michael. *Myths of the Greeks and Romans*. 1962. New York: Meridian, 1995. Very full handbook on myths and their afterlife. Updated bibliography.

Mayerson, Philip. *Classical Mythology in Literature, Art and Music*. Waltham, Mass.: Xerox College Publishing, [1971].

Powell, Barry B. *Classical Myth*. Prentice, 1995. College textbook with wideranging presentation; extensive bibliographies.

* * *

Brown, Norman O. *Theogony, Hesiod*. Indianapolis: Bobbs, 1953. Introductory essay, translation.

Clarke, Howard. *The Art of the Odyssey*. 1967. Wauconda, Ill.: Bolchazy-Carducci, 1989.

Dodds, E.R., ed. *The Plays of Euripides: Bacchae*. 1944. Oxford: Clarendon Press, 1960. Important introductory essay; Greek text.

Edmunds, Lowell. *Myth and Poetry in Homer*. Highland Park, N.J.: December Press, 1993.

Edwards, Mark. *Homer, Poet of the Iliad*. Baltimore: Johns Hopkins University Press, 1987.

Galinsky, G. Karl. *Ovid's Metamorphoses: An Introduction to the Basic Aspects*. Oxford: Blackwell, 1975.

Green, Peter, ed. *The Argonautica, by Apollonios Rhodios*. Trans. with introduction, commentary, and glossary. Berkeley: University of California Press, 1997.

Henry, Elisabeth. *The Vigour of Prophecy*. Carbondale: Southern Illinois University Press, 1989. Virgil's *Aeneid* seen largely through its mythology.

Hine, Daryl, trans. *The Homeric Hymns, and The Battle of the Frogs and the Mice*. New York: Atheneum, 1972.

Lesky, Albin. Greek Tragedy. Trans. H.A. Frankfort. New York: Barnes, 1965.

Lord, Albert. *The Singer of Tales*. 1965. Cambridge, Mass.: Harvard University Press, 2000. This edition has audio and video CD.

Page, Denys. *Folktales in the Odyssey*. Cambridge, Mass.: Harvard University Press, 1973.

* * *

Burkert, Walter. *Greek Religion, Archaic and Classical*. Trans. John Raffan. Cambridge, Mass.: Harvard University Press, 1985.

Carpenter, Thomas H., and Christopher A. Faraone, eds. *Masks of Dionysus*. Ithaca, N.Y.: Cornell University Press, 1993. Besides Dionysos, Pan, Theseus (see below), numerous other figures and their afterlives are treated in books titled after them: check catalogues under, for example, Aeneas, Cadmus/ Kadmos, Heracles/ Herakles, Hermes, Narcissus, Oedipus, Orpheus, Pandora, Persephone, Sphinx, Zeus.

Dexter, Miriam Robbins. *Whence the Goddesses? A Source Book*. Elmsford, N.Y.: Pergamon, 1990.

Fitton, J. Lesley. *The Discovery of the Greek Bronze Age*. Cambridge, Mass.: Harvard University Press, 1996.

Gardner, Jane F. *Roman Myths*. Austin: University of Texas Press, 1993.

Goodison, Lucy, and Christina Morris, eds. *Ancient Goddesses: The Myths and the Evidence*. London: British Museum, 1998.

Grant, Michael. *The Ancient Mediterranean*. London: Weidenfeld and Nicolson, 1969.

Guthrie, W.K.C. *Orpheus and Greek Religion*. 1935. Princeton, N.J.: Princeton University Press, 1993.

Lefkowitz, Mary R. *Women in Greek Myth*. Baltimore: Johns Hopkins University Press, 1986.

Merivale, Patricia. *Pan the Goat-God; His Myth in Modern Times.* Cambridge, Mass.: Harvard University Press, 1969.

Meyer, Marvin W., ed. *The Ancient Mysteries, A Sourcebook: Sacred Texts of the Mystery Religions of the Ancient Mediterranean World.* New York: Harper, 1987.

Neumann, Erich. *Amor and Psyche: The Psychic Development of the Feminine: A Commentary on the Tale by Apuleius.* Trans. Ralph Manheim. New York: Harper, 1962.

Nilsson, Martin P. *The Mycenean Origins of Greek Mythology* [1932], with a new introduction and bibliography by Emily Vermeule. Berkeley: University of California Press, 1972.

Reeder, Ellen D., ed. *Pandora: Women in Classical Greece.* Princeton, N.J.: Princeton University Press, 1995. Exhibition catalogue with fine illustrations and extensive essays.

Seznec, Jean. *The Survival of the Pagan Gods: The Mythological Tradition and Its Place in Renaissance Humanism and Art.* Trans. Barbara Sessions. (Bollingen Series 38.) New York: Pantheon, 1953.

Vermeule, Emily. *Aspects of Death in Early Greek Art and Poetry.* Berkeley: University of California Press, 1979.

Ward, Anne, ed. *The Quest for Theseus.* New York: Praeger, 1970.

The following web sites are worth trying:
theoi.com
uvic.ca/grs/bowman/myth
romansonline.com

Biblical Indexes

1. SCRIPTURAL PASSAGES CITED

2. PERSONS, NAMES, AND TITLES

Bible names as we know them are much anglicized. Usual English pronuncia-
tions are indicated below. Only long vowels have been marked; all other
vowels are either short or diphthongs. The accented syllable is marked '.

Vowels: Long vowels are pronounced Ā (*make*), Ē (*feet*), Ī (*fine*), Ō (*low*),
Ū (*duly*). Short vowels are pronounced A (*mat*), E (*let*), I (*fit*), O (*dot*), U (*rut*).

Consonants: CH is usually pronounced *k*: an exception is Rachel. C and G
are hard, as in *cat* and *gate*, except in some obviously non-Hebrew names such
as Caesarea and Cyrus.

Diphthongs: AA (when stressed, *air*; unstressed, *an*); AE (*see*); AI (usually
fine, but occasionally *day*, as in Cain; AU (*saw*); EU (*Europe*).

3. EVENTS, SYMBOLS, AND THEMES
(Italicized page numbers refer to illustrations.)

animal, 48; female, 67–8; human, 47, 65, 67

Satan, 126. *See also* Index 2

scapegoat, 46, 106

sea, 23, 24, 46, 79; of fresh water, 33–4

Second Coming, 223. *See also* apocalypse

separation, ultimate, 250

serpent, 41, 94, 144

seven and twelve, in Rev., 235

seven mountains, 52

sex, 46, 144

sexual relation, 50–1

sheep, sheepfold, 47–8, 72, 78, 82

shepherd, 60, 72; Christ as Good Shepherd, 61

sin, 159, 198

sky, 74–5; demonic symbols, 81–2

sky-father and earth-mother, 139–40, 142

soul and spirit, 113–15

Spirit of God, 75–6

spiritual kingdom, 41, 216–18

stone, stones, 73, 76–7, 232, 237

"suffering servant," 104–5

sun and moon, 137

temple, 57

Temple, 28, 41, 63, 237; establishment, 25, 120; Holy of Holies, 26, 78, 177; opening, in Rev., 238; purification, 26; rebuilding, rebuilt, 26, 27, 36–7; Solomon's, 76

Temptation of Christ, *58*, 93

time and space, 216, 235; as "here" and "now," 217–18; as *kairos*, 225; in Revelation, 239

tongues of flame, 75

Transfiguration of Christ, *70*, 112

tree: and water of death, 44; and water of life, 22, 32, 36, 41

tree of death, 46

tree of knowledge, 46

tree of life, 37, 45, 46, 73, 232

twelve tribes, twelve disciples, 93

two brothers pattern, 117–18, 121, 125–6

two thieves, 112

two trees, 32, 144

two witnesses (Moses and Elijah), 28, 112, 150, 233

typology, 146. *See also* Index 4

urban state or symbolism, 25, 47, 56–7, 60, 62

vine, 73

wasteland, 83. *See also* desert; wilderness

water: above the firmament, 34–5; dead, 35, 37

water of death, 45–6

water of life, 22, 32, 34–7, 76, 234

wedding, 51

whore, 52–3

Whore, Great, 52, 55, 234. *See also* Index 2, Babylon

wilderness, 24, 31, 83, 84, 93, 94, 106, 120

wind, 75–6

wine, 61, 62, 79

wisdom, 133, 166, 222–3; attainment, 175–6; and community, 174; at Creation, 174–5; and creativity, 176; and faith, 176; and folly, 173–4; as individual's absorption of law, 166, 172; and knowledge, 172; and play, 175, 265; as practical sense, 166–70; and prophecy, 182; and social continuity, 168, 172–4

Women at the Sepulchre, *171*

Word. *See* Christ as Word

4. SPECIAL TOPICS RELATED TO BIBLICAL SCHOLARSHIP

5. GENERAL INDEX

Index of Classical Mythology

Tem'pē, Thessalian valley between
Mounts Olympus and Ossa, 431
Te'nedos, island opposite Troy, 358
Tē'reus, king of Thrace, married to
Procne, 311–12
Te'thys, wife of Oceanus, mother of
Rivers and Nymphs.
Thē'a (Goddess), Titaness, wife of
Hyperion, 280, 293
Thebes (*Theebz*), chief city of Boeotia,
320, 349–54
Thebes (*Theebz*), famous city in
Egypt.
The'mis (Order), Titaness, mother of
Prometheus, 292
Thersī'tēs, ugly mocking Greek
warrior at Troy.
Thē'seus, Athenian hero, killer of the
Minotaur, 323, 340–7, 420
Thes'saly, country of northern
Greece, 313
The'tis, daughter of Nereus, wife of
Peleus, mother of Achilles, 289,
335, 355, 357, 359–60, 364
Thrace, country north of the Aegean,
304, 311
Thy-e'stēs, prince of Mycenae, son of
Pelops and Hippodamei'a, brother
of Atreus, 369–70
thyrsus, 351, 425 n.3
Ti'ber, River, in Italy, on which Rome
is built, 373
Ti'ryns, ancient Peloponnesian city,
338, 426
Ti'tans, twelve sons and daughters of
Uranus and Gaia, 280, 283–4
Titho'nus, Trojan prince loved and
carried off by Eos, by her the father
of Memnon; Eos begged Zeus to
make him immortal like herself,

but forgot to ask also for eternal
youth. When he grew old she tired
of him.
Ti'ty-us, giant punished in Tartarus
for trying to carry off Leto from
Olympus, 420, 421
Tmō'lus, Lydian mountain, 313
trident, 283, 419
tripod, 396, 431 n.1
Tripto'lemus, emissary of Demeter,
296, 421
Tri'ton, sea-god, son of Poseidon, 401
Trō'ilus, son of Priam and Hecabe,
killed by Achilles.
Trophō'nius, oracle of, in Lebadei'a,
Boeotia, 395–6
Trōs, ancestor of Trojan royal house,
428 n.15
Troy (Gk. and Lat. Troi'ā; also Gk.
I'lion, Lat. I'lium), city in Phrygia
beside Hellespont, 276, 355–67,
382, 426, 428
Tynda'reus, king of Sparta, husband
of Leda, foster-father of her children by Zeus, 356
Ty'phōn, monster, father by Echidna
of numerous pests; gives name to
hurricane, "typhoon," 276, 429
Tyre, ancient Phoenician seacoast
city, 348, 425

Ū'ranus (Sky, Lat. Coe'lus), son and
husband of Gaia, father of Titans,
280, 282, 290, 292

Vē'nus, Latin name of Aphrodite,
388–9, 391–4, 399–400, 401; planet,
418
Vir'bius (*vir bis*, twice a man?), Latin
name of revived Hippolytus, 346